The Official CompTIA Server+ Student Guide (Exam SK0-005)

Course Edition: 1.0

Acknowledgments

CompTIA

Damon Garn, Author

Thomas Reilly, Senior Vice President, Learning

Katie Hoenicke, Senior Director, Product Management

Evan Burns, Senior Manager, Learning Technology Operations and Implementation

James Chesterfield, Manager, Learning Content and Design

Becky Mann, Director, Product Development

Katherine Keyes, Content Specialist

Notices

Disclaimer

Trademark Notice

Copyright Notice

Table of Contents

About This Course

CompTIA is a not-for-profit trade association with the purpose of advancing the interests of IT professionals and IT channel organizations; its industry-leading IT certifications are an important part of that mission. CompTIA's Server+ Certification is designed for professionals with 18–24 months of work experience in a server environment, preferably with A+ certification or equivalent foundation.

> *The CompTIA Server+ exam will certify the successful candidate has the knowledge and skills required to install, configure, and manage server hardware and operating systems (OSs) by implementing proper security controls, successfully troubleshooting common server problems, and demonstrating an understanding of key disaster recovery concepts.*
>
> comptia.org/certifications/server

Course Description

Course Objectives

This course can benefit you in two ways. If you intend to pass the CompTIA Server+ (Exam SK0-005) certification examination, this course can be a significant part of your preparation. But certification is not the only key to professional success in the field of server management. Today's job market demands individuals with demonstrable skills, and the information and activities in this course can help you build your sysadmin skill set so that you can confidently perform your duties in any entry-level server administration role.

On course completion, you will be able to achieve the following:

- Understand server administration concepts.
- Understand virtualization and cloud computing.
- Understand physical and network security concepts.
- Manage physical inventory and assets.
- Manage server hardware.
- Configure storage management.
- Install and configure an OS.
- Troubleshoot OS, application, and network configurations.
- Maintain and manage servers post-installation.
- Manage data security.
- Manage service and data availability.
- Decommission servers.

Target Student

The Official CompTIA Server+ Guide (Exam SK0-005) is the primary course you will need to take if your job responsibilities include server administration, installation, and security within your organization. You can take this course to prepare for the CompTIA Server+ (Exam SK0-005) certification examination.

Prerequisites

To ensure your success in this course, you should have basic IT skills comprising 18 months to two years' experience. CompTIA A+ certification, or the equivalent knowledge, is strongly recommended.

The prerequisites for this course might differ significantly from the prerequisites for the CompTIA certification exams. For the most up-to-date information about the exam prerequisites, complete the form on this page: www.comptia.org/training/resources/exam-objectives

How to Use the Study Notes

The following notes will help you understand how the course structure and components are designed to support mastery of the competencies and tasks associated with the target job roles and help you to prepare to take the certification exam.

As You Learn

At the top level, this course is divided into **Lessons,** each representing an area of competency within the target job roles. Each Lesson is composed of a number of Topics. A **Topic** contains subjects that are related to a discrete job task, mapped to objectives and content examples in the CompTIA exam objectives document. Rather than follow the exam domains and objectives sequence, Lessons and Topics are arranged in order of increasing proficiency. Each Topic is intended to be studied within a short period (typically 30 minutes at most). Each Topic is concluded by one or more Activities, designed to help you to apply your understanding of the study notes to practical scenarios and tasks.

In addition to the study content in the Lessons, there is a glossary of the terms and concepts used throughout the course. There is also an index to assist in locating particular terminology, concepts, technologies, and tasks within the Lesson and topic content.

In many electronic versions of the book, you can click links on key words in the Topic content to move to the associated glossary definition and on page references in the index to move to that term in the content. To return to the previous location in the document after clicking a link, use the appropriate functionality in your eBook viewing software.

Watch throughout the material for the following visual cues.

Student Icon	Student Icon Descriptive Text
!	A **Note** provides additional information, guidance, or hints about a Topic or task.
⚠	A **Caution** note makes you aware of places where you need to be particularly careful with your actions, settings, or decisions so that you can be sure to get the desired results of an activity or task.

As You Review

Any method of instruction is only as effective as the time and effort you, the student, are willing to invest in it. In addition, some of the information that you learn in class may not be important to you immediately, but it may become important later. For this reason, we encourage you to spend some time reviewing the content of the course after your time in the classroom.

After the lesson content, you will find a table mapping the Lessons and Topics to the exam domains, objectives, and content examples. You can use this as a checklist as you prepare to take the exam, and review any content that you are uncertain about.

As a Reference

The organization and layout of this book make it an easy-to-use resource for future reference. Guidelines can be used during class and as after-class references when you're back on the job and need to refresh your understanding. Taking advantage of the glossary, index, and table of contents, you can use this book as a first source of definitions, background information, and summaries.

How to Use the CompTIA Learning Center

The CompTIA Learning Center is an intuitive online platform that provides access to the eBook and all accompanying resources to support The Official CompTIA curriculum. An access key to the CompTIA Learning Center is delivered upon purchase of the eBook. Resources include the following:

- **Online Reader:** An interactive online reader provides the ability to search, highlight, take notes, and bookmark passages in the eBook. Students can also access the eBook through the CompTIA Learning Center eReader mobile app.
- **Videos:** Videos complement the reading by providing short, engaging demonstrations of key activities in the course.
- **Assessments:** Practice questions help to verify a student's understanding of the material for each Lesson. Answers and feedback can be reviewed after each question or at the end of the assessment. A timed Final Assessment provides a practice-test-like experience to help students determine their readiness for the CompTIA certification exam. Students can review correct answers and full feedback after attempting the Final Assessment.
- **Strengths and Weaknesses Dashboard:** The Strengths and Weaknesses Dashboard provides you with a snapshot of your performance. Data flows into the dashboard from your practice questions, final assessment scores, and indicated confidence levels throughout the course.

The CompTIA Learning Center can be accessed at learn.comptia.org.

Lesson 1

Understanding Server Administration Concepts

LESSON INTRODUCTION

In order to effectively manage servers in an enterprise environment, you must understand the role of the systems administrator (sysadmin). You must also understand the differences between servers and workstations and how to manage the server lifecycle. Troubleshooting is a key skill for sysadmins. A troubleshooting methodology will make it more efficient to address server and network issues. Finally, in this lesson, you will learn about licensing models and compare open source and proprietary software licenses.

Lesson Objectives

In this lesson, you will:

- Understand server administration concepts.
- Understand troubleshooting methods.
- Manage licenses.

Topic 1A

Understand Server Administration Concepts

EXAM OBJECTIVES COVERED
This topic provides background information about the role of server administrators and does not cover a specific exam objective

The role of the systems administrator is key to understanding the management of servers. Systems administrators have many different job roles and responsibilities. You must also understand the difference between workstations and servers. You will also examine the server lifecycle and the four major subsystems of computers. Finally, you will compare the two major server operating systems (OSs), Linux and Windows Server.

Systems Administrator Job Roles and Responsibilities

Systems administrators are responsible for managing the server and network hardware lifecycles, documentation, and security. The sysadmin may also advise the business on emerging technologies and may have a role in capacity planning. The primary skill of a systems administrator is problem-solving. Sysadmins typically have a variety of skills and work with a wide range of technologies.

Common Sysadmin Responsibilities

- Installing, configuring, and managing server hardware, applications, and network components
- Managing the server lifecycle
- Monitoring server performance
- Providing capacity planning and growth
- Managing user and group accounts for access control
- Troubleshooting
- Working with other information technology (IT) teams, possibly including the service desk, developers, desktop support
- Accepting escalated service desk tickets
- Managing disparate technologies, such as databases, virtualization, cloud, backups, disaster recovery
- Managing network services, such as web, email, name resolution, Internet protocol (IP) address configuration
- Providing documentation

- Sharpening communications and presentation skills
- Advising the business on security policies, and implementing those policies

Take a few minutes to research the job descriptions and requirements for several server administrator jobs to discover a list of common responsibilities.

Sysadmins may possess the following:

- Formal technical training
- Vendor and vendor-neutral certifications
- College degree
- Years of experience

Take a few minutes to research the education and certification requirements for several server administrator jobs.

Servers Versus Workstations

Sysadmins must differentiate workstation computers and server computers. **Workstations** are usually assigned to end users. These devices do not tend to have redundant hardware and often do not have high-performance capabilities. Workstations also typically have a client OS installed. These OSs are optimized for a single user, support single-user applications, and often have a very elegant user interface. Client OSs include Microsoft Windows 10, Apple macOS, and Ubuntu Desktop Linux.

Server hardware is designed for high performance and redundancy. Often, a server includes multiple network interface cards (NICs), power supplies, and HDDs. The server may also have a great deal of random access memory (RAM) and multiple powerful central processing units (CPUs). The server's form factor may be measured in 1.75 inch (44.45 mm) units that permit it to be installed into standardized server racks. The server will be 19" wide and one or more units high. Servers typically have a server OS installed. These OSs are optimized for multiple users, support multiuser applications, and often have a more streamlined user interface. In fact, some server OSs do not use a graphical user interface (GUI) at all and instead are managed via a command-line interface (CLI). Server OSs include Microsoft Windows Server 2019 and Red Hat Enterprise Linux 8 (RHEL).

Workstation Characteristics	Server Characteristics
Assigned to end user	Secured in a server room
No redundant hardware	Redundant hardware
No high-performance hardware	High-performance hardware
Client OS optimized for a single user	Server operating system optimized for multiple users
Applications optimized for a single user	Applications optimized for multiple users
Elegant graphical user interface	Limited or no graphical user interface
Desktop or laptop form factor	Rack-mounted form factor

Comparing workstations and servers.

Workstation Operating Systems	Server Operating Systems
Microsoft Windows 10	Microsoft Windows Server 2019
Ubuntu Desktop Linux	Red Hat Enterprise Linux 8 (RHEL 8)
MacOS	

Workstation and server OSs.

Workstation and Server Security

Security is another factor that differentiates workstations and servers. End-user workstations are often exposed on the user's desk. Laptop computers may be removed from the business premises entirely. This represents a very significant security risk of damage, theft, loss, and dataexposure. Servers must be physically secured. Servers are usually housed in a locked server room that provides physical protection. They are also regularly backed up and equipped with redundant hardware to maintain a high degree of availability.

Sysadmins must understand how the different features of servers and server OSs necessitate a different management approach from end-user workstations.

Server Lifecycle

Server administrators are responsible for the lifecycle of the server. The term "lifecycle" normally specifies four phases: procurement, usage, end of life, and disposal/recycling. These phases are covered in more detail later in the course. At this stage, it useful for you to recognize that the server administrator's role is to maintain the server through its lifecycle.

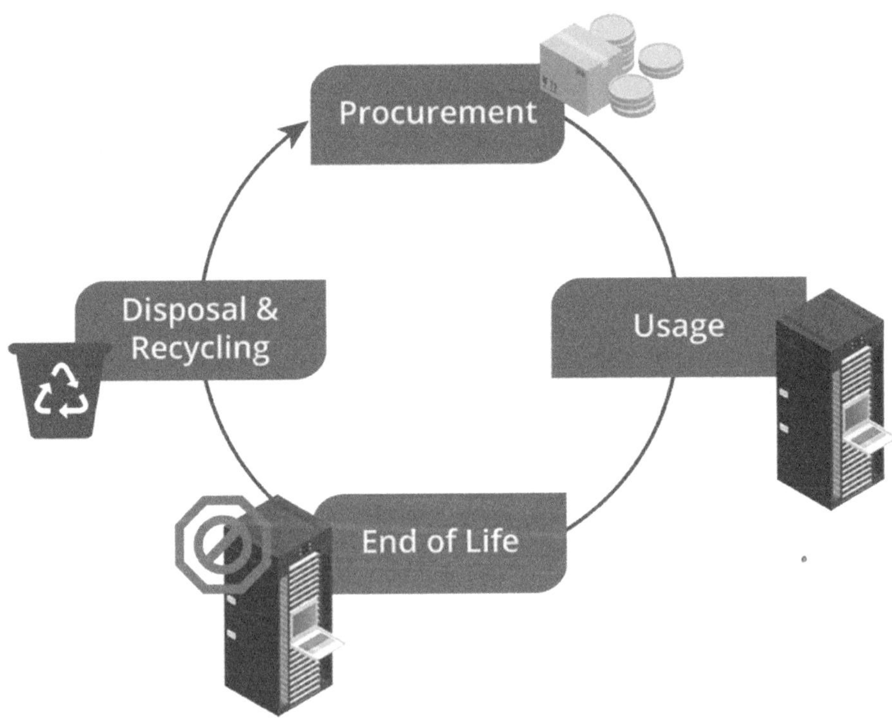

Server lifecycle illustration. (Images © 123RF.com)

The deployment of a server is often referred to as "standing up" the server.

The Four Major Subsystems

Computer systems are specified based on the four major subsystems, which are also useful measurements for the system's performance. Servers often require more available resources than do end-user workstations.

The four subsystems are the following:

- Processor—the CPU represents the amount of processing power the system has available.
- Memory—the RAM represents storage capacity available to the CPU for quick access to data.
- Storage—the storage drives represent storage capacity and access speeds available for the OS and user data.
- Network—the capacity for sending and receiving information across the network.

Server OSs—Linux and Windows

There are multiple OSs optimized for server roles, but this book focuses on Linux and Microsoft Windows Server. There are significant differences between the two.

Linux

Linux is actually a very big family of related OSs. Each version of Linux is referred to as a "distribution" (or "distro"). Each distribution is typically purpose specific. For example, Red Hat Enterprise Linux (RHEL) is designed to be used in a large-scale business deployment. Kali Linux is designed to be used in penetration testing situations.

Linux is licensed under the General Public License (GPL) and is an **open-source** OS. That means that the source code that makes up the OS is available to anyone to be modified and redistributed. The Linux OS is available for free download.

Use a web browser to connect to https://distrowatch.com/ to view the latest Linux distribution releases.

Most Linux distributions trace their lineage back to either Debian Linux or Red Hat Linux. The primary difference between the two branches of the Linux family is how software is managed.

Red Hat Linux Derivatives

- RHEL
- Fedora
- CentOS

Debian Linux Derivatives

- Debian Linux
- Ubuntu
- Kali

Two common areas of consideration for choosing between Linux and Windows Server OSs are device driver compatibility and software availability.

Windows Server

The Microsoft Windows Server OS is very common and is closely related to the Windows desktop OSs. Windows Server is designed to be used in a business setting to provide centralized administration.

Windows is a closed-source OS. That means that the source code that makes up the OS is not available to be modified or redistributed. The Windows Server OS is available for purchase from Microsoft or resellers.

Review Activity:

Server Administration Concepts

Answer the following questions:

1. **List several examples of systems administrator job roles.**

2. **List at least three differences between workstations and servers.**

3. **What are the four phases of the server lifecycle?**

4. **What are the four main subsystems of a computer?**

5. **What is a Linux distribution?**

6. **What are the two main branches of the Linux family of distributions?**

7. **How do these two branches differ?**

Topic 1B

Understand Troubleshooting Methods

EXAM OBJECTIVES COVERED
4.1 Explain the troubleshooting theory and methodology

One of the primary skills and duties of a systems administrator is to troubleshoot problems with servers, the network, and data access. It is important to have a methodology for troubleshooting. You should also recognize that troubleshooting methods may change by situation, skill level, and experience with the network environment.

Troubleshooting Methodology

A formalized and consistent **troubleshooting** methodology can make identifying issues and discovering fixes more efficient. While the steps can vary depending on the actual issue and components involved, there are several universal troubleshooting steps.

The following list represents the basic steps in a troubleshooting methodology:

- Identify the problem
- Determine the scope of the problem
- Establish a theory of probable cause/question the obvious
- Test the theory to determine the cause
- Establish a plan of action
- Implement the solution or escalate the issue
- Verify full system functionality
- Implement preventive measures
- Perform a root cause analysis

Document findings, actions, and outcomes throughout the process.

Identify the Problem and Determine the Scope

Identify the Problem

The first troubleshooting phase is to identify the problem. The problem may be discovered for you by the end users you support, exposed by log files, identified by monitoring software, or indicated by lights on the server. There are many ways in which the problem may be detected. Once a problem is identified, a service desk ticket is used to track it.

Determine the Scope of the Problem

Once a problem is identified, gather additional information to determine the scope of the problem. Start this process by asking users for additional details or examining log files. Attempt to replicate the problem by asking users to show you what they were doing when the problem was encountered, or to try to recreate the situation where the problem first arose. It is a good practice to back up data if there is any risk to the data during the troubleshooting phase. You must use your own judgment as to whether a data backup is necessary before you begin troubleshooting. Finally, consider whether you have the skills to address the problem or if you need to escalate the service desk ticket to another administrator.

One of the most important steps is to determine whether the problem exists on only one server, or on multiple servers. The scope of the problem could be hardware based and, if so, may be isolated to that device. It could be network based, in which case, multiple devices may be affected. It could be software based, such as a misconfiguration or a bug. This also may impact multiple servers.

Example: If one workstation cannot access a file server, but all other workstations can, the problem likely lies with that workstation. If many workstations cannot access the file server, the problem likely lies with that server or with the network between the workstations and the server.

Note: In Linux, the log file service is named "rsyslog." In Windows, the log file service is named "Event Viewer."

Establish and Test a Theory of Probable Cause

Establish a Theory of Probable Cause/Question the Obvious

The next troubleshooting phase is to establish a probable cause for the problem. It is essential to keep this step as simple as possible. Newer administrators may be tempted to believe that because the server and network are complex, the problem must also be complex. Troubleshooting often begins with very simple steps, such as confirming that the system is plugged in and powered on. More complex problems may require you to examine log files, talk to users or other administrators, or check the hardware.

When troubleshooting, identify any common elements or similar problems that might span multiple servers or network devices. Such common elements might include a new or updated piece of software, a new **device driver**, or a new configuration.

Check for any recent changes to the environment. These changes may have been implemented by another IT staff member or a stakeholder, such as a manager or other user. Recent changes are common culprits for issues.

Test the Theory to Determine the Cause

Next, test the theory by verifying that the likely cause is indeed the culprit. This phase involves research or other testing. Very simple problems may actually be solved during this step. If your theory is confirmed, then move on to the next phase, which is to establish a plan of action. If your theory is not confirmed, then you must establish and test a new theory.

Establish and Implement a Plan of Action

Establish a Plan of Action

The plan of action for addressing the problem must recognize that service interruptions and data loss should be avoided. If a server needs to be brought down to replace hardware, or if data has been lost due to a HDD failure, the end users must be notified. The plan of action defines the steps to be taken. These steps should be defined ahead of time rather than created during the implementation of the solution. It is useful to provide the impacted users with an expected duration of the outage.

Implement the Solution or Escalate

In this phase, follow the plan of action established earlier. It is important not to deviate from the plan. You may not have the knowledge to implement the plan and need to escalate the problem to the vendor's support team or other members of your own team.

When following a plan of action, be sure to only make one change at a time, and then test the result. If you make multiple changes simultaneously, it is difficult to identify exactly which change corrected the problem. If a given change does not solve the problem, reverse that change, and then try another option.

Verify, Prevent, Analyze, and Document

Verify Full System Functionality

Once the potential solution has been implemented, the next phase is to test for functionality. Your goal is to ensure that the server has returned to the service levels that are defined by the system parameters. The server performance baseline that you performed during the deployment portion of the server lifecycle will be very useful as a comparison.

Implement Preventive Measures

It may be possible to preemptively reconfigure other servers to avoid a repeat of the same problem. It may also be possible to implement additional technologies (such as a redundant array of independent/ inexpensive disks [RAID]) or additional practices (such as backups) to prevent future instances of failure. In some cases, additional training or documentation may also be necessary.

Perform a Root Cause Analysis

Once service is restored to your users, it is time to evaluate why the problem occurred. Identifying the root cause permits you to change processes or implement different technologies to avoid the problem in the future.

Document Findings, Actions, and Outcomes Throughout the Process

Documentation is maintained throughout the server's lifecycle, including during the troubleshooting process. Documenting the symptoms of the problem, the results of research into potential solutions, and the results of each step of the plan of action (whether the step was successful or not) permits you to understand your environment better and therefore helps to prevent possible future problems. Note that documentation is not a separate step but rather a good practice used during each phase of the troubleshooting process.

Some service desk management software requires the use of tickets. Such software may require that troubleshooting documentation be entered before the ticket can be closed.

Guidelines for Troubleshooting Methods

- Troubleshooting is a key skill for systems administrators.
- A troubleshooting methodology makes the process more efficient and accurate.
- A troubleshooting methodology may change somewhat depending on the situation.
- The following steps suggest a likely troubleshooting methodology:
    - Identify the problem
    - Determine the scope
    - Establish a theory of probable cause/question the obvious
    - Test the theory to determine the cause
    - Establish a plan of action/implement the solution or escalate
    - Verify full system functionality
    - Implement preventive measures
    - Perform a root cause analysis
    - Document findings, actions, and outcomes throughout the process

Review Activity:

Discuss a Troubleshooting Methodology

Answer the following questions:

1. **While troubleshooting a printing problem with a network print device, you check to see that the print device is powered, is turned on, has paper, and does not have an alarm indicating that the paper path is jammed. Which step of the troubleshooting methodology are you applying?**

2. **While troubleshooting a permissions issue on a file server, you check to verify that a user that should be able to access a particular folder can access that folder. You also check that a user that should not be able to access the folder cannot access it. It appears that you have successfully solved the permissions issue. Which step of the troubleshooting methodology are you applying?**

3. **The service desk escalates a ticket to you that indicates a user cannot access any network servers or any websites. While troubleshooting, you ask several employees near the user whether they can access the network servers and websites. Those users all indicate that they can access the requested resources. You have now determined that only one user is experiencing issues. Which step of the troubleshooting methodology are you applying?**

Topic 1C

Manage Licenses

EXAM OBJECTIVES COVERED
2.8 Explain licensing concepts

One of the responsibilities of a sysadmin is to properly understand and maximize software licensing. This can be a complex task, but it is an essential one. In the next section, you will compare open-source and proprietary licenses and investigate license models.

Licenses Versus Maintenance and Support

A software license is a legal contract that governs the distribution and use of software. Licenses typically define how many installations of the software are allowed or how many concurrent users are allowed to use the software.

Software is governed by two different licensing structures. The first is the traditional proprietary software license. This license protects the source code of the software from modification or redistribution. The second type of license governs free and open-source software (FOSS). Open-source software may be modified and redistributed within the terms defined by the license. Microsoft Windows Server is governed by a proprietary license, and Linux is governed by an FOSS license.

FOSS licensing—a licensing model where users are free to use, modify, and re-release software voluntarily manner to improve the software.

- No cost
- Free to modify and redistribute
- Not necessarily reliable vendor support
- Not necessarily reliable documentation

Proprietary—a licensing model where the source code for the software is hidden, and users are not allowed to freely modify and rerelease the software. Proprietary software may also have an associated purchase cost. Proprietary licenses may be subscription or volume based.

- Not free to use
- Not free to modify
- More likely reliable vendor support
- More likely reliable documentation

While FOSS does not require a formal license, many vendors utilize a subscription service to maintain the OS or software. Red Hat, for example, has a subscription service associated with RHEL8.

Earlier in the lesson you used a web browser to connect to https://distrowatch.com/ to view the latest Linux distribution releases. Reconnect to Distrowatch and select one of the distributions. Observe that you can download the distribution for free.

Maintenance and Support Plans

It is important not to confuse the licensing and maintenance concepts. Just because you have the legal right to use a piece of software or install an OS does not necessarily entitle you to vendor support for the product. Some licensing models may include support. Subscription license models are an example. Support plans are covered later in the book.

Licensing Models

There are many different license models. Licensing varies between on-premises and cloud solutions, OSs, applications, virtualization technologies, and even number of users. The following list is a summary of some common license types:

- Subscription—a license that permits the use of software hosted in the cloud. Subscription licenses are billed yearly or monthly. They may include support costs as part of the subscription.
- Volume licensing—a single license that covers a specified number of installations for the convenience of large businesses. This model simplifies the license management process.
- Per-instance—one license for each instance of the software installed. If you run twenty copies of the software, you will need twenty licenses.
- Per-concurrent-user—one license for each software instance in use by a user. This is typically less expensive than per-seat licensing. If your organization has ten of these licenses, and there are twenty copies of the software installed, then only ten users may use the software simultaneously.
- Per-seat license—one license for each potential user of the software. This is typically more expensive than per-concurrent-user licensing.
- Per-server—client access licenses (CALs) installed on the server. The number of licenses determines the number of simultaneous connections that clients may make to the server. A server with ten per-server CALs will permit up to ten simultaneous client connections.
- Per-socket—licenses allocated to each processor socket that is enabled on the server's motherboard. It is important to note that the motherboard may contain more sockets than are licensed, but the extra sockets are disabled.
- Per-core—licenses allocated to each processor core that is enabled on the CPU. It is important to note that the CPU may contain more cores than are licensed, but the extra cores are disabled.
- Site-based—licenses that permit the installation of software within a specified site, building, or organization.
- Node-locked—licenses stored on a single node or on a Universal Serial Bus (USB) dongle, and any number of instances of the software may run on that node. The goal is to permit the software to run only on one computer.
- Physical vs. virtual—not all licenses apply the same way between physical installations on a server and installations that are done on VMs. You need to further investigate the licenses when dealing with VMs.

Consider the possible complexity of managing licenses in a small organization. If your organization has five Windows Server installations, you need a license for each installation. If your organization also has 100 Windows 10 clients, you need 100 licenses for your Windows 10 installations. You also need CALs to permit the Windows 10 clients to connect to the Windows Server servers. Those CALs may be managed in a per-set or per-server model. In addition, you still need to account for the licensing of all software that runs on the servers and the clients. One piece of software installed on your servers may use per-socket licensing, while another piece of software may use per-core licensing.

Your organization must be able to prove license compliance if it is audited. "License count validation" refers to the ability to demonstrate that the number of installations or the number of users matches the license specifications. If a company exceeds the number of installations for which it has a license, the company must purchase the appropriate number of licenses to "true up" its compliance. Microsoft, for example, may audit organizations to ensure that they are compliant and then require those organizations to true up.

Electronic Signatures

In many cases, you may be required to provide a digital signature or e-signature acknowledging a license agreement. Organizations such as DocuSign provide electronic signing options for licenses, contacts, and other legal agreements.

The digital signatures referenced in this section are not the same thing as the digital signature function found with the Public Key Infrastructure. In this case, the focus is on signatures for legal documents.

Version Compatibility

Licenses may permit users to use a specified software version and any version previous to that one. For example, a current software license for version three of a software package might also enable the use of versions one and two. This is an example of license backward compatibility. Licenses that are forward compatible permit the use of the current software version and one or more future releases of the software.

As a systems administrator, you must understand the license requirements for OSs and software to ensure that your organization remains compliant. There can be legal and financial penalties for failing to maintain proper licensing.

Guidelines for Managing Licenses

- Remember that FOSS licensing allows for the modification of source code and the distribution of the modified software.
- Remember that proprietary licensing does not permit modification of the source code.
- Determine a means to track licenses to ensure compliance.
- Understand the licensing methods, and recognize that a vendor may offer several license models.
- Understand whether a license includes maintenance and support.
- Cloud-based services often utilize a subscription-based licensing model.

Review Activity:

Licenses

Answer the following question:

1. **List at least three attributes of FOSS licensing and at least three attributes of proprietary licensing.**

2. **Anne, a developer, creates a piece of software named "SuperSolver" and licenses the software as open source. She places the source code and the compiled software executable on her website. John, another developer, downloads the source code for SuperSolver and modifies the code to add several new features. He places the modified source code on his website. This is an example of what kind of licensing?**

3. **You are a systems administrator, and you are responsible for managing the licenses for a piece of cloud-based software. Currently, you have 100 users that access the software. Your organization is billed monthly for these users. Your organization hires an additional 50 users who also need access. You increase your licenses by using a web-based management tool. You also notice that the vendor has automatically given your users access to the newly released 2.0 version of the software. This is an example of what kind of licensing?**

4. **You are systems administrator, and you are responsible for managing the license for a piece of server-based software. The software license requires you to pay based on the number of physical CPUs enabled on the server's motherboard. This is an example of what kind of license?**

Lesson 1

Summary

Systems administrators have a broad range of responsibilities. The sysadmin's role includes understanding the server's place in the network as a component that provides services to end-user workstations or remote clients and requires a high degree of security. Effectively troubleshooting servers calls for a reliable troubleshooting methodology that quickly narrows the scope of the problem and helps to prevent future issues. Sysadmins are also responsible for licensing, which can become complex very quickly. Frequently, server environments rely on a mix of proprietary licenses, as with Microsoft Windows Server, and open-source licenses, aswith Linux distributions, such as RHEL or Ubuntu.

1. **Compare and contrast proprietary licensing versus open source. What are the benefits and drawbacks of each?**

2. **In what circumstances have you applied the troubleshooting method discussed in this Lesson?**

Lesson 2

Understanding Virtualization and Cloud Computing

LESSON INTRODUCTION

Modern server management is heavily integrated with virtualization and cloud-based deployments. In this section, you will understand virtualization concepts for on-premises deployments. You will then examine cloud computing concepts and how they relate to virtualization. Finally, you will look at the considerations for choosing between on-premises and cloud virtualized deployments.

Lesson Objectives

In this lesson, you will:

- Understand virtualization concepts.
- Understand cloud computing concepts.
- Understand on-premises versus cloud deployments.

Topic 2A

Understand Virtualization Concepts

EXAM OBJECTIVES COVERED
2.5 Summarize the purpose and operation of virtualization

Virtualization technologies revolutionized the delivery of IT services. In the past, businesses had to predict utilization trends, purchase expensive and dedicated hardware, and manage the physical lifecycle of that hardware. That deployment model was not agile and did not scale well. The rise of enterprise-class virtualization technologies has completely altered the server lifecycle. Today's sysadmins must understand virtualization concepts and be prepared to work with virtualized deployments.

Virtualization Concepts

Virtualization technologies revolutionized the delivery of IT services. In the past, businesses had to predict utilization trends, purchase expensive and dedicated hardware, and manage the physical lifecycle of that hardware. That deployment model was not agile and did not scale well. The rise of enterprise-class virtualization technologies has completely altered the server lifecycle. Today's sysadmins must understand virtualization concepts and be prepared to work with virtualized deployments.

Virtualization

Virtualization represents a very significant portion of modern server deployments. Many organizations opt to maintain just a few very powerful servers that host many VMs. Sysadmins are key players in deciding whether to deploy a traditional server installation or virtualize a server. It is increasingly difficult to justify the added costs and maintenance of traditional servers that have a single OS installed.

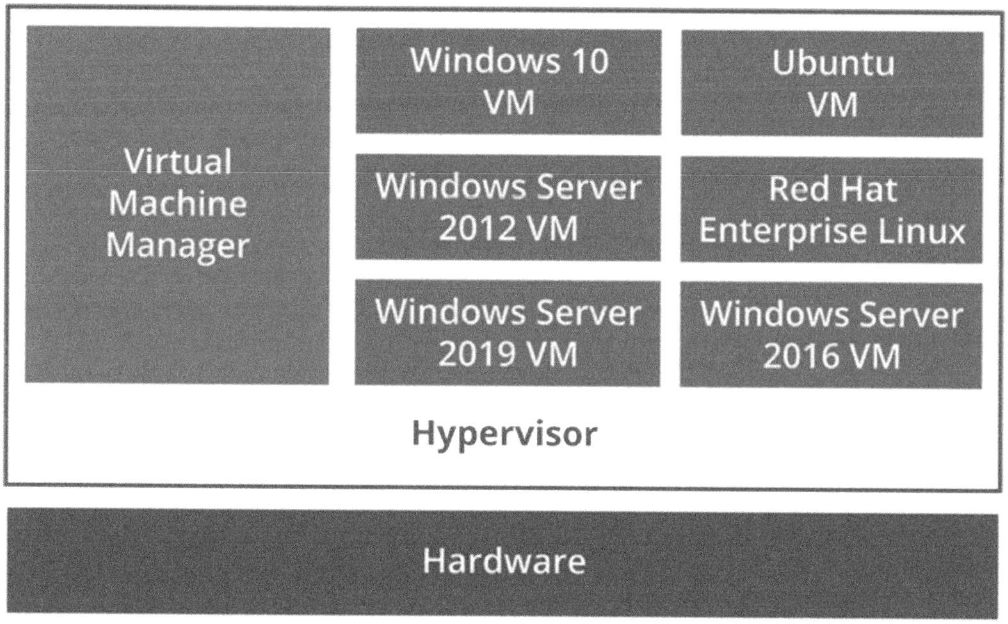

Hardware layer, a hypervisor, guest VMs, and a virtual machine manager.

Redundancy and High Availability

A basic virtualization deployment suffers from a single point of failure (the host system) that impacts every guest VM on that server. For this reason, redundancy and high availability are essential for virtualization. Many virtualization solutions include the ability to replicate VMs between two or more hosts. If one host fails, the other host will have a complete and up-to-date version of the guest VMs. In addition, virtualization hosts should have redundant hardware, such as HDDs, NICs, and power supplies.

Redundancy and high availability are discussed in greater detail later in the book.

Host System Versus Guest System

Virtualization begins with a single physical server, referred to as the "host system." The host is usually a powerful server with redundant hardware to help ensure performance and availability.

Next, a virtualization layer of software called a "hypervisor" is added to the hardware. The hypervisor allocates resources to VMs. There are two types of hypervisors.

- Type 1—the virtualization software is installed directly on the physical server, without using a traditional OS layer between the hardware and the hypervisor. The hypervisor acts as its own OS. Examples of Type 1 hypervisors include VMware ESXi, Microsoft Hyper-V, and Kernel-Based Virtual Machine (KVM).
- Type 2—a traditional OS, such as Windows Server, is installed directly on the physical server, and then the hypervisor software is added and runs within the OS. Examples of Type 2 hypervisors include Oracle VirtualBox and VMware Workstation.

Type 2 hypervisors are usually sufficient for smaller environments. Developers, IT students, and system administrators engaged in testing may all use Type 2 hypervisors, even on regular workstation hardware. However, enterprise-class virtualization requirements may justify the use of Type 1 hypervisors. These solutions may include a much more expensive licensing structure, but they also tend to include high availability solutions and more features.

Virtualization guests are the VMs carved from the physical host server's available resources by the hypervisor. VMs are individually allocated a portion of the hardware, including processor time, RAM, storage capacity, and network access. The specifications of a VM are much the same as the specifications for a regular physical computer. Once you create the VM, you install an OS and applications on it. The result is one or more fully functional VMs running on a single piece of hardware, with scalable hardware resource allocation.

Manage Virtualization Resources

Virtualization relies on a single hardware deployment that then supports one or more VMs. The VMs are each allocated some quantity of the hardware's overall resources. This allocation resembles the process of defining hardware specifications when purchasing a physical server. For example, if the server hosting the VMs has a total of 64 gigabytes (GB) of RAM, each VM running on that server is allocated a portion of that total. Let's say the first VM is allocated 16 GB of RAM, while the second is allocated 8 GB of RAM. In theory, that leaves an additional 40 GB of RAM available for other VMs that may be deployed. A similar process occurs with CPU time, storage capacity, and network bandwidth.

Some resources must also remain unallocated to the VMs and available to the host hypervisor or OS.

Overprovision

Systems administrators must ensure that the host server has enough physical hardware resources to meet the needs of the VMs. Therefore, the server is equipped with more hardware resources than the anticipated use requires.

For example, to provide the VMs with plenty of network bandwidth, the administrator installs multiple NICs and configures them to use network teaming. The combined bandwidth of the NICs is higher than the anticipated need.

Over-Allocate Resources

It is possible to deliberately over-allocate server resources. In fact, this feature is one of the main goals of virtualization. Different applications have different processor requirements. In many cases, physical server processors sit idle much of the time. By over-allocating processor resources to multiple VMs, it is possible to make better use of overall processor time. The decision to do so requires a great deal of monitoring to understand exactly what the processor requirements of the VMs are and when those requirements need to be met. Over-allocating without solid information can negatively impact the performance of the host server and all the guest VMs.

The quantity of hardware resources granted to VMs is managed dynamically to meet changing business needs. For example, during the early stages of an application server deployment, only a few users may access the VM to test the application. Once the application is fully tested and ready for deployment enterprise-wide, the system administrator allocates additional hardware to the VM to match the increased demand.

Virtual Networking

Virtualization also takes place at the network layer. **Virtual machines (VMs)** may have one or more virtual network interface cards (vNICs). These vNICs are configured like physical NICs and are attached to virtual switches. Each virtual NIC has its own MAC address and IP address to permit the VM to participate on a physical or virtual network as an independent node. In addition, the VM can join a Virtual Local Area Network (VLAN). Virtual switches are used to better manage network traffic.

Virtual machines can share a virtual **bridge** with the host device, which enables network access for the virtual machines. Virtual machines typically have four options for network access:

- None—as if they have no NIC installed
- Local—network access only to other virtual machines on the same host
- Host-only—access only to the host computer and not to the physical network or Internet
- Bridged—access to the physical network or Internet

Bridged or direct access is useful for virtual machines acting as production servers, such as Domain Name System (DNS) or webservers. From the perspective of the client computers, the virtual machines are normal servers on the network. Local or host-only access is useful in test or development environments where the virtual machines need to be isolated.

Network address translation (NAT) is a method for substituting public and private IP addresses in IPv4 packet headers. The private IP address ranges are only used on internal networks and not valid on the external public Internet. NAT is a service the runs on routers or within virtualization hypervisors to provide valid addressing between two networks.

The host hypervisor uses NAT to permit network traffic to move between network segments and even between the internal local area network's private IP address scheme and the public IP addresses of the Internet. The hypervisor also provides bridging between the host server's physical NIC and the vNICs for the VMs. For example, in Microsoft Hyper-V, vNICs are configured for public, private, and internal settings.

More details are provided on NAT in Lesson 7.

Management Interfaces for VMs

There are various management consoles available for VMs. Type 2 hypervisors likely have a basic console that runs locally and manages any local VMs. Enterprise virtualization solutions that rely on Type 1 hypervisors have a more centralized management interface.

Microsoft and VMware install consoles on the administrator's workstation that can then connect to one or more virtualization hosts and permit centralized remote administration. For a Microsoft solution, you install the Hyper-V console. For VMware, you use vSphere. Both platforms provide access to VMs hosted on other hypervisors.

VMs may also be managed from the command line. Such administration permits efficient, scheduled, consistent, and automated management.

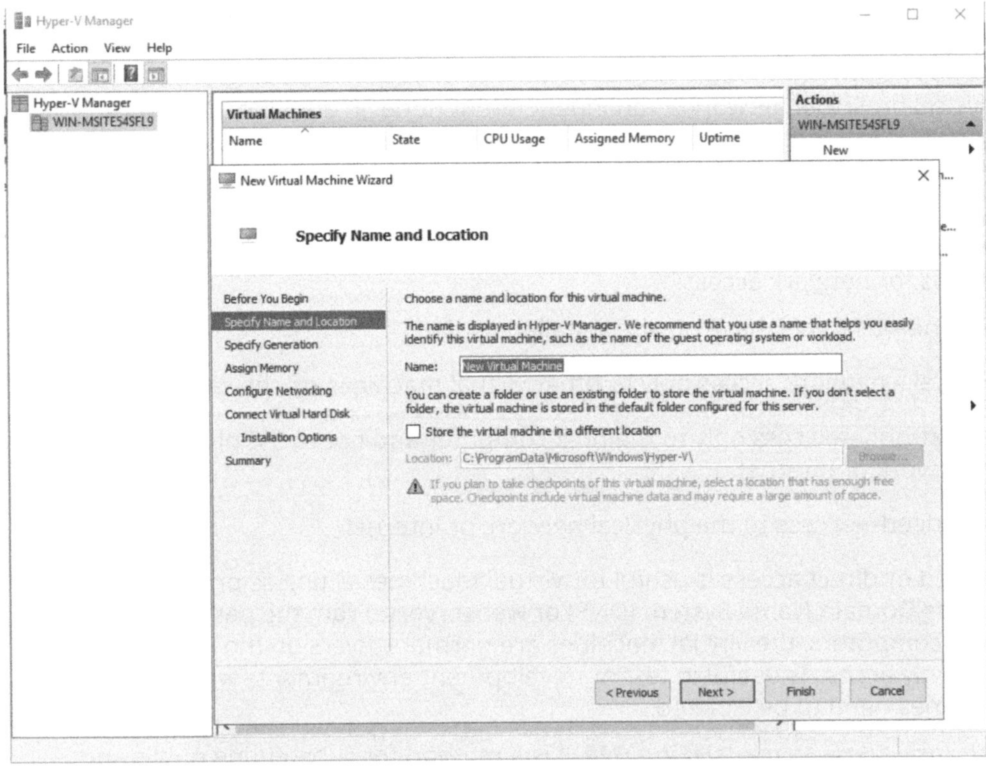

Windows Server Hyper-V console. (Screenshot courtesy of Microsoft.)

Review Activity:

Virtualization Concepts

Answer the following questions:

1. **How does virtualization improve scalability as compared to physical server deployments?**

2. **What is the difference between Type 1 and Type 2 hypervisors?**

3. **What is the role of virtual networking in virtualization?**

Topic 2B

Understanding Cloud Concepts

EXAM OBJECTIVES COVERED
2.5 Summarize the purpose and operation of virtualization

Cloud computing takes the concept of virtualization a step further. Servers hosted in the cloud are actually still VMs. Rather than running on physical servers on your premises, they are hosted in a cloud service provider (CSP) data center. Cloud computing offloads responsibility for various aspects of the server lifecycle from your enterprise to the CSP.

Cloud computing is prevalent in today's IT infrastructure. When standing up a new server, one of the earliest discussion points should be whether to deploy the server on-premises or in the cloud.

Cloud Characteristics

There are five characteristics defined by the National Institute of Standards and Technology (NIST) that describe cloud computing:

- On-demand self-service—resources are provisioned when needed by the consumer without relying on the CSP.
- Broad network access—services are available on the business network or the Internet from most kinds of network-connected devices (phones, tablets, workstations/laptops, servers, etc.).
- Resource pooling—compute resources are pooled together and then allocated to tenants on an as-needed basis.
- Rapid elasticity—resource use is scaled up and down as needed, permitting consumers to pay for the quantity of resources that they need at any given time.
- Measured service—resource utilization is monitored and billed based on actual use.

These five characteristics have revolutionized how IT services are provided. Cloud computing changes how organizations manage capital expenditure (CapEx), the skillsets required for sysadmins, and how software and hardware are maintained.

Cloud Deployment Models

There are three primary **cloud deployment models**, with a fourth that is simply any combination of the other three. These models define who is responsible for the data center that hosts the underlying infrastructure of the cloud services.

- Private cloud
- Public cloud
- Community cloud
- Hybrid cloud

Private Cloud

A **private cloud** consists of one or more data centers that provide services exclusively to a single organization, and these are owned and maintained by that organization. Private clouds offer significant data security because hardware resources are not shared across multiple clients, but they are very expensive for this same reason.

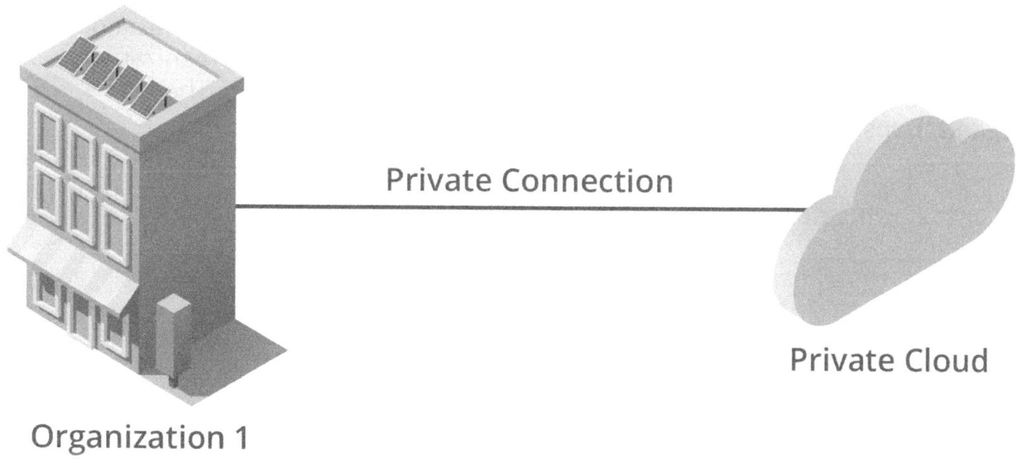

Private cloud model. (Images © 123RF.com)

For example, your organization owns two data centers and has hired an IT staff of cloud administrators to manage the data center. The IT staff uses cloud technologies to offer cloud services, such as Software as a Service (SaaS) and Platform as a Service (PaaS), to other employees of the organization. The data center, cloud, and personnel are internal organization resources.

Public Cloud

Public cloud solutions consist of data centers owned and maintained by CSPs that then share the resources of those data centers to customers. Customer data is dynamically allocated to available hardware resources as needed. Public clouds provide cost savings compared to private clouds, but there is an increased risk to data due to the shared resources.

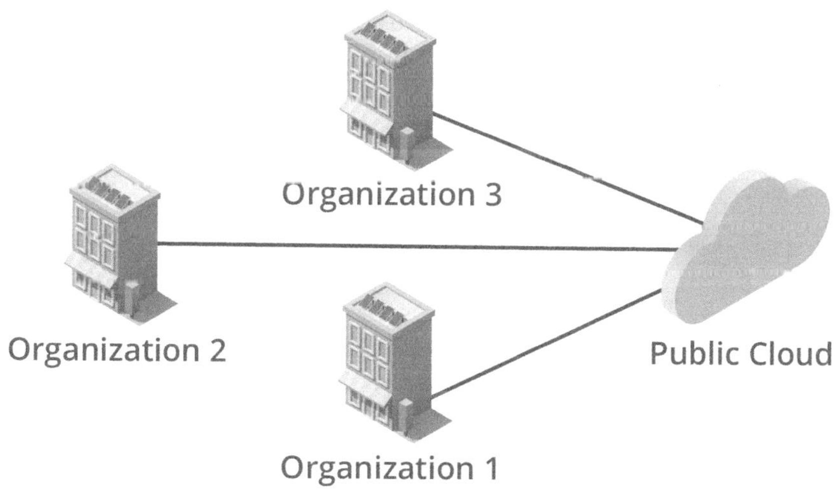

Public cloud model, showing three organizations sharing one publicly accessible cloud. (Images © 123RF.com)

In a public cloud example, your organization has established subscription-licensed relationship with a CSP, such as Amazon, Microsoft, or Google. The CSP maintains a data center and the staff to support it. Your organization accesses the data center resources to develop cloud services, such as Infrastructure as a Service (IaaS), PaaS, or SaaS.

Community Cloud

Community clouds exist in a data center owned and maintained by several organizations, and its resources are available exclusively to those organizations. This model takes advantage of the cost savings of having several organizations support the data center and maintains a higher degree of security. The organizations typically have similar security requirements.

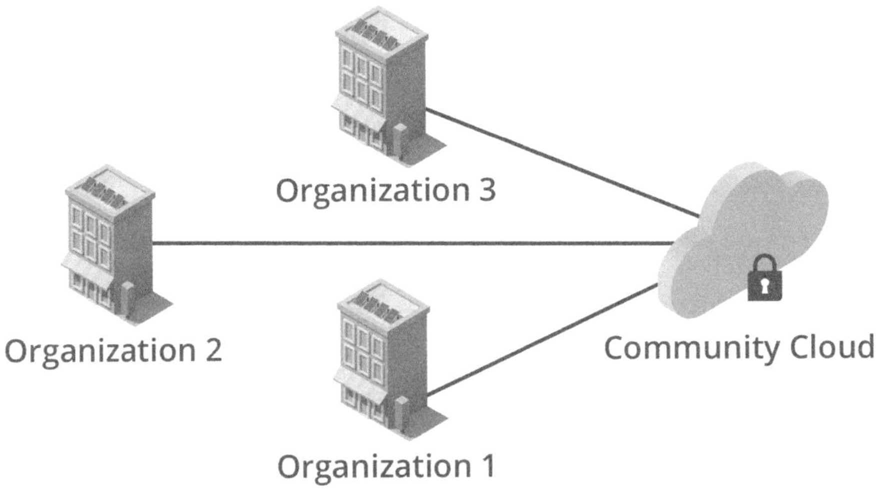

Community cloud model, showing three organizations sharing a secured cloud. (Images © 123RF.com)

As an example of a community cloud, your organization has partnered with three other organizations in your industry to invest in a data center and the IT staff to support it. That data center's resources are available only to the four organizations that have invested in it.

Hybrid Cloud

The **hybrid cloud** model is any combination of the above three cloud deployment models. An organization may choose to store some data in a private cloud deployment for security but other data in a public cloud deployment for cost savings.

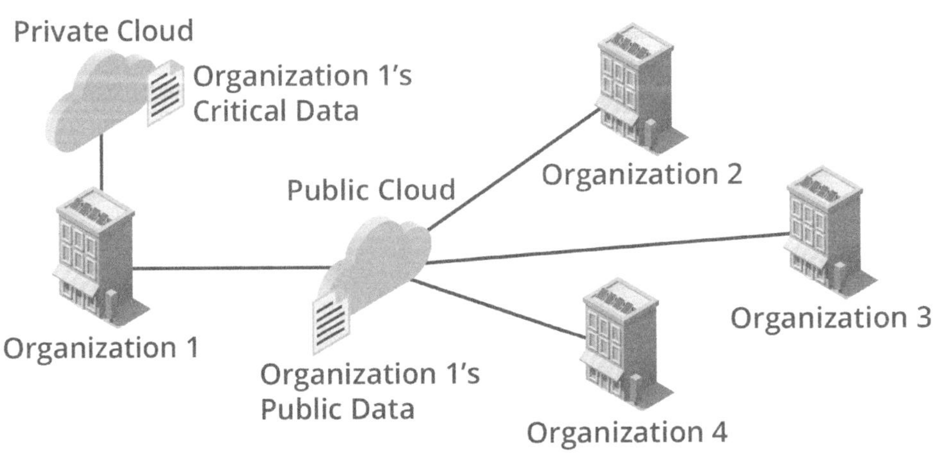

Hybrid cloud model. (Images © 123RF.com)

In a hybrid cloud scenario, your organization uses some combination of the other three deployment models. For example, your organization uses Microsoft's Office 365 SaaS cloud solution, which is part of Microsoft's public cloud. Your organization maintains its own data center and staff to maintain an IaaS environment that hosts highly secure proprietary data.

Cloud Service Models

There are many models available for **cloud services**. In fact, the "**Anything as a Service**" concept has been applied to a wide variety of IT functions. One way to understand the service models is to consider whether responsibility for support lies with the CSP or the organization. Let's consider the three basic cloud services.

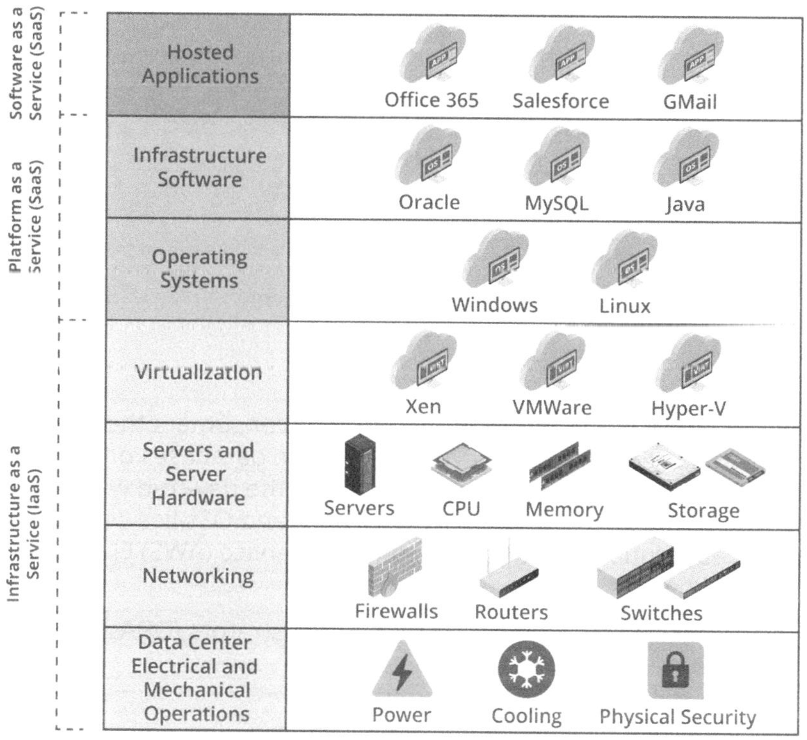

Three cloud service models. (Images © 123RF.com)

SaaS

SaaS—consumers have access to the software, but the responsibility for installing, maintaining, patching, and upgrading that software lies with the vendor. The vendor is also responsible for supporting the underlying hardware and OSs that run the software. Examples of SaaS solutions include Microsoft Office 365, Google Docs, and Netflix.

SaaS target audience: End users

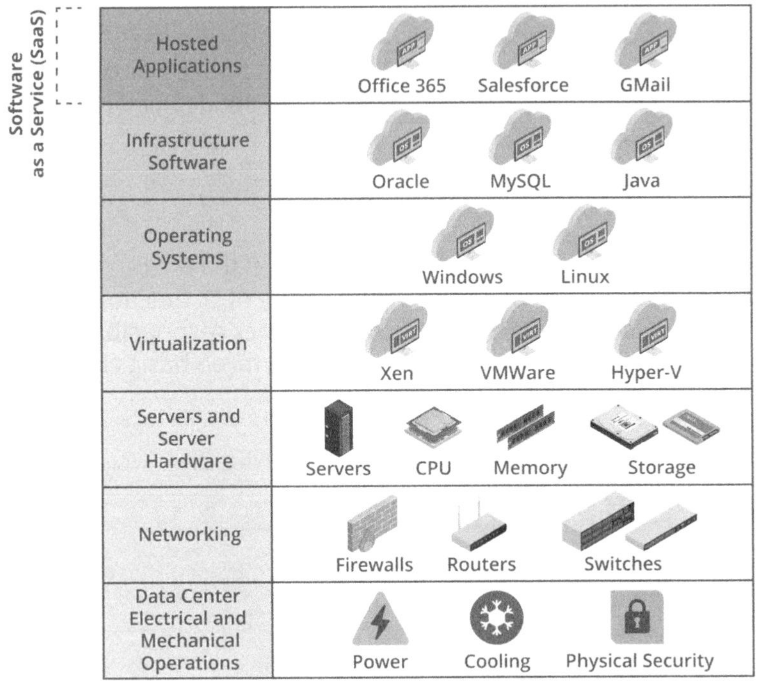

SaaS. (Images © 123RF.com)

PaaS

PaaS—the CSP supports the service structure, and consumers then populate and use that structure. The service structure may be databases or development environments. Consumers are also responsible for the day-to-day management of the platform. Support for the underlying hardware and OSs lies with the vendor. Examples of PaaS solutions include Amazon Web Service (AWS) Elastic Beanstalk and Google App Engine.

PaaS target audience: Developers, database administrators (DBAs)

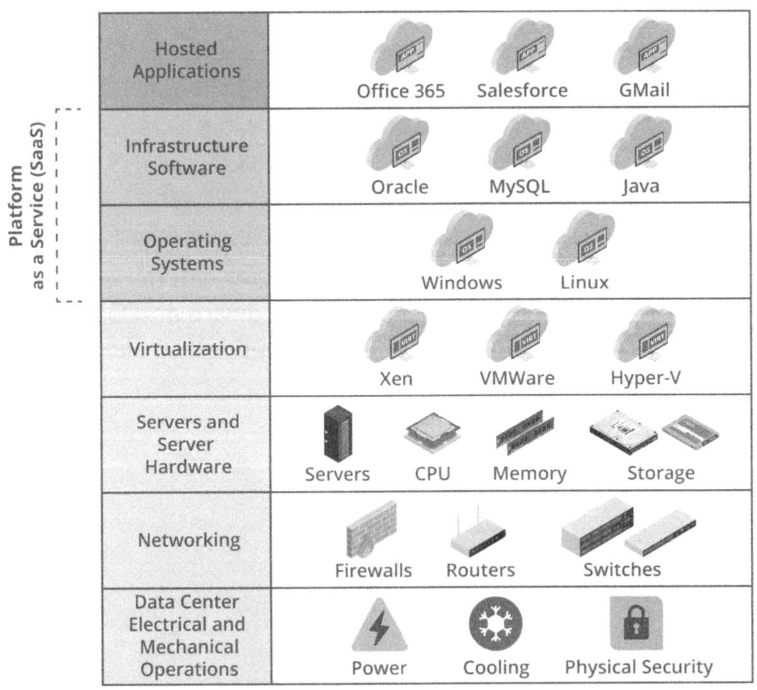

PaaS. (Images © 123RF.com)

IaaS

IaaS—consumers access hardware that is made available and maintained by the CSP. Consumers install and maintain OSs and applications on that hardware, without having to absorb the cost of hardware support. IaaS is essentially the use and control of VMs hosted in someone else's data center. Examples of IaaS solutions include AWS EC2, Microsoft Azure, and Rackspace.

IaaS target audience: Systems administrators

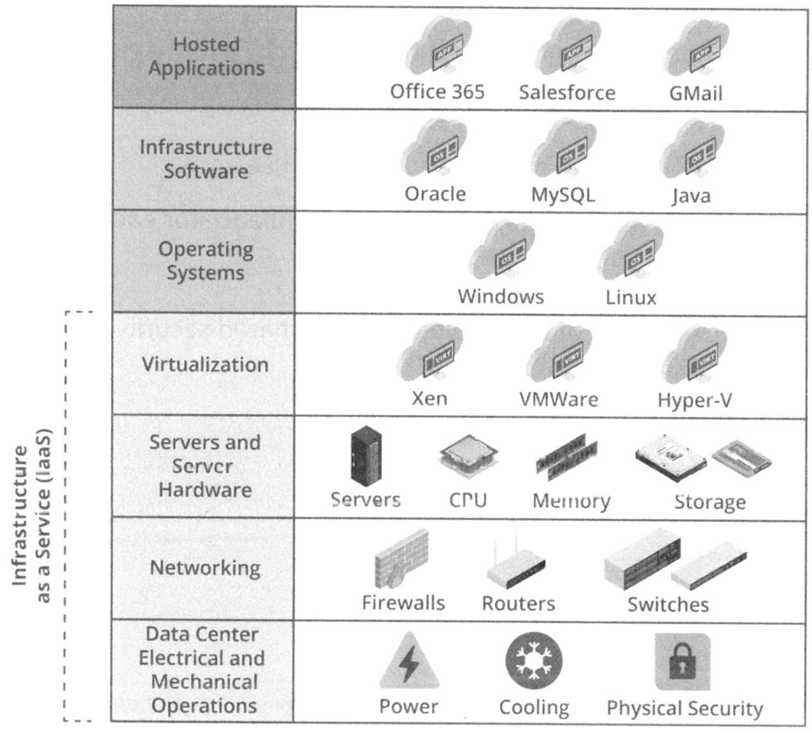

IaaS. (Images © 123RF.com)

Cloud Service Providers

There are many key players in the cloud services realm, but three of the most common are Amazon, Microsoft, and Google.

AWS offers a wide variety of services, including SaaS, PaaS, and IaaS solutions. AWS is hosted on Linux, and it can also support both Linux and Windows VMs. AWS data centers are distributed worldwide.

Microsoft Azure also offers a wide variety of available services that span all three of the service models. Azure is hosted on Windows, and it can also support Linux and Windows VMs. Microsoft has secured data centers worldwide.

Google Cloud Platform (GCP) provides SaaS, PaaS, and IaaS services, and it also supports both Linux and Windows VMs. Google's data centers exist worldwide.

All three of the major **CSPs** satisfy the three cloud service models. They each provide many different options tailored to meet the IT needs of almost any business. A vast number of organizations are migrating some or all of their IT services to the cloud.

The Shared Security Model

Cloud server administrators must understand the security responsibilities of the organization and the CSP. This relationship is called the "shared security model." The CSP is responsible for the physical security of the data center and hardware availability. The organization is responsible for the security of the data housed on that hardware.

Another way of putting this is that the CSP is responsible for the security of cloud resources, while the organization is responsible for the security of data in the cloud.

Guidelines for Understanding Cloud Concepts

- Know the five characteristics of cloud computing.
- Know the four deployment models and when to use each.
- Know the three service models and the target audience for each.
- Know the three major CSPs.
- Understand the division of responsibility in the shared security model.

Review Activity:

Cloud Computing

Answer the following questions:

1. **What are the five characteristics of cloud computing, according to NIST?**

2. **What are the four cloud deployment models?**

3. **What are the three cloud service models?**

4. **What is the cloud shared security model?**

Topic 2C

Understand On-Premises Versus Cloud Deployments

EXAM OBJECTIVES COVERED
2.5 Summarize the purpose and operation of virtualization

Systems administrators have many considerations when choosing between an on-premises or a cloud-based deployment. Concerns arise around service availability, cost, control, and security. Not all services and applications lend themselves to being hosted in the cloud, and not all industry regulations will permit cloud deployments.

On-Premises, Physical Server

The traditional server infrastructure has included a secured server room containing one or more racks of physical servers. Each server has a single OS installed on it. This sort of deployment allows for customized hardware and application solutions, though it is less flexible than on-premises or cloud virtual deployments.

The organization is responsible for all aspects of maintaining the servers, including provisioning, administration, security, troubleshooting, and purchasing.

One of the most important aspects of maintaining physical servers is the ability to retain control of the server itself and the data stored on it.

On-Premises, Virtual Server

On-premises virtual servers are similar to physical server deployments, but VMs often provide greater **scalability**, disaster recovery, and high availability. The use of custom hardware or custom applications may be more difficult with virtualized servers.

Like on-premises physical server deployments, on-premises virtual servers allow an organization to retain complete control of the hardware, OS, applications, and data.

Cloud, Virtual Server

Cloud-based virtualization provides many advantages over on-premises deployments, whether physical or virtual. Cloud services remove the direct support costs and effort for hardware, patching, and other administrative tasks. At the same time, cloud virtualization may increase disaster recovery and high availability.

Cloud services provide simplified licensing and a pay-as-you-go model that allows organizations to only pay for the resources that they use. Furthermore, these resources are easily scaled depending on business requirements.

It is worth noting that organizations lose a certain amount of control when it comes to cloud-based deployments. Sysadmins have less control over hardware, software, and resource access than they would with on-premises deployments. Access to resources is also dependent on a reliable and sufficiently fast Internet connection.

On-Premises versus Cloud Deployments

On-Premises Deployments

On-premises deployments are fully controlled but also fully funded by the organization.

Advantages of on-premises deployments:

- The organization retains complete control of the deployment environment.
- The organization retains complete control of administration and management.
- The organization retains complete control of data.
- Data may be maintained nearer to the users.
- A high degree of application customization and specialized hardware is available.

Disadvantages of on-premises deployments:

- The organization bears the entire cost of supporting the service, including hardware, installation, maintenance, and personnel.
- There is a higher initial CapEx.
- There is less flexibility with hardware utilization.
- It is difficult to scale based on demand.
- There is a slower deployment time.
- The organization bears the entire cost of securing data and providing security expertise.

Cloud Deployments

Advantages of cloud deployments:

- The organization only pays for the cloud resources that it consumes.
- The organization does not bear the cost of supporting the service.
- The organization retains control of most of the service administration and management.

Many CSPs are certified for personally identifiable information (PII), Payment Card Industry Data Security Standard (PCI DSS), Family Educational Rights and Privacy Act, and other industry standards.

- There is a simplified licensing and pay-as-you-go model.
- Data may be replicated worldwide and therefore be available nearer to geographically dispersed users.
- Geo-redundancy increases availability.
- It may reduce CapEx.
- It is much easier to scale based on demand.
- Deployment time is quicker.
- CSPs may offer security and administrative expertise.

Disadvantages of cloud deployments:

- The organization does not retain control of the deployment environment.
- The organization may lose access to data in the event of the loss of Internet connectivity or CSP downtime.
- It may increase operation expenditures (OpEx).
- Data may be maintained farther from the users.

Hybrid Deployments

Organizations may choose to deploy some services on-premises and others in the cloud. Such a deployment is known as a "hybrid cloud model." Data with high-security requirements are managed on-premises, while other data and services are deployed via a CSP. Organizations that utilize a hybrid deployment model take advantage of each solution's strengths and minimize the weaknesses.

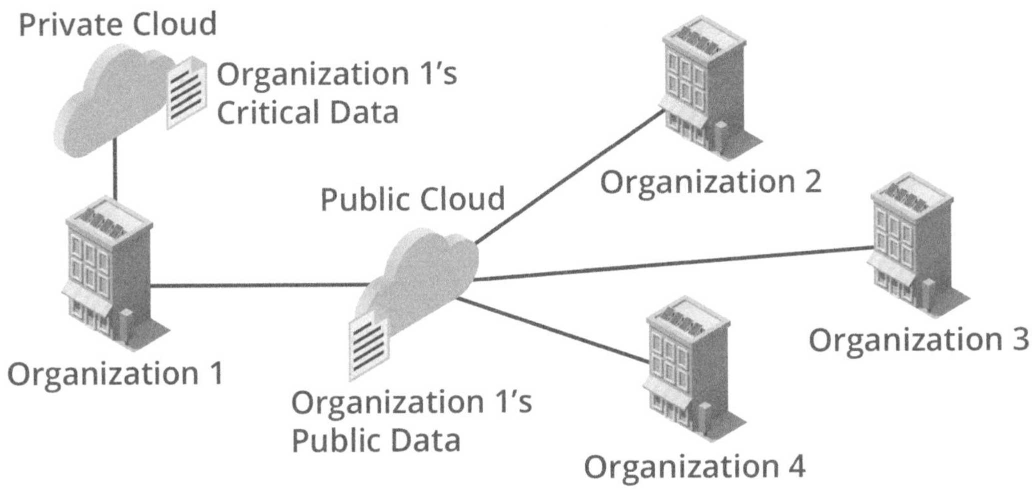

Hybrid deployment model. (Images © 123RF.com)

Choosing Between On-Premises and Cloud Deployments

Small and medium-sized organizations may prefer a cloud deployment due to its flexibility and low initial costs. Organizations with unique or high security requirements may choose an on-premises deployment to retain full control of the data and services.

Review Activity:

Deployment Models

Answer the following questions:

1. **List at least two advantages of on-premises deployments over cloud deployments.**

2. **List at least two disadvantages of on-premises deployments over cloud deployments.**

Lesson 2

Summary

- Today's modern network environments rely on physical servers, virtualization, and cloud-based services to fulfill the needs of users and customers.
- Organizations might choose to host VMs on on-premises physical servers or in the cloud.
- Virtualization provides many opportunities for high availability and scalability.
- While IaaS mostly just changes the location of the VM (from the premises to the cloud), PaaS and SaaS expand virtualization's functionality.
- Choosing between on-premises physical, on-premises virtual, and off-premises cloud solutions requires a good understanding of the benefits and drawbacks of each approach.
- Hybrid solutions will often maximize the benefits and minimize the drawbacks of any one solution.

1. **What cloud-based services are you using at home? At work?**
2. **What benefits does the scalability of virtualization bring to the services hosted on servers?**

Lesson 3

Understanding Physical and Network Security Concepts

LESSON INTRODUCTION

Systems administrators are responsible for basic security configurations to protect the confidentiality, integrity, and availability of services and data. Physical security is of paramount importance, and it is the foundation for all other security measures. Network security must also be guaranteed by using secure protocols, network segmentation strategies, and policies to manage data in transit across your network.

Lesson Objectives

In this lesson, you will:

- Understand physical security concepts.
- Understand network security concepts.

Topic 3A

Understand Physical Security Concepts

EXAM OBJECTIVES COVERED
3.2 Summarize physical security concepts

Physical security is the most fundamental form of computer security. It governs access to the server, the server's availability, and protection of the data stored on the server. In this section, you will examine how to implement physical security. You begin with an examination of the property where the data center resides, then move to the inside of the building, to the data center itself, the network operations center (NOC), and, finally, the actual server itself.

Many years ago, Microsoft published a document named "The 10 Immutable Laws of Security." Law #3 stated: "If a bad guy has unrestricted physical access to your computer, it's not your computer anymore." Keep this adage in mind as you review the concepts covered in this Topic.

Physical Security—An Outside in Approach

In this section, you examine physical security from outside of the data center working inward toward the actual physical servers. You begin with the data center building and property and then look at managing entryways into the facility. Next, you examine the interior of the data center itself, including the NOC or server room. Finally, you look at physical security controls for the actual servers.

Security is implemented in a layered approach. No single technology is meant to physically protect the server and its data. Instead, use layers of security to address specific threats.

Building and Property Security

Physical security begins with the data center building and the property where it resides. In high-security environments, the property may be gated and fenced. Landscaping, such as trees and boulders, are used to block access to the building. Exterior lighting is an essential deterrent to criminals. The facility may also use exterior cameras to display and record activity outside of the building. The property itself can effectively protect the data center.

Bollards

The building may also be protected by **bollards** that enforce a buffer zone between the building and motor traffic. These bollards help to prevent ramming attacks. Bollards are common near building entrances.

Bollards separate areas of motor traffic from buildings and pedestrian walkways. Some are powered, featuring lights and retractability, while other designs are static concrete or steel posts. (Image by Nikita Bylugin © 123RF.com)

The building's architecture may integrate other forms of security, including reflective glass, structural designs that block wireless signals, deceptive signage to camouflage the data center, and a lack of windows.

The building and property landscaping design are often tied to the physical security aspects of the data center.

Perimeter Security

The goal of perimeter security is to control the flow of people in and out of the building and separate visitors from regular employees. Many tools exist to help manage people's physical access within the data center.

- Exterior entry—require visitors to buzz in or request access to the perimeter doors.
- Interior entry—restrict interior doors and access points to employees and documented guests. Mark such doors with warnings, such as "Employees Only."
- Turnstiles—pass individuals through an entry one at a time. Turnstiles usually reach from ceiling to floor.
- Mantraps—install two doors, similar to turnstiles. Employees and visitors enter through the first door and then authenticate before proceeding through the second door. At any point, security personnel can stop the individual's entry.

A security station enforces the management of visitors. The security desk provides guest badges, notifies employees that their guests have arrived, ensures that all visitors are properly escorted, and requires all visitors to sign in and sign out of the facility. The entryway is also under surveillance.

Emergency doors that exit the building should be one-way doors without exterior door handles. These doors should also be alarmed and under surveillance.

Interior Data Center

The area of the building that houses the actual data centers and server rooms has restricted access and will likely have specific physical security measures. Visitors are certainly escorted, and all personnel are authenticated before entering the area. The facility is under surveillance.

Network closets contain network devices, such as switches, routers, and wireless access points (WAPs) that may not be able to be physically installed in the server rooms. Such closets must remain locked because the devices inside provide direct access to network traffic. These devices also have complex configurations that should not be accessible to visitors or unauthorized employees. In addition, you should route network cable through conduits to provide physical protection.

Patch panel in a network closet. (Image by Svetlana Kurochkina © 123RF.com)

Often, interior walls in business buildings are really only partitions between sections. The partition walls only rise as high as a hanging ceiling, which allows access between building sections by going over the walls. The interior of the data center may be designed with full walls that rise from floor to ceiling and stop such access via hanging ceilings. The data center will likely not have windows.

Heat, Ventilation, and Air Conditioning (HVAC)

Proper air circulation is essential to maintaining servers, especially in server rooms, where large numbers of devices may be generating heat. Server racks are organized in aisles to facilitate air flow, and air conditioning maintains an optimal temperature. Proper humidity levels must also be maintained to reduce static electricity.

- Target temperature: 68–71 degrees Fahrenheit (20–21.6 degrees Celsius)
- Maximum temperature range: 60–82 degrees Fahrenheit (15.5–27.8 degrees Celsius)
- Target humidity level: 40–60% rH (relative humidity)

The data center interior will typically have redundant utilities and electrical circuits, eliminating any single points of failure. There may be generators that support this portion of the building, too. Air monitoring and **HVAC** systems may be isolated to this section of the facility.

Additional environmental controls are covered later, including information regarding hot and cold aisles in server rooms.

Network Operations Center/Server Room

The location that houses the servers is referred to as the NOC, or, more informally, the server room. Server rooms are specifically designed to house the servers. The rooms are air-conditioned, are humidified to cut down on static electricity, and have multiple electrical circuits. The server rooms store the business's most valuable IT devices.

The most fundamental way to secure the server room is by locking the door and controlling access to the room's interior. There are many possible types of locks:

- **Biometric** scanners—identifies users by using fingerprints, handprints, facial recognition, retinal/eye maps, etc.
- **Radio frequency identification (RFID)**—identifies users by using a chipped access card that transmits a signal on a designated frequency. The card reader accepts the signal.
- Card readers—identifies users by reading chipped cards that contain authentication certificates.
- Electronic keyless locks—open only for an authorized combination, which may include alphanumeric characters or specific patterns.
- Multifactor Authentication (MFA)—identifies users by using combinations of the above factors.

Fire Suppression

Temperature, smoke, and fire sensors protect the server room and alert administrators to a fire. **Fire suppression** in server rooms differs from fire suppression elsewhere in the building because water sprinkler systems put the servers at risk. Modern fire suppression works to protect the equipment in the server room and any people that might be present. Fire suppression using inert gasses, such as argon and nitrogen, reduces the oxygen level from the standard 21% to a range of 10–15%, suffocating the fire but still providing oxygen for people. These inert gasses are non-corrosive and non-conductive.

Secure Storage for Backup Media

You must provide secure storage for backup media, but that storage is typically away from the NOC. Separating the backup media from the servers helps to maintain the data's availability in the event of a disaster in the server room. Use fireproof safes to protect important documentation or even backups.

The server room, like everywhere else in the data center, is usually under surveillance.

Physical Server Security

The server room is protected by the layers of physical security discussed above, but there are additional protections inside it.

Signing in to the server may require MFA. For example, the administrator might have to insert a smart card into a card reader and provide a personal identification number (PIN). This example relies on "what you have" (smart card) and "what you know" (PIN) to verify the administrator.

The servers are typically mounted in standardized racks. These racks provide stability, cable management, and access to the servers, but they also provide physical security. The racks may be locked to stop anyone from touching the servers, accessing their removable media slots (such as USB), or removing their HDDs. Rack-mounted servers are much easier to secure than tower-style server cases.

You will learn more about server racks in a later section.

Rack-mounted servers behind a locked door. (Image © 123RF.com)

Review Activity:

Physical Security Concepts

Answer the following questions:

1. **Explain the outside-in approach to physical security.**

2. **List at least three examples of building or property security measures:**

3. **List at least three examples of perimeter security measures:**

Topic 3B

Understand Network Security Concepts

EXAM OBJECTIVES COVERED
2.2 Given a scenario, configure servers to use network infrastructure services

Network security is associated with server management and the role of the systems administrator. Like physical security, network security is organized into layers. Administrators use network segmentation, different types of network devices, firewalls, and network protocols to secure data.

Intercept Network Traffic

It is relatively easy to intercept network traffic. This is one of the key concepts to keep in mind with network security. Because most network traffic is not encrypted, it can be easily read once it is intercepted. This is a fundamental idea—email, file transfers, web browsing, print jobs, and other common network traffic are not usually encrypted and therefore vulnerable to being read by anyone on the network whocan intercept them.

You will examine the tools used for intercepting network traffic later in this section. At this point, the key is to understand that such interception is possible and relatively straightforward to accomplish.

Tools such as Wireshark and tcpdump are used to intercept network traffic. Both tools display packet header information, such as source and destination IP address, source and destination MAC address, and transport layer protocol. Both tools can also display the contents of the transmission. If the contents are not encrypted, anyone can read the data. For example, email message content that is not encrypted will be viewable.

Protocol analyzers, including Wireshark and tcpdump, can be excellent network troubleshooting utilities. They can also be used for security audits. However, these tools can be used maliciously to intercept confidential data, called eavesdropping attacks.

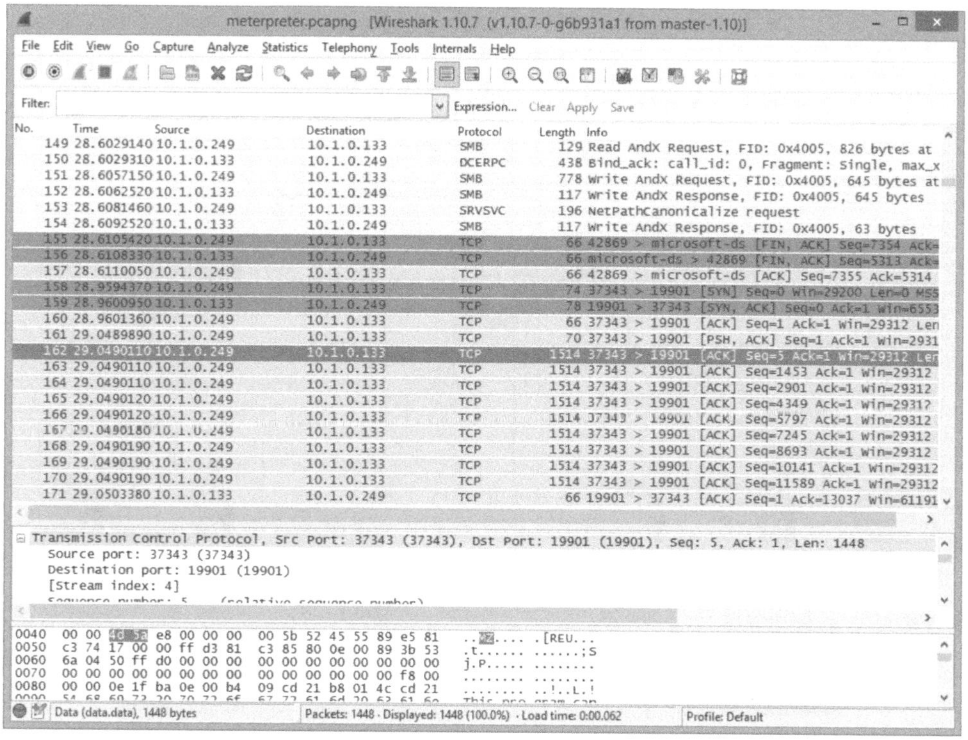

Wireshark packet capturing utility. (Screenshot courtesy of Wireshark.)

One way of mitigating the risk of eavesdropping attacks is to divide the network into segments and then isolate certain types of traffic to certain segments.

Segment Networks for Security

Network administrators divide networks into sections, which is known as segmentation. The purpose of segmentation is to isolate certain kinds of network traffic to certain areas of the network. Segmentation permits the administrators to exert greater control over the traffic. There are usually two reasons to segment a network: security and performance.

For example, if an administrator supports a network that includes a Finance Department with strict security requirements and an Engineering Department that transfers many large files across the network, the administrator may wish to segment the network. By segmenting the Finance network traffic away from the Engineering Department, the administrator provides additional privacy to that traffic. By segmenting the large Engineering file transfers away from the Finance Department, the administrator provides greater performance. In other words, the Finance Department network traffic is only in the Finance section of the network and therefore better protected from interception by the Engineering Department. In addition, the Engineering Department network traffic is only in the Engineering section of the network and therefore it only impacts the Engineering users with its performance hit from large file transfers.

There are several ways to accomplish segmentation. The most common methods are by subnetting using routers or switches (also known as virtual local area networks [VLANs]).

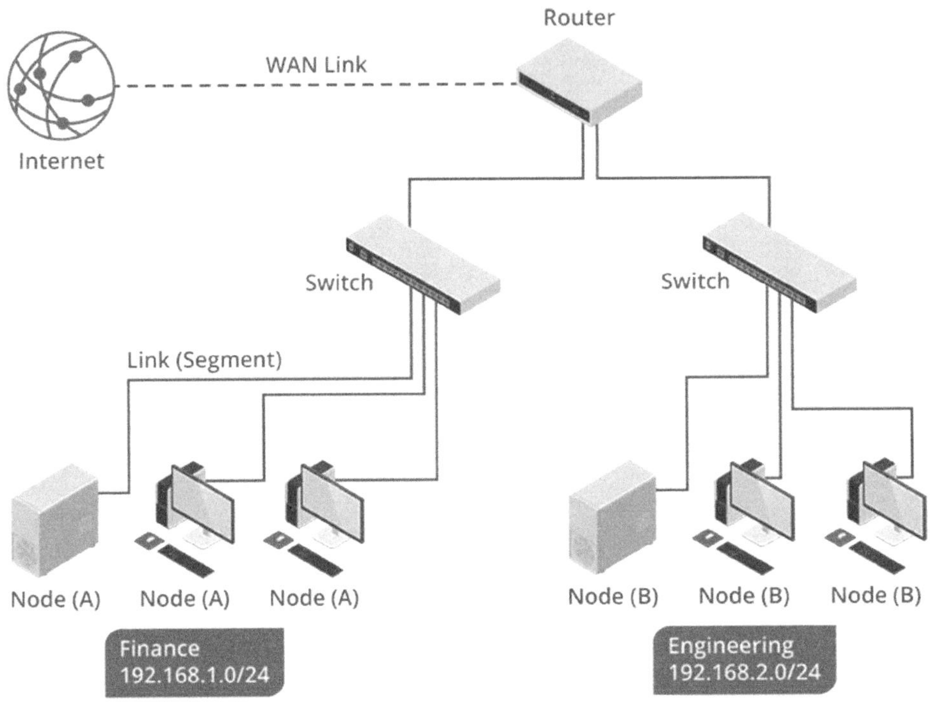

Two segments linked by a router. (Images © 123RF.com)

Demilitarized Zone (DMZ)

Some internal network services need direct Internet connectivity. Such connectivity makes the servers hosting the services vulnerable. It is a common practice to place those servers in an isolated network, referred to as a **demilitarized zone (DMZ)**. Services hosted in the DMZ include DNS, email, web, **virtual private network (VPN)**, FTP, and others. A DMZ is another example of an isolated network segment.

Guest Network

Some organizations provide a separate, isolated network for unauthorized or guest computers. For example, if your business frequently receives guests, it may be worthwhile to create a guest network to provide basic printing functionality and an Internet connection. Guests who need printing or Internet access do not have to connect to the production network to get it.

Air Gap

Administrators may choose to provide no connectivity whatsoever between two network divisions. Normally, this is done to enforce security measures in high-security environments. The two network segments are separated by an air gap so that there is no physical path available for network traffic to move from one network to another.

Network Maps

Network or infrastructure diagrams provide a visual reference to the major components of the network. Servers, routers, switches, firewalls, and network segments or subnets are all displayed. The diagram is useful for troubleshooting and understanding the flow of network traffic between endpoints.

Network Mapping Tools

Network diagrams can be created by using specific software and collections of icons. The drawings are created manually based on reference information. Tools such as Microsoft Visio Professional 2019 and draw.io can be used to create network diagrams manually.

Network diagrams can also be created automatically by various types of software. Utilities such as **Nmap** query network devices, collect information from those devices, and then construct diagrams based on that information.

Lesson 4 covers infrastructure diagrams in more detail.

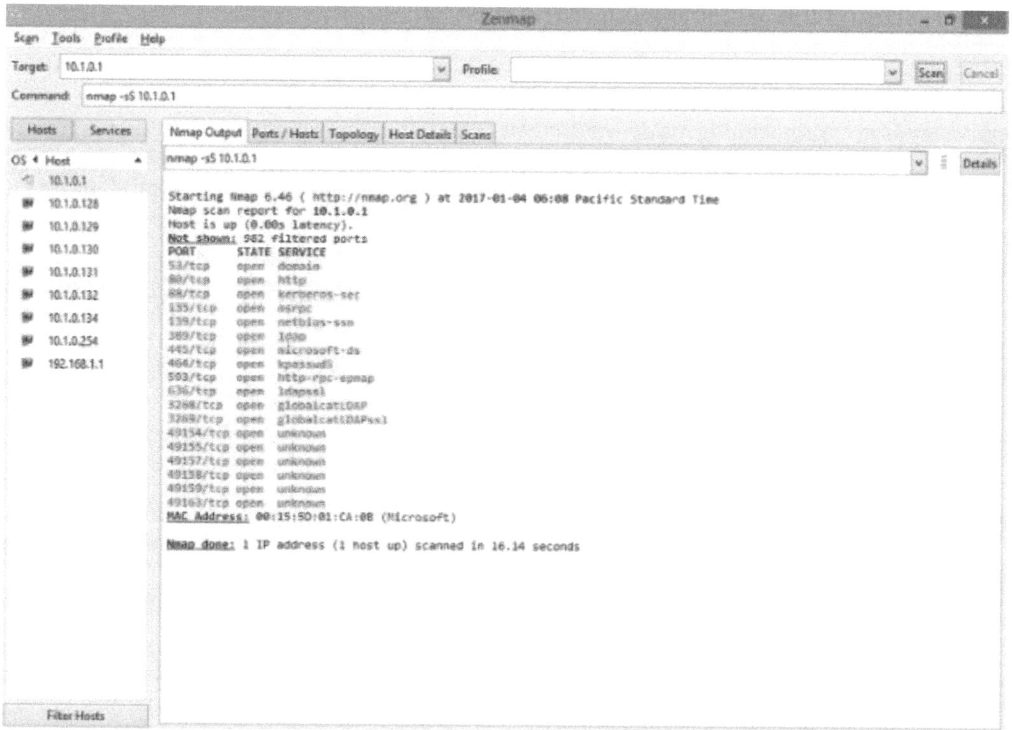

Results of an nmap scan. (Screenshot courtesy of Zenmap.)

IP Address Review

To better understand subnetting, let's quickly review some basic IP addressing concepts.

IP addresses are configured on each network node. At its most simple, the IP address contains two parts: the Network ID and the Host ID. The Network ID identifies which network segment or subnet the host belongs to, and the Host ID uniquely identifies a specific node within the subnet. The Network ID is to a telephone area code, which specifies a section of the telephone network. The Host ID is similar to a telephone number, which defines a particular telephone within the area code. A Network ID is assigned to each network segment. All nodes that exist within that network segment have the same Network ID. A Host ID is assigned to each computer, router, printer, etc. in the network segment.

If an administrator has divided the network into two segments—the Finance Department and the Engineering Department—then there are two Network IDs (one for each segment). The Finance Department might be given 192.168.1.0 as its Network ID. All computers in that segment, therefore, have an IP address that begins with 192.168.1. The Engineering Department might be given 192.168.2.0 as its Network ID. All computers in that segment, therefore, have an IP address that starts with 192.168.2.0.

Subnet Masks

An IP address is almost always displayed with an additional numeric value named the **subnet mask**. Subnet masks allow administrators and computers to recognize which portion of the IP address is the Network ID and which portion is the Host ID. For example, if a Finance Department server has an IP address of 192.168.1.15 and a subnet mask of 255.255.255.0, then the first three fields of the IP address are the Network ID, and the remaining one is the Host ID.

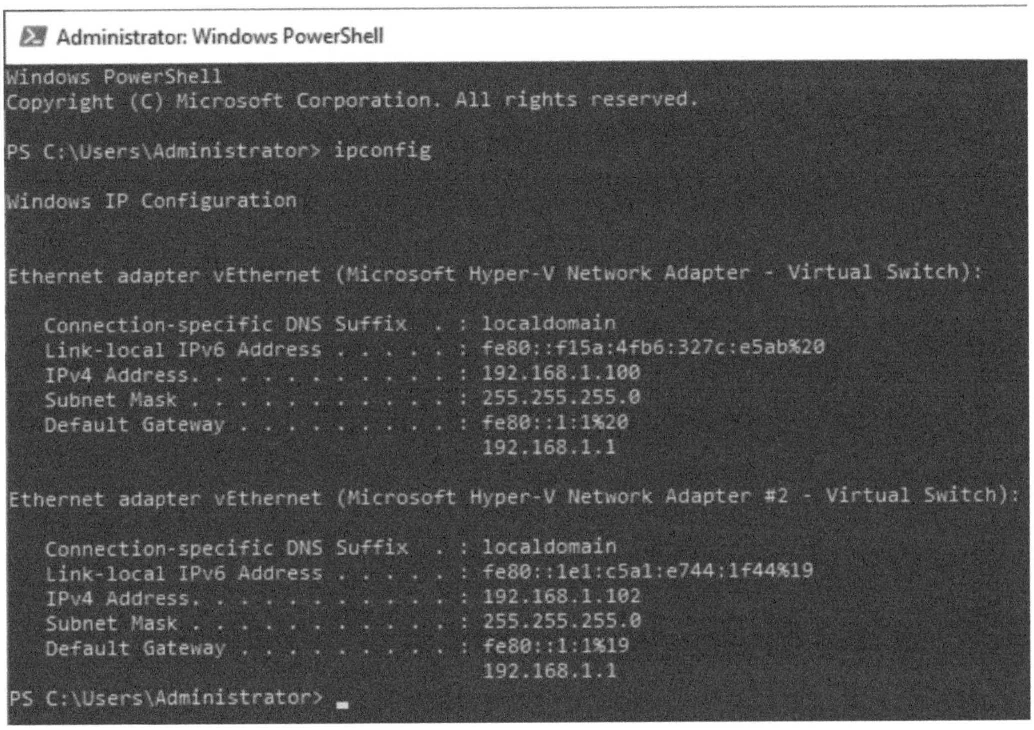

Output from ipconfig command. Note the Subnet Mask value. (Screenshot courtesy of Microsoft.)

Reserved IP Address Ranges

The **Request for Comment (RFC)** that defines IP version 4 addresses divides the roughly 4.3 billion available addresses into five classes. Three of the five classes (Classes A, B, and C) are commonly used in networking. Each of the three classes has a designated IP address range solely for internal use on private networks. Almost any internal network you encounter uses one of these private IP address ranges.

Class	Range
A	10.0.0.0/8
B	172.16.0.0/12
C	192.168.0.0/16

Internal IP address ranges.

Subnetting with Routers

Traditional subnetting relies on network segments that are connected by routers, which control the flow of traffic between two or more segments based on Network IDs. The disadvantage of segmentation with routers is that all of the nodes must be in close physical proximity. Such a design is not always convenient.

Subnetting with Switches

VLANs are configured on **switches** and segment at the switch level, instead of at the router level. Each connection port on the switch is configured as a member of a particular VLAN. The switches permit traffic only between ports that are part of the same VLAN. VLANs are identified by a tag. Network traffic is tagged for a specific VLAN, and the traffic is only passed to other ports that have the same tag.

VLAN tags are numbers between 0 and 4095. An administrator might assign computers that are part of the Finance Department to VLAN 10 and computers that are part of the Engineering Department to VLAN 20. Traffic tagged for VLAN 20 is passed to nodes that are also part of VLAN 20 and not to nodes that are part of VLAN 10. The result is that traffic is managed and isolated based on VLAN membership.

VLANs are much more flexible than traditional router-based segmentation and very common in today's networks.

Network Hardware, Protocols, and Tools

Servers participate on the business network, and therefore server administrators need to have a basic understanding of the different kinds of network devices and protocols.

Network devices, including routers, switches, and firewalls, all play a role in network security. One of the primary functions they provide is segmentation, as discussed above.

Network Devices

There are many types of network devices. In addition, some network appliances combine several functions into a single device. These devices are part of the network security configuration.

Lesson 7 covers network devices in more detail, including routers, switches, and firewalls.

Routers

Routers operate at Layer 3 of the OSI model, function based on IP addresses, filter traffic, and link together one or more network segments.

Switches

Switches operate at Layer 2 of the OSI model, function based on **Media Access Control (MAC)** addresses, link network nodes that are near each other, and filter traffic between one or more network VLANs.

It is assumed that you are already familiar with the seven layers of the OSI model and the responsibilities of each layer.

Gateways

Gateways link two or more networks and may translate between network protocols. Routers are a type of gateway.

WAPs

WAPs are gateways that link wireless devices together and attach the wireless network to the wired network.

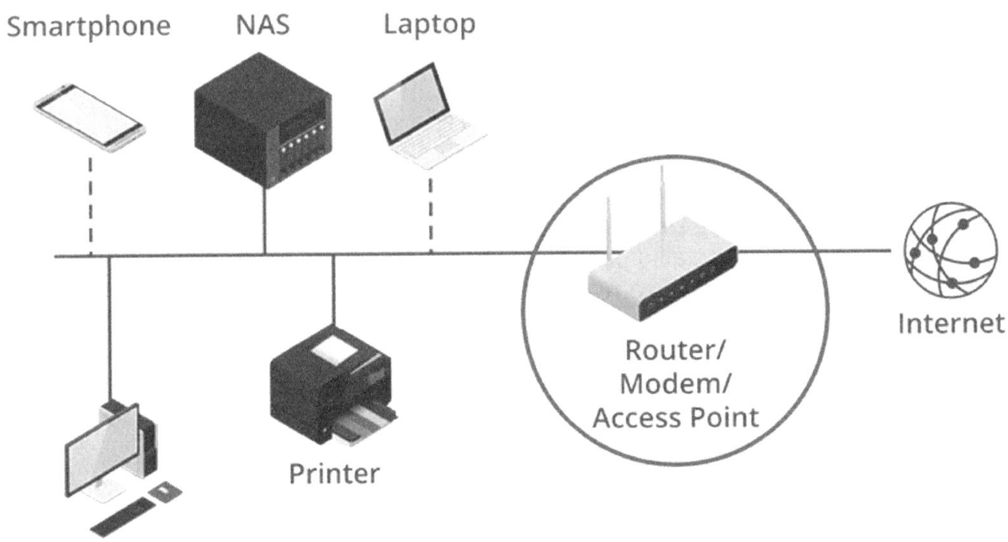

Wireless access point attaching the wireless network to the wired network. (Images © 123RF.com)

Media

Media consists of the network cabling that links computers to routers, switches, and gateways. Common media types include twisted pair Ethernet cable, co-ax cable, and fiber optic cable.

You will learn more about network media in a later section of this course.

Network Firewalls

Firewalls filter network traffic, allowing administrators to control traffic that moves between two networks, between two network segments, or even in and out of an individual workstation or server. Firewalls may be software running as a service on a computer or a dedicated hardware device.

Like any other service or device, firewalls need to be kept current. In addition, you should regularly review their configurations to ensure that they match the requirements for your network environment.

Most firewalls generate log files. Regularly review these log files for suspicious activity, for frequently blocked connection attempts, and to ensure the accepted connections are from expected sources using expected protocols. Some firewalls can alert administrators to suspicious activity.

Network firewalls are found between network segments or between two separate networks. For example, an administrator might implement a simple packet filtering firewall between the Financial Department's segment and the Engineering Department's segment. A more complex stateful firewall might be installed at the perimeter to govern the flow of traffic between the company's trusted internal network and the untrusted external Internet.

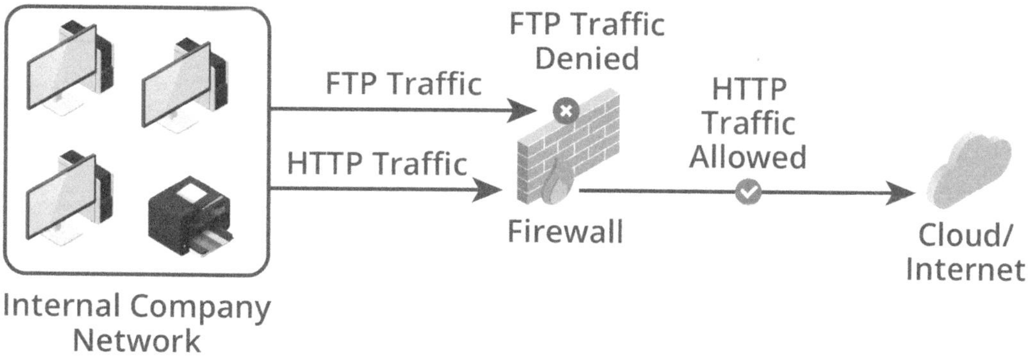

Network firewall separating an internal LAN and the Internet. (Images © 123RF.com)

Host-Based Firewalls

Host-based firewalls control traffic flow in and out of the host server's NIC. Host-based firewalls protect the server from different threats than do network firewalls. Network firewalls protect the perimeter, while host-based firewalls protect each individual host inside the perimeter. Both are important.

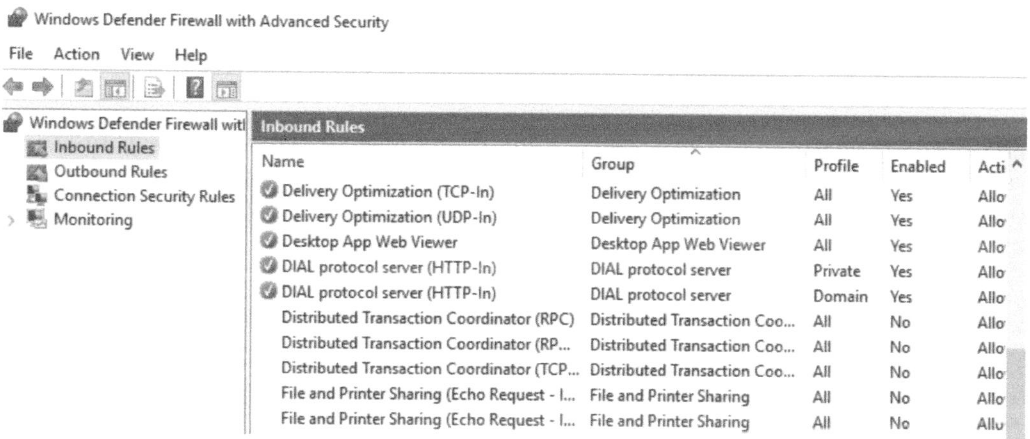

Windows Defender Firewall with Advanced Security. (Screenshot courtesy of Microsoft.)

Network Protocols

Protocols are rules that govern network communications. The primary suite of protocols for modern networks is **Transmission Control Protocol/Internet Protocol (TCP/IP)**, which is actually a family of many different protocols.

The following table displays basic attributes of some of the common TCP/IP protocols:

Protocol	Use	Port Number
IP	Logical addressing	n/a
Hypertext Transfer Protocol (HTTP)	Web traffic	TCP 80
Hypertext Transfer Protocol Secure (HTTPS)	Encrypted web traffic	TCP 443
File Transfer Protocol (FTP)	File transfers	TCP 21
Secure File Transfer Protocol (SFTP)	Encrypted file transfers	TCP 22
File Transfer Protocol Secure (FTPS)	Encrypted file transfers	TCP 990
Secure Shell (SSH)	Encrypted remote command line administration	TCP 22
IPsec	Encrypted network traffic	UDP 500, UDP 4500
Secure Copy (SCP)	Encrypted file transfers	TCP 22
Common Internet File System (CIFS) or Server Message Blocks (SMB)	Network access to shared folders	TCP 137, 139, UDP 137, 139

TCP/IP protocols.

Firewalls, log files, network mappers, configuration files, and other settings may reference these port numbers. It is critical that you recognize the common port numbers listed here, as well as any additional ports that are used in your network environment.

```
[user01@CentOS7-A ~]$ ssh root@192.168.1.100
root@192.168.1.100's password:
Last login: Mon Aug  3 15:15:09 2020 from 172.20.0.2
[root@CentOS7-A ~]# █
```

SSH connection to 192.168.1.100.

Network Access Control (NAC)

NAC defines rules for valid computer configuration and then enforces those rules when a device attempts to connect to the network. For example, the NAC might state that all devices must have a firewall enabled and an antivirus program installed before being permitted to connect to the network. The NAC service will check each device to ensure that those two requirements are met. If so, then the connection is permitted. If not, either the connection is denied completely or the device is placed on an isolated network until it can be made compliant.

Review Activity:

Network Security Concepts

Answer the following questions:

1. **Why might it be useful to intercept network traffic as a server administrator, and what are two tools you could use to accomplish this task?**

2. **List two reasons an administrator might segment a network.**

3. **What types of services might reside on servers located in a DMZ?**

4. **What is the purpose of the IP address subnet mask?**

5. **What are the Class A, B, and C reserved IP address ranges, and what is their purpose?**

6. **What is the difference between a host-based firewall and a network-based firewall?**

7. **What is the default port for the SSH protocol, and when might you need to use that port number?**

Lesson 3

Summary

- Sysadmins are responsible for maintaining the physical security and availability of servers and network devices.
- Network protocols, services, and segmentation are all network security mitigation tools.
- Physical and network security are critical to server maintenance.

1. **What physical security measures have you observed at your workplace?**

Lesson 4

Managing Physical Assets

LESSON INTRODUCTION

Servers are critical physical assets for the organization. They have a specific lifecycle and must be properly inventoried. In addition, supporting documentation must be created, updated, and made accessible to those that need it. In this Lesson, you will learn the server lifecycle and the associated documentation.

Lesson Objectives

In this lesson, you will:

- Understand asset management concepts.
- Manage documentation.

Topic 4A

Understand Asset Management Concepts

EXAM OBJECTIVES COVERED
2.7 Explain the importance of asset management and documentation

Servers are maintained through a lifecycle that includes procurement, OS and software installation, and decommissioning. During this lifecycle, an accurate inventory is necessary to ensure the server is effectively managed.

Server Lifecycle

Like software, hardware also has a lifecycle. In the case of servers, the lifecycle begins with the procurement process. Next comes the usage phase, which is the majority of the server's lifecycle, when it fulfills its role providing services. The server reaches its end-of-life phase when the hardware is too outdated for continued support. At that point, the server is disposed of.

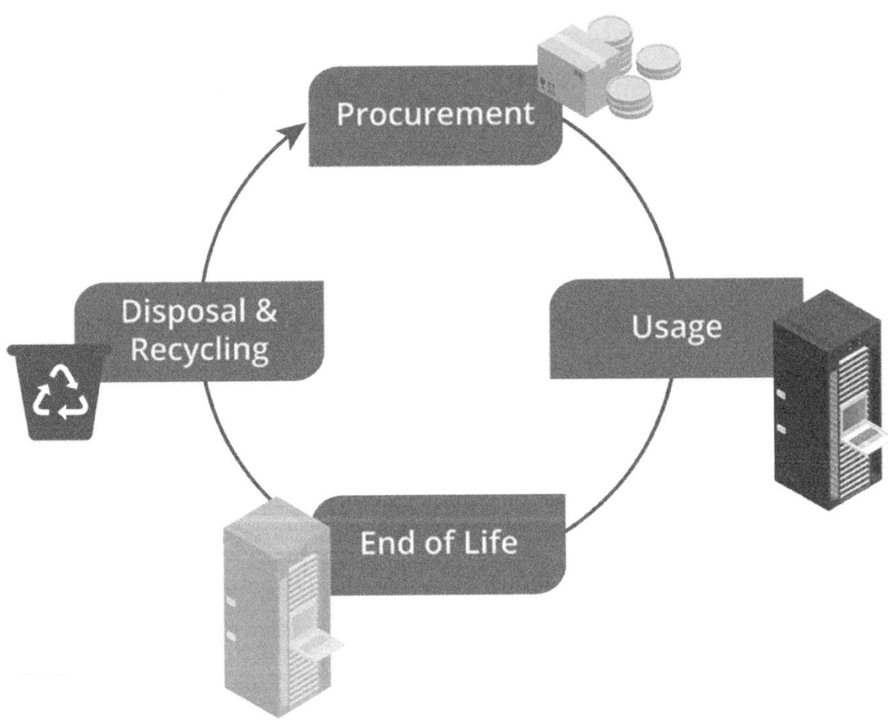

The server lifecycle. (Images © 123RF.com)

Procurement

The administrator defines the server's specifications based on its intended use and then decides whether to deploy the server as a new physical device, a new on-premises VM, or a new cloud-based VM. Hardware capabilities, such as storage capacity and available memory, must also be decided.

The procurement process includes the following:

- Understanding the business requirements
- Identification of supplies, perhaps through a Request for Proposal (RFP) process
- Pricing and contract negotiation
- Finalization and shipping of the product

Choices are made to either purchase or lease server hardware during the procurement phase. Security concerns and warranty/service plan options are considered at that time as well.

Many organizations are proactively building security requirements into the procurement process. These requirements may be written into the RFP or other documentation. Examples of requirements include the use of MFA , encrypted network protocols, and a mature patching mechanism.

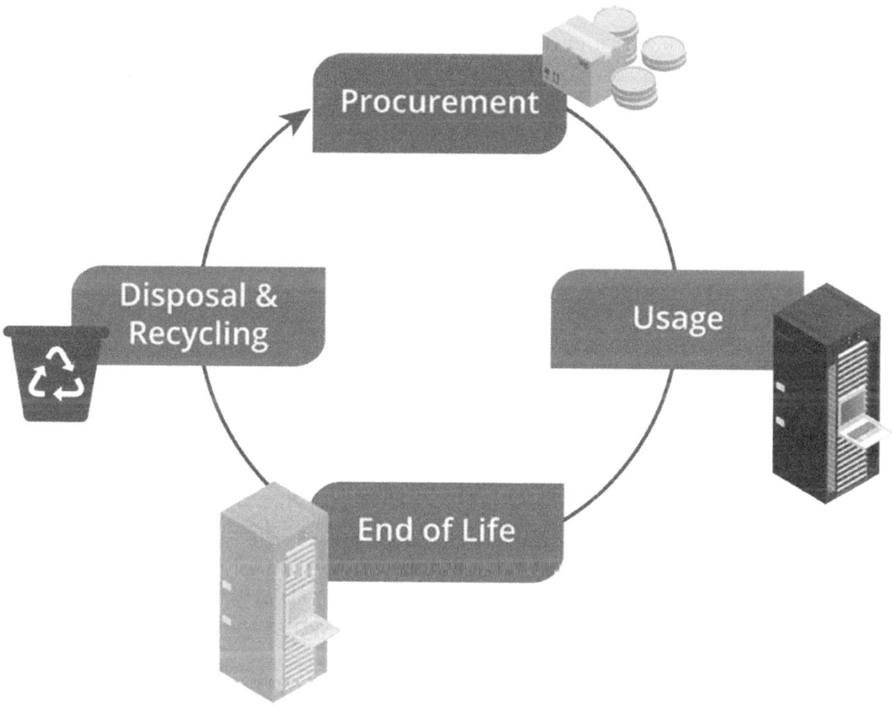

Server procurement. (Images © 123RF.com)

Usage

A physical server is installed in the rack, provided with power, network connectivity, and adequate cooling. VMs, whether deployed on-premises or in the cloud, are provisioned with resources to meet the anticipated workload. Next, the appropriate server OS is installed, updated, and configured. Server applications are installed and updated at this time, too. Finally, the server's performance baseline is measured and documented.

The usage phase includes the following:

- Hardware performance testing and baselining
- Standing up the server in production, including OS installation, configuration management, and security settings.
- Patching, upgrading, and maintaining the hardware and software
- Firmware management

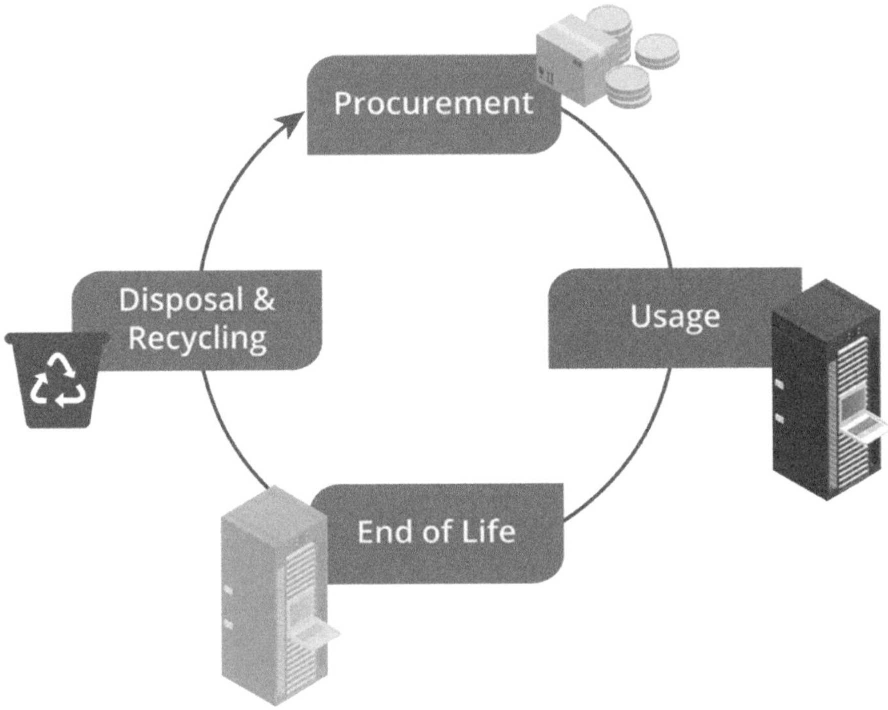

Server usage. (Images © 123RF.com)

End of Life

Server hardware usually has a useful life span of 3–7 years. This estimate is based on replacement components for the server, device driver and application compatibility, and OS support for older hardware. In addition, older hardware does not tend to provide adequate performance compared to newer devices. Older servers may be reprovisioned and given a new role in the organization. Many functions do not require powerful hardware, which allows older servers to be reused.

Microsoft supports for its Windows Server OSs for about 12 years after the initial release. Microsoft announces the "end of life" for products well in advance. Linux tends to have a very long OS lifecycle with a great deal of backward compatibility.

Servers may reach their end-of-life phase earlier due to virtualization. In many cases, a server that was initially deployed on physical hardware may later be converted to a VM hosted on-premises or in the cloud. Virtualized servers often have many advantages over physical servers.

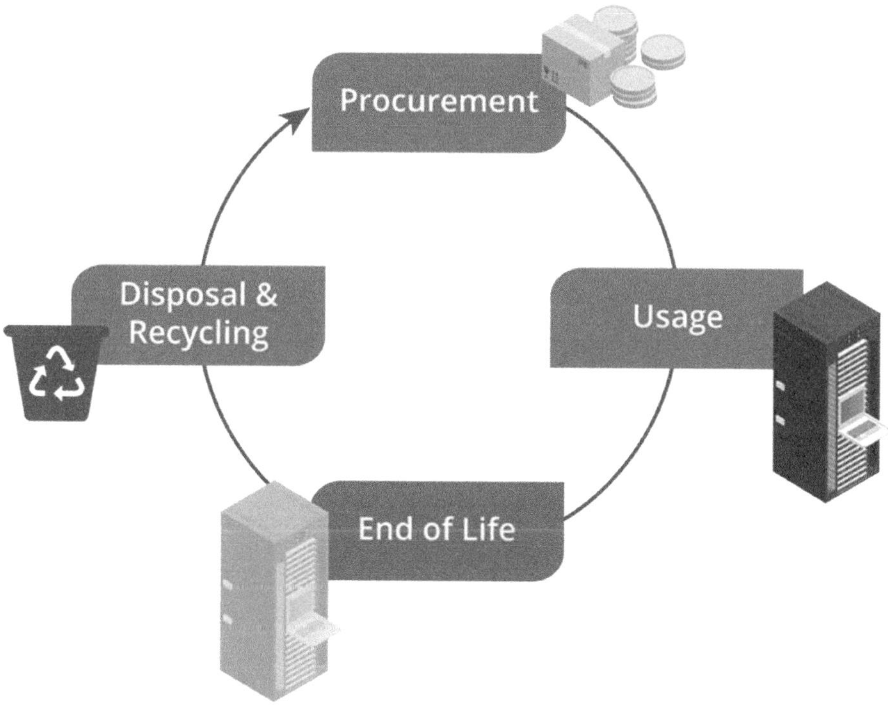

End of server life. (Images © 123RF.com)

Disposal/Recycling

Most computer hardware, including servers, must be disposed of according to specific standards. Some computer components are potentially hazardous. Check with disposal or recycling centers to ensure that they are properly equipped to deal with server hardware. Some companies manage the disposal of IT hardware for you.

One of the most critical aspects of server disposal is data protection. For this reason, HDDs are usually removed and physically destroyed, and then the rest of the server is disposed of. Hard disk destruction can be done with specialized shredders. In some cases, it may be sufficient to encrypt the HDD rather than physically destroying it.

It is not enough to delete data on a hard drive or to reformat the drive. The data that was stored on the drive is still present after a delete or a reformat task and may be recovered relatively easily.

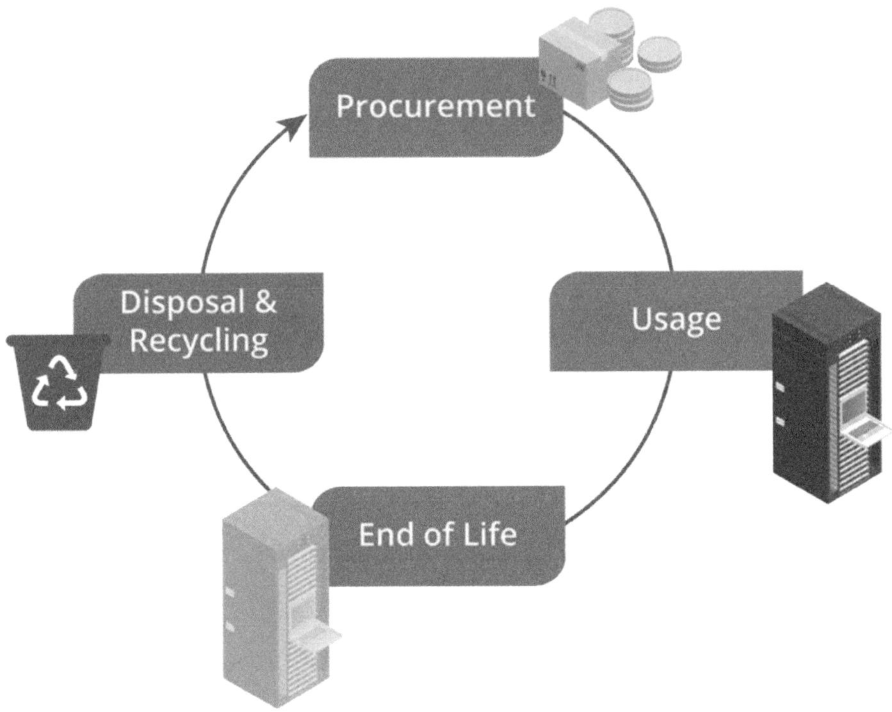

Disposing of discarded server. (Images © 123RF.com)

Leasing Versus Owning and Service Plans

Traditionally, organizations purchased servers and related hardware outright. These purchases represent a significant CapEx or upfront cost. Such a purchase may be a risk because agile services and business initiatives frequently change during the server's lifecycle, rendering the server unsuited to the demand placed upon it. However, ownership of the server hardware may also provide tax benefits if the investment is spread out over several years.

Leasing server hardware may be an attractive option for your organization. Some hardware providers have lease options that include lease-to-own or a more traditional temporary lease.

The possible benefits of leasing server hardware include the following:

- Reduced CapEx/low upfront cost
- Reduced total cost of ownership (TCO)
- Simplified budget with predictable monthly payments
- Protection against hardware obsolescence
- Possible ownership of the hardware at the end of the lease

Your organization is still responsible for configurating and managing the server hardware, although there may also be a service plan negotiated as part of the lease.

Warranty and Service Plans

Server hardware typically includes a warranty against manufacturer defects. During the procurement phase of the server's lifecycle, you should understand and document the warranty details so that you can quickly reach out to the vendor in the event of a suspected hardware defect.

Many vendors offer tiered service plans that help to ensure the availability of your servers. Replacement components may be delivered and possibly even installed by the vendor, depending on the service plan.

The following are examples of possible repair locations and response times that may be built into service plans:

- On-site, four-hour response time, same business day
- On-site, same business day
- On-site, next business day

Inventory Management

Accurate management of an IT inventory is critical and can mitigate various risks. The benefits include accurate licensing and informed purchasing. Servers include multiple methods by which they can be inventoried.

Importance of Inventory Management

Accurate IT asset management is an essential part of the sysadmin's job. There are risks, both financial and technical, when assets are not well inventoried or labeled. Conversely, there are many benefits to be accrued from proper IT asset tracking. In very small IT environments, it may be possible to track IT assets manually, but most organizations use an automated system to manage server, workstation, and network device inventory.

Risks of Not Tracking Assets

Consider the following list of possible risks of not correctly tracking IT assets:

- License violations—a disorganized record of OSs and applications makes it very difficult to manage licenses properly. Your organization may be paying too much for licenses that it is not using or be violating license agreements and subject to penalties.
- Misinformed purchasing decisions—without accurate knowledge of the IT assets already on hand, it is likely that your organization will purchase duplicate devices or devices that are not well suited to their desired role.
- Inadequate security—you can't secure what you don't know about. Devices, especially network devices and Internet-connected servers, that the administrator is unaware of are not managed by the company's security policy and do not have regular security updates and configurations applied.

It is crucial to track IT assets to ensure that all resources are correctly licensed, understand what resources are available, and know what resources need to be secured.

Benefits to Tracking Assets

In addition to addressing the risks documented above, there are many benefits to tracking assets. An accurate understanding of your resources makes for more efficient utilization, greater security, and increased service agility. Also, the accounting department may require an asset inventory to depreciate IT expenditures correctly.

Depreciation is an accounting term. The practice allows accounting and tax benefits that reflect the actual value of tangible resources.

Asset Management Systems Features

Automated systems can be used to help you manage your IT assets. There are many different systems, each with their own specific features. Here are a few common considerations:

- Automation—a high degree of automation permits accurate inventory tracking in modern data centers, where devices are replaced very rapidly. Automation also allows for more accurate results with virtualization and cloud deployments.
- Reporting—the point of asset management is to know what resources exist. Reporting and filtering your inventory to display the information you need is a critical component of asset management.
- Comprehensive—many inventory solutions are capable of tracking different kinds of devices. For example, you need inventory information for servers, workstations, printers, tablets, routers, and switches.
- Coverage throughout the device's lifecycle—devices need to be tracked from when they are purchased until they are completely decommissioned.

Microsoft's System Center Configuration Manager (SCCM) is a very common inventory solution. While SCCM does far more than just track inventory, the ability to manage assets and query the inventory data is an important feature.

Tracking Servers

There are many aspects of the server to be tracked, and the organization needs a consistent way of identifying the server. Remember, the server's host name and IP address are not likely to be consistent throughout its lifecycle.

Tracking servers:

- Make and model—the vendor assigns a model to the server. You may track the device based on this model and by the vendor that manufactured it.
- Serial number—the vendor also assigns a unique serial number to the server that identifies it.
- Asset tags or labels—physical tags are attached to the server and scanned with a barcode reader to uniquely identify the machine.
- **Basic input/output system (BIOS)** asset tags—the BIOS of the server probably has a place to enter a unique asset number. This value remains unchanged, even if the server's OS is reinstalled.
- OS—usually, this will be Microsoft Windows Server or a Linux distribution, such as Ubuntu Server or RHEL.

Review Activity:

Asset Management Concepts

Answer the following questions:

1. **What are the four phases of the server lifecycle?**

2. **What are some risks of not tracking inventory?**

3. **What inventory information might you track for servers?**

Topic 4B

Manage Documentation

EXAM OBJECTIVES COVERED

2.3 Given a scenario, configure and maintain server functions and features
2.7 Explain the importance of asset management and documentation

Documentation that supports the server and network infrastructure is an effective tool for troubleshooting and day-to-day management. Baselines, workflow diagrams, and change management also help you to understand your environment better. In this Topic, you examine different types of documentation and consider situations where documentation might be useful.

Configurations and Baselines

As discussed in Lesson 1, standing up or deploying a new server should be documented and standardized. Standardization is easily accomplished with VMs by using templates, which allow for consistent and efficient deployments.

```
[root@CentOS7-A ~]# virt-install --name=LinuxSvr1 --vcpus=1 --memory
=1024 --disk size=10 --cdrom=/media/cdrom/rhel8 --os-variant=rhel8
```

Use virt-install to define a virtual machine configuration.

Standardized components:

- OS versions, such as Windows Server 2019 or RHEL 8.
- Security software, such as antivirus or anti-malware solutions.
- Local account configuration, especially for the administrator and root accounts.
- Storage and RAID array configuration.
- BIOS password configuration (if using physical hardware).

Each server should have a performance **baseline** that documents its normal behavior; this permits administrators to empirically understand whether its performance has changed radically. Comparing an original baseline to the server's current performance is much more useful than saying "The server seems slower than it used to be."

Baselines, and the related performance monitoring, begin with the four major subsystems of the server: processor, memory, storage, and network. Each subsystem is monitored, although the relative importance of each varies depending on the services the server provides. Monitoring a Microsoft SQL Server deployment includes different information than monitoring an Active Directory (AD) Domain Controller or a Linux Apache webserver.

Here are a few examples of Microsoft **Performance Monitor** objects and counters that are used for an initial server baseline:

- Processor—% Processor time
- Processor—% User time

- Memory—Pages/sec
- Network Interface—Transfers/sec
- Physical Disk—Disk Transfers/sec
- Physical Disk—Average disk queue length

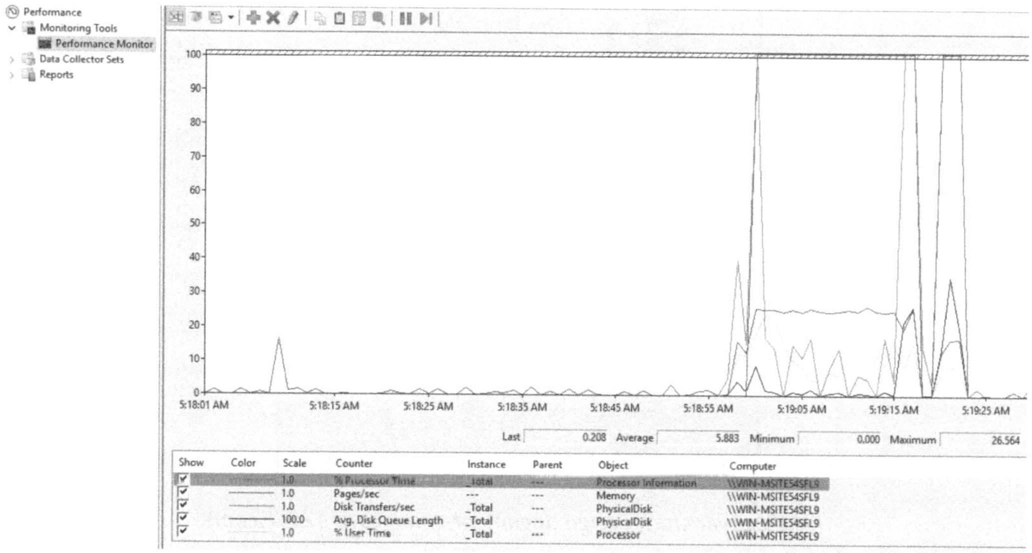

Performance Monitor with server baseline counters. (Screenshot courtesy of Microsoft.)

Gather real-time performance information by using various built-in Windows Server and Linux tools. While these tools are not part of baselining, they may help you to understand your server's overall performance better.

Windows Tools:

- Task Manager
- Resource Monitor
- Reliability Monitor

Linux Tools:

- Sar
- Top
- Uptime

Design Documents

Architectural diagrams allow sysadmins to better understand the components of a service solution and the flow of data. Such information is essential for troubleshooting, capacity planning, and the ability to scale up services to meet demand. Architectural diagrams usually include specific hardware components, such as storage area network (SAN) hardware, and software solutions, such as web or authentication services.

The following example is a LAMP server (Linux, Apache, MySQL, PHP) that provides basic web application functionality. All of the services and storage are contained within the single server.

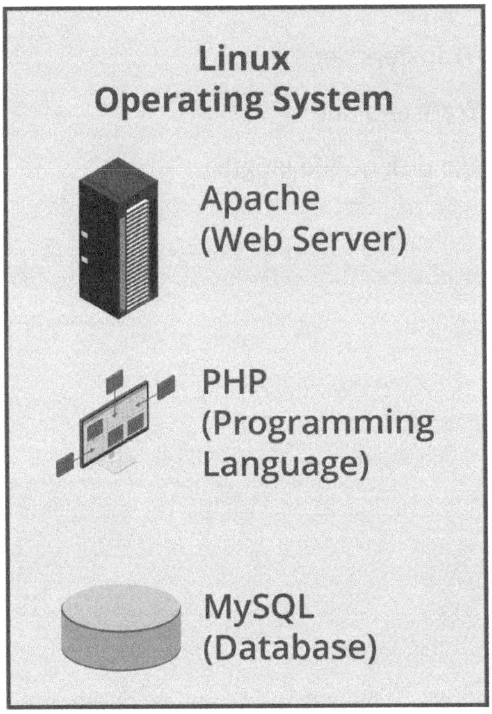

LAMP server stack design document. (Images © 123RF.com)

The following example is a slightly more complex architectural design. It includes devices such as the firewall, server, and SAN, as well as the services provided.

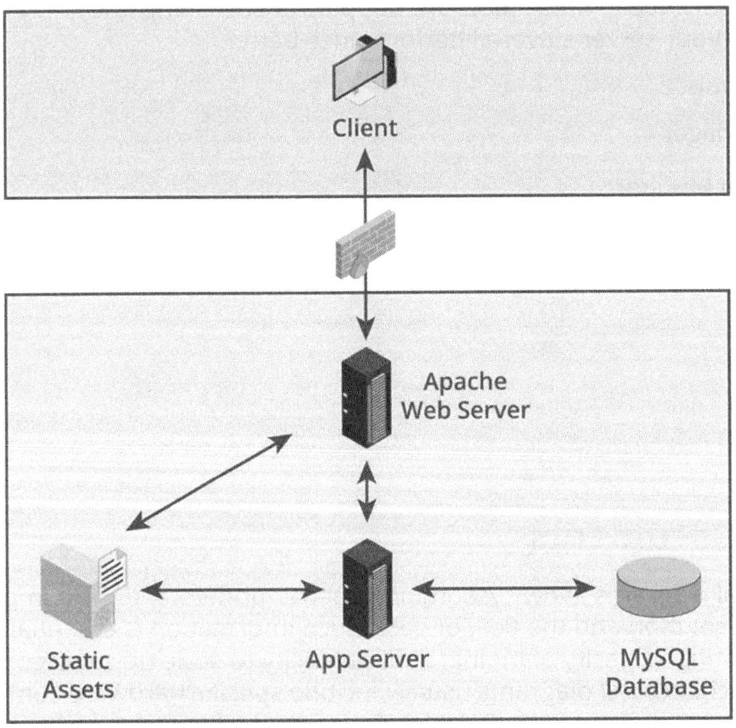

Architectural diagram for a web application. (Images © 123RF.com)

Software exists, both proprietary and open source, to create architectural diagrams. These diagrams are also essential for depicting the structure of your network, including subnets, routers, and WAPs.

Standard Operating Procedure (SOP)

Service management documents help your business maintain and manage its services, recovery requirements, and customer obligations.

SOP

The purpose of an SOP document is to state detailed instructions for how to complete a specific task. These instructions are clear enough to be followed by anyone and produce consistent results.

Most organizations create SOPs from standard templates, which will usually contain similar information. Here are several content areas you are likely to find in an IT SOP:

- Clear, descriptive title
- Statement of purpose
- Author/owner and contact information
- Scope of the document
- Detailed step by step instructions, possibly containing screenshots, links, command or code examples, and options.

SOPs may be generated for tasks that IT staff members are commonly responsible for, such as the following:

- Putting a web server into production
- Removing a file server from production
- Building standard end-user workstations
- Building developer workstations
- Installing OSs on servers (physical or virtual)
- Managing user accounts, including creation, maintenance, and deletion

Business Continuity Plan (BCP)

The purpose of a BCP is to address how to maintain business obligations in the case of a large-scale disaster (natural or caused by humans). The focus is on the business as a whole, rather than on the areas for which IT is responsible.

Business Impact Analysis (BIA) and **Disaster Recovery Plans (DRPs)** are subsets of the BCP.

BIA

A BIA is a component of your company's overall BCP. The purpose of the BIA is to identify the potential consequences of an interruption to your business due to a disaster or other unplanned events. These consequences may include the following:

- An impact on income
- An effect on the business's reputation

- Penalties that result from fines or contract breaches
- Additional expenses to address the interruption

The BIA identifies interdependent systems, interdependent business processes, potential failure points, staffing requirements, etc. The server infrastructure, including redundancy (or lack thereof) and security, are critical components of the BIA.

Disaster Recovery Plan (DRP)

The Disaster Recovery Plan (DRP) specifies responsibilities, tools, procedures, and supporting policies for recovering IT services in the event of a disaster. While the BCP focuses on the business as a whole, the DRP focuses on IT services.

The DRP typically consists of the following topics. The goal is to help predict, mitigate, and prioritize service outages. These may be broken down on a per-service basis.

- **Mean Time Between Failures (MTBF)**
- **Mean Time to Repair/Replace/Recovery (MTTR)**
- **Recovery Point Objective (RPO)**
- **Recovery Time Objective (RTO)**
- **Service Level Agreement (SLA)**

The DRP should consist the following components:

- DRP team designated, with contact information
- Scope of the plan
- Risk identification
- Service catalog, including dependencies among services
- Backup infrastructure and remote site configuration (hot, warm, cold)
- Test processes, including updates based on service changes
- Automation of processes

One of the available cloud services is Disaster Recovery as a Service (DRaaS), which focuses on providing a disaster recovery infrastructure for organizations.

MTBF

This calculation estimates the average time between server or system failures. It is vital to define what a failure is in this context, as well. For example, routine maintenance where the system is unavailable is not defined as a failure.

For example, your organization has three file servers, and they suffer a storage disk failure at 1,000, 3,000, and 4,000 hours, respectively. The MTBF for the storage disks in those servers is approximately 2,666 hours. (1,000 + 3,000 + 4,000 = 8,000 / 3 = 2,666 hours)

MTTR

MTTR estimates the amount of time necessary to return a service to fully operational status. This value is used to calculate SLAs and related penalties.

RPO

An RPO measures the quantity of time between a disaster and the most recent backup or recovery point. The amount of time represents how much data the organization can acceptably lose, which defines how frequently to run backups or what redundancy is needed.

Consider the lost revenue associated with a failed service, such as a website, or lost data, such as customer PII. Factor in the cost of recovery, as well.

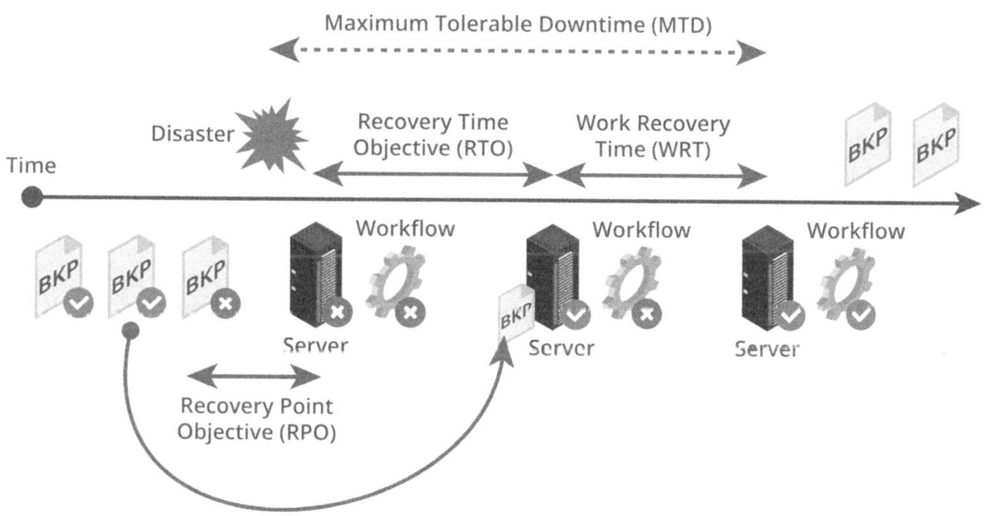

Disaster recovery - note RPO and RTO information. (Images © 123RF.com)

RTO

An RTO defines the recovery time needed to maintain an organization's business continuity. It measures how long the organization can continue to meet its obligations in the event of a disaster. Such an understanding allows the organization to prioritize disaster recovery processes.

RTO values may vary by service. Your organization's public web services may be more important than an internal archiving service. For each service, determine the associated risks and the recovery time to generate an RTO.

SLA

SLAs define service requirements and expectations between a consumer and a provider. For example, if your servers are hosted by a cloud-based IaaS CSP, such as Amazon or Microsoft, then you will have an agreement with them that outlines the expected availability of your hosted services. If the CSP suffers an outage, then there may be penalties against them to compensate your organization for potential lost revenue.

SLAs may also be established between the IT department (service provider) and the rest of the organization (service consumer). In such a case, the IT department guarantees a certain level of service availability.

The components of an SLA may include the following:

- Version and change history information
- Key terms
- Purpose statement
- Key performance indicators (KPIs) and metrics
- Priorities
- Exceptions or limitations

An example of a simple internal SLA might focus on the Help Desk. The SLA defines how the Help Desk prioritizes tickets, provides timely responses, and communicates with the rest of the organization.

Uptime Requirements

Uptime means the amount of time that the server is powered on and running. It is important to differentiate between uptime and availability. Availability means that the service used by consumers is working as required. Just because a server is powered on (and therefore up) does not mean that it is reachable or usable by your employees.

You have several ways of gathering uptime information on a Windows server. If you open Task Manager and then select the Performance tab, the uptime is displayed.

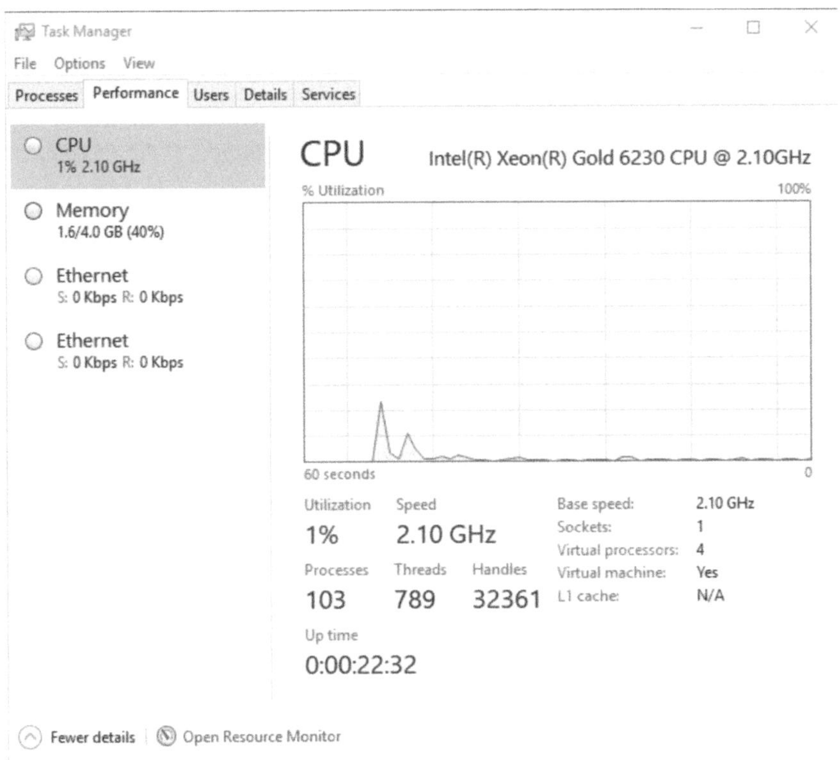

Task Manager, Up time displayed at the bottom. (Screenshot courtesy of Microsoft.)

You can run a simple command on a Linux server to discover uptime information: uptime. The output of this command displays how long the server has been up since the last restart, the number of users logged on, and an estimate of processor utilization.

```
[root@localhost ~]# uptime
 12:24:12 up  1:29,  1 user,  load average: 0.00, 0.00, 0.00
[root@localhost ~]# █
```

The uptime command in Linux.

Troubleshooting Documents

Service Manuals

Service manuals provide vendor documentation for the server. This information includes physical specifications, diagrams, part numbers for replacement components, safety considerations, etc. Most service manuals come in an electronic format and are available at the vendor's website.

Infrastructure Diagrams

Diagrams that depict the entire network infrastructure are essential for troubleshooting and understanding the environment where your servers reside. Such documentation allows troubleshooters to view network segments, what network devices are accessible in each segment, and where servers are in relation to client machines.

For example, a user opens a service desk ticket that indicates they have lost access to three particular servers. The ticket is escalated to you. You use the infrastructure diagram to understand where in the network the user's workstation and the three destination servers are located. The diagram shows the three servers exist in a network segment isolated by a firewall. You may now begin troubleshooting the path between the user's computer and the servers, giving particular attention to the firewall.

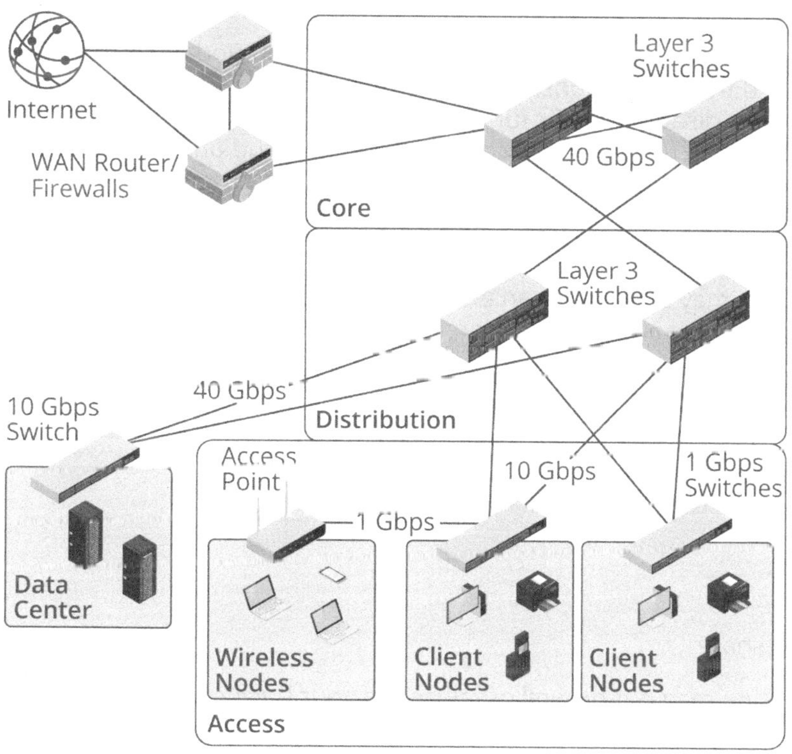

Network infrastructure diagram. (Images © 123RF.com)

Workflow Diagrams

A workflow diagram provides a visual reference for following business processes through their lifecycle. Workflow diagrams are used to automate business processes for efficiency and consistency. The workflow includes a trigger that starts the process, actions taken throughout the process, and roles for the people who manage the process.

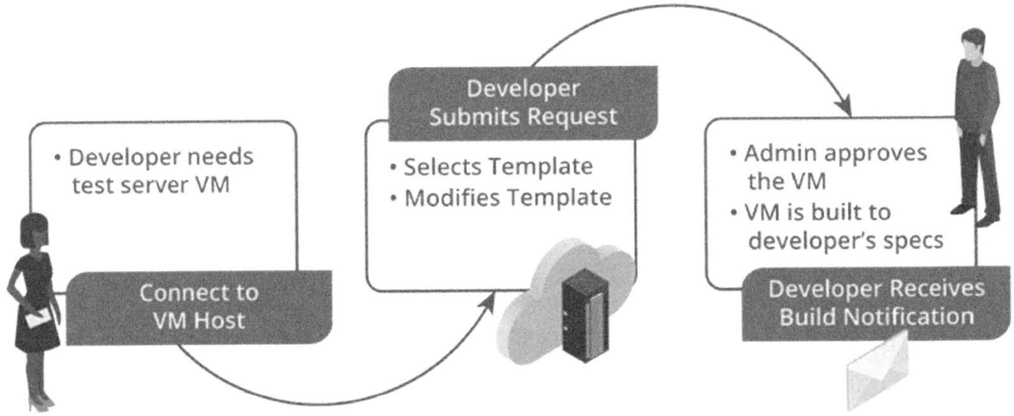

Server deployment workflow. (Images © 123RF.com)

Change Management Documents

Your organization may utilize a **change management** process to ensure that all potential changes to a server's configuration or a service's deployment are documented, tested, and accepted by the organization before being put into place. Change management provides a standardized approach to making changes within the infrastructure to minimize service disruptions.

Change management also includes OS and application updates. Depending on the OS and the applications, some updates may provide significant feature enhancements, disable specific functions, or significantly alter backward compatibility. Such updates, service packs, hotfixes, and other incremental changes are tested and approved via the formal change management process.

Document Storage, Access, and Security

Your company may implement an enterprise document management system to aid in the organization and dissemination of information.

Goals of an enterprise document management system:

- Capture
- Store
- Locate
- Update
- Securely share

Documentation may not be well organized in your business. Departments often have their own standards and storage locations for their data. Some departments may store data on on-premises file servers, while others may use cloud-based storage from one or more vendors.

Secure storage could be as simple as implementing effective permissions for files and shared folders. More complex document management solutions include the ability to check out documents, submit proposed updates or improvements, and even automatically expire and archive older documents.

Guidelines for Managing Documentation

The following list of documentation types enables more effective scaling, risk mitigation, security, and troubleshooting:

- Accurate, secure, and accessible documentation is essential.
- Windows Server and Linux include built-in tools to help develop some documentation and baselines.
- Architectural documents allow administrators and developers to understand the application environment.
- BIA documents enable an organization to understand the consequences of a significant service interruption by identifying interdependent systems and processes.
- MTBF enables the business to anticipate hardware lifecycles.
- MTTR allows the business to understand how long it will take to return a service to fully operational status, which allows the organization to alter procedures to improve that time if it is unsatisfactory.
- RPO enables the organization to understand the amount of time between the most recent backup and a disaster, which indicates how much data might be lost in the event of a disaster.
- RTO provides the recovery time after a disaster for the business to meet obligations before penalties or negative consequences arise.
- SLAs set the expectations of the service support staff and the service consumer for downtime, recovery time, response time, etc.
- Infrastructure diagrams allow administrators to understand the physical and logical paths between components, including servers, workstations, routers, and switches.
- Workflow diagrams allow administrators and developers to understand how parts of a software solution interact with each other.
- Change management improves uptime and service availability by defining a specific testing and approval process for changes to services, network configurations, and applications.

Review Activity:

Documentation

Answer the following questions:

1. **List server components (hardware and software) that are commonly standardized.**

2. **What is the purpose of an architectural diagram?**

3. **Explain the difference between MTBF and MTTR.**

4. **Explain the difference between RPOs and RTOs.**

5. **What information is contained on an infrastructure diagram?**

6. **What are the goals of a document management system?**

Lesson 4

Summary

Maintaining a server through its lifecycle is a vital task for sysadmins. Arguably, it is the reason the sysadmin role exists. The server must be properly inventoried, and all associated documentation needs to be kept current.

1. **How is the lifecycle of a server different from that of an end-user workstation or laptop?**

2. **Have you worked with organizations that fail to keep current and accurate documentation? What impact did that have on the effectiveness of the IT department?**

Lesson 5

Managing Server Hardware

LESSON INTRODUCTION

Server hardware is managed differently than workstation hardware. The server chassis is usually designed to fit in a server rack, which helps to manage server power, networking, cable management, and security. Servers often contain redundant components. In this Lesson, you will also learn common troubleshooting problems and their related causes.

Lesson Objectives

In this lesson, you will:

- Manage the physical server.
- Administer the server and storage.
- Troubleshoot server hardware.

Topic 5A

Manage the Physical Server

EXAM OBJECTIVES COVERED

1.1 Given a scenario, install physical hardware

The form factor for most servers is rack mountable, meaning the server chassis is designed to be installed into a rack in the server room. The chassis is designed to house redundant components, such as power supplies, HDDs, and NICs. Racks also help to organize power and network cabling (also known as network media).

Server Chassis Types

Servers are available in a tower **form factor**, much like a standard workstation, or in a rack-mounted form factor. They could also be deployed as blades. In this section, you will understand the differences between the chassis types.

Tower Form Factor

A server with a tower form factor fits easily into space not normally designed for large servers. This is useful in small offices or other settings where a traditional NOC is not available. **Tower servers** are arranged on shelves or tables, where they are easily accessed. Tower form factors are less space efficient than rack-mounted servers, however. Towers consume space vertically. Rack-mounted servers, discussed in the next section, consume space horizontally.

Server in the tower form factor, very similar in size and appearance to a typical workstation. (Image © 123RF.com)

Blade Form Factor

Servers may also be deployed as blades. Multiple **blade servers** are installed in a single chassis, or blade enclosure. Each blade has its own CPU, memory, and storage connections, but all share redundant power supplies, cooling, and other components. The blades themselves are hot swappable in the event of a failure or a need to scale the system.

Blade enclosures are often standardized into units for installation in racks. The enclosures provide the blades with redundant power, network connections, and cooling. Because there are fewer supporting components, the blade systems are more heat efficient. These supporting components are frequently used more efficiently, as well.

Blades and blade enclosures are particularly useful for web servers, virtualization servers, and clustering.

Several blades in an enclosure consume less power, generate less heat, and use less space than do standalone rack-mounted or tower servers.

For example, a small organization has a single rack and needs ten servers. In a traditional rack-mounted deployment, the organization purchases and installs ten separate physical servers, each of which includes two power supplies for redundancy. That's a total of twenty power supplies. The equivalent blade deployment contains ten blade servers in a single enclosure. The enclosure itself houses two larger power supplies, which generate less heat than the twenty smaller power supplies. Similar efficiency is realized with physical space, power consumption, and overall cooling.

Server in the blade form factor, installed within a chassis. (Image by Mikhail Starodubov © 123RF.com)

Rack Form Factor

The rack form factor is standardized and offers a great many advantages. The racks are 19 inches wide, and their vertical height is measured in units. A single unit is 1.75 inches (44.45mm) tall and is written as "1U." The result is that this form factor consumes space horizontally.

The servers mounted in a rack are stacked very tightly together for cooling and space efficiency. The rack may also support other network devices, such as routers and switches, that are the same standardized size.

Such standardization makes it much easier to store, organize, and secure the servers and related devices. The racks themselves are mounted to the floor. Aisles in front of and behind the servers provide administrators with access to physical connections, etc.

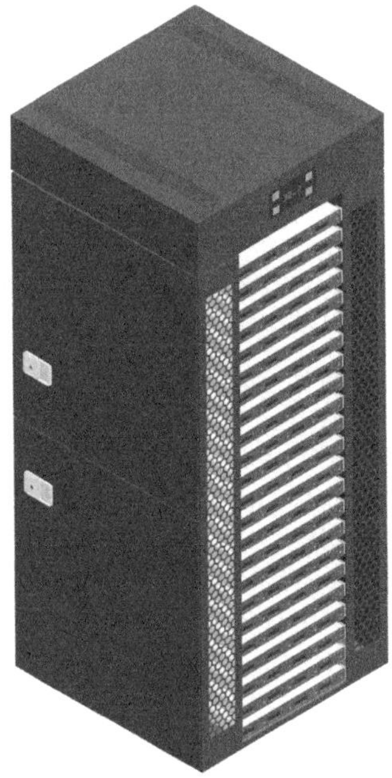

Server rack holding multiple components. (Image © 123RF.com)

Mounting Server and Network Devices in Racks

Rack mounting is the most common form factor for most server rooms. These deployments start with a standardized storage **rack**. The rack is secured to the floor for stability. It is also usually installed into an isolated server room to provide physical security, dedicated power, and cooling. Once the rack is installed, power is brought to it, and then servers and network devices are placed in it.

The number of available storage units defines rack size. As noted earlier, rack-mounted servers are one or more units in size. For a very small facility, a 6U or 8U rack may be sufficient to house one or two servers, a router, and an **uninterruptible power supply (UPS)**. For larger environments, a rack as tall as 42U may be deployed. Larger server rooms and data centers may have a great many of these full-sized racks.

Small racks may also be used in network closets for devices such as routers, switches, **patch panels**, and telecom devices.

Rail Kits

Rails are attached to the server's chassis and then the rack. These rails permit the server to slide forward out of the rack for service or removal. Rail kits may be universal or proprietary, so check with the manufacturer of your rack to find the proper fit.

Be careful when sliding servers out of the rack on rails that you do not overbalance the rack! For your safety, the rack should be anchored to the floor.

Rack Layout for Cooling

Adequate air circulation is essential to keep the devices mounted in the rack cool. Heat is detrimental to the performance and lifespan of electronic devices.

Best practices for cooling rack-mounted devices:

- Provide air circulation through the rack doors (front and back).
- Use fans to circulate air through the rack. Take care to address dust and other contaminants that might cause additional issues.
- Do not fill a rack to capacity. Too many devices may provide a heat load that the rack cannot dissipate.
- Monitor temperature. Some servers, for example, include temperature sensors on the motherboard and chassis. These components may also include alert capabilities. For centralized administration, monitoring software aggregates temperature and other environmental concerns (humidity) into a single dashboard.

Environmental Sensors

Environmental sensors may be installed in racks to better manage the server. Running servers with optimal environmental conditions extends their lifespan. The sensors also alert you to potential problems before downtime is generated.

Examples of environmental sensors:

- Temperature—it is critical to monitor temperature to ensure the server's current availability and extend its lifespan.
- Humidity—suboptimal humidity may shorten the server's lifespan.
- Water—damage from broken pipes, leaking ceilings, and other sources can physically damage servers.
- Door closure—sensors on rack doors ensure air is flowing as designed and the server's physical security.
- Airflow—airflow sensors prevent technicians from having to regularly check for failed cooling fans.

The sensors may communicate via simple mail transfer protocol (SMTP) or through proprietary interfaces. They may participate on wired or wireless networks.

Air Conditioning

An air conditioner is one critical method to control server room temperature. Air conditioner units must be sized properly to provide the appropriate amount of cooling. The target temperature for most server rooms is between 68 and 71 degrees Fahrenheit (25–27 degrees Celsius). The maximum temperature range should be 50–82 degrees Fahrenheit.

Calculating the capacity of the Computer Room Air Conditioning (CRAC) unit requires you to multiply the IT load x 1.3. The IT load is the power consumption of all devices, measured in watts. Device vendors provide the power consumption values in their documentation. This calculation results in a system rating for the CRAC unit measured in **British Thermal Units (BTUs)**. Air conditioner units are rated for a number of BTUs. Remember that all devices in the server room will generate heat, as will any administrators in the room.

Hot and Cold Aisles in the Server Room

Server racks are organized into rows with aisles in between them. The aisles are there not only to provide physical access to the racks for administrators but also to act as conduits for air ventilation. Organize the server racks to blow hot air into one aisle and pull cold air from another aisle. Orienting all the servers the same way maintains a flow of hot or cold air in the aisles to ensure efficient cooling.

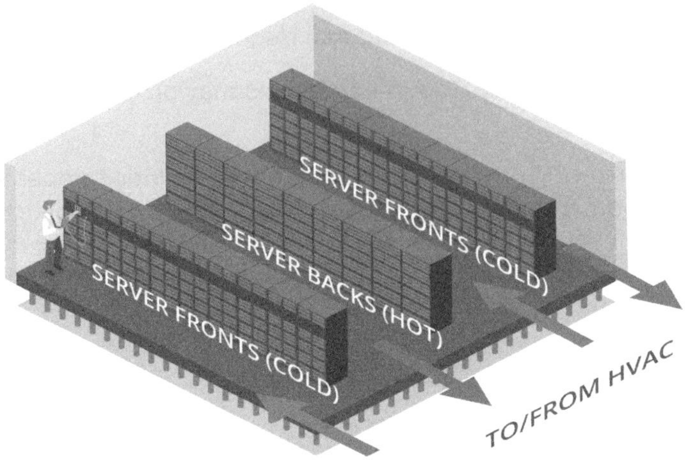

Server orientation with hot and cold airflow. (Images © 123RF.com)

Safety

Servers, especially the multi-unit devices, are very heavy. Tall racks require you to lift a server to or over the level of your head. Proper lifting techniques, including team lifting, are recommended. There are also specialized devices designed to lift servers to the appropriate height for rack mounting.

Hydraulic trolley, one type of equipment used for safely lifting servers to the appropriate height in a rack. (Image by grispb © 123RF.com)

It is essential to ensure to secure the rack to the floor. This prevents servers that are pulled forward on rails from overbalancing the rack and causing it to tip over. Floors must also be rated to properly support the weight of the servers, the rack, and any other IT equipment.

Power Distribution Unit (PDU)

PDUs allocate power from the UPS to the rack-mounted devices. The PDUs are much more complicated than a simple power strip. They may include power monitoring, circuit breakers, and consumption measurements. It is a best practice to provide balancing and redundancy. For example, a server with two power supplies has each one attached to a different PDU (which is attached to different UPS devices). Ensure that the devices connected to the PDU do not exceed its rating, especially in a failover situation.

Keyboard Video Mouse (KVM) Placement

It is not realistic to have an individual keyboard, mouse, and video display for each server in the server room. Instead, the servers mounted in a rack connect to a single device that switches its attention among the servers. This device, known as a **KVM switch**, has a single keyboard, monitor, and mouse attached to it, with connections to many servers.

KVM switches provide keyboard, video, and mouse functionality to a great many servers while consuming very little space. USB and audio connections may also be available.

KVM switches may be mounted in the rack and connected to a standard keyboard, display, and mouse, which may be kept on a shelf or a cart. This is the simplest solution.

Dedicated consoles are another alternative. The console integrates a keyboard, monitor, and mouse into a single 1U tray that stows in the rack when not in use.

Rack-mounted KVM. (Image © 123RF.com)

IP KVM switches use ethernet network connectivity to communicate with servers. These switches allow for remote administration from any distance. Traditional PS2/USB KVM switches operate within the limits of the server room.

It is worth noting that remote administration via Remote Desktop Protocol (RDP) and Secure Shell (SSH) connections is very common. Use KVM connections when a more direct connection is required.

To decide on which KVM solution is best, evaluate the size of your server room and the number of servers you are supporting.

Power Cabling

One of the hallmarks of the server is high availability. The most fundamental availability begins with electricity. Clean and consistent electricity must be provided to the server for it to function. Any interruption in power may result in system crashes.

Redundant power is provided in many ways. First, the data center may have multiple electricity sources. Next, the server room connects to two or more electrical circuits in the building. The server room has one or more **UPS** devices, the racks have multiple PDUs, and each server has multiple power supplies installed.

Ways to implement power redundancy:

- Electricity brought in by two different service providers (power companies)
- Electricity available via generators during an outage
- Multiple electrical circuits in the building that are isolated from the rest of the building's power
- UPSs
- Multiple PDUs
- Multiple power supplies installed inside the server

Power conditioners, either as separate devices or integrated into the power distribution devices, help to ensure the flow of electricity is steady.

Power Connections

You may see a variety of power connectors form factors, but it is particularly common to see the National Electrical Manufacturing Association (NEMA) 5-15P and International Electrotechnical Commission (IEC) C13/C14 connectors.

NEMA 5-15P/R

NEMA sets standards in the United States for electrical components. The common electrical plugs and outlets found in many homes and businesses are the NEMA 5-15P (plug) and NEMA 5-15R (receptacle).

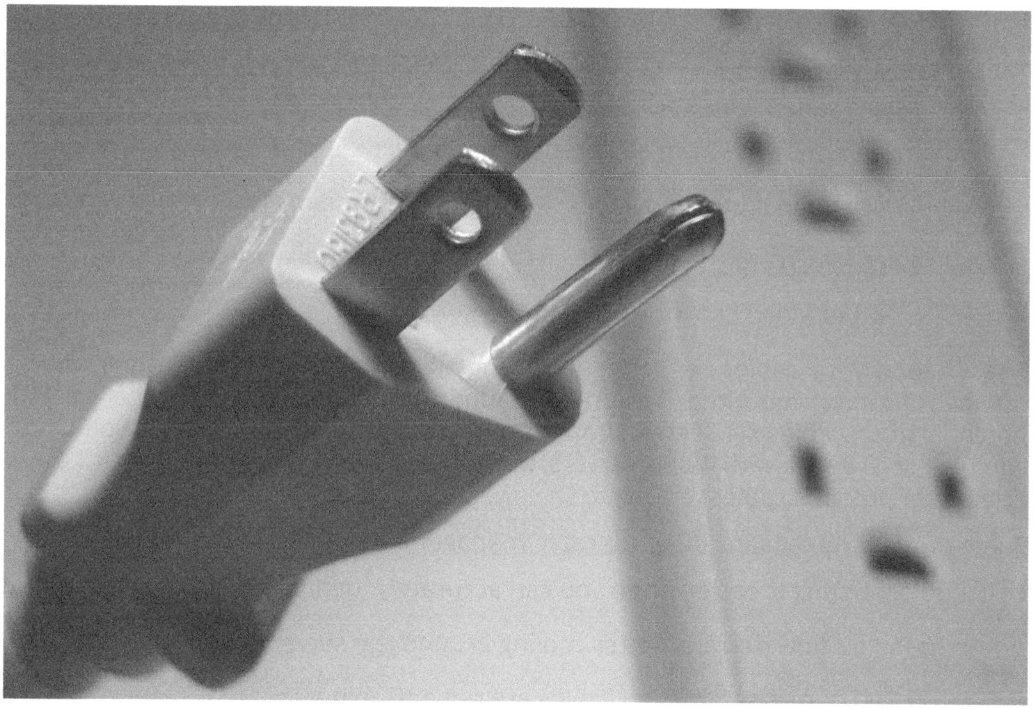

NEMA 5-15P (a three-prong plug) and NEMA 5-15R (a three-prong receptacle). (Image © 123RF.com)

IEC C13/C14

IEC sets international standards. Many server and network components use the IEC C13 and C14 connectors. It is also common to find these connectors used with PDUs.

IEC C13 and C14 cable terminals. (Image by Andrii Zhezhera © 123RF.com)

Cable Management

There may be a great many cables coming out of the back of a rack-mounted server. Let's assemble a brief list of some possible cables:

- Two power cords (one from each redundant power supply)
- Multiple twisted pair network cables—at least one for each NIC
- USB cables leading to the KVM switch for the mouse and keyboard
- HDMI or other video cables leading to the KVM switch

That's a total of six cables per server (counting only one network cable), times the number of servers mounted in the rack. Assuming a full-sized 42U rack, that's a potential of six cables x 42 servers for a total of 252 cables! You probably would not completely fill a rack with 42 1U servers, but this equation gives you an idea of the number of possible cables.

There are several reasons effective cable management is essential:

- Troubleshooting is easier when you can accurately identify and chase each cable.
- Increased air flow permits better cooling around the servers.
- The server room is safer when cables are not a tripping **hazard**.
- It minimizes potential cable damage.
- It reduces crosstalk and electrical interference.

There are plenty of tools to help you organize cables. First, many cables are available in different colors, which permits you to color-code them. This practice is especially common with twisted pair network cables. You can use horizontal and vertical cable managers in racks to help guide cables. You can also use trays to guide cables over aisles (you don't want the weight of hanging cables to stress the connectors in the network devices).

Horizontal cable managers can be used for power and for network cables. (Image by Kjetil Kolbjornsrud © 123RF.com)

Overhead cable tray supporting bundles of cable. (Image by Pisit Khambubpha © 123RF.com)

Network Cabling

Sysadmins may be responsible for managing network cabling and connectivity. While some IT departments have a separate network team, often, the server admin team still manages some parts of networking.

The network segment to which the servers are directly attached may include **redundancy** to help ensure availability and performance. In addition, connectivity might include twisted pair or fiber optic network media. Such media has standards that you need to know for successful management.

Redundant Networking

Redundant networking refers to eliminating single points of failure in the network infrastructure. Such redundancy is usually implemented in a mesh topology, where there are multiple communications paths through multiple network devices. Redundancy is particularly important for servers.

Most organizations don't need a mesh topology or redundancy for the workstation network. Redundancy for server-to-server communication (database replication, etc.) and between the server LAN and the workstation LAN is usually sufficient.

Server Redundancy

The first area of network redundancy for a server is multiple **NICs**. Like any other component, NICs can fail, which would take a server with a single NIC offline. For this reason, many servers ship with multiple NICs integrated into the motherboard. In addition, administrators may choose to install additional NICs in the motherboard's expansion slots.

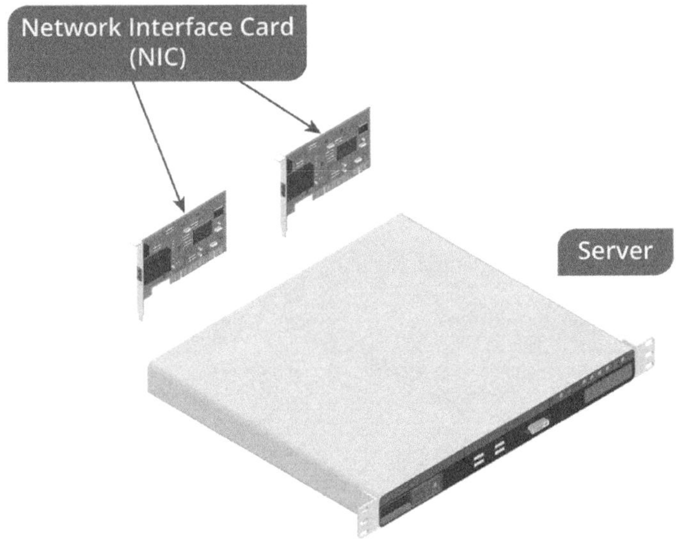

Server with redundant NICs. (Images © 123RF.com)

Media and Switch Redundancy

Once redundancy is achieved in the server, the next component is redundant network media. Because the server has multiple NICs, network media, such as twisted pair cable, is attached. This helps to eliminate a disconnected or damaged cable as a single point of failure.

The next layer of redundancy is network switching. Two server NICs, with one network cable each, could be plugged into a single switch. When configured for NIC teaming, this design can increase **bandwidth**. That switch, however, is still a single point of failure.

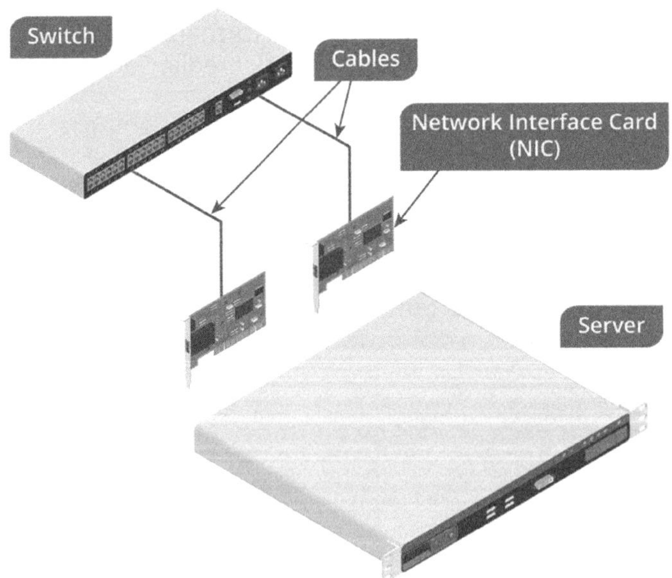

Server with redundant NICs plugged into one switch. (Images © 123RF.com)

To mitigate the risk, the cable from one server NIC could be plugged into a different switch than the cable from the second NIC. In this case, if a switch fails, the server still has connectivity to the rest of the network via the redundant switch.

Don't forget to provide redundant power sources to your network devices.

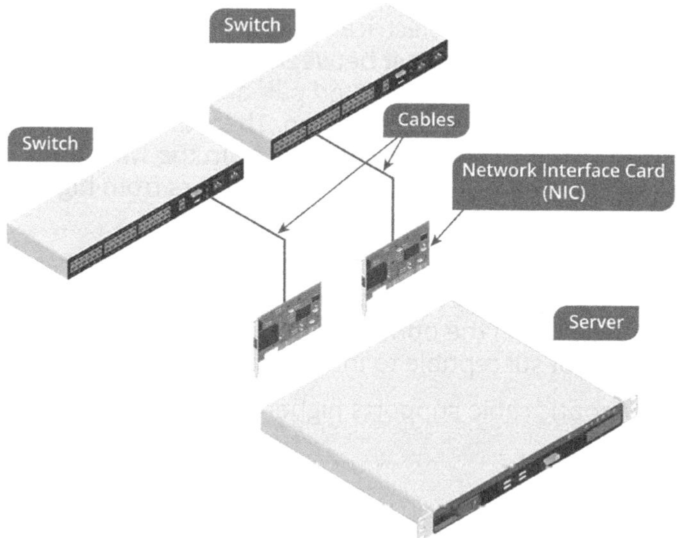

Server with redundant NICs plugged into redundant switches. (Images © 123RF.com)

Router Redundancy

Each network segment is connected to other segments via a router. If the router fails, the network segment is isolated from the rest of the network. A standby router may be configured to take over if the primary router goes offline.

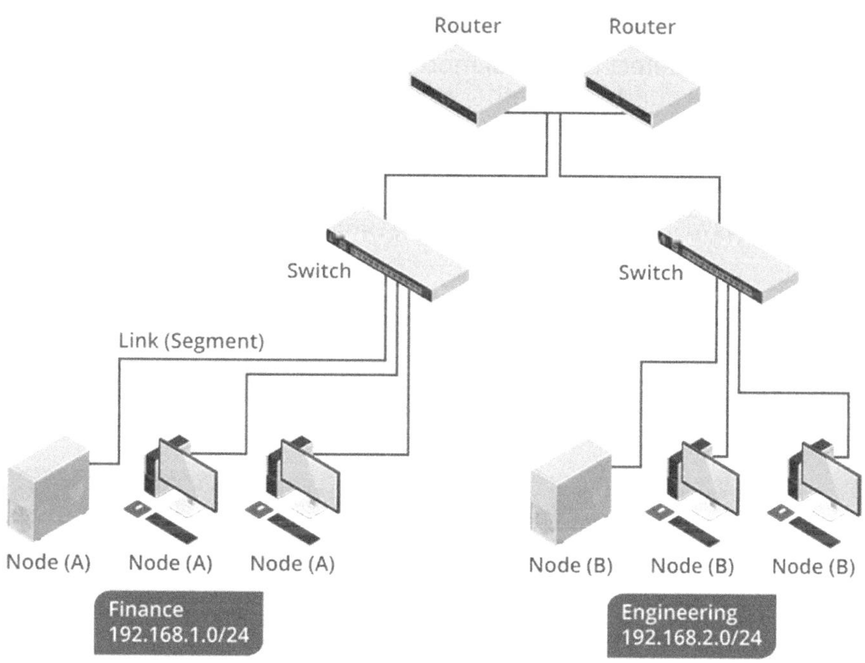

Redundant routers between network segments. (Images © 123RF.com)

Ensure network components, such as firewalls or routers, are not configured to block traffic in a manner that interferes with redundancy.

Transmission Media Types

Most data networks use either copper or fiber optic cable media or radio-based wireless media.

Copper cable is used to transmit electrical signals. The cable between two nodes creates a low-**voltage** electrical circuit between the interfaces on the nodes. There are two main types of copper cable: twisted pair and coaxial (coax). Electrical signals are susceptible to interference and dispersion. There is some degree of impedance in the copper conductor; signals can leak easily from the wire, and noise can also leak into the wire. This means that copper cable suffers from high attenuation: that the signal loses strength over long links.

Fiber optic cable carries very-high-frequency radiation in the infrared light part of the electromagnetic spectrum. Even though high frequencies are used, they are very closely contained within the optical media and can propagate more easily. The light signals are also not susceptible to interference or noise from other sources.

Consequently, fiber optic cable supports higher bandwidth over longer links than copper cable does.

Twisted Pair Cable

Twisted pair cable is relatively inexpensive, easy to work with, common, and standardized. There are two main types: **unshielded twisted pair (UTP)** and **shielded twisted pair (STP)**.

Unshielded Twisted Pair

Twisted pair is a type of copper cable that has been extensively used for telephone systems and data networks. One pair of insulated wires twisted together forms a balanced pair. The pair carries the same signal but with different polarity; one wire is positive, and the other is negative. This allows the receiver to identify any noise affecting the line and detect the signal more strongly. Two or four twisted pairs are themselves twisted around one another to form a twisted pair cable. The pairs are twisted to reduce external interference and crosstalk, whereby one wire causes interference in another as a result of their proximity. Twisting the wires ensures the emitted signals from one wire are cancelled out by the emitted signals from the other. Each pair is twisted at a different rate to ensure the pairs do not interfere with one another.

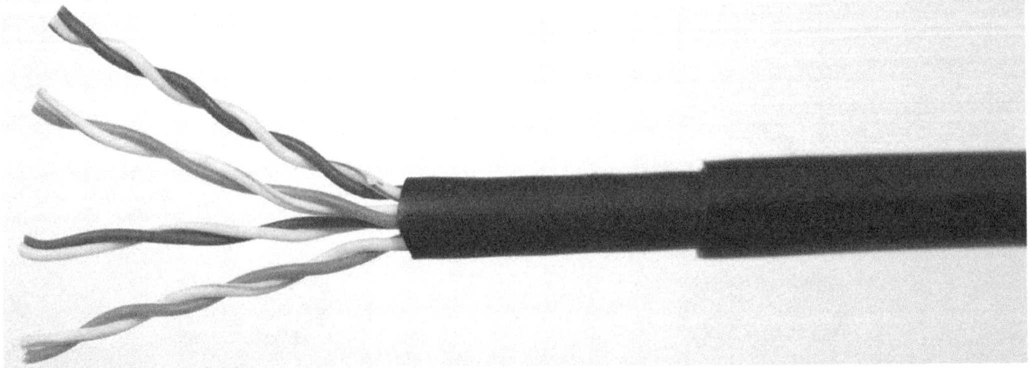

Twisted pair cable with four pairs, twisted at different rates. (Image by Thuansak Srilao © 123RF.com)

Most twisted pair cable currently used in networks is UTP. A major reason for UTP's popularity is because this form of cabling is used in many telephone systems. Modern buildings are often flood-wired using UTP cabling. This involves cables being laid to every location in the building that may need to support a telephone or computer. These cables can then be used for either the telephone system or the data network.

Shielded Twisted Pair

When twisted pair cabling was first used in networks based on IBM's Token Ring product, it was usually shielded to make it less susceptible to interference and crosstalk. Each pair was surrounded by a braided shield and was referred to as STP. This type of cabling is no longer widespread.

RJ-45 Connectors

RJ-45 connectors are used with four-pair (eight-wire) cables. The connectors are also referred to as 8P8C, standing for eight-position/eight-contact. This means that all eight potential wire positions are supplied with contacts, so that they can all carry signals if needed. RJ-45 is used for **Ethernet** twisted pair cabling.

Cat Standards

The American National Standards Institute (ANSI) and the Telecommunications Industry Association (TIA)/Electronic Industries Alliance (EIA) have created categories for twisted pair to simplify selection of a suitable quality of cable, known as **cat cable standards**. These categories, along with other aspects of telecommunications wiring best practices, are defined in the ANSI/TIA/EIA 568 Commercial Building Telecommunications Cabling Standards (tiaonline.org).

Cat	Frequency	Capacity	Max Distance	Network Application
3	16 MHz	10 Mbps	100 meters	10BaseT
5	100 MHz	100 Mbps	100 meters	100BaseTX
5e	100 MHz	1 Gbps	100 meters	1000BaseT
6	250 MHz	1 Gbps	100 meters	1000BaseT
6A	500 MHz	10 Gbps	100 meters	10GBaseT
7	600 MHz	10 Gbps	100 meters	10GBaseT

Cat cable standards.

Here are some details about the categories used for network media:

- Cat 5 cable is no longer available. Cat 5e is tested at 100 megahertz (MHz; like Cat 5 was) but to higher overall specifications for attenuation and crosstalk, meaning that the cable is rated to handle **Gigabit Ethernet** throughput. With Gigabit Ethernet, all four pairs are used for bidirectional data transfer. Cat 5e would still be an acceptable choice for providing network links for workstations.
- Cat 6 can support 10 Gbps but over shorter distances—nominally 55 m, but often less if cables are closely bundled together.
- Cat 6A is an improved specification cable that can support 10 Gbps over 100 m. It is mostly deployed in data centers or as backbone cabling (links between servers, switches, and routers). Cat 6A cable is bulkier than Cat 5e, and the installation requirements more stringent, so fitting it within pathways designed for older cable can be problematic.

- With Cat 6A, there are UTP and F/UTP variants. Both types are bulkier than Cat 5e or Cat 6, though, in fact, the diameter of Cat 6A UTP is slightly larger than 6A F/UTP. The components of F/UTP are more expensive, but UTP requires more testing to ensure proper performance. Also, F/UTP can be bundled more tightly together than UTP.
- Cat 7 cable is fully screened and shielded (S/FTP) and rated for 10GbE applications up to 100 m (328 feet). The cable supports transmission frequencies up to 600 MHz. Cat 7 is not recognized by TIA/EIA but appears in the cabling standards created by the ISO (ISO/IEC 11801).

Gigabit

Gigabit Ethernet builds on the standards defined for Ethernet and Fast Ethernet. The bit rate is 10 times faster than Fast Ethernet. The Gigabit Ethernet standard over fiber is documented in IEEE 802.3z. There are variants for long wavelength optics (LX), required for long distance transmission, and short wavelength optics (SX). The various fiber standards are collectively known as 1000BASE-X. The IEEE also approved 1000BASE-T, a standard utilizing Cat 5e (or better) copper wiring. This is defined in IEEE 802.3ab.

10GbE

10 Gigabit Ethernet (10GbE) multiplies the nominal speed of Gigabit Ethernet by a factor of 10. It is not deployed in many access networks, however, as the cost of 10GbE network adapters and switches is high. The major applications of 10GbE Ethernet are the following:

- Increasing bandwidth for server interconnections and network backbones, especially in data centers and for SANs.
- Replacing existing switched public data networks based on proprietary technologies with simpler Ethernet switches (Metro Ethernet).

General-purpose office buildings are less likely to deploy 10GbE for client connectivity. It might be used where a company's business requires very high bandwidth for data transfers, such as TV and film production. It is standardized under several publications with letter designations, starting with 802.3ae, which are periodically collated. At the time of writing, IEEE 802.3-2018 is current.

Fiber Optic Cable

Copper wire carries electrical signals, which are subject to interference and attenuation (the reduction of signal quality over distance). **Fiber optic cable** uses pulses of infrared light for signaling, which are not susceptible to interference, cannot easily be intercepted (eavesdropped on), and suffer less from attenuation. Consequently, fiber optic cabling supports much higher bandwidth (multiple gigabits per second) and longer cable runs (measured in kilometers, rather than meters). A single optical fiber is constructed from three elements:

- Core provides the transmission path for the light signals (waveguide).
- Cladding reflects signals back into the waveguide as efficiently as possible so that the signal travels along the waveguide by multiple internal reflections. The core and cladding can be made from glass or plastic. The cladding is applied as a thin layer surrounding the core. Cladding is made of the same material, but it has a different refractive index than the core. The effect of this is to create a boundary that causes the light to bounce back into the core, facilitating the process of total internal reflection that guides the light signal through the core.

- Buffer is a protective plastic coating. It may be of a tight or loose configuration, with the loose format using some form of lubricant between the strand and the sheath.

In basic operation modes, each fiber optic strand can only transfer light in a single direction at a time. Therefore, multiple fibers are often bundled within a cable to allow simultaneous transmission and reception of signals or provide links for multiple applications. There are many different outer jacket designs and materials suited for different installations (indoor/plenum, outdoor, underground, undersea, and so on). Kevlar (Aramid) strands and sometimes fiberglass rods (strength members) are often used to protect the fibers from excessive bending or kinking when pulling the cable to install it. For exposed outdoor applications, a steel shield (armor) may be added to deter rodents from gnawing the cable.

Single Mode and Multimode Fiber Optics

Fiber optic cables are specified using the mode, composition (glass/plastic), and core/ cladding size; for example, 8.3 micron core/125 microcladding single mode glass or 62.5 micron core/125 microcladding multimode plastic. Fiber optic cables fall into two broad categories: single mode and multimode. **Single Mode Fiber (SMF)** has a small core (8–10 microns) and a long wavelength, near infrared (1310 nm or 1550 nm) light signal, generated by a laser. Single mode cables support data rates up to 10 Gbps or better and cable runs of many kilometers, depending on the quality of the cable and optics.

Multimode Fiber (MMF) has a larger core (62.5 or 50 microns) and shorter wavelength light (850 nm or 1300 nm) transmitted in multiple waves of varying length. MMF uses less expensive optics and consequently is less expensive to deploy than SMF. However, it does not support such high signaling speeds or long distances as SMF and so is more suitable for LANs than WANs.

Optical transceivers for SMF are now only slightly more expensive than ones for MMF. Consequently, SMF is often used for short-range applications in data centers, as well as for long distance links. SMF still comes at a slight price premium, but it provides better support for the next generation of 40 Gbps and 100 Gbps Ethernet standards.

Fiber Optic Connector Types

Fiber optic connectors are available in many different form factors. Some types are more popular for multimode and some for single mode.

Straight Tip (ST) is an early bayonet-style connector that uses a push-and-twist locking mechanism. ST was used mostly for multimode networks, but it is not widely used for Ethernet installations anymore.

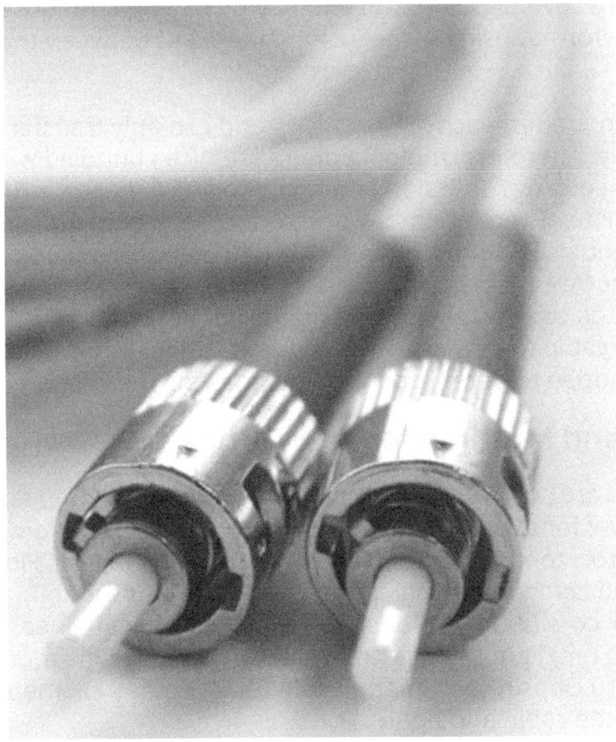

Two single-mode ST connectors. (Image by Aleh Datskevich © 123RF.com)

The Subscriber Connector (SC) is a push/pull design, allowing for simple insertion and removal. It can be used for single mode or multimode. It is commonly used for Gigabit Ethernet.

The **Lucent Connector (LC)** is a small-form-factor connector with a tabbed push/pull design. LC is similar to SC, but the smaller size allows for higher port density. LC is a widely adopted form factor for Gigabit Ethernet and 10GbE.

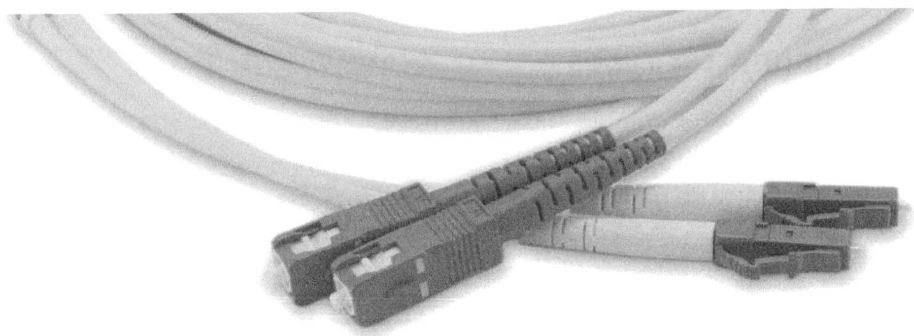

Fiber optics single-mode patch cord with different connectors, SC to LC. (Image by Yanawut Suntornkij © 123RF.com)

Transceivers and Small Form Factor Pluggable (SFP), SFP+, Quad SFP

A network might involve multiple types of cabling. When this occurs, switch and router equipment must be able to terminate different cable and connector types, and devices must convert from one type to another. Enterprise switches and routers are available with modular, hot-swappable transceivers for different types of fiber optic patch cord connections. Historically, these were based on the Gigabit Interface Converter (GBIC) form factor, which used SC ports and was designed (as the name suggests) for Gigabit Ethernet. GBIC was very bulky and has largely been replaced by **SFP**, also known as mini-GBIC. SFP uses LC connectors and is also designed for Gigabit Ethernet. SFP+ is an updated specification to support 10GbE but still uses the LC form factor. XFP represents another standard for small form factor, hot-swappable transceivers capable of supporting 10GbE. XFP also uses the LC form factor.

GBIC, SFP, and SFP+ are all duplex interfaces, with one transmit port and one receive port. BiDi SFP and BiDi SFP+ are newer types of transceiver supporting transmitting and receiving signals over the same strand of fiber (simplex port). This uses a technology called Wavelength Division Multiplexing to transmit the Tx and Rx signals over slightly shifted wavelengths, such as 1270 nm for TX and 1330 nm for RX. BiDi transceivers must be installed in matched pairs tuned to the wavelengths used for the link. BiDi links are documented in Ethernet standards (1000BASE-BX and 10GBASE-BX).

Quad SFP (QSFP and QSFP+) is a transceiver form factor designed to support 40GbE along with other high-bandwidth applications (including InfiniBand and SONET). Essentially, it combines 4 SFP or SFP+ links to support either 4 x 1 Gbps or 4 x 10 Gbps, which can be aggregated into a single 4 Gbps or 40 Gbps channel. QSFP uses a few copper and fiber optic cable and connector types.

Do not neglect the importance of proper cable management. As you saw in an earlier section, well-organized cabling promotes easier troubleshooting, more efficient cooling, safety, reduced risk of cable damage, and less interference.

Review Activity:

Physical Server Management

Answer the following questions:

1. **What are the standard width and height measurements for rack-mounted devices?**

2. **List at least two benefits of using rack-mounted devices:**

3. **What are hot and cold aisles in a server room?**

4. **How is a KVM switch useful in a server room?**

5. **List at least three ways of providing redundant power to servers:**

Topic 5B

Administer the Server and Storage

EXAM OBJECTIVES COVERED
1.1 Given a scenario, install physical hardware
1.3 Given a scenario, perform server hardware maintenance

Server administration may be performed locally (logged in to the server directly) or remotely (logged into the server over a network connection). Each method has its advantages, though as a general rule, remote connectivity is preferred and usually the most convenient.

Components such as CPUs, graphics processing units (GPUs), memory, and storage are often specialized for servers. These components often tolerate higher workloads and provide greater resiliency compared to workstation components. Some components, such as storage disks, may be hot swappable.

Local Hardware Administration and Out-of-Band Management

It is a best practice for administrators to manage servers and other network devices remotely, which is often done over the production network using protocols such as SSH, Virtual Network Computing (VNC), and Remote Desktop. These connections utilize the same network as the data transfers used by the company's employees. Mixing the two traffic types isn't usually a problem. The network connection is available for the administrators as long as the server or other network device is online. What happens when the network is down or the server is off or hung?

Out-of-band management uses a second, dedicated physical connection to the server known as a console port. This connection provides administrative functionality through specialized software that allows for control of the device independently of the OS. A sysadmin can, therefore, manage a server even if the OS is offline or uninstalled.

Reasons for out-of-band access a device:

- Increased security by separating administrative traffic away from production network traffic
- Remote power on and power off of servers and other network devices
- Additional remote connection if the primary remote management tool is unavailable
- Unified Extensible Firmware Interface (UEFI)/BIOS-level access to servers
- Remote drive access
- Remote console or terminal access that is used for troubleshooting or configuration
- Virtual administrative console that is used for access to VMs

Connection types:

- IP Keyboard/Video/Mouse (IP KVM)
- RS-232 serial ports
- USB
- Modem that permits remote dial-up

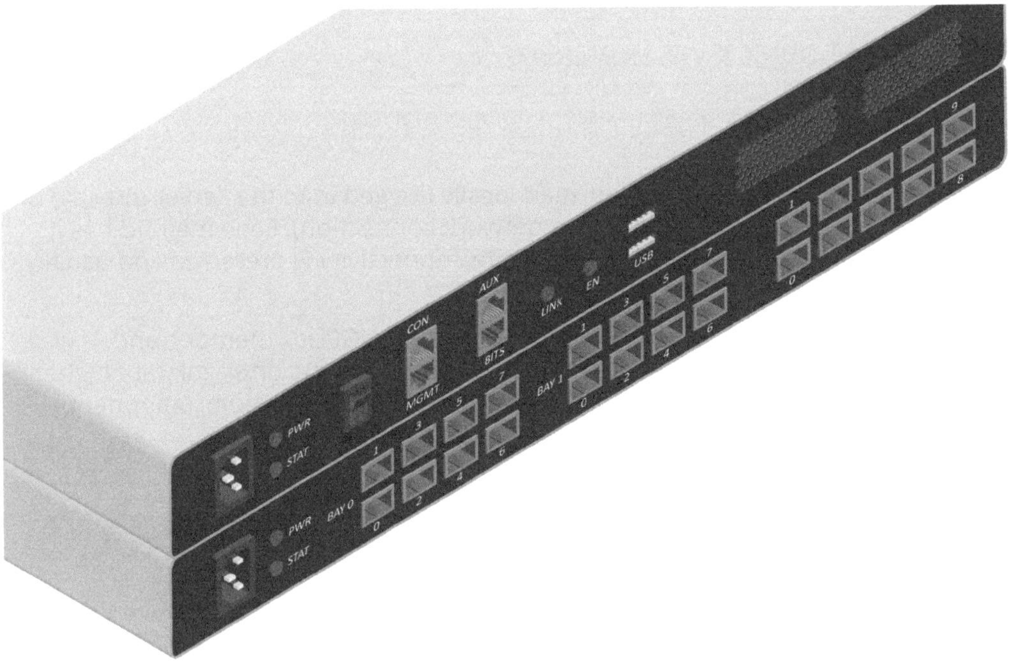

RJ-45 ports for out-of-band management. (Image © 123RF.com)

The Simple Network Management Protocol (SNMP) allows for network monitoring to help you anticipate and address problems. What will you do when the network devices are down and SNMP information is no longer available? That's when out-of-band management is essential.

Crash Cart

Your server room may be equipped with a crash cart for local out-of-band management. The cart contains a secured laptop that is used solely for out-of-band connectivity to servers and network devices. Alternatively, the cart may have a keyboard, full-sized monitor, and mouse that can be directly connected to the server.

The crash cart is mobile and ergonomically designed for an administrator to stand and use the laptop comfortably. The cart includes all necessary cables for establishing an out-of-band connection to any device in the server room.

Some vendors, such as Dell and Oracle, have created their own out-of-band connectivity standards and tools. The Dell product is called "Dell Remote Access Controller" (DRAC), and the Oracle product is called "Oracle Integrated Lights Out Manager" (iLOM).

Crash cart in a server room. (Image by Aleksei Gorodenkov © 123RF.com)

Local hardware administration includes the physical replacement and reconfiguration of failed components. Often, this reconfiguration is accomplished by connecting to the server with a KVM switch or a crash cart equipped with a laptop and the appropriate connection cables. While most server administration takes place over the standard network, out-of-band management uses a dedicated connection with greater access to the server's BIOS/Unified Extensible Firmware Interface settings, NIC configurations, RAID controllers, and other firmware management tools.

The KVM connection may be accomplished by using a KVM in a rack drawer. The server's interface, whether GUI or CLI, will be displayed on the KVM. The KVM device may be connecting to the server via an IP-based network connection or a serial connection, such as USB.

KVM devices were covered in the Topic 5A.

Manage Server Components

Hardware Compatibility List (HCL)

Vendor HCLs permit sysadmins to discover hardware that may or may not function correctly with a given OS. It is beneficial to check the HCL if you're dealing with a custom-built or nonstandard hardware configuration. Server vendors strive to make their products compatible with the major server OSs.

Microsoft provides the Windows Server Catalog website to consolidate information about server hardware tested for Windows Server products. Products that have passed Microsoft testing are badged as "Certified for Windows Server." Criteria include security, stability, and drivers. You can browse by hardware component or OS. The Windows Server Catalog is found here: https://www.windowsservercatalog.com/

Red Hat provides a website where sysadmins can search for hardware and vendor compatibility for the various RHEL: https://access.redhat.com/ecosystem/search/#/category/Server

Ubuntu Linux also provides a web site where hardware compatibility may be checked for Ubuntu Server: https://certification.ubuntu.com/server

For example, your organization has asked you to purchase a server that contains industry-specific hardware. This hardware is uncommon, so before you make the purchase, you must ensure the hardware meets the requirements for your company's standard OS (e.g., Windows Server or RHEL).

Central Processing Unit (CPU)

Obviously, one of the critical components is the server's **CPU**. The processor handles the actual "thinking" for the server. Server CPUs are often more powerful, complex, and expensive than the CPUs found in end-user workstations.

For example, Intel's primary server CPU is the Xeon processor. This processor usually has a much larger L3 **cache** than an Intel i7 processor does. This cache helps increase performance. In addition, Xeon processors are designed to work longer under the heavy loads that servers experience. Finally, and perhaps most importantly, Intel Xeon processors support the use of EEC RAM. EEC RAM is covered in more detail below. These features permit server-class CPUs to operate more quickly and more reliably than a typical workstation CPU does.

Modern processors have multiple cores, or processors within the processor package. Server CPU packages have many cores, which permits code to be processed simultaneously. Modern processors also support multi-threading, in which each core is capable of working with two processing threads. Applications believe that there are multiple processors (or cores) installed, and the workload is distributed across them.

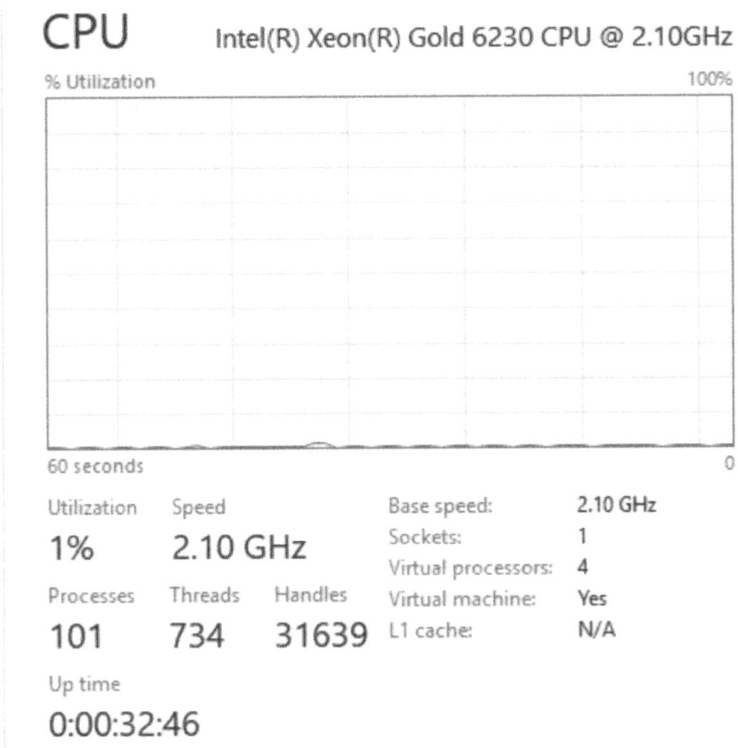

Windows Task Manager with four virtual processors displayed at lower right. (Screenshot courtesy of Microsoft.)

Hardware-assisted virtualization is an essential feature to be aware of for server CPU selection. Because so many of today's servers are virtualized, it is critical to ensure that your server hardware platforms can host VMs. Hardware-assisted virtualization is a set of virtualization instructions for the CPU. Virtualization is important enough that manufacturers clearly state when a CPU supports this function. It is also something that you can check on your existing servers. It is unlikely, however, that you'll find a modern processor that does not support virtualization.

An example of a modern server processor can be seen by examining an Intel Xeon Gold6240R Processor, which offers up to 24 cores to the OS. This processor supports multi-threading and Intel **Virtualization Technology (VT)** for hardware-assisted virtualization.

GPU

When sysadmins think about servers, they rarely consider graphics processing. Many server OSs have no **GUI** whatsoever or may have only a basic GUI. Graphics-intensive activities, such as gaming or graphics rendering, are done on workstations. The same processing power required for high-end graphics, however, can be directed toward other processing tasks. The idea is the same in both a gaming computer and a server with one or more powerful **graphics processing units**—to offload processing away from the CPU, freeing up the CPU for processing only it can do. If some tasks are carried out by the GPU, then the CPU has more time for other jobs.

These devices are often referred to as General Purpose GPUs.

Memory

Memory, or **RAM**, is a temporary storage location used by the CPU (and by some GPUs). RAM is a standard benchmark for anticipating a server's capabilities. Workstations also utilize RAM, but often a server requires far more RAM and better performance.

RAM speed is measured in MHz, and its quantity is usually measured in gigabytes (GB). The third common performance attribute of RAM is its bandwidth, which is measured in Mega Transfers/second (MT/s). Modern server memory is usually available in **Double Data Rate (DDR)** format.

For example, a Dell PowerEdge 940 rack-mount server contains 48 RAM slots for DDR4 memory, for a maximum of 6 terabytes (TB) of memory depending on the type of RAM installed.

It is important to try to predict the quantity of RAM required for a server. Such a calculation begins with the desired OS. Next, consider any applications that will run on the server. Finally, understand how those applications use memory. Some services are far more RAM intensive than others. Database servers and virtualization hosts require a great deal of memory, while file servers and basic web servers use significantly less.

OS Memory Requirements

Windows Server 2019 memory requirements:

- 512 MB minimum/2 GB minimum of EEC RAM if the Server with Desktop Experience feature is installed.

RHEL 8 memory requirements:

- 768 MiB minimum recommended

Ubuntu Server memory requirements:

- 4 GB minimum recommended

Notice that the Windows Server recommendation is the actual minimum, while the RHEL and Ubuntu minimums are recommended for a functional server.

VMs need the same quantity of memory allocated to them as if they were physical servers. One advantage that VMs have is that the sysadmin can reallocate RAM among them to ensure efficient memory use.

Expansion

Not every physical server has the exact specifications or hardware configuration that you may require. Like a workstation computer, servers usually have at least one expansion slot. These slots allow additional hardware cards to be inserted, extending the functionality of the server. The most common card type is **Peripheral Component Interconnect Express (PCIe)**. One common example of a PCIe expansion card is an NIC. You might add an NIC to a server if you need to connect the server to multiple networks or an integrated NIC has failed or is not fast enough for your needs.

Version	Transfers in Gigatransfers/sec	Year
3.0	8 GT/s	2010
4.0	16 GT/s	2017
5.0	32 GT/s	2020
6.0	64 GT/s	2021

PCIe versions. Note that overall throughput also depends on the number of lanes available in the motherboard's bus. A 16-lane bus has higher throughput than a 4-lane bus, for example.

Server Motherboard Buses

The platform controller hub on modern server motherboards manages the data **buses** that are not integrated into the CPU. These buses include peripherals. The CPU itself is responsible for PCIe graphics management as well as access to RAM.

Older motherboards had two integrated communications paths, or buses. The first, the Front Side Bus, provided a connection between the CPU and the motherboard's northbridge and was often used for external communications. The Back Side Bus connected the CPU to RAM. This path was used for internal communications. Intel's QuickPath Interconnect technology replaced the FSB. In 2017, QuickPath was replaced by the UltraPath Interconnect.

Expansion Bus Types

The primary expansion buses on the server are the Universal Serial Bus (USB) and the **PCIe**. Each of these buses permits additional devices to be attached to the server. In the case of PCIe, the devices include other USB connectors, NICs, storage controllers, or graphics cards. For USB, the devices include input devices (mice and keyboards) or external storage devices (flash drives).

Storage buses, such as Serial Advanced Technology Attachment (SATA), Small Computer System Interface (SCSI), and Serial Attached SCSI (SAS), are discussed later in this Lesson.

Interface Types

There are a variety of different ports on the back of your servers. These interfaces connect additional peripheral devices, provide network connectivity, or attach to the KVM switch.

Common ports:

- USB for storage devices, keyboards, and mice
- RS-232 for console management
- VGA/HDMI for video
- RJ-45 for Ethernet, console management.

RS-232 COM port. (Image by Yuri Minaev © 123RF.com)

Server components are constructed for durability and longevity under intense workloads. Processors, memory, storage devices, and expansion cards are designed to handle the demands of servers. Many vendors construct their server systems to be compatible with Microsoft Windows Server or particular Linux distributions. If you upgrade components or build a custom server solution, be careful to reference the HCLs that apply to your chosen OS.

Storage Drives

Most servers utilize at least some internal storage in the form of one or more HDDs. These drives attach via SATA, SAS, or SCSI controllers. A Linux or Windows OS is installed on one of these drives. Servers may also be connected to external storage, such as network attached storage (NAS), SAN, or Just a Bunch of Disks (JBOD) devices.

Most storage drive maintenance consists of discovering sections of the drive that may no longer be writable and anticipating drive failures. Storage disk failures are a common issue that plagues most computers, including servers.

Storage Disk Maintenance

Storage disk failures are often related to human error, firmware issues, or physical damage. Because human error is a common issue, ensure any BIOS/UEFI configuration changes are tested and documented before implementation. Test and apply manufacturer firmware updates, too. Storage disks are susceptible to heat damage, so proper cooling and ventilation are essential. This ventilation is necessary for many of the server's components, not just for storage disks.

Both Windows Server and Linux include a variety of disk maintenance utilities.

Windows has the **chkdsk** tool to aid administrators with disk maintenance. Chkdsk scans a storage disk for errors within the NTFS file system. It can report errors or both report and correct errors, depending on the switches selected when it is run.

Use the following chkdsk syntax to verify the M: drive and fix any errors found:

```
chkdsk m: /f
```

Linux includes a similar utility named "fsck" to check disk file systems. This tool also includes the option to fix discovered errors.

Use this fsck syntax to verify the /home **directory** file system (note that the file system must be unmounted first):

```
fsck /home
```

Misconfigured settings in the BIOS or OS configuration files may also cause storage disks not to be recognized. Take care when working in the BIOS to ensure that all settings are correct. Typically, the BIOS automatically detects disk settings (and it should be left that way). Mistakes in the Windows Registry or the Linux /etc/fstab file may also cause disks to be unrecognized or inaccessible.

Log files, such as Windows Server Event Viewer or Linux dmesg kernel log, provide clues about storage disk issues or imminent failures.

Administrators use many strategies to mitigate storage disk failures. Backups, RAID arrays, and data redundancy are all examples of mitigation techniques. Proper disk maintenance practices are also part of these strategies.

Hot-swappable Hardware

Hot-swappable devices are added or removed from the server without a reboot. This is essential for servers because reboots are downtime. The most common device is a USB flash drive, but servers can support many other hot-swap components. In some instances, power supplies, HDDs, RAM sticks, and even CPUs may be added or removed without restarting the server. Check the hardware specifications, as well as the OS requirements, to better understand exactly what devices are hot swappable on your systems.

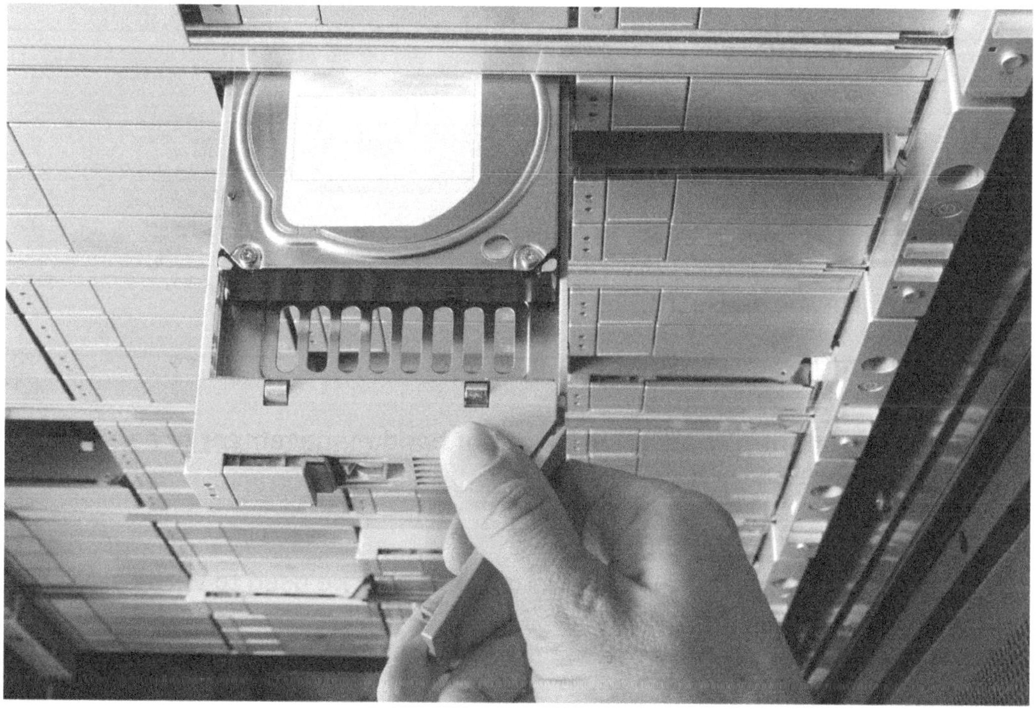

Hot-swappable HDD tray. (Image by kubais © 123RF.com)

When it comes to hard disk drives, the term hot-swappable is something of a misnomer. There is nothing specific about the disk drive itself that makes it hot swappable. Instead, replacing HDDs without restarting the server is a combination of the capabilities of the physical server bays, the OS, the RAID controller, and the file system.

Hot-Swap Cages

Some systems use HDD cages installed into the server chassis as bays for multiple storage devices. These cages maximize drive density. More importantly, they enable quick HDD changes in environments where hot-swap storage is used.

Hot-Swap Cards

Storage arrays may be made accessible or be controlled by **Host Bus Adapter (HBA)** and RAID controller cards. These cards are essential server components and therefore, may also be hot swappable. NICs may also be hot swappable, depending on the system configuration. Check your expansion card specifications and OS features to find out whether these cards can be hot swapped.

Hot-Swap Power Supplies and Fans

The server may contain other devices that are also hot swappable. Most servers are configured with dual power supplies to help ensure uptime. When one of the power supplies fails, the other one continues to power the server. The failed power supply is replaced with a functional one. Usually, this can be accomplished without powering down the server. Internal **cooling devices**, such as fans may also be hot swappable, depending on how they are powered. Check your server's documentation.

Review Activity:

Administration and Storage

Answer the following questions:

1. **List at least one situation where out of band management of a server may be necessary:**

2. **List one Linux and one Windows tool that may be used to verify storage disk file systems for errors:**

3. **What is the advantage of using an HCL when considering a server purchase?**

Topic 5C

Troubleshoot Server Hardware

EXAM OBJECTIVES COVERED
4.2 Given a scenario, troubleshoot common hardware failures

Hardware failure indicators can take many forms. Initially, predictive failure analysis might inform your troubleshooting—what has commonly failed in the past? There may be visual or auditory indicators, such as lights or **beep codes**. System failures such as crashes or lockups also indicate possible hardware issues.

Hardware failures may be caused by technical issues or environmental issues, such as temperature or static electricity. Failures may also be caused by misconfigurations by sysadmins, which can occur in the the BIOS settings, the OS, or applications.

A clean workspace is vital to troubleshooting, as is protection against static electricity. You should have access to not only the proper physical tools but also memory diagnostic tools. Finally, log files may be useful in troubleshooting hardware failures.

Indicators of Common Hardware Problems

There are many signs of imminent failure. Servers can communicate a vast amount of information to systems administrators. Log files, visual indicators, performance monitoring, and predictive failure analysis can all be used to anticipate problems.

Predictive Failure Analysis

Predictive failure analysis uses evidence from component use and direct experience to anticipate (and therefore mitigate) hardware failures. Storage device vendors, for example, may provide statistics that indicate the potential lifespan of devices. Your organization may also be able to generate predictive failure information by examining trends with service desk software, log files, and other internal measures.

Visual, Auditory, and Olfactory Indicators

Servers and their related components provide many visual and auditory clues about problems. Many devices have indicator LEDs that communicate their status. Green usually indicates that all is well, while amber or red may indicate problems. Check the documentation to interpret these colors correctly.

LED indicators on a switch. (Image by sbmh765 © 123RF.com)

For example, you see a log file entry in Event Viewer that indicates a possible HDD failure. Upon entering the server room and examining the server housing the suspect drive, you notice that of the six HDD bays in the hot-swap cage, five are displaying a green LED, while the sixth shows a red LED. The logs and the indicator lights help to identify exactly which HDD has failed.

A burned smell may originate from power supplies and other electrical equipment, indicating a problem. Components that overheat may give off the scent of burned plastic or wiring.

Some devices, such as network switches, use colors to indicate performance information rather than status information. For example, a network switch may display a green LED on a port if the connection is operating at 1 Gbps but an amber LED if the port is operating at 100 Mbps. Check the device's documentation to interpret the colors correctly.

System Crashes and Lockups

System crashes or lockups can indicate various issues, including problems with power supplies, RAM, the motherboard, and other devices. These lockups can also suggest problems with device drivers or other software, rather than hardware. Further investigation will be necessary.

Memory Failures

Memory sticks are particularly susceptible to power fluctuations and static electricity. Failed or failing RAM causes OS instability. With Windows Server, this usually causes a **Blue Screen** to occur. This Windows crash screen provides some clues as to the problem on screen or via a memory dump file that can help identify problems leading up to the crash. If the server successfully restarts, check the log files for more information. On VMware ESXi systems, memory errors may trigger a Purple crash screen. On Linux servers, a kernel panic error may indicate problems with RAM.

CMOS Battery Failure

A small battery, such as the kind used in watches, provides a trickle of power to the motherboard's CMOS chip. This chip holds basic configuration information for the server. The battery will eventually fail. When that occurs, settings stored in the BIOS on the CMOS may be reset. The date and time may also not display correctly in the BIOS (the server's OS probably acquires its time from the network). The battery is typically inexpensive and easy to replace. When BIOS or startup errors occur or settings do not appear to be configured correctly, be sure to check this battery. In some cases, when there is a problem with the battery, the server's chassis may display an amber or red LED.

It is a good idea to document when the CMOS battery is changed for each server.

Many different types of errors generate similar symptoms. Crash screens, lockups, and visual indicators all inform you that you need to further investigate the system's stability. Information gathered from sources such as log files and kernel dumps help to lead you toward memory, power supply, motherboard, device driver, and other issues. Virtually all the problems defined here indicate that additional research is required to discover the root cause.

Indicators of failure include the following:

- LEDs may display in different colors indicating full functionality, possible errors, or complete failures.
- The system failing to maintain the correct time or BIOS settings may indicate a CMOS battery failure.
- Vendors may provide predictive failure analysis data, or you may be able to generate your own data from log files and service desk tickets.

Causes of Common Hardware Problems

When troubleshooting, it is useful to divide problems into technical, environmental, or misconfiguration issues.

Technical

Temperature issues can cause many problems. The temperature may be too high in the server room or within the server's chassis. Within the chassis, cooling fans may fail, and heat sinks may be improperly seated. Internal cable routing for power, HDDs, and other devices may interfere with proper air flow. When diagnosing events such as random shutdowns or unexplained performance problems, consider the server's internal temperature.

Power supplies within the server chassis may fail with no warning. If the server only has a single power supply, it obviously becomes immediately unavailable. Most servers are equipped with dual power supplies for redundancy. Many of those power supplies are also hot swappable and can, therefore, be replaced without bringing the server down. However, before installing a new power supply, verify that all power connections to the motherboard and the devices are correctly seated.

Firmware exists on an embedded chip on controllers such as motherboards, graphics cards, and even NICs. The manufacturer may update such firmware to correct problems or expose new functionality. However, it is possible to render a device unusable if an incorrect firmware update is applied to it or the application process is interrupted by a power failure. When updating the firmware, make sure that the version is correct.

Use system documentation to ensure that any replacement or upgraded components you install in your server are compatible. Vendors' HCLs can also aid in confirming that you are using the right devices. This is particularly true for components such as RAM sticks. Devices that attach to the USB or PCIe busses may be more flexible.

The server's **backplane** provides a communications bus among devices that you may install. The backplane is an additional circuit board attached to the motherboard, and not all servers have one. Damage to the backplane—either physical or electrical—may keep devices on this bus from communicating correctly.

Environmental

Dust and other small particulates are a significant environmental concern in the server room. Dust builds up on fan blades, slowing the fans and preventing them from providing sufficient cooling. The fans also wear out more quickly. On the motherboard, dust is an insulator, keeping heat from dissipating as efficiently. It is vital to make sure that dust does not impede cooling in any manner.

It may surprise you that humidity plays an essential role in the server room. Humidity needs to be correctly balanced. Too little humidity, and static electricity may build up. Too much, and moisture in the air may condense on components. The recommended humidity level is between 40 and 60% rH. A hygrometer helps you to regulate server room humidity.

Environmental sensors can alert administrators. (Image by primagefactory © 123RF.com)

The recommended server room temperature is 68–71 degrees Fahrenheit (20–21.6 Celsius), though the range may fall as low as 50 degrees (10 Celsius) or as high as 80 degrees (27 Celsius). Regulating the server room temperature is a key part of maintaining server availability and prolonging the server's lifespan. Some servers have temperature sensors that alert you when the device is overheating, and a thermometer in the server room will help, as well.

CPU and GPU overheating may be caused by applications overutilizing resources or if the processor is being over clocked. Overheating can also be caused by an inadequate heat sink or a server chassis that does not have the appropriate air flow.

Cooling and other environmental factors were covered earlier in this Lesson.

Configuration

Misconfigurations are an additional cause of server problems. These misconfigurations may be due to typographical errors or other mistakes by administrators. They may also be caused by sysadmins who are not well versed on the technologies that they are supporting. Common misconfigurations include the following:

- Incorrect device drivers installed
- Incorrect hardware installed
- Incorrect BIOS/UEFI settings
- Mistakes in the Windows Registry
- Errors in Linux configuration files
- Incorrect service settings
- Incorrect firewall configurations

When troubleshooting hardware issues, it is valuable to categorize the problem as technical, environmental, or configuration to better narrow the scope. Such categorization helps guide you toward the next steps in the process.

Tools and Techniques for Troubleshooting Hardware

In this section, you examine some tools and techniques that help with the troubleshooting process. The first section discusses preparing a workspace, the second section covers physical hardware considerations, and the third section provides information on firmware and diagnostic tools. Finally, the fourth section includes log files for both Windows Server and Linux.

Preparing a Workspace for Troubleshooting

When troubleshooting hardware, provide yourself with a workspace that is convenient and protects the hardware. A well-organized workspace, with plenty of room to spread out components, is essential. You also need a good tool kit and containers to keep track of screws and other small parts.

In particular, dust can damage or degrade components, such as fans. Static electricity can also damage sensitive components, such as RAM sticks.

A static electricity shock that is powerful enough to ruin a stick of RAM is not necessarily powerful enough for you to feel. In other words, you can destroy a stick of RAM and not even feel it!

Troubleshooting tools:

- Large, well-organized workspace
- Tool kit
- Antistatic mat
- Antistatic wrist strap
- Antistatic bag
- Compressed air

Physical Hardware Troubleshooting

Now that you have an effective workspace, compressed air for cleaning, and antistatic equipment to protect your server's components, you can open the case and perform an upgrade. Let's say you want to install more RAM. During troubleshooting (and during installation), ensure that RAM sticks, expansion cards, and cable connectors are properly seated.

For example, after your RAM upgrade, you discover the server's NIC does not seem to work. Ensure that the NIC was not accidentally dislodged from the PCIe expansion slot where it is installed. Firmly but carefully press down on the components to be certain they are seated correctly and making a good electrical connection. Also, confirm that power cables and data cables (such as SATA data cables to HDDs) are well seated and have not been dislodged.

It might be a useful habit to make the last task you do inside an open server chassis be to check that all components are firmly seated, even if you don't believe you removed or disconnected anything.

Firmware and Diagnostic Tools

Firmware is used to manage individual server components, including RAID controllers, NICs, and other specialized hardware. Firmware is very specific to the vendor and the device. You should only upgrade the firmware with the updates recommended by the vendor.

Do not interrupt the firmware update process by stopping the process or restarting the server. Doing so can render the device inoperable.

Hardware vendors make firmware updates available online and include instructions to apply the updates. In addition, many hardware vendors provide tools to diagnose problems with the hardware devices that they have created. Downloading and using such tools helps to identify issues or misconfigurations.

One of the components you may wish to test during hardware troubleshooting is RAM. The memory sticks are vulnerable to **electrostatic discharge**, physical damage, or heat, which may cause the RAM to ultimately fail. Unfortunately, such problems may also cause intermittent failures, which are much more challenging to troubleshoot.

The complete failure of RAM is relatively easy to diagnose. If you know that the server has 32 GB of RAM installed, but the OS only recognizes 16 GB, you can be reasonably certain that something is wrong with the memory. Intermittent failures cause the system to become unstable. The OS may identify all 32 GB of RAM but fail when it tries to use some of the memory for storage.

Software such as the Windows Memory Diagnostic tool tests RAM and identifies specific memory sticks that are not functioning correctly. For a Linux server, download and install the memtester tool.

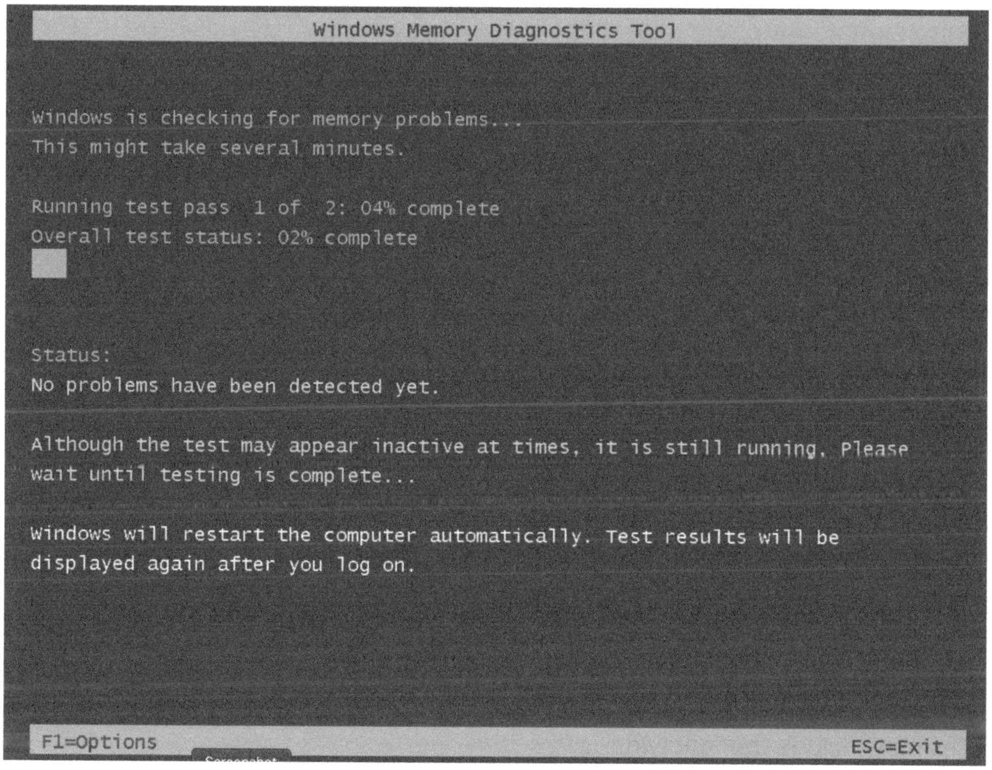

Windows Memory Diagnostic Tool. (Screenshot courtesy of Microsoft.)

Earlier in this Lesson, you learned about diagnostic tools for storage drives. Windows Server uses chkdsk to search for damaged areas of the HDD. Linux relies on fsck to accomplish the same task.

Check NICs by using a hardware loopback device. Use the ping utility to verify that the NIC is functioning correctly. While using ping is not entirely effective in diagnosing hardware issues, it can be a useful first step.

- Windows: ping 127.0.0.1
- Linux: ping -c 4 127.0.0.1

Log Files

Log files are one of the most useful troubleshooting tools available to sysadmins. While log files will be covered in more detail elsewhere in the course, a few logs specific to hardware are noted here.

The Windows log file system is named "Event Viewer." The primary part of Event Viewer to check for hardware issues is the System log. Event Viewer has many features for filtering and searching log files to help you discover exactly the information you need.

Linux log files are generated by a service named "rsyslog." By default, rsyslog stores log files in the /var/log directory. That directory contains many log files, though its exact contents vary depending on the Linux distribution and the installed applications.

When the Linux system boots, kernel messages are gathered by dmesg. You can run this command, along with a wide variety of options, to display information about hardware that was discovered by the **kernel** during the boot process. Here are some examples of using dmesg:

- dmesg | less—breaks the output of dmesg into pages (the output is very long)
- dmesg | grep network—searches the dmesg output for the keyword network

```
[root@localhost ~]# dmesg | grep network
[    0.876171] drop_monitor: Initializing network drop monitor service
[    4.396153] SELinux:  policy capability network_peer_controls=1
[    4.396154] SELinux:  policy capability always_check_network=0
[root@localhost ~]#
```

Gather network information with dmesg.

Linux and Windows log files are covered in much more detail later in the course.

Power-On Self-Test (POST) Codes

When the system boots, firmware runs a series of tests to ensure the expected components exist and are functional. This process is known as a **POST**. A series of codes are generated when the system fails its POST. These codes are specific to the BIOS vendor and provide significant clues as to the cause of the failed start process. Codes may include the following:

- Failed or missing CPU
- Failed or missing memory
- Motherboard failure
- Power supply failure

LCD Panel Readouts

POST codes may be stored for later reference or communicated via LED or sound. Some servers include an LCD panel that offers troubleshooting information if the server cannot boot normally, such as POST codes, temperature settings, or indicators of failed hardware.

Misallocation of Resources for VMs

Virtualization allows organizations to more efficiently use the compute power available in a server. However, it is possible to overallocate resources to VMs.

For example, three VMs on a host server could each be allocated 4 GB of RAM. The host OS also needs RAM—let's say 4 GB. That's a total of 16 GB of RAM that has been allocated. However, the physical server may only have 8 GB of RAM installed. Such overallocation can overheat components, such as CPUs, and reduce the system's overall effectiveness.

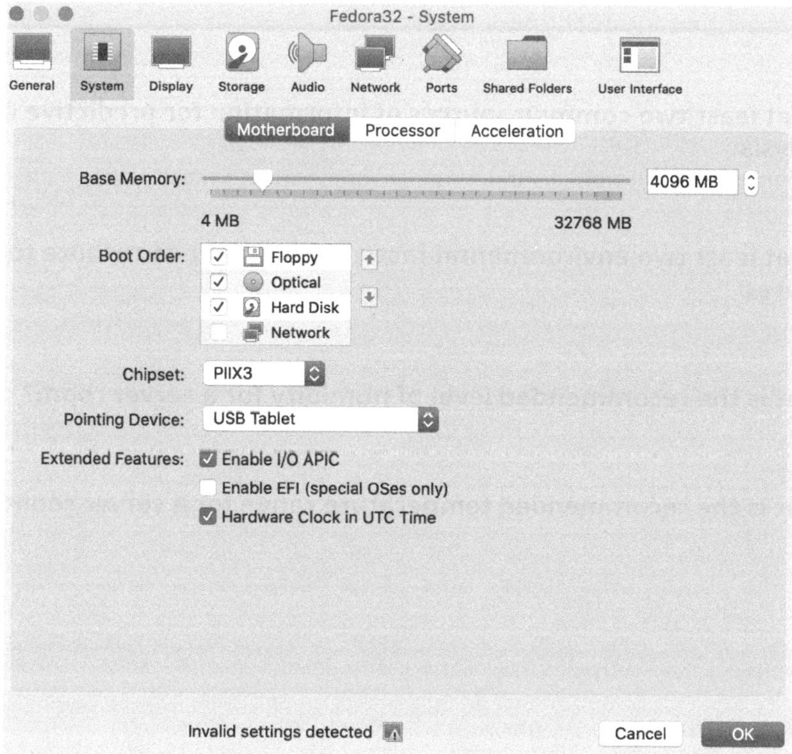

VirtualBox VM with a Base Memory allocation of 4 GB.

Review Activity:

Server Hardware

Answer the following questions:

1. **List at least two common sources of information for predictive failure analysis:**

2. **List at least two environmental factors that might contribute to server failures:**

3. **What is the recommended level of humidity for a server room?**

4. **What is the recommended temperature range for a server room?**

Lesson 5

Summary

Server management methods:

- A crash cart with a secure laptop is a convenient way of achieving out-of-band management.
- A KVM console is a space-efficient way of managing servers.
- For day to day remote management, use SSH, Remote Desktop, and VNC.
- Use a console connection for out-of-band management when the server is down or has no OS.
- Hot-swappable components can be replaced without powering down the server.
- Use fsck (Linux) and chkdsk (Windows) to verify HDD functionality.

It is useful to categorize common causes of failures.

Technical issues:

- A failed power supply that results in system downtime or periodic restarts
- Firmware update failures or interruptions that result in a nonfunctional device
- Devices that are not listed on the OS's HCL
- Backplane or motherboard failures that result in downtime or periodic restarts

Environmental issues:

- Dust that permits heat to build up
- Humidity that is too low and allows static electricity to build up
- Temperatures that exceed the recommended 68–71 degree F range

Configuration issues:

- Mistakes made by administrators who are not well trained on the technologies they support

Physical troubleshooting tools and practices:

- Have a clean, clear, large workspace and a quality tool kit.
- Use compressed air for cleaning the insides of computers.
- Use antistatic tools, such as mats, wrist straps, and bags, to protect components.
- Ensure that expansion cards, RAM sticks, power connectors, and data connectors are firmly seated in motherboard slots.
- Download firmware or diagnostic tools for specialized controllers from the vendor.

- The Windows tool to test RAM is the Windows Memory Diagnostic tool, and the Linux tool is memtester.
- The Windows tool to check the hard disk drive is chkdsk, and the Linux tool is fsck.

Log files:

- Windows Event Viewer System log contains hardware events.
- Linux /var/log/messages log contains hardware events.
- Linux dmesg displays hardware events encountered by the kernel during the boot process.

1. **What tools or methods discussed in this Lesson have you applied while troubleshooting server failures?**
2. **Does your organization's server room manage environmental concerns, such as temperature and humidity?**

Lesson 6

Configuring Storage Management

LESSON INTRODUCTION

Administering server storage can be one of the most challenging tasks for sysadmins. There are choices between traditional HDDs and solid-state drives (SSDs), as well as choices for connectivity. These choices impact speed and resiliency for data reads and writes.

This Lesson also covers common troubleshooting areas for storage and the tools that may help you discover and resolve storage problems.

Lesson Objectives

In this lesson, you will:

- Manage storage.
- Troubleshoot storage.

Topic 6A

Manage Storage

EXAM OBJECTIVES COVERED
1.2 Given a scenario, deploy and manage storage
2.3 Given a scenario, configure and maintain server functions and features

Storage management must include several factors, including capacity planning and what type of storage solution to use.

Capacity planning may be difficult, especially with the transition to cloud-based storage. Traditional HDDs are falling out of favor, with an increased reliance on SSDs. There are many ways of connecting storage devices to servers, both internally and externally. Redundancy, in the form of Redundant Array of Inexpensive Disk (RAID) configurations, is essential to protecting user data. Finally, network-based storage, including file shares, NAS, and SAN solutions are common in today's environments.

Capacity Planning

Server administration frequently requires lots of attention to storage. Storage capacity planning is the first step in effectively managing storage. **Capacity planning** measures current utilization in order to predict storage needs before all the space is consumed.

Capacity Planning Considerations

The key factor in capacity planning is the role of the server. File servers often require lots of storage capacity. These servers may store several different kinds of information:

- User home directories
- Department project directories
- Multimedia content
- Archived content
- Collaboration software content

Other server roles, such as database or network infrastructure services, may have different capacity requirements.

While this section focuses on capacity, don't forget that many of these services also have performance requirements that must also be considered.

Automated software suites help sysadmins understand current storage consumption and track trends to predict future storage requirements.

Enforce Capacity Management

Several technologies help administrators enforce capacity management rules.

- Disk quotas—enforce a consumption limit
- Data deduplication—eliminates duplicate information found in blocks of data for more efficient storage capacity use
- **Compression**—reduces the space consumed by files by using compression algorithms

Storage Capacity and the Cloud

The common use of STaaS has changed how sysadmins manage HDD space. Services such as Dropbox, Google Drive, AWS, Microsoft OneDrive, and others provide scalable, inexpensive, and managed storage solutions that may reduce the amount of on-premises storage required.

Hard Drive Media Types

Modern HDD storage uses two media types. There are also hybrid solutions that combine the two media types. Magnetic HDDs containing rotating disks and access arms have been the dominant form of server storage for decades. SSDs have become more prevalent in the last ten years in both servers and end-user workstations.

HDDs

Traditional **hard disk drives** use magnetic disks to store data. The content is read and written with an access arm. The disks spin to allow the arm to retrieve the requested information.

HDD rotation speeds, measured in rotations per minute (RPM):

- 5400 RPMs—common in laptops and desktops
- 7200 RPMs—common in laptops and desktops
- 10,000 RPMs—common in servers
- 15,000 RPMs—common in servers

Spin speeds also impact the disk's cost and battery consumption (for laptops).

In general, traditional HDDs tend to have higher capacity, slower access speeds, and cheaper cost than SSDs.

SSDs

Solid state drives use flash memory to store data, much like RAM or USB flash drives. The result is that SSDs are much faster at reading and writing data than HDDs. The performance benefit is important, especially when it comes to busy servers.

SSDs are available in several different form factors, which are discussed in a later section.

Solid-state drive. (Image © 123RF.com)

The use of SSDs in servers is becoming much more common. Some aspects of SSD must be carefully considered. For example, SSDs have a lower number of reads and writes compared HDDs. The reason for this is that SSDs store data in memory cells, and each time data is written to a cell, the oxide layer that actually stores the information is degraded. Eventually, depending on the number of writes, the cell is no longer capable of storing information accurately. This limit is referred to as an SSD's endurance. SSDs use software to implement wear leveling (the even use of all the storage cells). As the technology continues to evolve, this limit is changing.

One way of calculating SSD endurance ratings is Drive Writes Per Day (DWPD). The formula assumes an overwrite of the entire drive once per day for a given number of years (the years might represent a manufacturer warranty, for example).

Consider a 100 GB SSD with a DWPD rating of one and an estimated five years of usable life:

100 GB overwritten per day x 365 days in a year x 5 years = 182.5 cumulative writes.

SSDs designed for enterprise use are more durable, with a higher associated cost.

Hybrid Drives

Hybrid drives combine the best attributes of HDDs and SSDs. Specifically, the speed benefit of SSDs is maximized by using that storage as a cache for frequently accessed data, and the cost-effective higher capacity of traditional HDDs is maximized for overall storage.

There are two primary types of hybrid drives:

- Dual-drive hybrid—two physical drives are installed (one SSD, one HDD). The user or the OS then manages what data is stored on each drive.
- SSD hybrid—the SSD is contained in the same physical device as the HDDs. Data management is handled by the storage device itself.

Hybrid drives may be an effective solution for some file servers.

Scenarios for Choosing SSD or HDD

When it comes to selecting a storage solution for servers, there are several points of comparison. As a general rule, the following considerations must be made:

- Noise—SSD is quieter

- Power—SSD consumes less power
- Capacity—SSD and HDD are about equal
- Cost—HDD is cheaper per GB of capacity
- Durability—SSD is less susceptible to physical damage

SSDs are appropriate in servers that support performance-oriented applications, especially those without too many write functions. HDDs are appropriate for servers that demand a high capacity at an economical rate, especially when performance is less of a concern. Archived data, for example, might be a good choice for HDD.

HDD Interface Types

Storage requirements on a server are significantly different from those of a standard workstation. First, a server may be required to have far more storage capacity. Next, the data on the server's storage devices may need to be accessed more quickly and by many more clients. Finally, server storage needs a very high degree of redundancy.

While a basic server configuration might start with a single internal HDD, it is much more likely that the server will have multiple drives installed to increase capacity.

There are several interfaces for attaching storage to a server. Some are internal, others are external. The choice between HDDs versus SSDs is fairly straightforward. The choice of what interface is required is much more difficult. Server motherboards will support specific interface connections, and you must choose storage disks that are compatible.

Direct Attached Storage (DAS)

Internal storage, also known as DAS, begins with an evaluation of performance and cost, which leads you to choose the appropriate interface for the disk controller and the disks themselves. The considerations are pretty simple—the better the performance, the bigger the cost.

- SATA—Serial Advanced Technology Attachment
- SAS—Serial Attached SCSI
- NVMe—Non-Volatile Memory Express

DAS Controllers and Drives

SATA

The **Serial ATA** specification uses a dedicated connection for reading from the drive and a separate dedicated channel for writing to the drive. Unfortunately, SATA is a **half-duplex** technology, meaning that it can manage either a read or a write transaction at a given moment, but it cannot do both simultaneously.

SATA is commonly found in end-user workstations, where performance is far less of a concern. It may also be found in servers in situations where cost is more important than speed. In many cases, certain data do not have to be accessed extremely quickly.

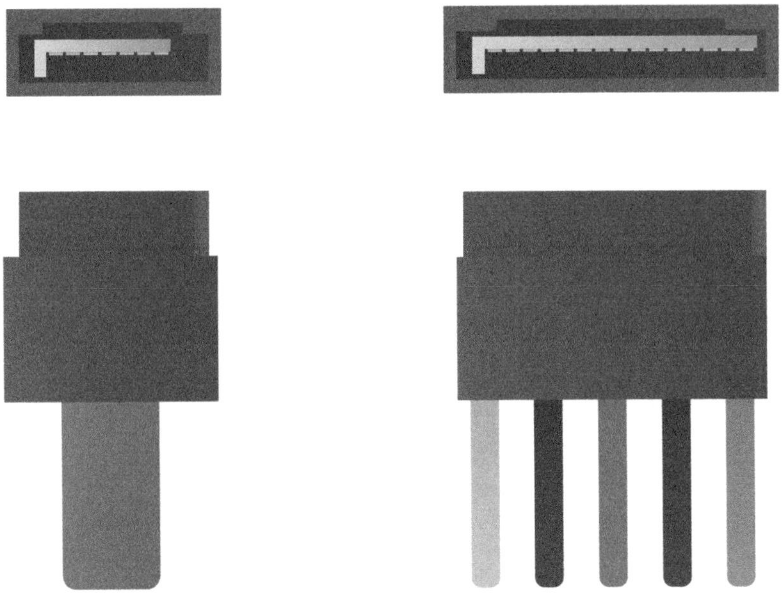

SATA cables. SATA data cables are typically smaller and usually contain 7 pins, whereas SATA power cables are larger and contain 15 pins. (Images © 123RF.com)

SAS

SAS will almost always be a better choice for enterprise server solutions than SATA is. It has a much better performance-to-cost relationship, it includes error checking capabilities, and it is much faster for both reads and writes. Part of how it achieves this better performance is through full duplexing, or the ability to read and write data simultaneously. SAS is also much more scalable—it supports up to 128 devices.

SAS utilizes SCSI commands, but unlike SCSI, it moves data serially rather than in parallel. This is another attribute that gives it better performance. SAS is a great choice when performance is important but cost is still a consideration.

Many servers will support both SATA and SAS, and therefore one practice is to use SAS for hot or frequently accessed data, while using SATA for cold or less commonly accessed data. This strategy uses the best features of each of the technologies by balancing cost and performance based on the type of data.

NVMe

NVMe implementations are a far more expensive endeavor, but the performance benefit over SAS is immense. This is the future standard for server drive interfaces, so keep that in mind when you're making purchase decisions. What makes NVMe so powerful is its reliance on the PCIe bus, rather than a dedicated storage bus like SAS and SATA use. This bus carries a great deal more data and is full duplex. NVMe transfers are basically 1 Gbps per PCIe lane. Therefore, a 16-lane bus (which is a motherboard specification) provides a 16 Gbps transfer rate. The potential downside of NVMe, besides its cost, is that the benefits are usually only realized for large file transfers. Basic small transfers, such as booting the OS, will not necessarily display any significant increase.

Comparison of the three DAS implementations:

- SATA when cost is more important than performance, less need for scalability
- SAS to balance cost and performance, scalability

- NVMe when performance is more important than cost, especially on servers that see large file transfers

Interface	Speed	Relative cost
SATA III	6 Gbps	Cheaper
SAS	12 Gbps	Cheaper
NVMe	32 Gbps (on a 32-bit PCIe bus)	More expensive

Comparing DAS implementations.

DAS Drive Connectors

The M.2 specification, also known as the "Next Generation Form Factor," defines an interface connection for SSDs, SATA, and NVMe drives.

This standard provides a more flexible form factor to permit the design of drives that will connect easily to server, laptop, and desktop motherboards by using the USB, PCIe 3.0, and SATA interfaces.

M.2 connectors are notched, or keyed, so that they can only fit into the motherboard slot one way. The drives and boards will be labeled as B, M, or B+M. These connectors are the standard for current SSDs.

- M.2 B standard—6 pins on the smaller tab
- M.2 M standard—5 pins on the smaller tab

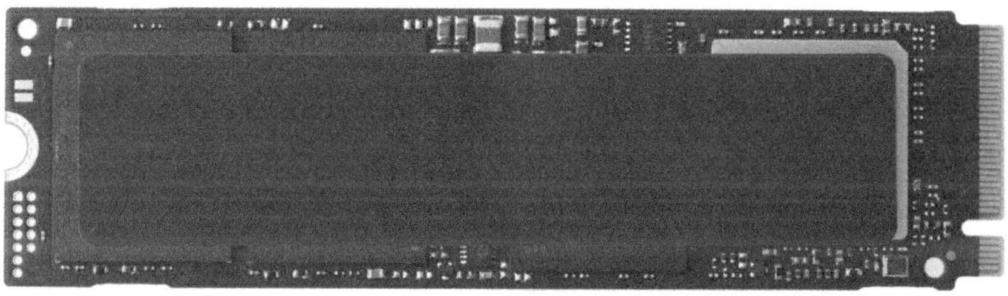

SSD M.2 form factor. (Image by Vitaly Pozdeyev © 123RF.com)

SSDs that utilize the M.2 standard come in different physical sizes. This can matter when trying to fit them into server cases. One of the key considerations is heat dissipation.

SSD with M.2 Standard	Size
2240	22mm wide x 40mm long
2260	22mm wide x 60mm long
2280	22mm wide x 80mm long

M.2 form factors.

PCIe

PCIe is an expansion bus on the motherboard. A variety of different expansion cards may be attached to the bus, including NICs, graphics cards, and SSD controllers.

Servers containing a PCIe bus may have SSDs added to increase storage capacity and performance. PCIe-compatible SSDs have the appropriate form factor to be used in the motherboard expansion slot.

Devices connected to the PCIe bus may communicate at up to 15.75 Gbps, which represents a significant improvement over other communication busses. These devices also tend to be more expensive than the more common SATA III storage solutions.

External Serial Advanced Technology Attachment (eSATA)

It is not always practical for all storage devices to be contained inside the body of the server. External storage may be used to mitigate concerns over heat, physical space inside the server, or portability.

The **external serial advanced technology attachment** storage device transfers data at the 6 Gbps rate defined by SATA III.

USB3 and USB-C have largely replaced eSATA as external storage busses, and eSATA is considered to be a workstation-level technology, rather than a server solution.

USB

USB solutions have been around for a very long time. The modern implementation is USB-C. This expansion bus may be used for a great many different peripherals, including Ethernet connectivity, displays, input devices, and storage devices.

Standard	Connector	Speed
1.0	Type A or B	Up to 12 Mbits/s
2.0	Type A or B	Up to 480 Mbits/s
3.0	Type A or B (SuperSpeed) or Type C	Up to 5 Gbits/s
4.0	Type C	Up to 40 Gbits/s

USB specifications.

USB Type C connector. (Image by tevarak11 © 123RF.com)

Most sysadmins will not choose to add USB drives to a server for security, performance, and reliability reasons. External drives can be helpful in some situations, including backups, restores, and data transfers.

Secure Digital (SD) cards

Another storage media type is **Secure Digital** cards. These storage devices are mostly found in tablets, laptops, cameras, and other peripheral devices. Servers may have SD card slots to facilitate data transfers from external devices. External card readers may also attach to servers via USB connectors.

RAID Levels and Types

To provide greater redundancy and **fault tolerance**, the server's storage may be managed by a **redundant array of independent/inexpensive disks** controller. There are many types of RAID arrays, and you will choose which types are appropriate depending on your needs.

Number	Name	Attributes	Drive Failures
0	Disk striping	Very fast, no fault tolerance	Loss of data with 1 failed drive
1	Disk mirroring	Fault tolerance, inefficient use of capacity	Protects data even with the loss of 1 drive
5	Disk striping with parity	Speed, fault tolerance	Protects data even with the loss of 1 drive
6	Double parity	Fault tolerance with parity information written twice	Protects data even with the loss of 2 drives
10	Disk mirroring and striping	Mirrored striped drives for speed and fault tolerance	Protects data even with the loss of 1 drive

RAID array types.

RAID 0 Disk Striping

This RAID design provides a great deal of speed but no redundancy whatsoever. The lack of redundancy means that there should never be mission-critical information stored on it. It may be appropriate for caching and other non-critical data.

RAID 0 requires a minimum of two disks.

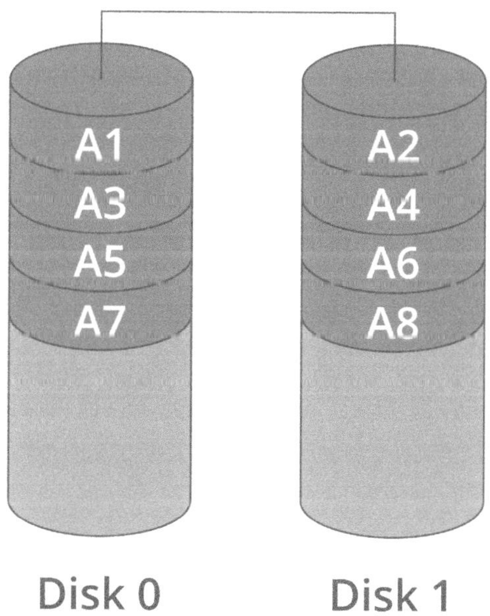

RAID 0 disk striping. (Images © 123RF.com)

RAID 1 Disk Mirroring

This RAID design provides a very high degree of redundancy. All content is written to both disks, and if one disk fails, the other disk has everything. This solution is excellent for mission-critical situations. The downside to **mirroring** is that drive space is not very efficiently used (if you buy two disks that are 1 TB each, you've paid for 2 TB of storage but will only have the effective capacity of 1 TB).

RAID 1 requires a minimum of two disks.

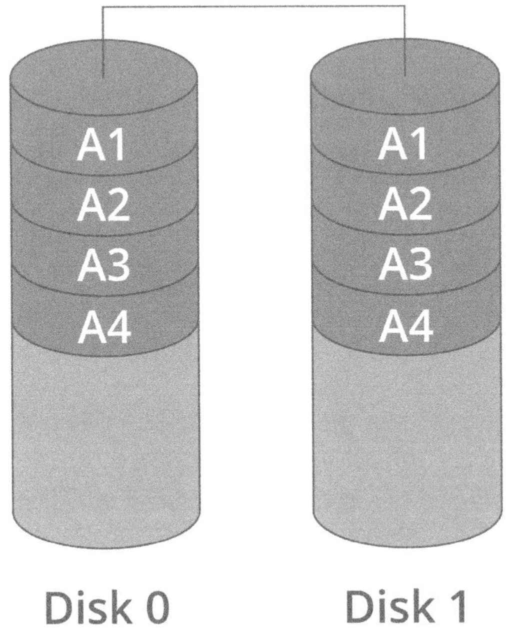

RAID 1 disk mirroring. (Images © 123RF.com)

RAID 5 Disk Striping with Parity

This RAID 5 design provides a good balance between performance, redundancy, and cost-effective capacity. Data is distributed across the stripes on the disks, as with RAID 0, but additional **parity** information is also written to the disks, which permits data to be recreated if one of the drives in the array fails. RAID 5 is a good general solution for most servers, though the performance of its writes is dependent on the RAID controller used.

RAID 5 requires a minimum of three HDDs.

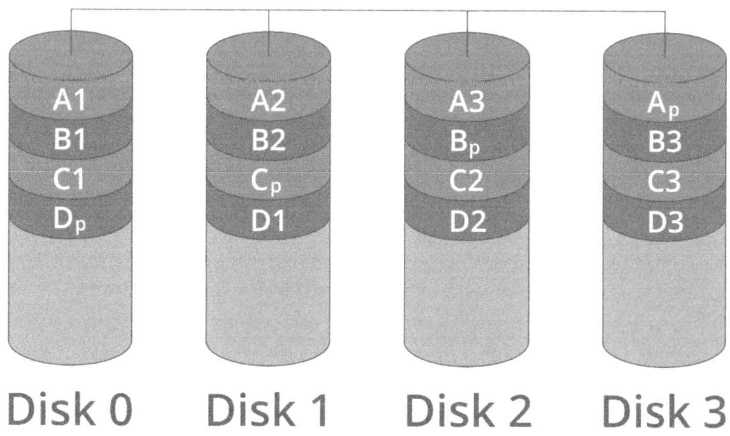

RAID 5 Disk striping with parity. (Images © 123RF.com)

RAID 6 Disk Striping with Double Parity

The RAID 6 design distributes data across a minimum of four HDDs the same way that RAID 0 and RAID 5 do, but it also distributes parity information across two disks. The result is that a RAID 6 array can recover data even with the failure of two HDDs. Reads are quick, like RAID 5, but writes are slower due to the duplication of the parity data. It is a good general solution as long as the performance hit on write tasks is not a problem for your environment.

RAID 6 requires a minimum of four HDDs.

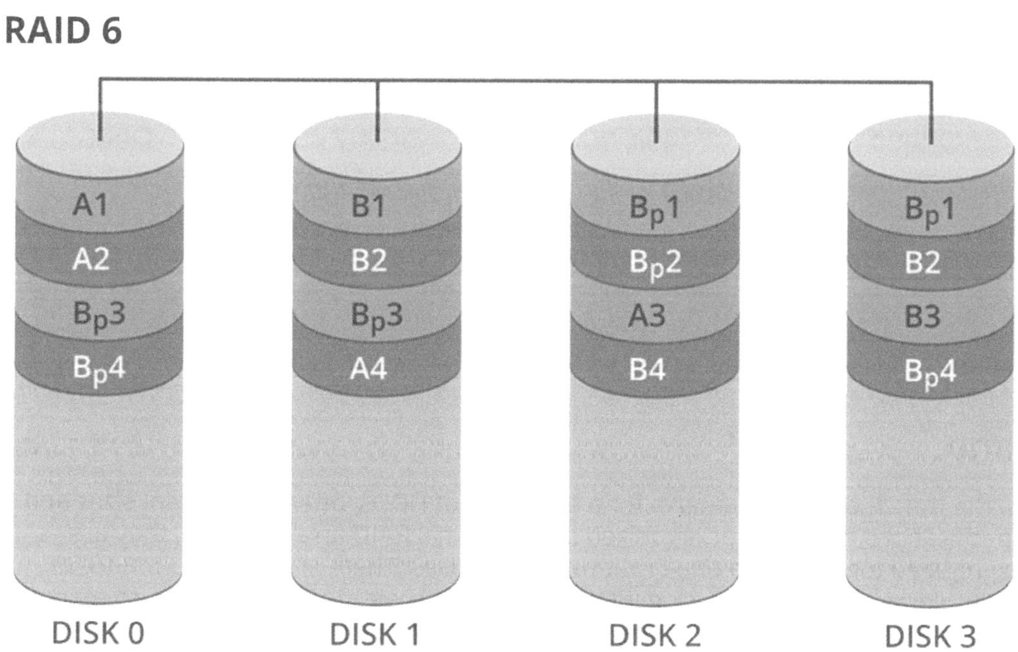

RAID 6 disk striping with double parity. (Images © 123RF.com)

RAID 10 Disk Mirroring with Striping

The last RAID solution that we'll look at is RAID 10. Basically, this is a RAID 0 stripe set that is mirrored. Rebuild times are fast, but the per-gigabyte storage costs are not as efficient as with RAID 5 or RAID 6.

RAID 10 requires a minimum of four HDDs.

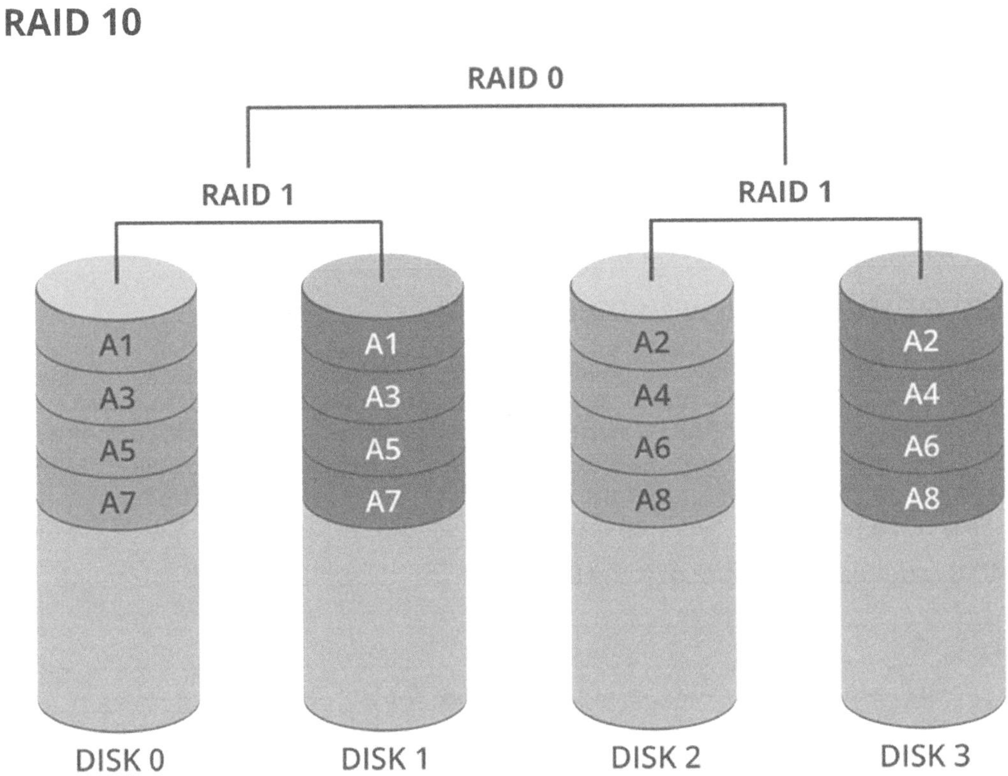

RAID 10 disk mirroring with striping. (Images © 123RF.com)

Recall that a RAID array is only one layer of data protection plan. You should still be doing data backups on a regular basis, and in fact, you may also be using other data protection tools, such as Windows Volume Shadow Copies.

JBOD

Just a Bunch of Disks is a term for a collection of HDDs, often of different sizes and specifications, that are not organized into a normal RAID array. Instead, they are aggregated together into one or more logical drives. There are no performance or fault tolerance benefits to using JBOD. It is easy to scale, flexible, and easy to manage.

Software RAID vs. Hardware RAID

Software RAID relies on the OS to manage the RAID array. First, that assumes the OS is capable of doing so—most server OSs can, but most client systems cannot. The computer's primary processing power handles the array. However, software RAID is usually cheaper that hardware RAID (it's rolled into the cost of the OS).

Hardware RAID relies on a separate controller to manage the array. This RAID solution does not consume resources from the system. It is typically faster, more reliable, and more flexible. Those advantages mean a higher cost, however.

Software RAID advantages:

- Less expensive
- Fewer components to manage

Disadvantages:

- Less flexible
- Consumes system and OS resources

Hardware RAID advantages:

- Faster
- More flexible
- Does not consume server resources

Disadvantages:

- More expensive
- More components to manage
- More complex

Shared Storage

Direct attached storage (DAS) inside of a server is not the only storage solution. Network-based storage may also provide a cost-effective and scalable way to add capacity. NAS and SAN solutions may be used to extend storage in the enterprise.

Network File Sharing Protocols

One of the most common servers on the network are **file servers**. These devices are designed to store large numbers of files. Workstations access to these files from across the network. Application layer protocols manage file access. The two most common protocols are the Network File System (NFS) and Server Message Blocks (SMB).

NFS

The **NFS** is common in Unix-based environments, though Microsoft Windows Server can share out directories to **Unix** Linux clients with it. NFS includes the ability to protect the shared directories by using **permissions**.

NFS is configured in Linux by using the /etc/exports file. You must also reload the NFS daemon after making changes to this file. In this example, you make a directory named /projects available to a network client named workstation01. The client will have read and write access:

```
/projects workstation01 (rw,sync)
```

You will also control access to the file by using standard Linux permissions, so you set NFS permissions to be open.

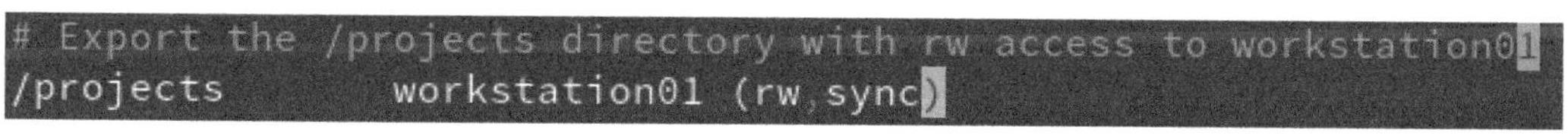

Exporting the /projects directory for network access.

If a user is logged on with root (administrative) privileges to a Linux client workstation, the user may retain root privileges across the NFS connection. This is a very bad security practice, so you may consider using the "root_squash" option to remap their connection to the local nfsnobody account on the NFS file server.

NFS client for Windows

To install the NFS Client on Windows 10, use the Windows Features function of Control Panel. To install NFS services on Windows Server, use the Add and Remove Services console in Server Manager.

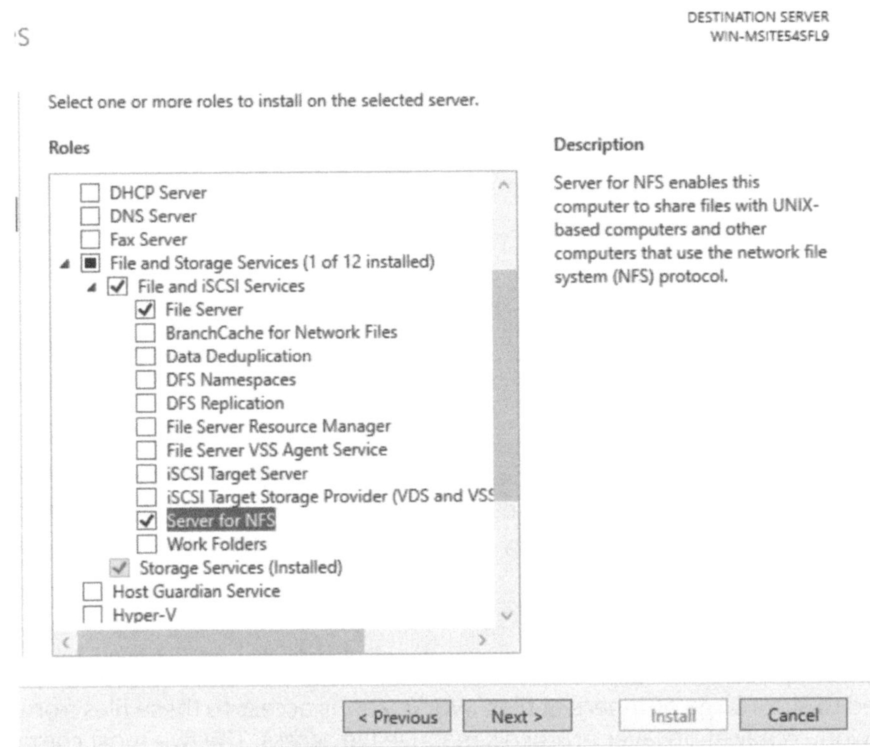

Add the Server for NFS Role to Windows Server 2019. (Screenshot courtesy of Microsoft.)

SMBs

The **Server Message Block** protocol also may be used to share out folders from a NAS (as well as from a traditional file server). SMB is the standard Windows protocol for sharing, though there is an SMB client that can be installed on Linux computers to permit them to access resources shared from a Windows server. You can also install a service named Samba on a Linux server to share out directories from the Linux box to Windows clients using this native Windows protocol.

To share a folder from a Windows Server system, right click on the folder, select the Sharing option from the context menu, and then configure access. Alternatively, you can select Advanced Sharing for more options.

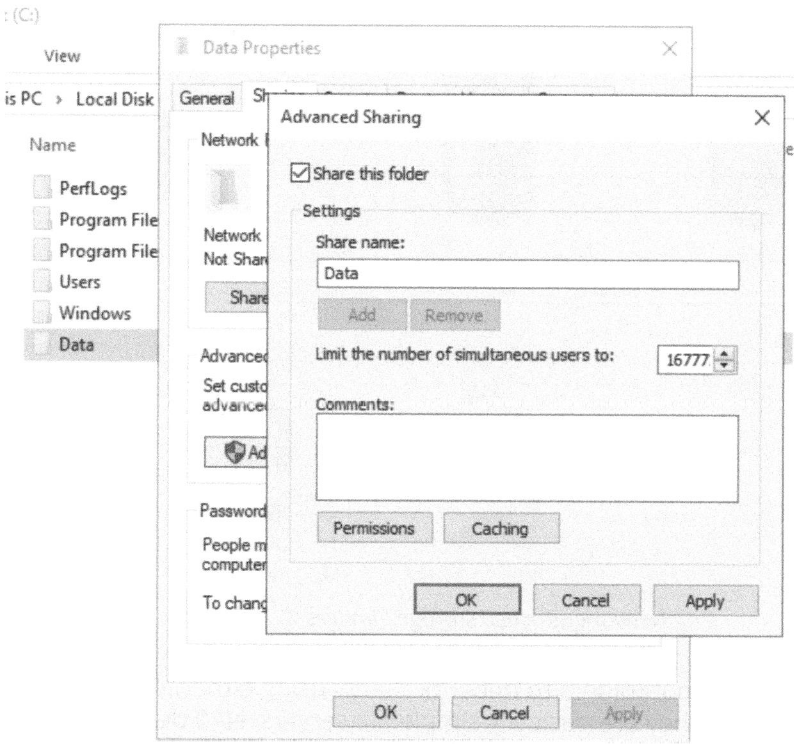

Sharing a folder in Windows. (Screenshot courtesy of Microsoft.)

The Common Internet File System (CIFS) is a dialect or an implementation of the SMBs protocol. Most references will be to SMB, and that is the proper term by today's standards.

Network Attached Storage (NAS)

An **NAS** device is essentially a group of storage drives with an NIC. NAS can be used to quickly and easily add capacity. Some NAS solutions can even be deployed with RAID configurations in order to better protect your stored data.

NAS storage adds another node to the network. The storage device consumes at least one IP address. It relies on available network bandwidth for performance. Adding an NAS to an already overwhelmed network increases network traffic and may result in unacceptable delays for users and applications to access data. On networks with adequate bandwidth, however, NASs are quick and easy ways of adding storage.

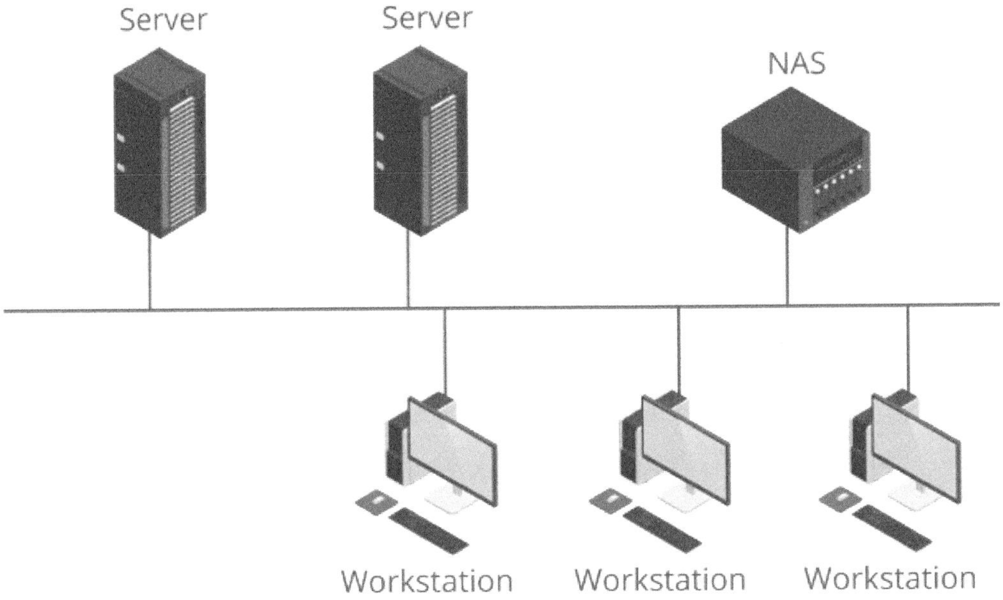

Network attached storage. (Images © 123RF.com)

NAS devices share out folders to network clients using either NFS or the Windows solution of SMBs. They are basically simple file servers. NAS devices are easy to add to the network and relatively inexpensive, but their performance is affected by the overall network performance. As such, an NAS may not be the best choice for an enterprise storage solution.

SAN

Storage area network devices provide greater scalability, fault tolerance, and performance than do NAS devices. SANs, however, are also significantly more complex and more expensive.

While the SAN is technically the supporting network between the servers and the storage devices, a complete SAN solution is made up of three primary components, in addition to the client workstations. The first component is one or more servers that manage access to the data. The second component is an isolated network between the servers and the storage infrastructure. The final component is the storage infrastructure itself. SANs allow organizations to connect disparate types of storage, such as tape and optical media. SANs also connect data storage across physical boundaries, such as remote data centers.

The SAN infrastructure is transparent to the end user. In the case of a Windows user, they may simply have a drive mapped on their computer and will have no idea what the storage structure actually looks like.

- The servers may be Microsoft Windows Server installations. The server hardware will likely contain HBA cards for access to the storage infrastructure.
- The isolated network is the communications path between the servers and the storage infrastructure. There is typically a great deal of redundancy in the network to ensure that data access is highly available.

- The storage infrastructure includes the actual storage drives which are housed in separate boxes from the servers. The disk arrays consist of many HDDs, controllers, and the supporting components to connect to the SAN network.

HBA

An HBA card provides an interface between the motherboard's PCIe bus and a data bus that is usually external to the server, such as an SAN. HBAs are not typically intelligent expansion cards, but they can come with additional features, such as RAID controllers, to extend their functionality. At their most fundamental, however, they are simply bus adapters. When you purchase a server, it is very likely to include the option for HBA expansion cards.

Connector Types for SANs

The **Fibre Channel** protocol is usually implemented over fiber optic media. Connecting the server HBA cards, the SAN switches, and the storage devices requires the appropriate fiber optic ports. Common connectors are SFP and its variations, or **quad small form factor pluggable**. Both types of connectors are hot swappable.

Connector	Speed
SFP	100/1000 Mbps
SFP+	10 Gbps
QSFP	1000 Gbps

Comparing connectors.

Small form-factor pluggable (SFP) connectors. (Image © 123RF.com)

SAN Protocols

There are two primary communications protocols used to support SAN solutions. The first is Fibre Channel, and the second is **Internet Small Computer Systems Interface (iSCSI)**.

Fibre Channel

This SAN design uses Fibre Channel protocols to carry SCSI commands over fiber optic cables. This implementation requires specialized network devices. This is the most common SAN structure.

The spelling of "fibre" is a deliberate choice designed to differentiate the technology from an older specification that used the traditional "fiber" spelling.

Fibre Channel is a protocol that provides block-level data transfers over optical media (it can use copper-based media, but that's less common). The Fibre Channel protocol carries SCSI or NVMe commands between server nodes and storage devices.

Fibre Channel SANs may be organized in a point-to-point (direct) or a switched topology. The point-to-point design is simple but not fault tolerant or scalable. It consists of a simple connection from the server to the storage device. The switched topology adds a layer of switches between the nodes and the storage. The advantage is scalability and multiple paths between the SAN components. The switches may optimize the data transfer traffic and provide redundancy.

Many enterprises will implement a homogeneous SAN solution from a single vendor. These SAN switches operate in native mode. The SAN vendor may provide additional proprietary software for these solutions. SANs that utilize components from different vendors have an open fabric heterogeneous design.

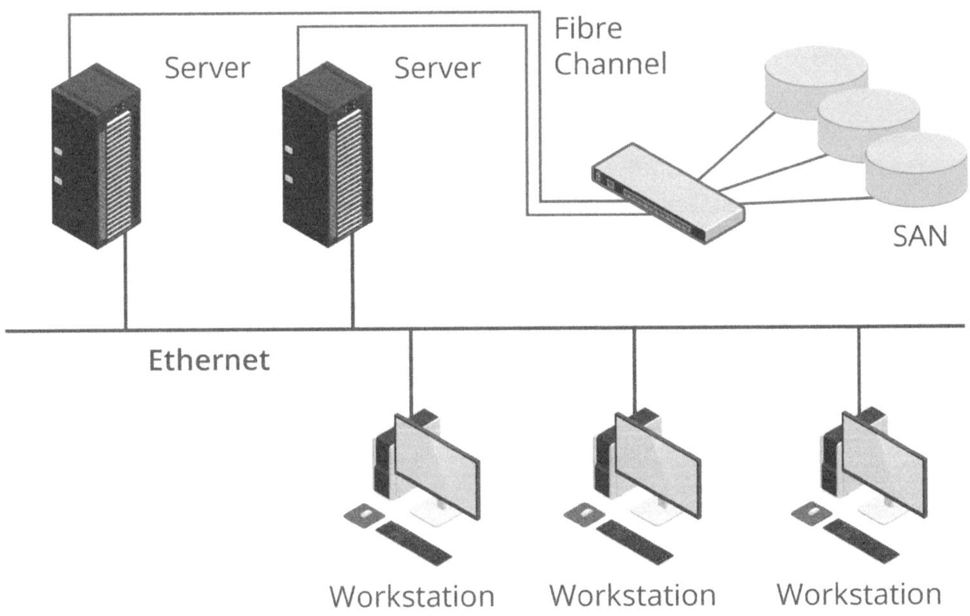

Switched SAN. (Images © 123RF.com)

Fibre Channel over Ethernet (FCoE)

FCoE represents a significant improvement in the SAN implementation. The FC protocol is embedded in Ethernet frames. The advantage to FCoE is in the network infrastructure, which is simplified, using the same 802.3 Ethernet-based network that the standard data network uses. There are fewer specialized devices, a single standardized Ethernet cable in the data center, and an overall lower cost. The SAN traffic uses the same path as regular network traffic. While traditional Fibre Channel may have greater performance, FCoE is rated up to 40 Gbps, which is often sufficient for most enterprises.

Connectivity in a FCoE SAN is provided by Converged Network Adapters (CNAs). These expansion cards integrate the role of a Fibre Channel HBA and a standard Ethernet NIC into a single component.

Internet Small Computers Systems Interface (iSCSI)

The **iSCSI** protocol is a common SAN solution for small and medium-sized organizations. It provides block communications by using SCSI commands over a traditional Ethernet network.

iSCSI implementations have a client component and a target component. The client component may be a software-based iSCSI Initiator. Such software is often integrated into the server OS. It is inexpensive and relatively easy to configure. An HBA may be added to the server itself and provides a hardware solution. HBA implementations are faster, more complex, and more expensive. You'll have to evaluate whether such additional complexity and cost is worth it for your environment. The target component is the iSCSI Target. This is the storage device itself, or the target for the iSCSI connection from the initiator or HBA.

The Windows Server OS provides an iSCSI client (initiator) and server (target) component.

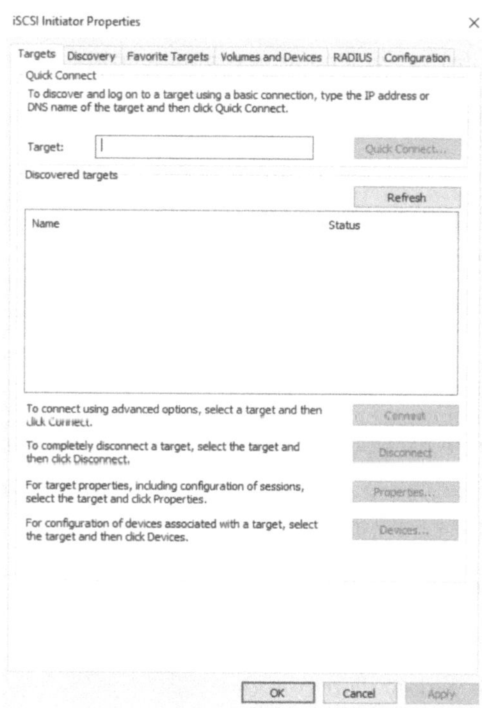

iSCSI Initiator Properties in Windows Server 2019. (Screenshot courtesy of Microsoft.)

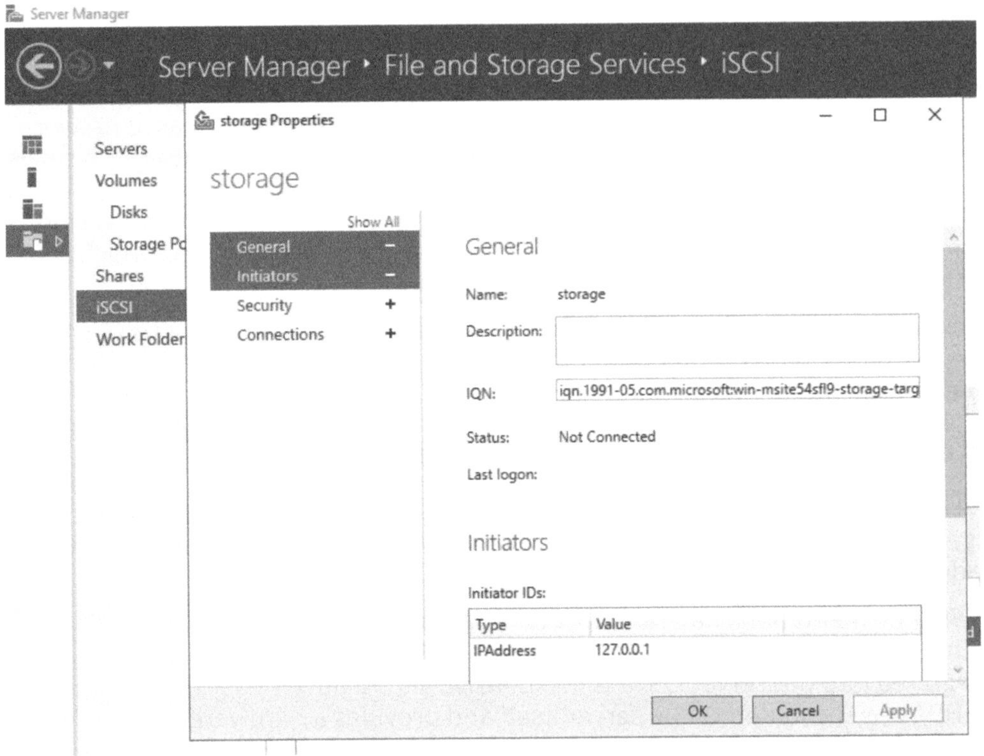

Configuring Windows Server as an iSCSI target. (Screenshot courtesy of Microsoft.)

iSCSI performance relies heavily on the underlying network infrastructure. iSCSI can be implemented on a network as slow as 1 Gbps, but the recommendation for an enterprise production network is 10 Gbps using either copper or fiber optic media. The iSCSI standard also includes some ways of speeding up the data transfer, including multipathing. It is also suggested that the iSCSI network be dedicated to server to storage traffic only. Another reason to use a dedicated network is that your data is traveling in IP packets, which are susceptible to packet sniffing attacks. Data can be protected by using **Internet Protocol security**, but that adds an additional layer of complexity, which can negatively impact performance.

Choosing iSCSI or Fibre Channel for Your SAN

The following table summarizes the main considerations for choosing between an iSCSI and a Fibre Channel solution.

Choose iSCSI for the following:

- Cost is an issue.
- You're connecting many hosts to one storage target (several servers storing different data on a single storage server).
- Training is not available for your IT staff for the complexities of a Fibre Channel solution.
- You need or want a less complex infrastructure.

Choose Fibre Channel for the following:

- Performance is paramount.
- SAN components are widely distributed.

Guidelines for Managing Storage

- RAID 0 disk striping provides a performance increase.
- RAID 1 mirroring provides complete redundancy.
- RAID 5 disk striping with parity provides a good balance of fault tolerance and cost.
- When considering direct attached storage, consider SATA for cost, SAS for a balance of cost and performance, and NVMe for performance when cost is no issue.
- NFS is the standard Unix directory sharing protocol.
- SMB is the standard Windows folder sharing protocol.
- Fibre Channel and iSCSI are competing SAN protocols.
- SAN performance depends heavily on the network connection.
- Choose iSCSI when cost is an issue.
- Choose iSCSI when you're connecting many hosts to one storage target (several servers storing different data on a single storage server).
- Choose iSCSI when training is not available for your IT staff for the complexities of a Fibre Channel solution.
- Choose iSCSI when you need or want a less complex infrastructure.
- Choose Fibre Channel when performance is paramount.
- Choose Fibre Channel when SAN components are widely distributed.

Review Activity:

Storage Management

Answer the following questions:

1. **List at least two ways to mitigate storage capacity issues:**

2. **What is the balance of cost versus performance between SATA, SAS, and NVMe drives?**

3. **Which RAID solution writes data to two drives simultaneously, so that if one drive fails, the other contains all of the data?**

4. **List at least four differences between software RAID and hardware RAID:**

5. **What is the common file sharing protocol for Linux? For Windows?**

6. **List at least one advantage and one disadvantage of using NAS:**

Topic 6B

Troubleshoot Storage

EXAM OBJECTIVES COVERED
2.3 Given a scenario, configure and maintain server functions and features
4.3 Given a scenario, troubleshoot storage problems

This Topic covers common storage problems and their related causes. Storage problems are divided into categories and then listed with common causes. In addition, common disk management tools are discussed.

Common Storage Problems

There may be many causes of storage problems on a server or its related components.

Common storage troubleshooting categories:

- Physical connectivity, power cables, data cables, physical functionality of storage disks.
- Configuration of the drive and its partitions—partition configuration, OS configurations for drive mounting.
- RAID arrays—disk failures, controller/HBA failures, misconfigurations, mismatched drives.
- Capacity—insufficient disk space results in poor performance, data reliability.

Common Problem	Common Causes
Boot errors	Misconfigured RAID array Drive failure Controller or HBA failure Loose connections or cable failures Corrupt boot sector Corrupt file system table Backplane failure
OS not found	Drive failure Controller or HBA failure Corrupt boot sector Boot loader misconfiguration Corrupt file system table
Sector block errors	Drive failure Bad sectors
Read-write errors	Drive failure Bad sectors Controller or HBA failure Loose connections or cable failures

(continued)

Common Problem	Common Causes
Failed drives/failed multiple drives	Drive failure Array rebuild Misconfigured RAID array Controller or HBA failure Mismatched drives
Slow access/slow IO	Disk space utilization Insufficient disk space Misconfigured RAID Array rebuild Drive failure Controller or HBA failure Loose connections or cable failures Backplane failure
Cache failure	Cache battery failure on RAID array Cache turned off
Virtual memory configurations	Disk space utilization Insufficient disk space Misconfigured page/swap/scratch file or partition
Partition errors	Improper disk partition Misconfiguration in OS
Unable to mount partitions or logical drives	Misconfiguration in OS Improper RAID configuration
Unable to mount physical drive	Drive failure Misconfigured RAID array Controller or HBA failure
Loss of data on a RAID array	Cache battery failure Misconfigured RAID Array rebuild HBA failure Drive failure
Failed backups	Media failure Drive failure Misconfiguration in backup software
Failed restorals	Media failure Drive failure Misconfiguration in backup software

Tools and Techniques for Troubleshooting Storage

Some storage management tools are built into the OS, and other are used independently of the OS. One category of tool manages partition configurations, while others manage RAID configurations or storage access.

Partition Management

Once a storage disk is physically installed, it must be divided into usable sections, known as partitions. Usually, these partitions are created to store specific types of data.

The difference between the terms partition and volume varies by OS and configuration. In Windows, Basic Disk configurations use "partition," and Dynamic Disk configurations use "volume." Windows Storage Pools also use "volume." In Linux, standard disk configurations include partitions, but Logical Volume Manager (LVM) storage uses "volume" instead.

During the initial configuration of the server, partitions are managed before the OS is installed (or during its installation). There are two common partitioning tools: fdisk and parted. Both tools create, delete, and manage partitions for storage disks that will host Windows or Linux OSs. In addition, Windows Server has other tools to manage partitions, including Disk Management, **diskpart**, and several PowerShell cmdlets. It is much more common to manage storage in Windows by using these tools.

```
Command (m for help): m

Help:

  DOS (MBR)
   a   toggle a bootable flag
   b   edit nested BSD disklabel
   c   toggle the dos compatibility flag

  Generic
   d   delete a partition
   F   list free unpartitioned space
   l   list known partition types
   n   add a new partition
   p   print the partition table
   t   change a partition type
   v   verify the partition table
   i   print information about a partition

  Misc
   m   print this menu
   u   change display/entry units
   x   extra functionality (experts only)

  Script
   I   load disk layout from sfdisk script file
   O   dump disk layout to sfdisk script file

  Save & Exit
   w   write table to disk and exit
   q   quit without saving changes

  Create a new label
   g   create a new empty GPT partition table
   G   create a new empty SGI (IRIX) partition table
   o   create a new empty DOS partition table
   s   create a new empty Sun partition table
```

fdisk options menu.

Disk Management/Drive Monitoring

Both fdisk and parted are used to manage partitions after Linux is installed. Depending on the Linux distribution, there may be other built-in tools to configuration partitions. In Windows, the Disk Management utility is used to create and manage partitions.

Linux includes many tools to display and monitor storage space.

Tools	Description
du -h	Displays storage capacity in specific directories or partitions
df -h	Displays storage capacity for filesystems or partitions
cat /var/partitions	Displays existing partitions and disks

Linux disk management tools.

Most administrators use the GUI Disk Management console to create, delete, and otherwise manage partitions.

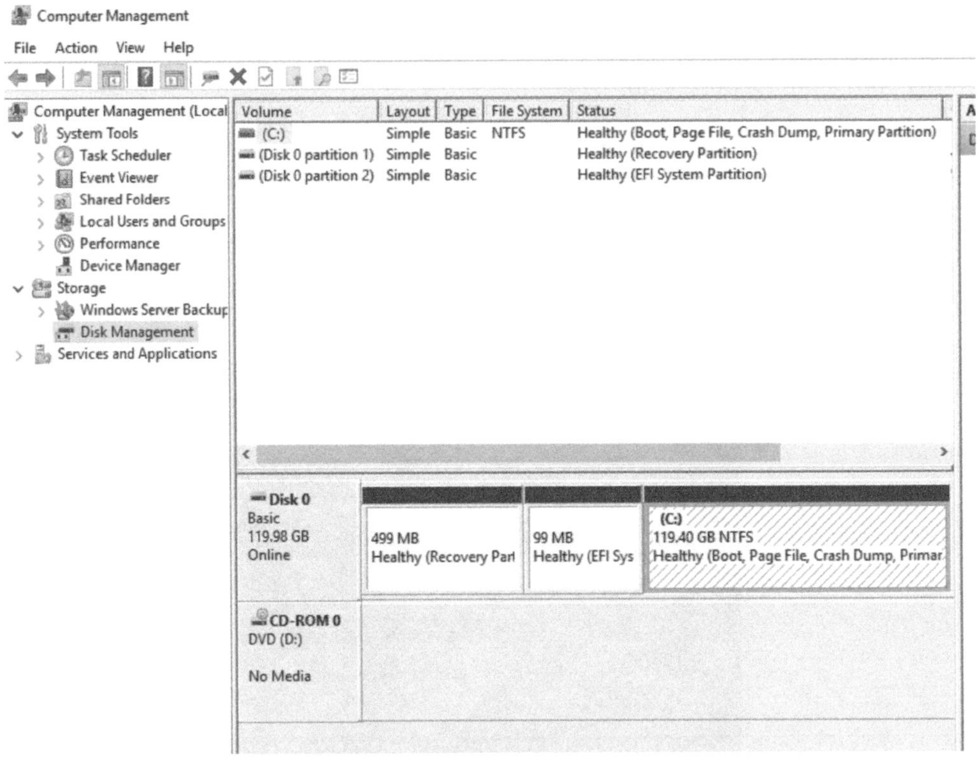

Windows Server Disk Management. (Screenshot courtesy of Microsoft.)

RAID Array Configuration

Software RAID is configured and managed within the OS. The Windows Disk Management console can be used to configure software RAID arrays on available disk partitions. Windows can manage RAID 0, 1, and 5 arrays.

Hardware RAID controllers use proprietary software to manage the array independent of the OS. Hardware RAID is usually faster and more flexible than software RAID, but the configurations may be more complex.

Partition Mounting Commands

Windows automatically connects to partitions on local storage disks and displays them via File Explorer. It also labels the partitions by using drive letters, beginning with the C: drive. You can also map or mount folders that are shared on the network by using File Explorer or the net use command.

The syntax of the net use command is

```
net use z: \\servername\sharename
```

*A **Universal Naming Convention (UNC)** path consists of the name of the remote network server, followed by the name of the folder shared out from that server. For example, if a folder named SalesData is shared from a server named FileServer3, the UNC would be \\FileServer3\SalesData*

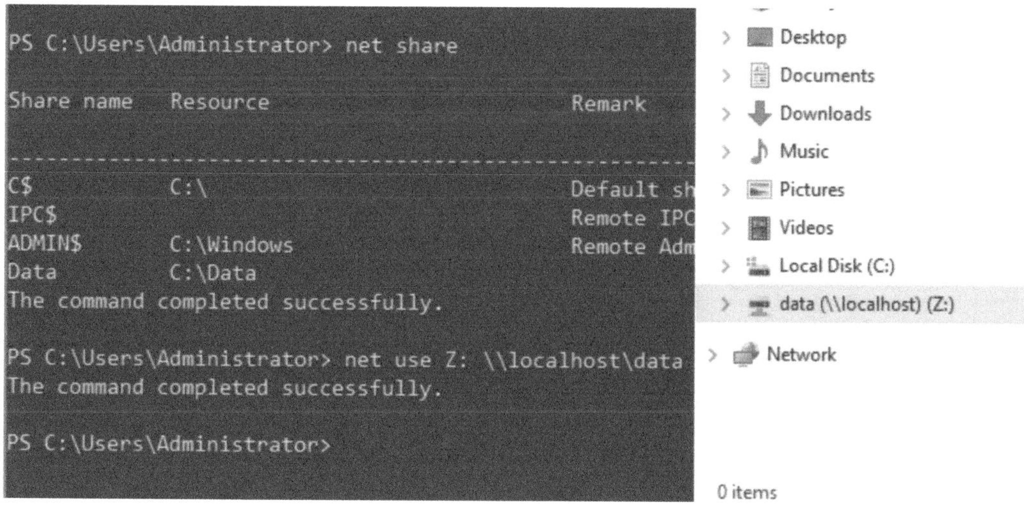

net share and net use commands, with mapped Z: drive. (Screenshot courtesy of Microsoft.)

Linux also mounts partitions and remote shares to the file system. It does not, however, use the concept of drive letters. Instead, the connected partitions are given user-friendly names. The mount command is used to attach to these partitions, and the umount command is used to detach (note that the command is not unmount, but umount).

The syntax of the mount command is

```
mount /dev/sdb1 /sales-data
```

Where /dev/sdb1 is the second storage device, first partition, and /sales-data is a directory in the Linux filesystem.

System Logs

System log files, such as the Linux rsyslog service or Windows Event Viewer, may alert you to potential drive failures or degraded performance. RAID controllers may also provide log file entries. Reviewing these logs should be a regular part of your sysadmin routine.

There is a second concern when it comes to log files and storage capacity. Log files can grow very rapidly in the event of a failure or other alert condition. Unattended logs can quickly consume available HDD space.

It is a common practice in Linux to place the /var directory on a separate partition. Rsyslog log files are stored at /var/log, and if these logs grow uncontrolled, they can consume the entire partition and potentially crash the system. Placing the logs on their own partition prevents such a crash. By default, Windows logs, stored in Event Viewer, cannot crash the system if they reach their maximum capacity.

```
[root@localhost ~]# ls /var/log
anaconda    chrony            firewalld   journal  README             tallylog                wtmp
audit       cups              gdm         lastlog  samba              vboxadd-install.log
blivet-gui  dnf.librepo.log   glusterfs   libvirt  speech-dispatcher  vboxadd-setup.log
boot.log    dnf.log           hawkey.log  ppp      sssd               vboxadd-setup.log.1
btmp        dnf.rpm.log       httpd       private  swtpm              vboxadd-uninstall.log
[root@localhost ~]#
```

The Linux /var/log directory.

Visual and Auditory Inspections

The housing for storage disks in the server may include indicator lights. For example, a green light may indicate the drive is functioning normally, an amber light might indicate the drive is performing slower than anticipated, and a red light might indicate a drive failure. There may also be auditory alarms to alert you to drive failures.

Traditional HDDs (not SSDs) may also click in the event of a drive failure.

Review Activity:

Common Storage Problems

Answer the following questions:

1. **What storage failure causes are often associated with the OS not being found?**

2. **What storage failure causes are often associated with failed backups or restores?**

3. **List at least two partitioning tools:**

4. **What Linux command is used to attach a partition to a directory so that users can access the partition?**

Lesson 6

Summary

- RAID 0 disk striping provides a performance increase.
- RAID 1 mirroring provides complete redundancy.
- RAID 5 disk striping with parity balances fault tolerance and cost.
- Consider SATA for cost, SAS for a balance of cost and performance, and NVMe for performance when cost is no issue.
- NFS is the standard Unix directory sharing protocol; SMB is the standard Windows folder sharing protocol.
- SAN performance depends heavily on the network connection.
- Fibre Channel and iSCSI are competing SAN protocols.
- Choose iSCSI when cost is an issue.
- Choose iSCSI when you're connecting many hosts to one storage target (several servers storing different data on a single storage server).
- Choose iSCSI when training is not available for your IT staff for the complexities of a Fibre Channel solution.
- Choose iSCSI when you need or want a less complex infrastructure.
- Choose Fibre Channel when performance is paramount.
- Choose Fibre Channel when SAN components are widely distributed.

1. **What RAID level seems most appropriate for file servers at your organization?**
2. **Does your organization use DAS, NAS, SAN, or some combination of the three?**

Lesson 7

Installing and Configuring an OS

LESSON INTRODUCTION

There are many deployment options available to you as a systems administrator when standing up a new server. You will view both manual and automated installation methods for both Windows Server and Linux. You will also view installation differences for virtualized versus bare-metal installations. Server storage is much more complex than standalone workstation storage, and you will gain knowledge of storage options, including partition and file system settings. Servers must be properly configured to participate on the network. You will briefly review basic network concepts before examining network settings and the TCP/IP protocol suite. Finally, scripted server configuration help to make server deployments quicker and more consistent. You will see both Bourne Again Shell (bash) and PowerShell scripting concepts.

Lesson Objectives

In this lesson, you will:

- Install an OS.
- Configure storage.
- Configure network settings.
- Use scripts to configure servers.

Topic 7A

Install an Operating System

EXAM OBJECTIVES COVERED

2.1 Given a scenario, install server operating systems

To install the server OS, you must first acquire the source files. Each OS uses a different installer to manage the installation process. The process may be accomplished manually or automated with options such as unattended installations or imaging. In other cases, an existing server will be migrated from one hardware device to another. All of these installation options could be used with bare-metal installations or VMs.

Installation Process

There are many methods for installing an OS. In some cases, the server hardware vendor may offer you a choice of preinstalled OSs. Your organization may instead mandate that the OS is to be installed and configured in house.

Some devices have an OS embedded in the device. The OS is usually installed by the manufacturer as part of the manufacturing process rather than directly installed. Examples include automated teller machines (ATMs), routers, self-service checkout machines, and some robotic devices.

OS Source Files

Several media types may be used to deploy OSs. Most users have installed OSs from optical media, such as CDs or DVDs. Today, it is common to receive the installation source files on a USB flash drive instead of an optical disk. In addition, the source files can be pulled from across the network or the Internet. Finally, the OS source files may be stored in an embedded format directly on the server or network appliance.

Live Installations

Some OSs, such as Linux, can be installed to a USB drive. The machine is booted from the USB drive, and the OS runs from the drive. There are many advantages to this method:

- Multiple OSs on one USB drive
- Supports Ubuntu, CentoS, Fedora, Kali, and many others
- Portable, so you have your preferred OS available
- Use borrowed or public computers without changing the OS installed on the HDD
- Repair local installations

In addition, live installations can be used to deploy images of the OS on the USB drive to one or more destination machines.

The Installer

The OSs use software called an installer to manage the installation process. The installers vary a lot, even within the Linux distributions. In general, however, the installer manages partition and file system choices, some OS features, and the creation of an initial administrator account.

The following table displays two installation options, along with their common attributes:

Installation Method	Features
Graphical	Guided via a mouse-driven interface Easy and self-explanatory Practical for occasional installations where speed and consistency are not essential
Command-line	Installation commands and options typed in manually Non-intuitive and assumes knowledge of required commands Typically faster than graphical installations Practical for occasional installations where speed and consistency are not essential

Manual Versus Unattended Installations

Unattended, or automated, installations use a text file as a reference for installation options. The text file, referred to as an answer file, contains all of the information needed for the installation to complete. The installer references the text file rather than the user for any needed options.

For example, if the installer requires partition information, it finds that information in the answer file instead of asking the user to enter the information manually. Answer files generate much faster installations. The installations are also much more consistent, since many OS instances can be created using the same answer file as a reference.

```
[root@localhost ~]# cat anaconda-ks.cfg
# Generated by Anaconda 33.25.4
# Generated by pykickstart v3.29
#version=F33
# Use graphical install
graphical


# Keyboard layouts
keyboard --xlayouts='us'
# System language
lang en_US.UTF-8

# Network information
network  --hostname=localhost.localdomain

# Run the Setup Agent on first boot
firstboot --enable

# Generated using Blivet version 3.3.0
ignoredisk --only-use=sda
autopart
# Partition clearing information
clearpart --none --initlabel

# System timezone
timezone America/Denver --utc

#Root password
rootpw --lock
```

Linux Kickstart files are used for automated, unattended installations.

Imaging is another form of automated installation. Imaging will be covered in more detail below.

Unattended installations may also have additional installation options added to the answer file. For example, updated device drivers, applications, utilities, and patches can be added to the automated installation. By the time this scripted installation completes, the OS is fully installed, is patched, and contains the additional applications necessary for the end user to begin work immediately.

Microsoft refers to automated deployments that contain patches, drivers, and applications as slip-stream installations.

In some cases, installations can occur across the network. The destination computer, where the new OS is to be installed, is booted from removable media or an existing OS, and then the source files for the new OS are transferred from a network server and executed.

Imaging

One form of automated installation is **imaging**, which consists of three components. The first component is a perfectly configured and updated server known as a source computer. An **image** of that source computer's configuration is then copied and uploaded to the imaging server. The imaging server is the second component. It stores images and OS source files. The final part is the destination servers. The OS image is downloaded to these servers and installed, resulting in one or more servers that are configured identically to the source computer. Imaging is a very efficient and consistent method of deploying server OSs.

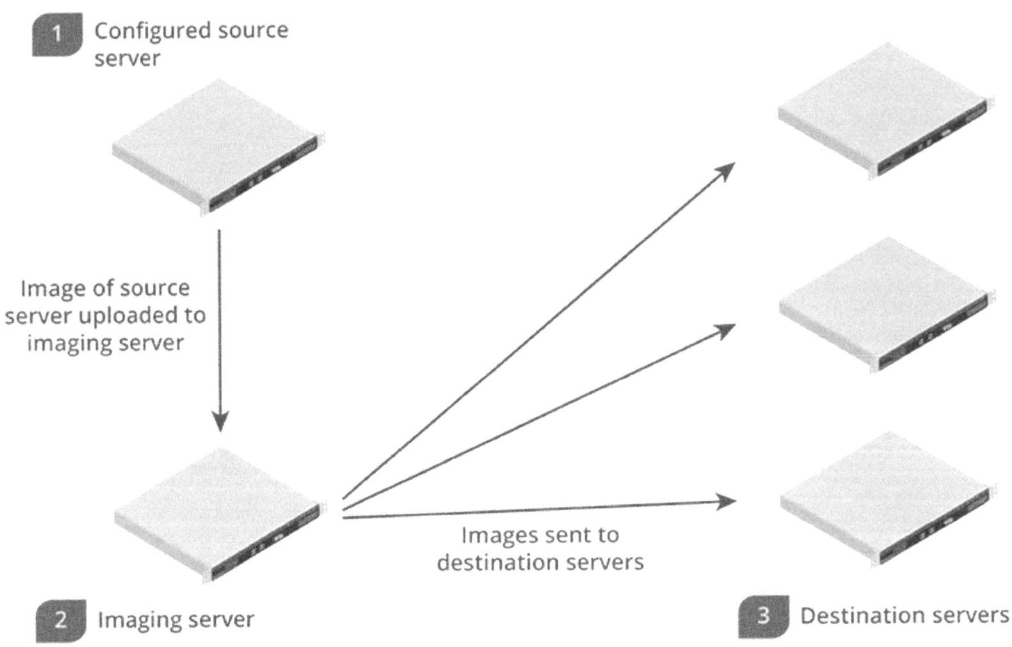

The source computer's configuration is uploaded to a deployment server. The image is then deployed to a destination server. (Images © 123RF.com)

Imaging is also a very common way of deploying workstation OSs.

VMs may also be cloned. The VM is really just a file defining its configuration. That file can be used as a reference for other VMs. For example, if five VMs each use a copy of a single configuration file, then their configurations will all be the same. Such cloning, which can even include the OS, applications, and data, is a very easy way to create multiple identical VMs.

VM templates are pre-generated VM configurations that can be used in a self-service environment. For example, a developer might need a test environment. The administrator creates a VM template that meets the developer's needs. The developer can then create a VM from the template on demand, without having to wait for the administrator to have time to deploy the VM. Such installations are very efficient and require very little human involvement.

Server Migrations

Once VMs are thought of as simple configuration files, then the options for how to use those files become very flexible. VMs can be created based on existing bare-metal installations. This is referred to as a Physical-to-Virtual (P2V) migration.

The table below shows some migration options and attributes

Migration Option	Acronym	Attributes
Physical-to-virtual	P2V	Migrates a physical server to a VM
Virtual-to-physical	V2P	Migrates a VM to a physical server
Virtual-to-virtual	V2V	Migrates a VM from one virtualization platform to another

P2V migrations are very common as businesses move their physical server infrastructure into virtualized cloud environments.

Bare Metal Versus Virtualized Installations

The following table displays installation targets. You may use the graphical or command-line methods above to install OSs on the various targets below.

Method	Attributes
Bare Metal	OS installed directly on the server hardware Traditional installation option Resources not shared among multiple installations Provides the security, reliability, and performance required by some industries May be more costly than virtualization
Virtualized	OS installed in a virtualized environment managed by a hypervisor Newer and common installation option Physical server resources shared among multiple VMs Provides fault tolerance, scalability, very efficient use of hardware May not provide the security required by some industries May be less costly than bare metal

Bare metal and virtualized installation attributes.

Managing the Server with a GUI or CLI

One of the choices made during the OS installation is whether to use a graphical or command-line user interface. While a graphical interface may be easier, a CLI may be faster and more secure.

Linux Servers

Historically, Linux servers have been managed at the command line. Such administration is usually much faster (it's quicker to enter commands than to navigate menus with a mouse—assuming you know the commands!), requires far fewer resources than a GUI, and may be more secure. Linux servers can have a variety of different GUI environments installed.

For example, a Linux sysadmin is tasked with standing up a web server that will host a static web site. The site will require little maintenance and only periodic changes. The sysadmin decides to deploy the web server as a VM with few compute resources. To maximize performance, and because there will be minimal administration, a command line–only deployment is selected. There's no reason to waste resources on a GUI.

```
[root@localhost ~]# uptime
 07:58:31 up 54 min,  1 user,  load average: 0.00, 0.07, 0.04
[root@localhost ~]# hostname
localhost.localdomain
[root@localhost ~]# ip addr show enp0s3
2: enp0s3: <BROADCAST,MULTICAST,UP,LOWER_UP> mtu 1500 qdisc fq_codel state UP group default qlen 1000
    link/ether 08:00:27:12:67:76 brd ff:ff:ff:ff:ff:ff
    inet 10.0.2.15/24 brd 10.0.2.255 scope global dynamic noprefixroute enp0s3
       valid_lft 83120sec preferred_lft 83120sec
    inet6 fe80::4ba0:590f:a7ca:1827/64 scope link noprefixroute
       valid_lft forever preferred_lft forever
[root@localhost ~]# █
```

Linux administrative commands.

Windows Servers

Windows servers have traditionally been managed via a GUI. Beginning with Windows Server 2008, Microsoft has offered the Server Core installation option. Server Core is a command line–only OS. It has a much smaller hardware footprint on the server and can provide significant performance benefits.

A Windows sysadmin has been tasked with setting up a file server for the applications team to test software. Because various applications team members will be accessing the server to install, modify, and remove software, the sysadmin chooses to install the Windows GUI. The interface is relatively easy to navigate and familiar.

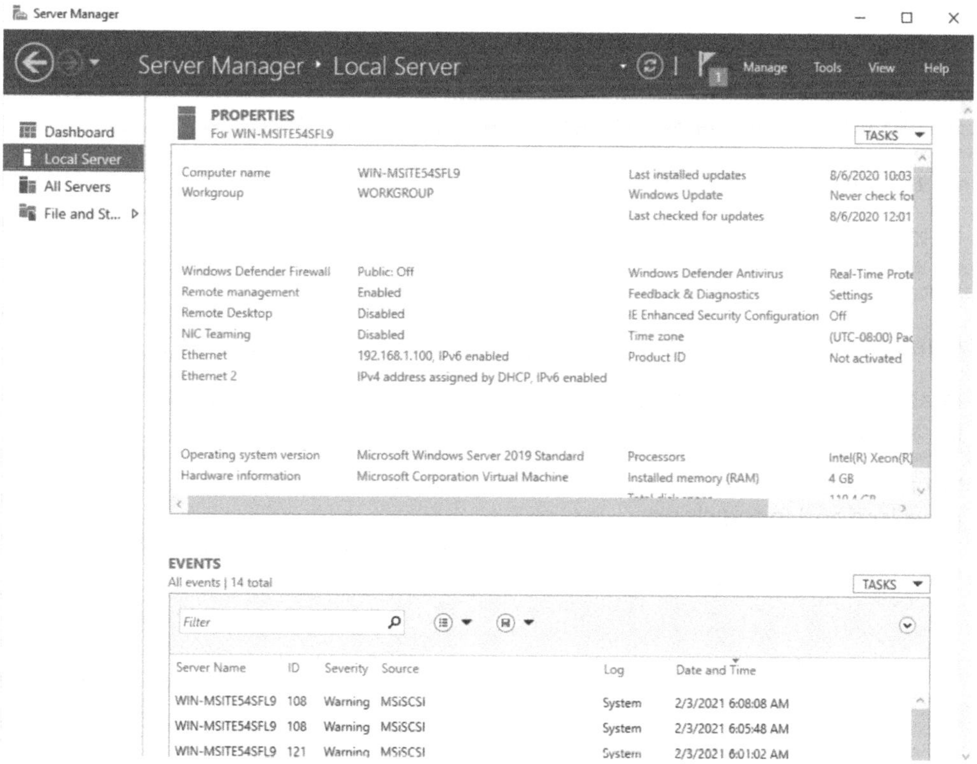

Windows Server Manager. (Screenshot courtesy of Microsoft.)

Remote Administration

It is worth noting that most servers should be administered remotely anyway. That usually means that the administrator is relying on the admin workstation GUI to produce the working environment for the remote server. In the case of Windows Server Server Core, you may remotely configure the server using a local GUI, which allows the server itself to operate with the more efficient command line–only environment.

Option	Notes
SSH	Remote, secured command-line administration, often on a Linux server
Remote Desktop Protocol (RDP)	Remote, secured connection to a graphical interface, usually on a Windows Server
Virtual Network Computing (VNC)	Remote, secured connection to a graphical interface, used with Linux and Windows

Remote administration options.

Guidelines for Installing an Operating System

- Confirm hardware requirements before beginning the installation.
- Consider minimum hardware versus recommended hardware.
- Confirm hardware is on the OS's HCL.
- Installations should be efficient, consistent, and automated.
- Vendor-installed OSs are not necessarily customizable.
- Manual installations with DVD or USB drives are slow, inconsistent, and simple.
- Image deployments are fast, consistent, and customizable but require more infrastructure.
- VM templates are fast, consistent, and customizable and can be used on-premises and in the cloud.
- Cloud deployments are fast, consistent, and customizable.

Review Activity:

OS Installation

Answer the following questions:

1. **List common attributes of manual installations:**

2. **List common attributes of automated installations:**

3. **Why might an administrator conduct at V2V conversion?**

4. **List at least three advantages of command-line administration:**

5. **What is an advantage of GUI administration?**

6. **List at least three remote administration methods:**

Topic 7B

Configure Storage

EXAM OBJECTIVES COVERED
2.1 Given a scenario, install server operating systems

Servers typically have greater storage capacity than workstations. In addition, the storage configurations for servers are typically more complex and provide for greater scalability and fault tolerance.

Server storage is set when the physical server is purchased or the VM is configured. By the time you are ready to install an OS on your server, you will have already made design decisions about storage, such as whether to use hardware RAID arrays. The next steps include partition management, disk configuration, and file systems.

Volumes and Partitions

Volumes and partitions are the fundamental divisions of traditional HDD storage. These divisions are configured to better manage storage on servers. There are different best practices and options available between Windows Server and Linux.

Partition Tables

Master Boot Record (MBR) and GUID Partition Table (GPT)

HDDs are partitioned to organize data, and the location of these partitions must be maintained. There are two different types of tables used to relate partition locations on storage disks. The older method is the **MBR**, and the newer way is the **GPT**. The primary difference between the two is that the GPT is far more flexible and practical on modern servers.

The following table displays storage options:

Storage Type	Attributes
GPT	Supports a larger number of partitions on the HDD Recognizes drives that are larger than two TB
MBR	Supports only four partitions on the HDD Recognizes drives that are two TB or smaller

Modern servers will likely exceed both of these requirements, and therefore a GPT configuration is the best bet. Server firmware must support UEFI system configurations to utilize a GPT structure.

Older servers may be configured with the MBR if their drive space is more limited or they need fewer partitions. MBR cannot manage more than 2 TB of storage space.

Partition and Volume Management

Primary and Extended Partitions

When disks are managed by the MBR, you have two types of partitions to select from. The first type is a **primary partition**. The system boots up off of primary partitions. Alternatively, the drive can be configured with a single extended partition, which itself can then be subdivided into **logical partitions**. Recall that MBR can only recognize a total of four partitions (up to three primary partitions and one extended partition).

Linux and Windows work with MBR and GPT formats.

Basic and Dynamic Disks in Windows

Once the OS is deployed, additional partitions may be created. Windows Server uses two different methods of organizing storage: Basic Disks and Dynamic Disks. By default, Windows uses the Basic Disk configuration, even though Dynamic Disk configurations are more flexible.

Dynamic disk attributes:

- Manages simple, spanned, striped (RAID 0), mirrored (RAID 1), and striped with parity (RAID 5) volumes.
- Simple and spanned volumes may be expanded to include more storage capacity.
- Mirrored and RAID 5 configurations can be repaired after a failure.

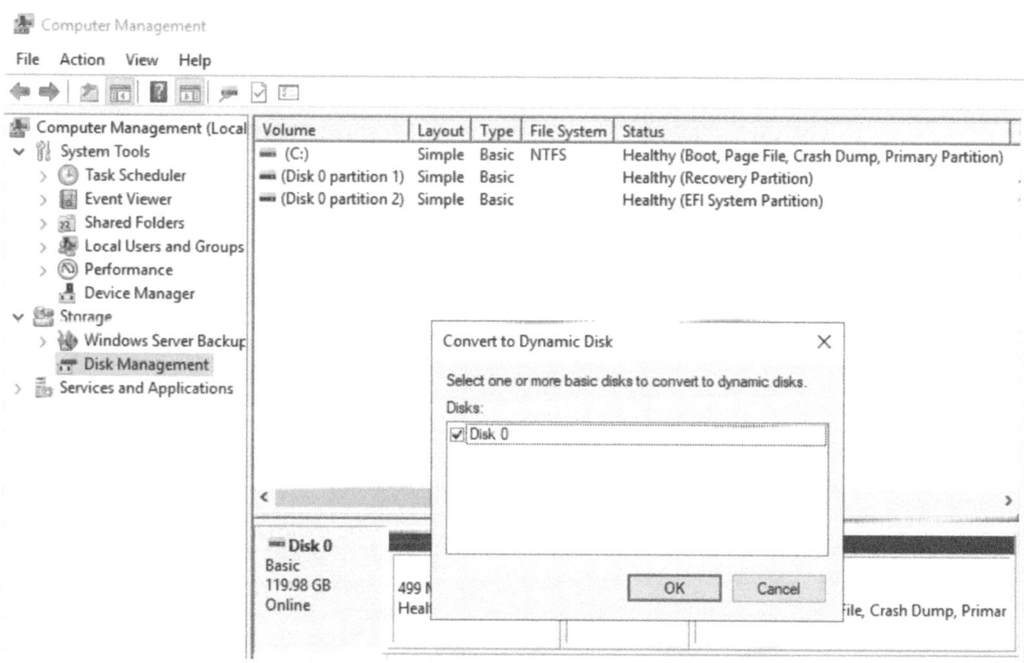

The conversion option in the Windows Server Disk Management console. (Screenshot courtesy of Microsoft.)

Basic and Dynamic Disk configurations are specific to Windows. Microsoft uses the term "partition" for disk divisions with traditional Basic Disk partitioning. Microsoft uses the name "volume" for disk divisions with the Dynamic Disk configuration option.

MBR and GPT tables can each be used with either Microsoft Basic or Dynamic Disk configurations.

LVM in Linux

LVM is more flexible than traditional partitioning and allows admins to manage storage capacity more easily. LVM organizes storage into three layers physical volumes (PVs), volume groups (VBs), and logical volumes (LVs) and permits increasing or decreasing storage space within those layers.

PVs

The lowest layer of LVM is one or more PVs. This layer represents the actual HDDs physically installed in the server. These drives do not have to be identical or contain the same capacity.

VGs

This layer represents the aggregation of capacity from one or more physical volumes and is known as a VG. This combined capacity represents the total storage space available to LVM.

LVs

The top layer of LVM consists of one or more volumes that are carved from the available space in a VG. The LVs are then formatted with a file system such as ext4 or XFS, and available as storage for the Linux system and users.

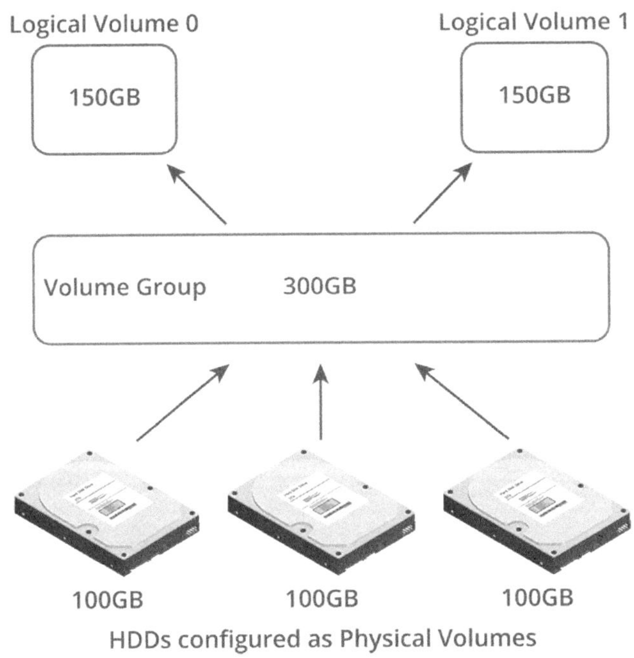

The three layers of LVM. (Images © 123RF.com)

The most significant benefit of LVM is its flexibility. To increase storage, an administrator adds a physical disk (PV), adds its storage capacity to the VG, and then extends the size of the LV. The administrator modifies the storage without rebooting the server or any repartitioning (which would remove access to the existing data). Such an extension of storage space is accomplished very quickly with almost no downtime (the volume cannot be mounted while it is being extended, so it would be unavailable for a few minutes).

Partition Strategies

There are some common strategies for managing storage space on Windows and Linux servers. These strategies vary depending on the purpose of the server, but this section presents some general guidelines.

Windows Guidelines

The C: drive is usually reserved for the OS and applications. It is large enough for the OS, applications, pagefile, and updates installed through the server's life cycle. Sufficient space for Event Viewer log files must also be considered. The NTFS file system is used for security (permissions) and stability.

The D: drive is usually reserved for data. If performance is a concern, the D: drive may be a second physical HDD. This partition is large enough to support the amount and type of data stored (user home folders and files, website files, graphics files). The file system is NTFS for security and stability.

Linux Guidelines

Linux servers often have a significantly more complex partition scheme than Windows servers do. The root of the file system, which is depicted with a / (forward slash), usually consumes one partition, while user home directories (/home) and system log files (/var/log) are stored on separate partitions. Linux systems usually use a dedicated partition named swap for virtual memory. The file system will probably be XFS, although ext4 is a possibility.

There are many possibilities for server partitions and drive formats. The final design depends on the role of the server.

Windows File Server Example

For example, a Windows sysadmin has been asked to set up a file server for the sales team, which is large and expected to continue growing. The team accesses their files frequently throughout the day, and the files are critical to business continuity.

With these requirements in mind, the sysadmin uses the Windows Disk Management tool to configure three physical HDDs as Dynamic Disks. Next, the drives are associated together in a RAID 5 array, managed by Windows (this is an example of software RAID). This configuration provides some speed and some fault tolerance to the servers storage.

Linux Web Server Example

A Linux sysadmin is deploying a web server. The server will host a static web site that does not change much. The site is important to daily business functions, however, so reliability is key. No standard users will access the server itself, just the web site it hosts.

The administrator creates a partition for the root of the Linux file system (represented with a forward slash), another partition for swap (virtual memory), and a final relatively large partition for /var. The /var directory hosts log files (which are important to reliable web services) and the files that make up the web site itself. No separate partition is used for /home because no users will store data on this server.

File systems

File systems manage data storage and retrieval on HDD partitions (or volumes). Data is broken into chunks, and each piece is labeled for ease of organization and retrieval.

File systems are OS-specific, though there is some cross-compatibility. There are many file system options for Windows and Linux servers.

The ext4 File System

The ext4 file system is the default for many Linux distributions. The file system is stable and has existed for many years.

The command to format a volume with the ext4 file system is

```
mkfs.ext4 /dev/sdb1
```

The XFS File System

The XFS file system is another common Linux file system, especially in enterprise environments. It provides high performance and stability. XFS is the default file system for RHEL8.

The command to format a volume with the XFS file system is

```
mkfs.xfs /dev/sdb1
```

```
[root@CentOS7-A ~]# xfs_info /dev/sda3
meta-data=/dev/sda3              isize=512    agcount=4, agsize=1310720 blks
         =                       sectsz=4096  attr=2, projid32bit=1
         =                       crc=1        finobt=0 spinodes=0
data     =                       bsize=4096   blocks=5242880, imaxpct=25
         =                       sunit=0      swidth=0 blks
naming   =version 2              bsize=4096   ascii-ci=0 ftype=1
log      =internal               bsize=4096   blocks=2560, version=2
         =                       sectsz=4096  sunit=1 blks, lazy-count=1
realtime =none                   extsz=4096   blocks=0, rtextents=0
[root@CentOS7-A ~]# 
```

XFS configuration information on a Linux server.

The ZFS File System

Sun Microsystems created the **ZFS file system**. It is a scalable and efficient file system that supports very large partitions, ACL permissions, and compression. The open-source implementation of ZFS is Open-ZFS. Many Unix and Linux systems use ZFS, especially for enterprise-class servers.

The name ZFS is not actually an acronym.

The New Technology File System (NTFS) and Resilient File System (ReFS)

Windows typically uses two different file systems: **NTFS** and **ReFS**. Older Windows versions, as well as removable media, also use **File Allocation Table (FAT)**. These file systems have different attributes.

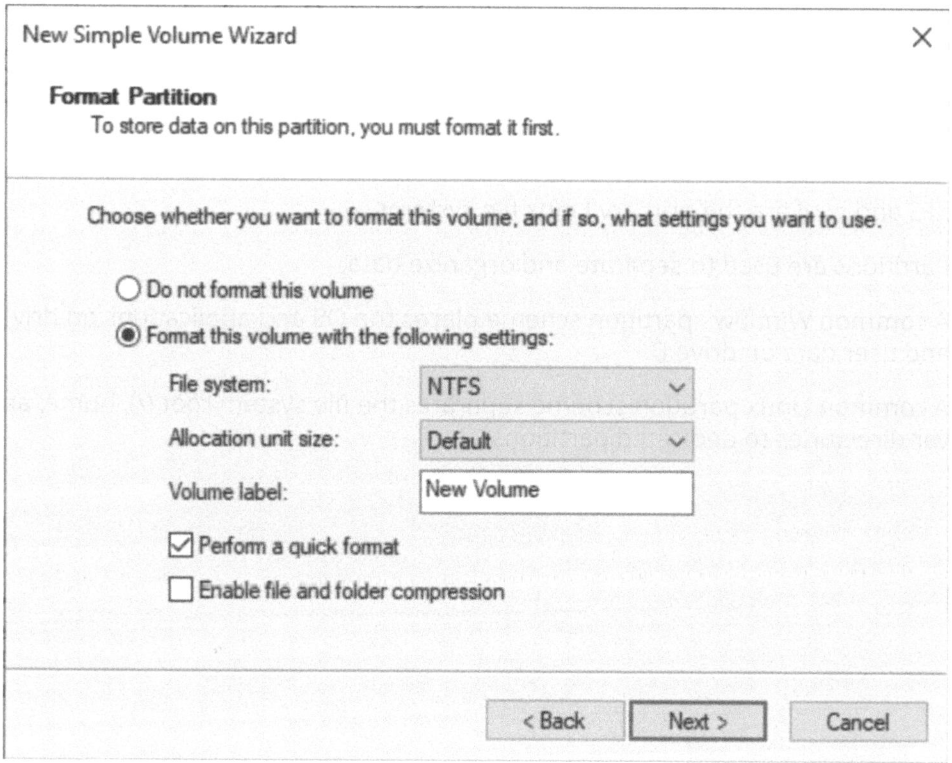

Format a new volume with the NTFS filesystem. (Screenshot courtesy of Microsoft.)

The Virtual Machine File System (VMFS)

VMware developed the **VMFS** to host multiple VM disk images. Each image is only writable by its own VM, but multiple servers can write to file system itself. This feature allows multiple VM hosts to have exclusive access to their own VM files. The entire file system is not locked exclusively to one VM host.

File System	Platform	Attributes
ext4	Linux	Journaling, large drive support, extended attributes
XFS	Linux	Journaling, scalability, large file support, fast repairs, extended attributes
ZFS	Linux	Massive storage (1 billion terabytes), scalability, flexible, enterprise-class management
NTFS	Windows	Journaling, scalability, BitLocker
ReFS	Windows	Journaling, scalability, large drive and file support, BitLocker
VMFS	ESXi	Optimized for virtual machines, multiple VMs can read/write, scalability

File system options.

Guidelines for Configuring Storage

- Choose GPT if drives are 2 TB or greater or more than four partitions are required.
- Windows Server includes Basic or Dynamic disk configurations.
- Linux uses LVM to enable flexible storage options.
- LVM consists of three layers: PVs, VGs, and LVs.
- File systems organize data on storage partitions or volumes.
- NTFS is the primary Windows file system.
- XFS and ext4 are the primary Linux file systems.
- Partitions are used to separate and organize data.
- A common Windows partition scheme places the OS and applications on drive C: and user data on drive D:.
- A common Linux partition scheme separates the file system root (/), home, and var directories to dedicated partitions.

Review Activity:

Storage Configuration

Answer the following questions:

1. **List two advantages that the GPT format has over MBR:**

2. **What are the three components of a Linux LVM deployment?**

3. **What content is typically stored on the C: drive on a Windows Server? On the D: drive?**

4. **List three common Linux file systems. List two common Windows file systems.**

Topic 7C

Configure Network Settings

EXAM OBJECTIVES COVERED
2.2 Given a scenario, configure servers to use network infrastructure services

Server administration requires a basic understanding of networking. It is useful to begin with the functions of the seven layers of the OSI model. Next, the TCP/IP protocol suite is covered, including protocols and port numbers. Nodes on the network have three identities: a physical address, a logical address, and a hostname. Each node is configured with a unique IP address that relies on either IPv4 or IPv6. Finally, IP address allocation and name resolution are critical to understanding how the nodes participate on the network.

General networking is an assumed skill for CompTIA Server+ candidates. This topic briefly summarizes some of the key concepts.

Review Network Fundamentals

Networking skills are essential for server administrators. You must understand where in the network your servers will reside and how to configure them to participate in network communications. In this section, you will review a few basic network fundamentals, including the OSI model and the TCP/IP protocol suite.

Review the OSI Model

The OSI Model

The **Open Systems Interconnect (OSI) model** conceptualizes network communications by dividing the process into a series of steps that are organized into seven layers. These layers define what information is sent and received in each step of network communications.

Layer	Name	Function
7	Application	Provides applications with the ability to access the network, including email, web browsing, file transfers, network sharing, and other services
6	Presentation	Converts application layer data into a form that can be used by servers and clients
5	Session	Establishes, maintains, and tears down the network connection between two nodes Controls when each node can send data
4	Transport	Manages reliable communications and error checking

Layer	Name	Function
3	Network	Provides logical addressing of nodes so that they may be uniquely identified on the network
2	Data Link	Provides physical addressing of network devices so that they may be uniquely identified on the network Organizes data into a form that an be transmitted on the media type (802.3 Ethernet, 802.11 wireless, and others)
1	Physical	Defines the physical network standards, including the actual transmission of data on the media

The seven layers of the OSI model.

The OSI model provides a single frame of reference for networking professionals, developers, and manufacturers. For example, if an issue is stated as being a layer 3 problem, everyone involved understands what that means.

In addition, the OSI model is a framework for the development of network protocols. In the 1980s and 1990s, there were several families of network protocols, including AppleTalk, NetBEUI, IPX/SPX, and TCP/IP. These protocol suites could be understood by using OSI model concepts. Modern internal networks today almost exclusively use TCP/IP.

Review the TCP/IP Suite

Today, nearly all private home and business networks, as well as the Internet, use the TCP/IP protocol suite, which contains far more than just the two protocols listed in its name. TCP/IP governs the flow of traffic among network nodes on internal networks and the Internet.

The TCP/IP stack combines functions of the seven layers of the OSI model into four layers.

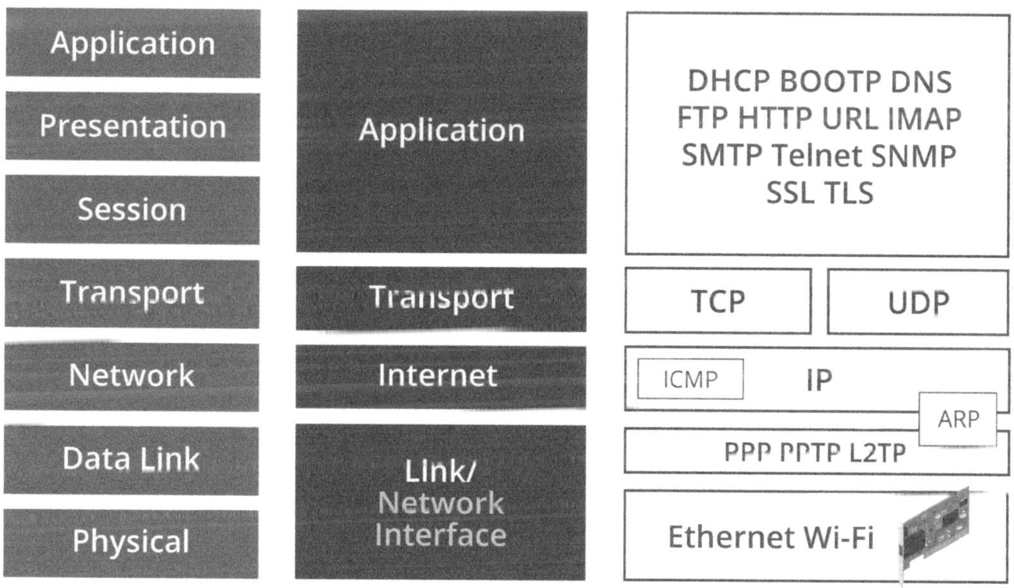

The Application, Transport, Internet, and Network Access Layers of TCP/IP. (Images © 123RF.com)

Layer	Function
Application	Provides access to network resources Common protocols: HTTP, HTTPS, FTP, SMTP, POP3, IMAP, DNS, TFTP, SNMP
Transport	Manages reliable communications Common protocols: TCP and UDP
Internet	Governs the movement of data between the source and destination, including IP addresses Common protocols: IP, ICMP, IGMP, ARP, RARP
Network Access	Transmits data on the network based on the network type, such as Ethernet

The TCP/IP Stack.

Port Numbers

Recall that computers use numbers as identifiers, and humans use names. For example, a human interprets the **File Transfer Protocol** as a protocol that manages file transfers. A computer cannot understand those words, so it uses a **port** number to represent the protocol. The FTP service uses port 21 as its identifier. Port numbers are associated with specific Transport layer protocols.

Port/Protocol	Service
21/tcp	FTP
22/tcp	SSH
25/tcp	SMTP
53/tcp and 53/udp	DNS
67/udp	DHCP
69/udp	TFTP
80/tcp	HTTP
110/tcp	POP3
123/udp	NTP
143/udp	IMAPv4
161/udp	SNMP
443/tcp	HTTPS
3389/tcp	RDP

Common port numbers, protocols, and services.

There are many other protocols and associated port numbers. You will recognize and memorize many that are specific to your environment.

It is crucial to be able to recognize standard port numbers. These numbers are used when configuring firewalls or displayed when interpreting log files.

Addressing

Nodes are identified on TCP/IP networks by using logical address. In this section, you will briefly review basic IP address concepts.

IPv4 Addresses

The IP is located at the Internet layer of the TCP/IP suite. This layer is responsible for logical addressing. From 1981 until recently, these addresses were 32 bits in length. Each address is divided into four fields of eight bits, each called octets. Mathematically, the result is approximately 4.3 billion IP addresses.

The 4.3 billion addresses are divided into five classes: A, B, C, D, and E. Class E is experimental and not used in standard networking. Class D is used for a one-to-many communication process called "multi-casting." Classes A, B, and C are used in standard networking.

The difference between the three standard classes is the number of available networks compared to the number of possible hosts per network.

Class	Number of Networks	Number of Hosts
A	126	16,777,214
B	16,384	65,534
C	2,097,152	254

The three standard IP address classes, number of networks, and number of hosts.

The first octets (eight bits) identify to which class a given IP address belongs by default.

First Octet	Class
1-126	A
128-191	B
192-223	C
224-239	D
240-255	E

Identifying IP address classes.

The 127.0.0.0 address range is reserved for the loopback address of 127.0.0.1, which is why 127 does not appear in the table above.

Unfortunately, the 4.3 billion available addresses have been depleted. Each identity on the Internet—every email server, email client, FTP server, FTP client, web server, web client—must have a unique IP address. You can see how those 4.3 billion addresses would be quickly consumed!

To make IP address utilization more efficient, a range of Class A, Class B, and Class C addresses are reserved for use on internal networks. This private IP address standard is specified in RFC 1918. An organization's internal IP address structure is almost certainly allocated from one of these ranges:

Class	Reserved IP Address Range
A	10.0.0.0-10.255.255.255
B	172.16.0.0-172.31.255.255
C	192.168.0.0-192.168.255.255

Reserved IP address ranges.

Be prepared to see the words "reserved," "private," or "internal" to describe these ranges.

The Loopback and APIPA Addresses

There are two additional IP addresses you should also be able to recognize.

Address	Name	Function
127.0.0.1	Loopback address	Network troubleshooting, IP address refers the computer to itself
169.254.0.0	Automatic Private IP Address (APIPA)	Self-assigned address when the client fails to lease an address from a DHCP server

The loopback and APIPA addresses.

Network ID, Host ID, and the Subnet Mask

IPv4 addresses are divided into two portions: the network identifier and the host identifier. Classes A, B, and C have clearly defined default divisions between the network ID and host ID.

Class	Network ID	Host ID
A	First octet	Remaining three octets
B	First two octets	Remaining two octets
C	First three octets	Remaining three octets

Classes, Network IDs, and Host IDs.

For example, if a host has an IPv4 address of 192.168.2.200 and a subnet mask of 255.255.255.0, then the network ID is 192.168.2.0, and the host ID is 0.0.0.200.

These defaults are changeable, however, depending on the needs of the network administrator. A second value, called the "Default Subnet Mask," identifies which part of the IPv4 address is the network ID and which is the host ID.

Bit Count Notation

Class	Decimal	Bit Count Notation
A	255.0.0.0	/8
B	255.255.0.0	/16
C	255.255.255.0	/32

Subnet mask in decimal and bit count notation.

Network Address Translation

As discussed, the reserved IP address ranges are for use inside company (and home) networks. The addresses in this range are not routable on the public Internet. If a company workstation or server with a reserved IP of 192.168.2.200 tried to access a public webserver hosted at 2.219.13.186, Internet routers would refuse the packets because of the reserved IP address. So how do machines on internal networks access public Internet resources?

The answer is NAT. NAT is a service on some servers and routers that substitutes the organization's single public IP address for any traffic originating from or addressed to internal devices that have reserved IP addresses. As far as Internet resources can tell, the network connection originated with the NAT device, and the internal resources behind the NAT device are hidden.

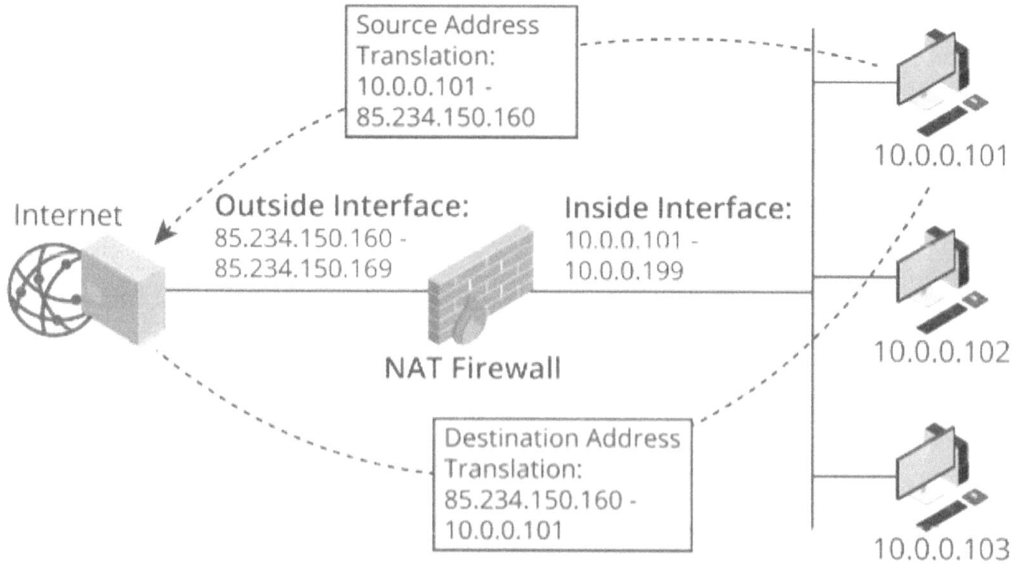

NAT device translating between public and private IP addresses. (Images © 123RF.com)

IPv4 Address Depletion

As noted above, the 32-bit structure of IPv4 addressing provides approximately 4.3 billion available addresses, and most of those are consumed. Reserved IP address ranges don't really offer additional addresses, just more efficient use of existing addresses. So, what's the solution?

IP Address Management

Organizations often use IP address management software to help keep track of subnets, consumed addresses, available addresses, etc. As branch offices open and close, employees transition to working from home, and mobile devices come and go, IP address tracking becomes much more difficult.

Some companies even specialize in brokering and selling IP address blocks. For example, when Nortel went bankrupt, Microsoft purchased over 600,000 IPv4 addresses from it.

IPv6 Addresses

IP version 6 (IPv6) rectifies many of the shortcomings of IPv4. The most obvious improvement is that it provides a great many additional addresses.

IPv6 addresses are 128 bits in length, providing approximately 3.4×10^{38} addresses, and the addresses are allocated more efficiently. IPv6 also includes benefits related to routing and data encryption.

The addresses are displayed using hexadecimal (base 16). The addresses are more difficult to work with, but hexadecimal simplifies the notation somewhat.

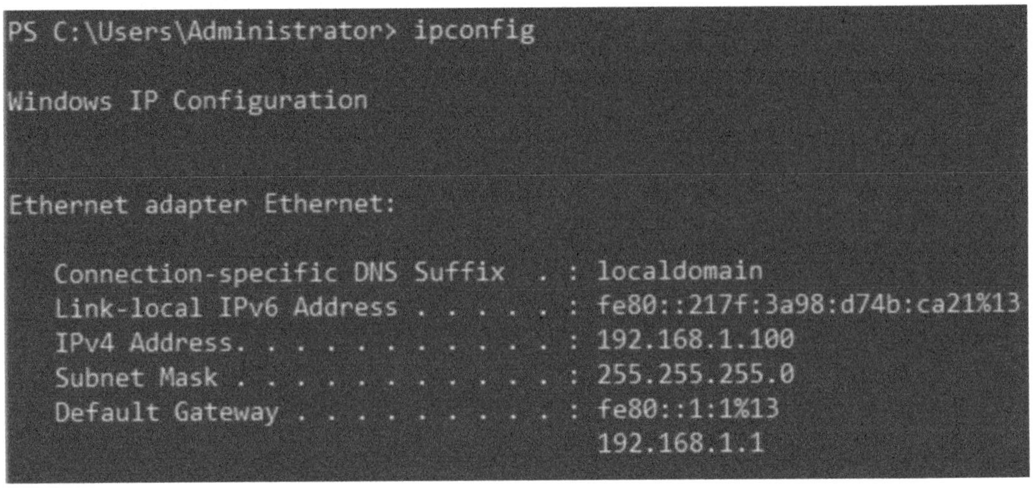

Output from the ipconfig command displaying the IPv6 address.

Range	Name	IPv4 Equivalent
::1/128	Loopback Address	Similar to 127.0.0.1
FE80::/10	Link-Local Address	Similar to 169.254.0.0 APIPA
FEC, FED, FEE, FEF	Site-Local Address	Similar to Reserved IPv4 addresses
2000:/3	Global Unicast Address	Internet-routable, similar to Public IPv4 addresses

IPv6 Addresses.

Transitioning to IPv6

Major ISPs, mobile carriers, website hosts, retailers, and other organizations have largely moved to IPv6 for their public presence. Internal business networks and home networks have largely remained on IPv4. Many of these internal networks do not need to take advantage of the benefits of IPv6.

Network Identities

Nodes are devices that have an identity on a network. Servers, workstations, smartphones, network printers, and other similar devices are all examples of nodes. There are three different types of identities the nodes might have. Many nodes will have all three types.

Identities	Identifiers	Example
Media Access Control address	Physical address	00:0a:97:9e:86:16
Internet Protocol address	Logical address	192.168.2.3/24
Hostname	Human-friendly name	webserver03

The three network identities.

MAC Addresses

MAC addresses are examples of physical addresses. Each NIC has a unique identifier hardcoded into it. This identity is used by other nodes on the same network segment to address network communications. MAC addresses occur at the Data Link layer (layer 2) of the OSI model. Switches and NICs reference MAC addresses.

MAC addresses are displayed in hexadecimal (base 16). The first half of the address identifies the device vendor, and the second half uniquely identifies the device itself.

```
PS C:\Users\Administrator> ipconfig /all

Windows IP Configuration

   Host Name . . . . . . . . . . . . : WIN-MSITE54SFL9
   Primary Dns Suffix  . . . . . . . :
   Node Type . . . . . . . . . . . . : Hybrid
   IP Routing Enabled. . . . . . . . : No
   WINS Proxy Enabled. . . . . . . . : No
   DNS Suffix Search List. . . . . . : localdomain

Ethernet adapter Ethernet:

   Connection-specific DNS Suffix  . : localdomain
   Description . . . . . . . . . . . : Microsoft Hyper-V Network Adapter
   Physical Address. . . . . . . . . : 00-15-5D-01-80-08
   DHCP Enabled. . . . . . . . . . . : No
   Autoconfiguration Enabled . . . . : Yes
   Link-local IPv6 Address . . . . . : fe80::217f:3a98:d74b:ca21%13(Preferred)
   IPv4 Address. . . . . . . . . . . : 192.168.1.100(Preferred)
   Subnet Mask . . . . . . . . . . . : 255.255.255.0
   Default Gateway . . . . . . . . . : fe80::1:1%13
                                       192.168.1.1
   DHCPv6 IAID . . . . . . . . . . . : 100668765
   DHCPv6 Client DUID. . . . . . . . : 00-01-00-01-25-B2-71-FD-00-15-5D-01-80-08
   DNS Servers . . . . . . . . . . . : 8.8.8.8
                                       4.4.4.4
   NetBIOS over Tcpip. . . . . . . . : Enabled
   Connection-specific DNS Suffix Search List :
                                       localdomain
```

ipconfig /all output, note the physical (MAC) address.

IP addresses

IP addresses are examples of logical addresses. NICs are assigned an IP address by the systems administrator, depending on the rest of the network's configuration. IP addresses occur at the Network layer (layer 3) of the OSI model. Routers reference IP addresses to direct network traffic.

```
PS C:\Users\Administrator> ipconfig /all

Windows IP Configuration

   Host Name . . . . . . . . . . . . : WIN-MSITE54SFL9
   Primary Dns Suffix  . . . . . . . :
   Node Type . . . . . . . . . . . . : Hybrid
   IP Routing Enabled. . . . . . . . : No
   WINS Proxy Enabled. . . . . . . . : No
   DNS Suffix Search List. . . . . . : localdomain

Ethernet adapter Ethernet:

   Connection-specific DNS Suffix  . : localdomain
   Description . . . . . . . . . . . : Microsoft Hyper-V Network Adapter
   Physical Address. . . . . . . . . : 00-15-5D-01-80-08
   DHCP Enabled. . . . . . . . . . . : No
   Autoconfiguration Enabled . . . . : Yes
   Link-local IPv6 Address . . . . . : fe80::217f:3a98:d74b:ca21%13(Preferred)
   IPv4 Address. . . . . . . . . . . : 192.168.1.100(Preferred)
   Subnet Mask . . . . . . . . . . . : 255.255.255.0
   Default Gateway . . . . . . . . . : fe80::1:1%13
                                       192.168.1.1
   DHCPv6 IAID . . . . . . . . . . . : 100668765
   DHCPv6 Client DUID. . . . . . . . : 00-01-00-01-25-B2-71-FD-00-15-5D-01-80-08
   DNS Servers . . . . . . . . . . . : 8.8.8.8
                                       4.4.4.4
   NetBIOS over Tcpip. . . . . . . . : Enabled
   Connection-specific DNS Suffix Search List :
                                       localdomain
```

ipconfig /all output, note the IPv4 Address.

Hostnames

Hostnames are user-friendly computer names. The network protocols do not reference these names, but they make it easier for people to understand the devices they interact with. For example, it's much easier to recognize the Color-Sales-Printer hostname than the 192.168.2.55 IP address.

```
PS C:\Users\Administrator> ipconfig /all

Windows IP Configuration

   Host Name . . . . . . . . . . . . : WIN-MSITE54SFL9
   Primary Dns Suffix  . . . . . . . :
   Node Type . . . . . . . . . . . . : Hybrid
   IP Routing Enabled. . . . . . . . : No
   WINS Proxy Enabled. . . . . . . . : No
   DNS Suffix Search List. . . . . . : localdomain

Ethernet adapter Ethernet:

   Connection-specific DNS Suffix  . : localdomain
   Description . . . . . . . . . . . : Microsoft Hyper-V Network Adapter
   Physical Address. . . . . . . . . : 00-15-5D-01-80-08
   DHCP Enabled. . . . . . . . . . . : No
   Autoconfiguration Enabled . . . . : Yes
   Link-local IPv6 Address . . . . . : fe80::217f:3a98:d74b:ca21%13(Preferred)
   IPv4 Address. . . . . . . . . . . : 192.168.1.100(Preferred)
   Subnet Mask . . . . . . . . . . . : 255.255.255.0
   Default Gateway . . . . . . . . . : fe80::1:1%13
                                       192.168.1.1
   DHCPv6 IAID . . . . . . . . . . . : 100668765
   DHCPv6 Client DUID. . . . . . . . : 00-01-00-01-25-B2-71-FD-00-15-5D-01-80-08
   DNS Servers . . . . . . . . . . . : 8.8.8.8
                                       4.4.4.4
   NetBIOS over Tcpip. . . . . . . . : Enabled
   Connection-specific DNS Suffix Search List :
                                       localdomain
```

ipconfig /all output, note the Host Name.

IP Address Configuration

Each of your servers will have three identities. The MAC address is preconfigured on the server's NIC by the vendor, so you won't have to configure that. The hostname is the computer name that you set when installing the OS. The primary identity you'll have to configure is the IP address and related information.

IP Address Configuration Methods

There are two methods for setting an IP configuration: the static method and the dynamic method. We'll examine both ways below, but for now, be aware that servers usually have a static IP address.

The IP address configuration contains several values, including the IP address itself, the related subnet mask, the IP address of the router in the subnet, and the IP address of at least one DNS name resolution server.

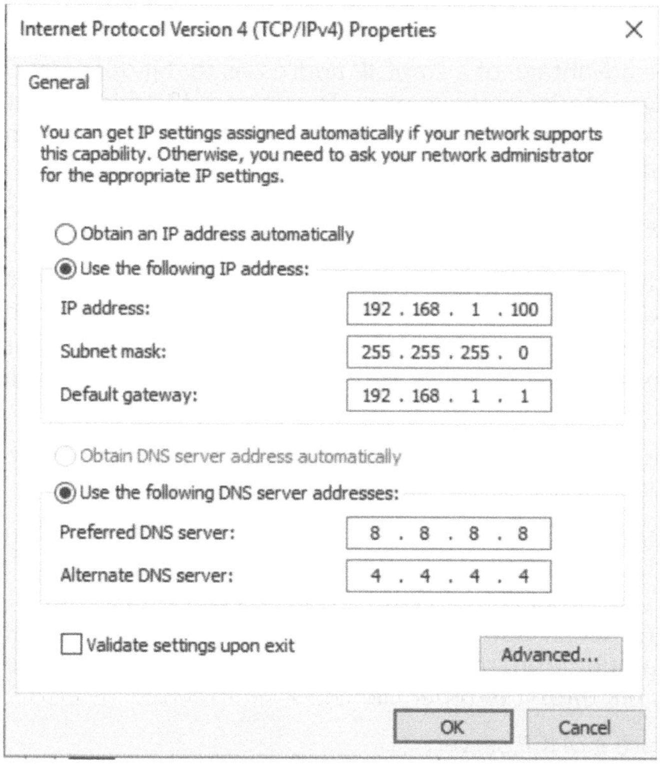

The configuration dialog box to statically set an IP address in Windows. (Screenshot courtesy of Microsoft.)

As a sysadmin, you need to determine a method for assigning these configurations to each server.

Static Method

Static IP address configurations are accomplished manually by the administrator. That means you need to log on to the server, select the appropriate console or command-line tool, and then manually enter the IP address, subnet mask, IP address of the default gateway, and IP address of one or more DNS name resolution servers. You cannot make any typographical errors, and you cannot configure the server with an IP address that is already in use on the network. Because of this restriction, you will have to have a method of tracking what IP addresses are already in use.

IP Address	MAC Address	Hostname	Status	Location
10.1.0.53	00:0a:95:9d:86:14	fileserver3	used	ServerRoom
10.1.0.99	00:0a:95:8a:68:16	webserver1	used	ServerRoom
192.168.2.200	00:0a:95:5b:54:11	client7	used	HQ
192.168.2.201	00:0a:95:68:14:4b	client102	used	Branch01
192.168.2.202	00:0a:95:18:9d:1a:11	client95	used	Branch01
192.168.2.203	00:0a:95:5d:42:11	client14	used	HQ
192.168.2.204	00:0a:95:1a:44:32	client27	used	HQ
192.168.2.205			unused	
192.168.2.206			unused	

Spreadsheet to track IP address assignments.

Static IP addressing is relatively cumbersome, but it is necessary on servers and many other network devices (routers, managed switches, and security appliances). The advantage of a static IP address is that it does not change (unless you deliberately reconfigure the server). The server's IP address is an identity on the network that is used and referenced by client computers, so it must remain unchanged, hence the label static.

Dynamic Method

Dynamic IP address configuration is automatic. It relies on a server that you configure with a scope of available IP addresses. Network clients then request the use of an IP address from the scope and periodically renew their request. The configuration includes values for IP addresses, subnet masks, default gateways, and DNS servers.

The service that manages IP addresses is named the **Dynamic Host Configuration Protocol** or DHCP service.

As the administrator, you determine what range of IP addresses you want to make available on your network. You install the DHCP service on a server and then create a DHCP scope that contains the addresses you've selected. Client computers contact the DHCP server during the boot process and request the use of an IP address configuration from the scope. The DHCP server leases the address to the client and does not offer it to other clients.

Steps to configure a DHCP server:

1. Install the DHCP service.
2. Configure a scope with a range of IP addresses and a related subnet mask.
3. Configure additional options, including default gateway and one or more DNS servers.
4. Start the service so that clients can lease an IP address configuration.

Client machines use the following four-step process to lease an IP address configuration:

1. The client broadcasts a DHCPDiscover message
2. The DHCP server broadcasts a DHCPOffer message
3. The client broadcasts a DHCPRequest message
4. The DHCP server broadcasts a DHCPAcknowledge message

The client configures its networking based on the information provided by the DHCP server.

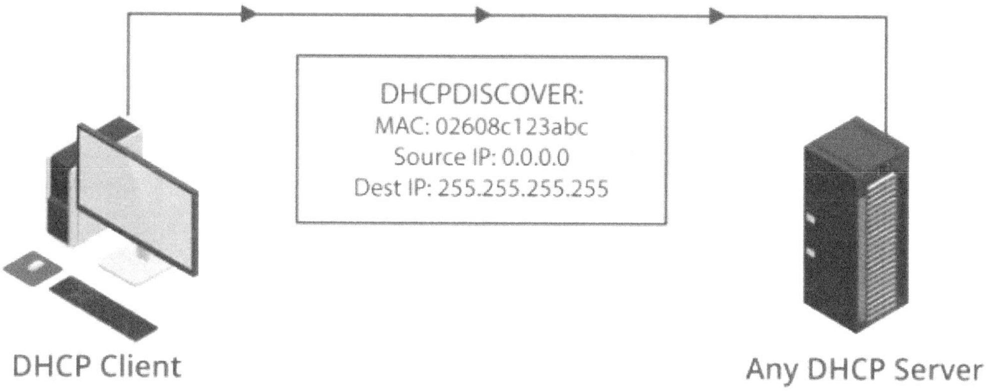

Step one of the four-step DHCP lease generation process: Discover (Images © 123RF.com)

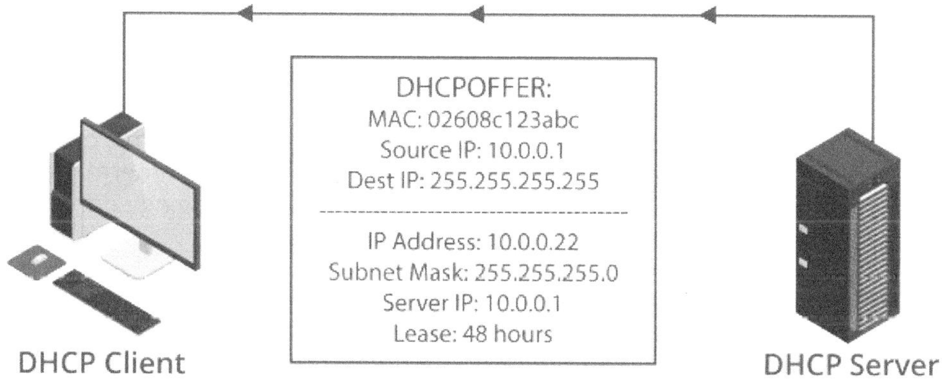

Step two of the four-step DHCP lease generation process: Offer (Images © 123RF.com)

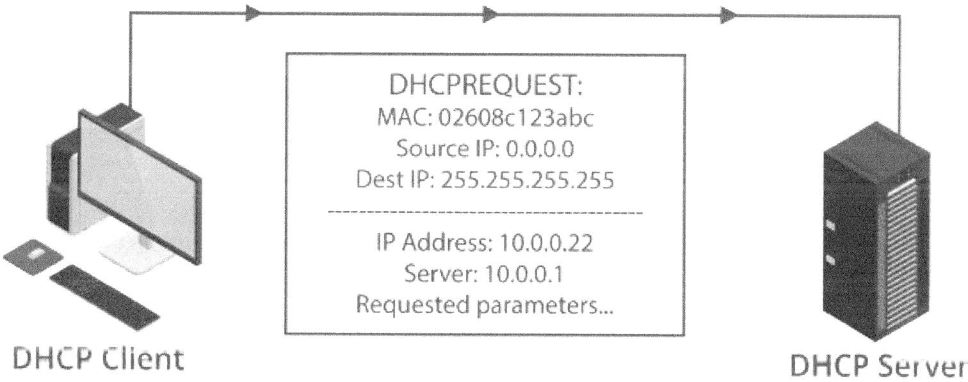

Step three of the four-step DHCP lease generation process: Request (Images © 123RF.com)

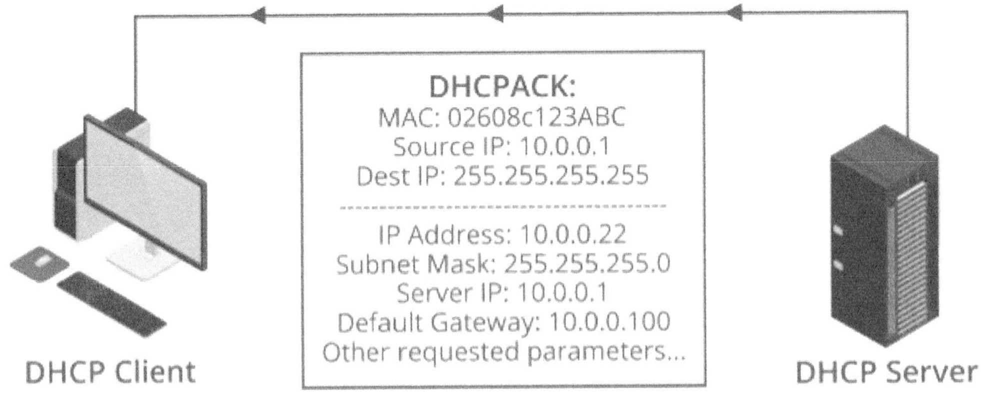

Step four of the four-step DHCP lease generation process: Acknowledge (Images © 123RF.com)

Periodically, the client must renew the lease, letting the DHCP server know that the address is still in use and should not be given to other clients. A client machine may use the same IP address configuration for a very long time (months, perhaps), but the address is not really permanent. For client computers, a non-permanent IP address is not an issue. However, servers usually need an unchanging address so that they may be consistently found on the network.

```
C:\Users\LabUser>ipconfig /all

Windows IP Configuration

   Host Name . . . . . . . . . . . . : DESKTOP-BT4131D
   Primary Dns Suffix  . . . . . . . :
   Node Type . . . . . . . . . . . . : Hybrid
   IP Routing Enabled. . . . . . . . : No
   WINS Proxy Enabled. . . . . . . . : No
   DNS Suffix Search List. . . . . . : localdomain

Ethernet adapter Ethernet:

   Connection-specific DNS Suffix  . : localdomain
   Description . . . . . . . . . . . : Microsoft Hyper-V Network Adapter
   Physical Address. . . . . . . . . : 00-15-5D-01-80-00
   DHCP Enabled. . . . . . . . . . . : Yes
   Autoconfiguration Enabled . . . . : Yes
   Link-local IPv6 Address . . . . . : fe80::35a2:35c7:3721:90fe%14(Preferred)
   IPv4 Address. . . . . . . . . . . : 192.168.1.101(Preferred)
   Subnet Mask . . . . . . . . . . . : 255.255.255.0
   Lease Obtained. . . . . . . . . . : Thursday, February 4, 2021 7:20:31 PM
   Lease Expires . . . . . . . . . . : Thursday, February 4, 2021 9:20:31 PM
   Default Gateway . . . . . . . . . : fe80::1:1%14
                                       192.168.1.1
   DHCP Server . . . . . . . . . . . : 192.168.1.1
```

DHCP lease information displayed by using the ipconfig /all command.

Automatic Private IP Address Range (169.254.0.0)

If the client computer fails to lease an IP address from the DHCP server for some reason, a reserved IP address will be automatically generated from the Class B range 169.254.0.0/16. This range, known as the **Automatic Private IP Address (APIPA)** range, helps with troubleshooting. The workstation will not have network connectivity. When you use the `i` or `ip addr` commands to verify the address and see this 169.254.0.0/16 setting, you should recognize that the DHCP lease acquisition process failed. That tells you where to begin troubleshooting.

Network Segmentation

Network administrators divide networks into segments. The purpose behind these divisions is usually a combination of security and performance. The segments are identified by different Network ID values in IP addresses.

Segmentation

For example, in a very simple network, an administrator may separate a development environment from a production environment by using segmentation. The development segment is assigned the 192.168.1.0 /24 IP address range, while the production segment is assigned 192.168.2.0 /24. All hosts in the development segment will have IP addresses that begin with 192.168.1.0. Similarly, all hosts in the production environment will have IP addresses that start with 192.168.2.0. These segments are also known as subnets.

In the above diagram, there is no connectivity at all between the two segments. That might be intentional, but the network administrator likely wants some traffic to pass between the two networks. The administrator links the two networks via a **router**. The router has two NICs, each connected to one of the segments.

Each NIC in the router must have an IP address that is local to the segment to which it is connected. By tradition, the NICs are given either the first or the last IP address in the range.

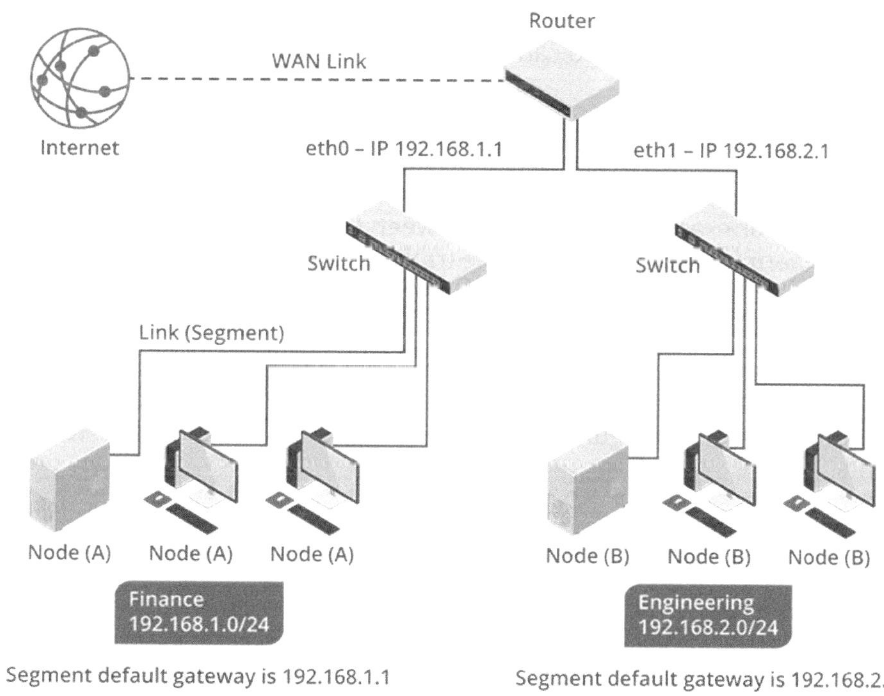

A simple network displaying the router's IP addresses for each NIC. (Images © 123RF.com)

For network traffic to pass from one segment to another, the sending computer directs the traffic to the router. One of the critical IP address configurations is the **default gateway** value. It informs the sending computer of the IP address of the NIC in the router connected to the host's segment of the network. In other words, clients in the 192.168.1.0 development network are configured to use 192.168.1.1 as the default gateway. Similarly, clients in the 192.168.2.0 production network use 192.168.2.1 as the default gateway. The default gateway is the door out of the local network segment and onward to remote segments.

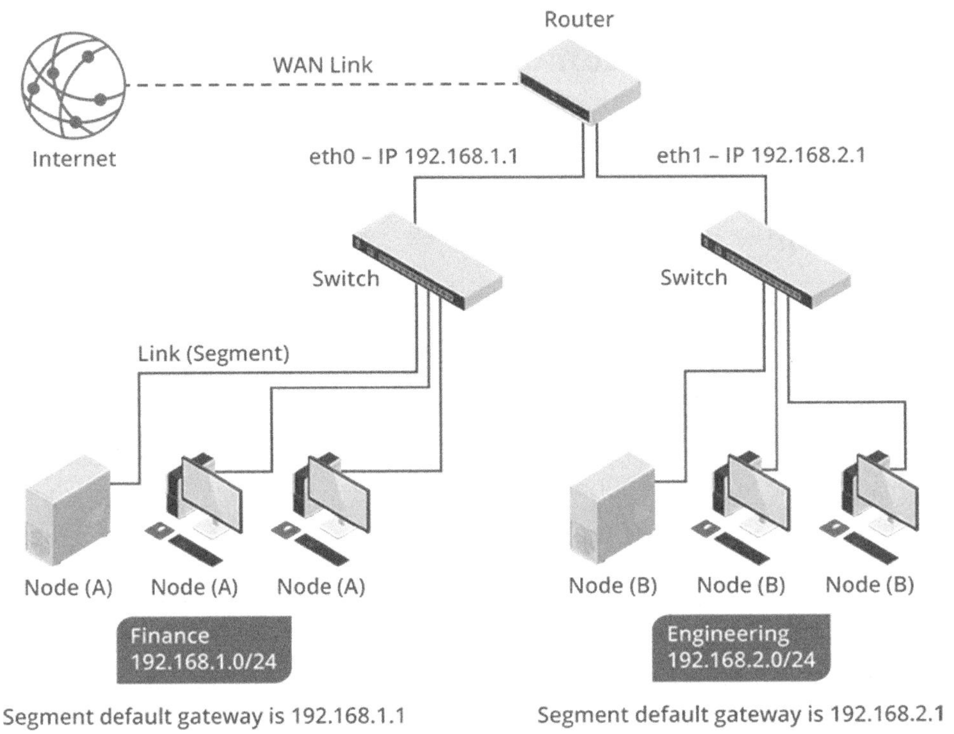

A simple network displaying the network IDs and default gateways. (Images © 123RF.com)

Based on the above figures, you can see how each segment is a subdivision of the network, or a subnet.

If the administrator's goal is to separate development traffic from production traffic, why does the router exist between the two network segments? Part of the router's value is that it can permit specifically designated traffic to flow between the two networks. For example, web traffic between the production and development segments is permitted, while file-sharing traffic is not allowed. By adding the router, the administrator can control what traffic may and may not pass between the segments.

Many environments, even small networks, might have several network segments to help manage and control traffic. The hosts within the segments must have a default gateway value configured for a local router's NIC to send traffic to any other segments.

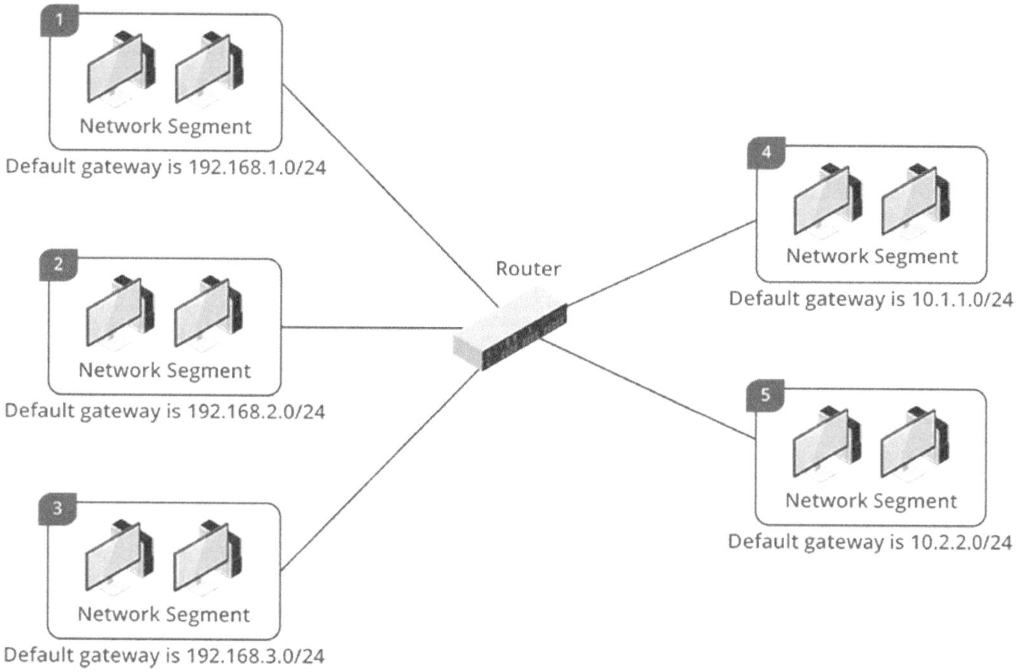

A network with five segments and one router. (Images © 123RF.com)

VLAN

One method of segmenting networks is with routers, as described above. A significant issue is that all of the hosts in the segment must be in fairly close physical proximity to each other. They connect to the same switches, which then connect to the router at the default gateway NIC. This design limits how physically distributed the hosts can be.

A VLAN design allows segmentation on a per-port basis within switches. The result is that hosts on the same logical segment can be physically placed in different areas of the network. Each port in the switch is configured as a member of a particular VLAN, and then that port can only communicate with other ports that are also members of that same VLAN. This configuration can span across multiple switches.

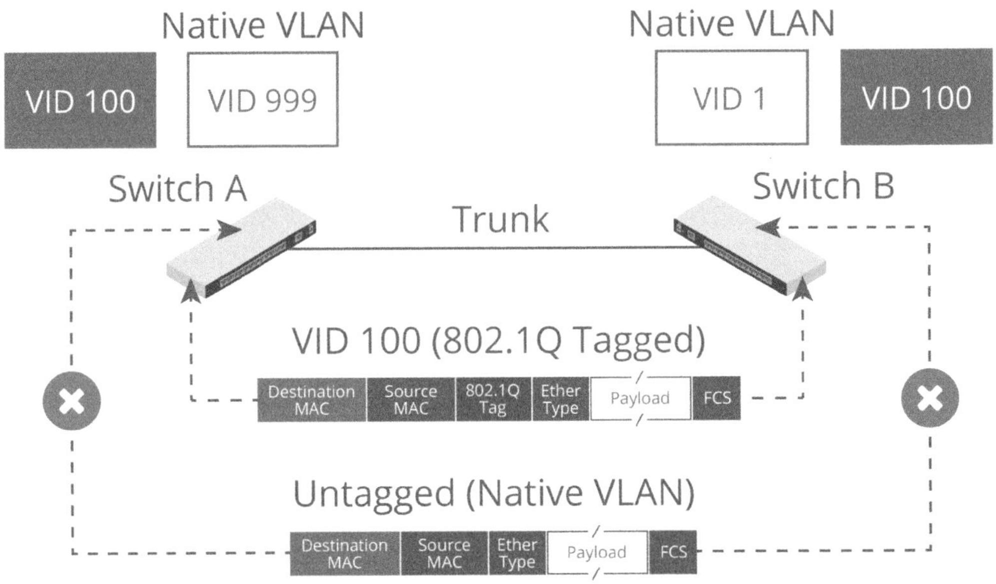

A VLAN with multiple switches. (Images © 123RF.com)

Subnets are divisions of a network based on routers. VLANs are divisions of a network based on switches.

Name Resolution

Humans identify devices by name, such as Sales-Printer-4 or Web-Server7. These names mean nothing to computers. Computers identify network devices by number—by either MAC address or IP address (or both). These numbers are relatively difficult for people to remember or work with.

For example, it's pretty simple to remember that if you want to learn more about CompTIA certifications, you should visit http://www.comptia.org. It is far more challenging to remember that you should visit http://52.165.16.154—the IP address of the www.comptia.org website. Imagine if all of your favorite bookmarked web sites were displayed by IP address rather than by name!

```
[root@localhost ~]# host www.comptia.org
www.comptia.org is an alias for production-comptiawebsite.trafficmanager.net.
production-comptiawebsite.trafficmanager.net is an alias for production-northcentral-www.comptia.org.
production-northcentral-www.comptia.org has address 23.96.239.26
[root@localhost ~]# nslookup 52.165.6.154
** server can't find 154.6.165.52.in-addr.arpa: NXDOMAIN

[root@localhost ~]# █
```

A website URL resolved to an IP address.

So, if you identify network resources by name, and your computers identify resources by number, then there must be a mechanism for relating the two. That mechanism is called name resolution, and there are several methods for accomplishing it.

Fully Qualified Domain Name (FQDN)

Network nodes are configured with a hostname. That name, however, is given context by including a domain name representing the host's location in a hierarchical network. For example, your company might be labeled internal and then labeled with the company name mycompany. So the network name is mycompany.internal. A host computer named computer1 has a **FQDN** of computer1.mycompany.internal.

If this looks familiar, it should. The Internet is organized by using DNS, too.

Hosts Files

The most fundamental approach to name resolution is the use of a text file, stored locally on each computer's HDD. The file contains a list of network resource hostnames and the IP address assigned to each of them. This file is called the hosts file.

An entry in the hosts file has the following syntax:

```
192.168.1.42 dev-server     #Development server
```

```
[root@localhost ~]# cat /etc/hosts
127.0.0.1   localhost localhost.localdomain localhost4 localhost4.localdomain4
::1         localhost localhost.localdomain localhost6 localhost6.localdomain6
192.168.2.200   workstation01 workstation01.localdomain        #User workstation
192.168.2.201   devworkstation devworkstation.localdomain      #Developer workstation
[root@localhost ~]#
```

The /etc/hosts file.

The hash # character indicates a comment. The OS ignores lines that begin with #. Commented lines provide instructions, examples, or other information to anyone that reads the files.

The problem with hosts files is that they are static. If even one network identity changes, either hostname or IP address, the hosts file on every computer in the network must be updated. If you recall from earlier, DHCP client computers do not necessarily keep the same IP address configuration for days or weeks. In older networks, which were typically very small, the hosts files were an acceptable means of providing name resolution. Modern networks are too large and too dynamic for hosts files to be the primary means of name resolution.

It is worth noting, however, that hosts files may still be beneficial in certain circumstances. For example, perhaps a developer is working on a project on an isolated server. No one else needs to access the server, and because it's in development, it is not yet registered on the network as a findable device. An entry for the name and IP address of the isolated server can be placed in the local hosts file on the developer's workstation. It is convenient for the developer, who can reference the server by name, but there is no reference to the server for the rest of the network.

OS	Path
Windows Server	C:\Windows\System32\drivers\etc\hosts
Linux	/etc/hosts

The location of the hosts file on Windows Server and Linux.

DNS

Typically, hosts files are not practical for name resolution in modern networks. A more dynamic, robust, and flexible system is used. The **Domain Name System** provides name resolution on the Internet and internal networks.

On internal networks, one or more DNS servers host a database identified by the company's network name. In the above example, the network name was mycompany.internal. The DNS database contains entries for each identity on the mycompany.internal network. The entries include the node's hostname and IP address. A network with 1,000 nodes has at least 1,000 entries in the DNS database, one for each node.

(same as parent folder)	Host (A)	192.168.0.102	30/12/2017
99servera	Host (A)	192.168.0.188	static
FileServer1	Host (A)	192.168.0.178	static
MailServer1	Mail Exchanger (MX)	[10] serverb99.widgets.co...	static
MailServer2	Mail Exchanger (MX)	[10] servera99.widgets.co...	static
ServerA99	Host (A)	192.168.0.12	static
serverb99	Host (A)	192.168.0.102	static
ServerC99	Host (A)	192.168.0.34	static
TestServer	IPv6 Host (AAAA)	2001:0001:3dfe:0001:0000:...	static
www	Alias (CNAME)	serverc99.widgets.com.	static

The DNS records on a Windows Server DNS server. (Screenshot courtesy of Microsoft.)

Most networks have at least two DNS servers that are replicas of each other for fault tolerance. DNS is an essential network service. If one internal host attempts to connect to another by name, DNS is used to resolve the name to an IP address.

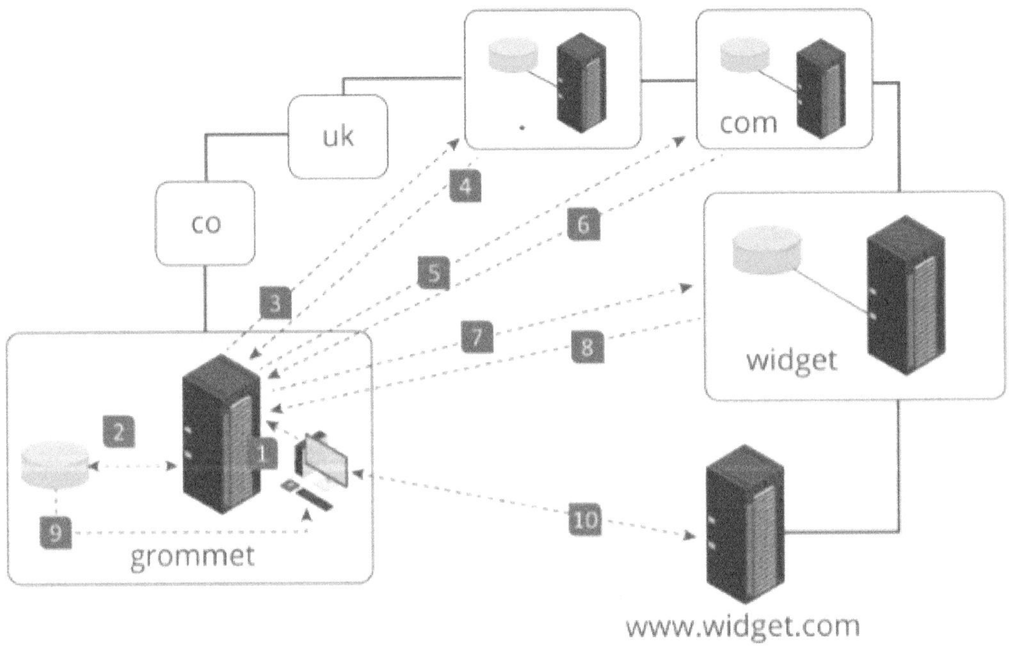

Example of a client computer querying DNS to resolve the IP address for a destination server identified by name. (Images © 123RF.com)

Network Devices

As a systems administrator, you must be able to recognize and understand the network devices your servers are attached to. The following table displays some fundamental information about several common network devices.

Device	OSI Model Layer	Function
Switch	Layer 2	Physical connectivity, concentrator
Router	Layer 3	Logical connectivity between segments
Wireless Access Point	Layer 1 and 2	Wireless connectivity, bridges wired/wireless networks

Network devices and their related OSI model layers.

Firewalls and Port Numbers

Firewalls often use IP protocol information to filter traffic. Packet filtering firewalls decide whether to pass traffic based on data contained in the packet header, specifically the source IP address, the destination IP address, and the port number.

Firewalls are a good example of why you should recognize standard port numbers as an administrator. Log files, for example, might indicate that packets destined for port 443 are filtered out. That means HTTPS connections are denied, which is useful troubleshooting information.

Guidelines for Configuring Network Settings

- Know the seven layers of the OSI model.
- Know the four layers of the TCP/IP stack.
- Recognize common port numbers.
- Nodes have three identities: MAC address, IP address, and hostname.
- The network identity in an IPv4 address identifies what part of a network the node is in.
- The host identity in an IPv4 address identifies the host in the network.
- The subnet mask is used to calculate which part of the IPv4 address is the network identity and which part is the host identity.
- Recognize the three reserved IP address ranges.
- The IPv4 loopback address is 127.0.0.1.
- The IPv4 APIPA address is 169.254.x.x.
- Clients lease IP address configurations from a DHCP server.
- The four steps of the DHCP lease generation process are Discover, Offer, Request, and Acknowledge.
- The default gateway is the IP address of the router in your part of the network.
- VLANs make it easier for administrators to associate nodes with similar network requirements without the devices being in close physical proximity to each other.
- Name resolution is relating an easy-to-remember name with a difficult-to-remember IP address.

Review Activity:

Network Settings

Answer the following questions:

1. **What are the seven layers of the OSI model?**

2. **What are the four layers of the TCP/IP stack?**

3. **List the Class A, B, and C reserved IP address ranges:**

4. **List the loopback address and the Automatic Private IP Address range:**

5. **What are the three identities a network node has?**

6. **What are two reasons a network administrator segments a network?**

7. **What is the purpose of name resolution?**

Topic 7D

Use Scripts to Configure Servers

EXAM OBJECTIVES COVERED
2.1 Given a scenario, install server operating systems
2.6 Summarize scripting basics for server administration

Scripting provides fast, consistent, and automated configurations or reporting. Scripts are useful for tasks that repeat frequently. There are several scripting languages to be aware of, including Windows PowerShell and bash.

What are scripts?

Scripts are text files containing one or more system commands and various system calls used to automate and simplify administrative tasks.

Basic script utilization:

1. The administrator writes commands into a text file.
2. The text file is given the executable permission so that the system processes the file rather than reading it.
3. The administrator executes the script manually or schedules it to be executed automatically by the system.
4. The system reads and follows the commands contained in the script.
5. The script completes.

Advantages of Scripts

First, scripts are consistent. Let's say that you need to back up a directory, and the process of doing so takes five steps. Normally, you would manually execute each step. But what if you were interrupted and forgot a step? Or repeated a step? What are the chances that you might make a typographical error in one of the steps? With a script, you carefully write each of the five steps into the script and double check your syntax and spelling, and you can be confident that the script executes the same five steps the same way, every time.

Second, scripts are fast. The five-step script described above executes much more quickly than you can manually type the five commands. While a task requiring five steps may not seem like much, many scripts are much larger, and the increased efficiency is very apparent.

Third, scripts can be scheduled. One commonly scripted task for administrators is data backup. Backups often run in the middle of the night, when files are not likely to be open or in use. You do not want to have to manually execute the script at 2 am every night. Instead, a utility such as cron (Linux) or Task Scheduler (Windows) is configured to automatically run the script at whatever time you wish.

Fourth, scripts can accomplish different tasks based on user input or discovered results. Initially, scripts are simple, but their functionality can be significantly extended by using variables, constructs, and data types. For example, a basic script might check a directory. If the directory is empty, the script deletes the directory. If the directory contains files, the script backs up the directory. The script adapts its functionality based on whether the directory has contents.

Shell Languages

Scripts are written using a shell language. The shell is the server's command-line environment. The default shell for Linux is **bash**. Windows has two shells: cmd.exe and **PowerShell**, although Microsoft emphasizes PowerShell. As a general rule, a script written for one shell, such as PowerShell, will not be understood by another shell, such as bash. The system must have the appropriate shell installed to process the script.

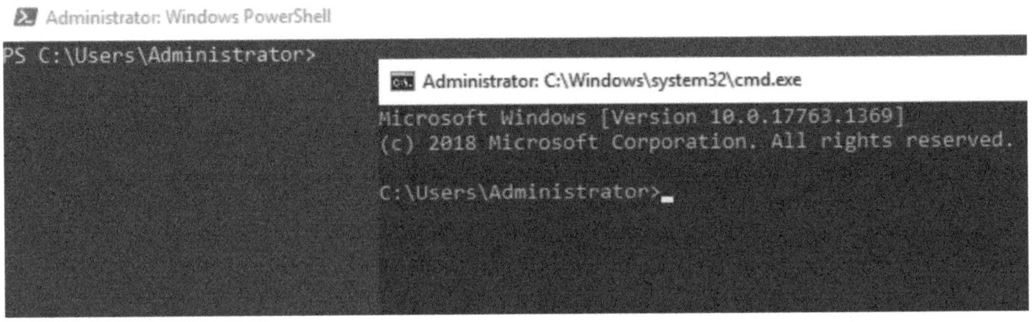

PowerShell/cmd.exe. (Screenshot courtesy of Microsoft.)

Types of scripts:

- Batch file—a series of commands, usually based on MS-DOS, that execute with limited additional functionality.
- Bash script—a script written in bash language that contains commands, variables, constructs, and other components. Bash scripts are almost always written for Linux systems.
- PowerShell script—a script written in the PowerShell language that contains cmdlets (PowerShell commands), variables, constructs, and other components. PowerShell scripts are almost always written for Windows systems.
- **VBS** script—a script written in the VBScript language. Microsoft has deprecated VBScript, but there have been many VBScript scripts written over the years. VBScript scripts are almost always written for Windows systems.

Comment Syntax

Before you examine scripts in any further detail, it is useful to understand comment fields. As noted above, the system reads a script and process the commands it finds. The system does not read commented lines. These lines provide guidance, example configurations, and other information that the system doesn't need but the script user might. Comment lines are delineated by using the hash character, or #.

```
#!/bin/bash

# This script displays the string "Hello World" on the screen.
echo "Hello World"
```

Script with commented lines.

It is a good practice to use comments extensively when creating your scripts.

Remember that you may not be the only user of the script over the years of its existence. Scripts are often shared over the Internet and among sysadmins, so comments provide information to other users.

Environment Variables

Variables are stored values. These values are not necessarily permanent, and they may change depending on the system, who is logged in, the current date and time, or other factors. There are two types of variables: shell and environment. Shell variables are specific to a single instance of the shell. Environment variables are systemwide.

Variable	Value
$HOSTNAME	The system's hostname
$USER	The currently logged-in user
$HOME	The current user's home directory

Bash shell environment variables.

```
[admin@localhost ~]$ echo $HOSTNAME
Fedora
[admin@localhost ~]$ echo $USER
admin
[admin@localhost ~]$ echo $HOME
/home/admin
[admin@localhost ~]$ _
```

Displaying variables.

Scripts can call or reference these variables. For example, a script might be written that backs up the current user's home directory. By identifying the current user by a variable, rather than by the specific username, the script will work for any logged-in user.

Basic Script Constructs

Scripts are capable of specific tasks, depending on what additional information is provided to them. Constructs provide this additional information.

These constructs include the following:

- Loops
- Conditionals
- Comparators

Loops

Loops are repeating sections of code. In bash, there are four different types of loops:

Loops	Example
For	The script repeats a specific number of times.
While	The script repeats as long as the criteria is true.
Until	The script repeats as long as the criteria is false.
Select	The script prompts the user for a duration value.

Types of loops.

Conditionals

Conditionals evaluate whether a particular statement is true or not, and then the script processes differently depending on that result. "If" and "else" are two examples of conditionals.

Conditional	Example
if	The block of code following the if statement processes if the statement is true.
else	The block of code following the else statement processes if the statement is false.

Types of conditionals.

Comparators

Comparison operators (sometimes called comparators) compare values. Scripts can use these operators to filter or differentiate data.

Comparator	Example
-eq	Equal to
-ne	Not equal to
-gt	Greater than
-ge	Greater than or equal to
-lt	Less than
-le	Less than or equal to

Types of comparators.

Functions

Functions are discrete sections of code within a script. The code section is named and can be called later in the script. For example, a script may create several user accounts. A function is placed at the start of the script that lists all of the various commands necessary to create and configure user accounts.

Basic Data Types

The basic data types include integers, strings, and arrays

Integers

Integers are whole numbers (not fractions or numbers that contain decimal points). These values are entered into a script so that comparisons or arithmetic processes can use them. For example, in a bash script, you could type a line reading echo $((2 + 2)), and bash would sum the two values and display a total of 4. The numbers involved in this example, 2 and 4, are integers.

```
[admin@localhost ~]$ echo $((2+2))
4
[admin@localhost ~]$ 
```

echo $((2+2)) value is summed and displayed.

Strings

A **string** is a combination of one or more alphanumeric characters. These characters may have a discrete meaning, such as a name, or a numerical value, such as a quantity. Strings are useful for searches, for example. A portion of your script might include a search for any file containing the string "sept" to discover files that reference the month September.

Arrays

An **array** is a list of values that can be referenced in the script. Usually, the values are all of the same type. Arrays simplify the storage and retrieval of values in situations where the values cannot be stored as variables due to the quantity. For example, if you needed to store 100 computer names, you could create a variable representing each computer name. However, it would be more efficient to create a single array that references all 100 names

Server Administration Scripting Tasks

There are many, many uses for scripts. Scripts may run during the startup or the shutdown of servers, at user login, or manually to complete administrative tasks.

Login and Logout Scripts

Some scripts execute based on the user. For example, a login script runs when a user logs in. The script customizes the user's environment, maps network drives, and automatically launches a particular application. Logout scripts execute when the user signs off. These scripts might delete temp files or copy the user's data to a network server.

Startup and Shutdown Scripts

These scripts execute based on the computer. When the computer starts, a startup script runs. The script checks for updates to programs or implements a particular security configuration. Shutdown scripts execute during the shutdown process. These scripts might copy data to a network server, for example.

Account Management Scripts

Administrators may need to create multiple user accounts, as well as custom files and directories. Scripting automates this process. Imagine that you are a sysadmin for an educational institution, and you need to prepare a lab environment for twenty students. Each of the twenty computers in the lab needs to have the same ten user accounts, groups, and lab directories installed. You could automate this process with a script that ensures efficiency and consistency.

Service Scripts

Administrators may write simple scripts to manage multiple services simultaneously. In the course of troubleshooting, for example, you may need to restart five different related services. You could create a script to restart each one, and you would only need to issue one command (the script name) to initiate the process.

Bootstrap Scripts

Bootstrap Protocol is a framework for quickly creating web pages in a scripted manner. It is used with HTML, pre-written JavaScript, and linking to content delivery networks.

Guidelines for Using Scripts to Configure Servers

Scripts enable the automation of frequent tasks. Scripts execute the tasks consistently and may be scheduled. Scripts are very flexible and powerful.

- Use scripts for repetitive tasks.
- Schedule scripts to run jobs during non-business hours.
- Scripts are written in a scripting language that the server must recognize.
- PowerShell scripts are primarily used with Windows.
- Bash scripts are primarily used with Linux.
- Use comment lines to provide instructions, notes, and examples.
- Comment lines begin with the # character and are ignored by the system.

Review Activity:

Configure Servers with Scripts

Answer the following questions:

1. **What is the difference between a for loop and a while loop?**

2. **Why are comments important in scripts?**

3. **You are configuring a server in a lab environment and need a script that clears user-specific information, such as temp files and downloaded files, after students ends their session. What kind of script would you write?**

Lesson 7

Summary

There are many deployment options for modern servers: manual versus automated, bare metal versus virtualized, manual versus scripted configurations, etc. Once the OC is deployed, storage and network configurations must be set. The deployment of services and data to the server may be automated through scripting. Windows Servers usually rely on Windows PowerShell scripts, and Linux servers usually rely on bash scripts.

1. **What advantages do automated deployments have over manual deployments?**

2. **What types of network configurations must be set on the server?**

Lesson 8

Troubleshooting OS, Application, and Network Configurations

LESSON INTRODUCTION

One of the most important steps in troubleshooting is determining whether a problem exists at the OS, application, or network layer. Troubleshooting methodology, and even responsibility, varies depending on which layer the problem resides in. In this section, you will examine OS and applications issues in the first section. Network issues are covered in the second section.

Lesson Objectives

In this lesson, you will:

- Troubleshoot an OS and applications.
- Troubleshoot network configurations.

Topic 8A

Troubleshoot an OS and Applications

EXAM OBJECTIVES COVERED
4.4 Given a scenario, troubleshoot common OS and software problems

Many factors may cause OS and application issues. How you begin troubleshooting depends on the symptoms of the problem. In this section, some common issues and causes are categorized for you. The first category is hardware issues that might become apparent through OS or application failures. The second category is OS misconfigurations or incompatibilities. Next, you view application problems and general misconfigurations. Another category is OS and application patching. Logon problems have their own category, and the section concludes with a discussion of user error.

General Categories

Help desk tickets may arise due to hardware, OS, applications, or networking failures or misconfigurations. In this section, you will examine various symptoms for each category.

Hardware

When **troubleshooting** OS and application issues, you may be dealing with a hardware failure. Corrupted files, failed network connectivity, unaligned system clocks, and other items could be indicators of hardware issues.

When troubleshooting servers, it may be valuable to determine whether the OS officially supports the components installed in the server. If it does not, then that may explain why the system is not working as expected. Earlier, you learned about the HCL at Red Hat Linux's web site and the Windows Server Catalog provided by Microsoft. Both tools can help you determine system compatibility.

OS

Once you're confident that you're not dealing with a hardware problem, the next layer to consider is the OS. These problems could include misconfigurations or incompatibilities. Windows stores its configurations in the system registry. Linux stores its settings in configuration files located in the /etc directory.

Applications

You may immediately recognize that you're troubleshooting an application problem. These problems could include incompatibilities with the hosting OS, hardware, or poorly written applications.

General Misconfigurations

Some configurations are not easily categorized as OS or application problems. These problems might include issues with log files, application permissions, or service management.

Patching

Operating systems and applications each need to be patched and managed throughout their lifecycles. Over time, bugs may be revealed or new features enabled. Vendors provide patches and other updates to address these concerns. Patch management, especially at the server level, is essential to stability and security.

User Error

Some issues might initially be diagnosed as OS or application problems when they are actually user error. When troubleshooting, don't forget to verify that the user interacts correctly with the OS and the applications. One of the best ways to do this is to ask the user to show you what they were doing when the problem occurred.

Common Problems

The following table provides an easy reference for several common categories of problems and possible causes.

Common Problem	Common Causes
Unable to log on	Server not joined to domain Clock skew User error
Unable to access resources or files	Incompatible drivers/modules Unstable drivers or software Server not joined to domain Inappropriate application-level permissions
System file corruption	Incompatible drivers/modules Improperly applied patches Missing or failed patches Missing dependencies Memory leak Buffer overrun Missing updates
End of life	Incompatibility due to dependencies or version control
Slow performance	Incompatible or missing drivers/modules Improperly applied or failed patches Memory leaks Buffer overrun Improper CPU affinity/priority
Cannot write to system logs	Inappropriate application-level permissions Architecture Server not joined to domain
Service failures	Missing dependencies Insecure dependencies Missing updates
System or application hanging or freezing	Incompatible drivers/modules Improperly applied patches Downstream failure due to updates
Cannot install OS or applications	Incompatible architecture
Patch update failure	Improperly applied patches Incompatible architecture Missing dependencies Insecure dependencies

Privilege Escalation

Recall that it is a security best practice NOT to sign on to the server with administrative credentials. Sometimes, it's necessary. The majority of the time, however, you should sign on as a non-privileged user and elevate your privileges when necessary.

Suppose you have been assigned to create a new user account and configure a profile on a Linux workstation for new developer. You need to have root administrative privileges to create these resources.

Privileged Account	Description
root	Linux local administrative account
Administrator	Windows local administrative account
Domain Administrator	Microsoft Active Directory administrative account

```
[root@localhost ~]# whoami
root
[root@localhost ~]# 
```

Linux root user.

Privilege Escalation in Windows

In the Windows GUI, you can right-click on an application and select the "Run As" option to run the program with different privileges. Depending on the application, you may need to hold down the Shift key to select a user other than the Administrator.

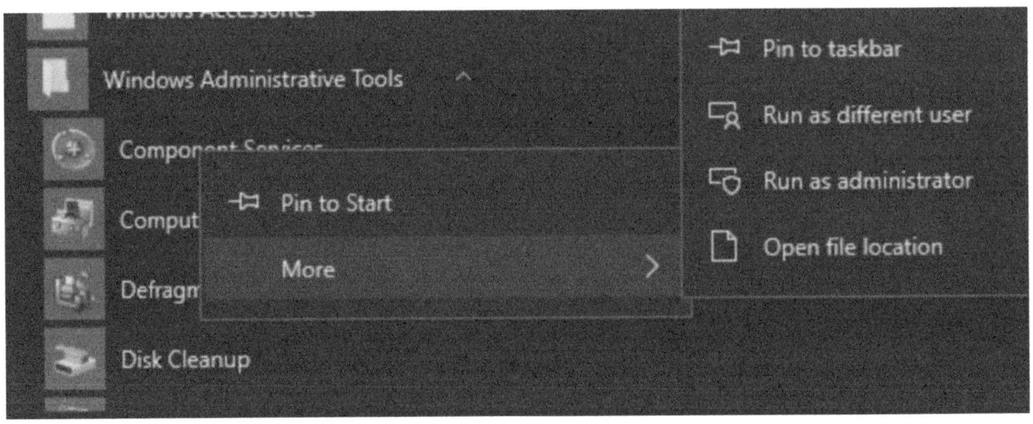

The Windows Runas graphical interface. (Screenshot courtesy of Microsoft.)

At the Windows CLI, use the "runas" command to execute a command or script as a different user.

```
C:\Users\Administrator>runas /user:administrator cmd.exe
Enter the password for administrator: _
```

The Windows runas CLI.

Privilege Escalation in Linux

There are two ways to elevating privileges in Linux. The first is to actually change your login credentials. The other is to exercise rights that were explicitly delegated to your standard account by the root user.

The su ("switch user") command allows you to change your credentials and environment to those of another user without signing out of the current user account. In daily practice, you would log on to your Linux server as a standard user. If you need to run a command that requires administrative privileges, you "switch" to the root user, execute the command, and then switch back to your standard user account.

```
[root@localhost ~]# su - devuser
[devuser@localhost ~]$ █
```

Root user switches to the devuser by using the su command.

There are two ways of using su:

```
su root
```

Switch to root user in the original standard user's environment (preferences, variables, etc.).

```
su - root
```

Switch to the root user in the root user's environment (preferences, variables, etc.). Observe that there is a space on either side of the dash.

> *If you merely execute su without specifying a user account, the system assumes you want to switch to the root user account. This shortcut saves a bit of typing. You can use this trick with the su - form of the command as well.*

The second way to change Linux privileges is for the root user to delegate privileges to a user account or group specifically, by editing the /etc/sudoers file. The file permits an administrator to identify one or more specific commands and then identify particular users and groups that may execute them.

For example, you could delegate the ability to run a script that normally requires root privileges to a standard user. If you give the user the root password so that they can use su, then they can sign on as root and do anything. It is better to delegate only the execution of that one particular script by using the /etc/sudoers file. They can then accomplish that one task as root, but no other.

To exercise their delegation, the user precedes the command with sudo. They may or may not be challenged for their password, depending on how the administrator has configured sudo.

```
[admin@localhost ~]$ useradd testuser
useradd: Permission denied.
useradd: cannot lock /etc/passwd; try again later.
[admin@localhost ~]$ sudo useradd testuser

We trust you have received the usual lecture from the local System
Administrator. It usually boils down to these three things:

    #1) Respect the privacy of others.
    #2) Think before you type.
    #3) With great power comes great responsibility.

[sudo] password for admin:
[admin@localhost ~]$ █
```

Using the sudo command in Linux.

You can use su to switch your identity to any user, whether that user has higher privileges or not. This identity change might be handy for testing whether specific users can execute certain commands.

Services

Services are long-running applications that usually provide the main functionality of the server. For example, services might include web site hosting, email services, file storage, and network printing.

Services may hang or stall. When this occurs, they often just need to be restarted. Novice admins are tempted to restart the entire server, but if you can diagnose which service is experiencing issues, it is usually better to only restart the service. Doing so acts as a kind of reset for the service.

Restarting a server is downtime, which is frowned upon. If possible, it's better just to restart a service than the entire box.

Restarting services is particularly important in Linux, which holds most service configurations in text files. When the service starts up, it reads the text file for its configuration instructions. If you later edit the text file to change the service's configuration, you must restart the service to force it to reread the configuration file and therefore receive the new configuration changes.

Starting and stopping services is also a useful part of system configuration. Your server does not necessarily need all of the services that are installed on it.

Manage Windows Services

You can use the Services console in Windows to manage services. You can verify the status of the service in this console and change its startup options.

Startup Option	Description
Automatic	Service starts when the server boots.
Manual	Service starts when it is needed.
Disabled	Service does not start when the server boots.

Windows Services can be configured to start (or not start) when the system boots.

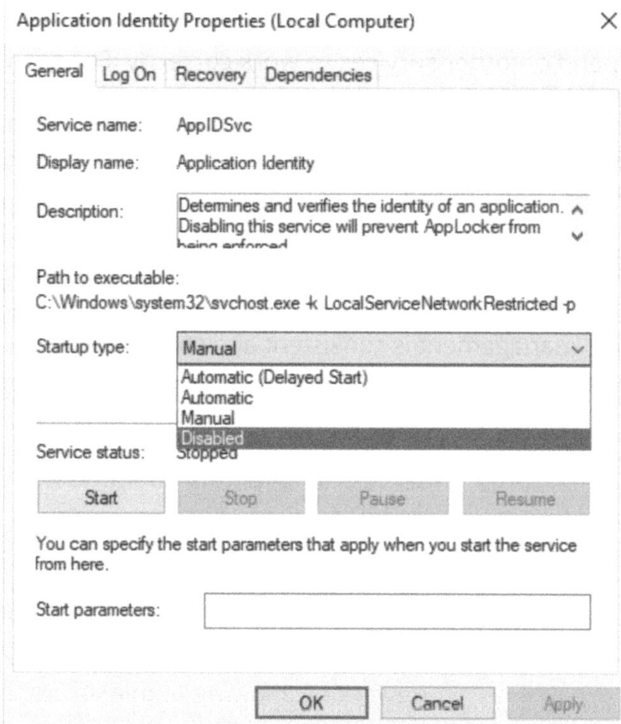

Configuring a Windows Service startup option. (Screenshot courtesy of Microsoft.)

Manage Linux Services

The current standard for managing services in Linux is the systemd mechanism. You can use the systemctl command to stop, start, restart, enable, and disable services. You can also check the status of a service using systemctl.

The following command displays syntax to manage Linux services:

```
systemctl restart firewalld
systemctl status sshd
```

Starting a service and checking its status in Linux.

Service Dependencies

Some services depend on other services to work correctly. For example, a Windows Server hosting the AD Domain Controller role (**domain controller**) runs the AD Domain Service (ADDS). That service depends on the DNS service (among others). If you restart the DNS service to correct a DNS configuration problem, the ADDS will also restart due to the dependency.

Common Categories

There are many ways to manage workstation and server configurations. The primary goal of configuration management is consistent and straightforward OS management.

Tool	Description
System Center Configuration Manager (SCCM)	Installs an agent on Windows workstations and servers to inventory, identify, and then manage systems
Microsoft Group Policy	Configures Windows workstations and servers with several thousand settings to manage security, software, services, and devices
Puppet	Open-source tool to manage Linux and Windows devices by allowing administrators to declare a desired configuration, which Puppet then causes the systems to match
Chef	Delivers a desired configuration to devices and then sets them to match the configuration
Ansible	Defines configurations in playbooks that are delivered to and processed by workstations and servers

Orchestration tools to manage configurations.

Configuration management tools are widely used in cloud and on-premises environments.

Configure the Firewall

Firewalls

Modern OSs, such as Windows Server, the various Linux distributions, and Apple macOS, use software firewalls to control network traffic flow in and out of the system. These host-based firewalls serve a different purpose than the perimeter firewalls between your internal network and the Internet. Host-based firewalls protect just the system where they are installed.

Host-based firewalls use zones to define different configurations. For example, your Windows firewall might be configured differently in the trusted Domain zone than the untrusted Public zone. If your Windows computer is on the business network, the Domain zone is used. If you're in a coffee shop, then the Public zone, with stricter rules, is used.

Windows usually configures the firewall automatically when you add a new network service or application. If it is not, access the Windows Firewall console and add the service by using either its name or port number. Adding services to the firewall by port number is particularly common if you are dealing with a network application that was developed internally by your organization.

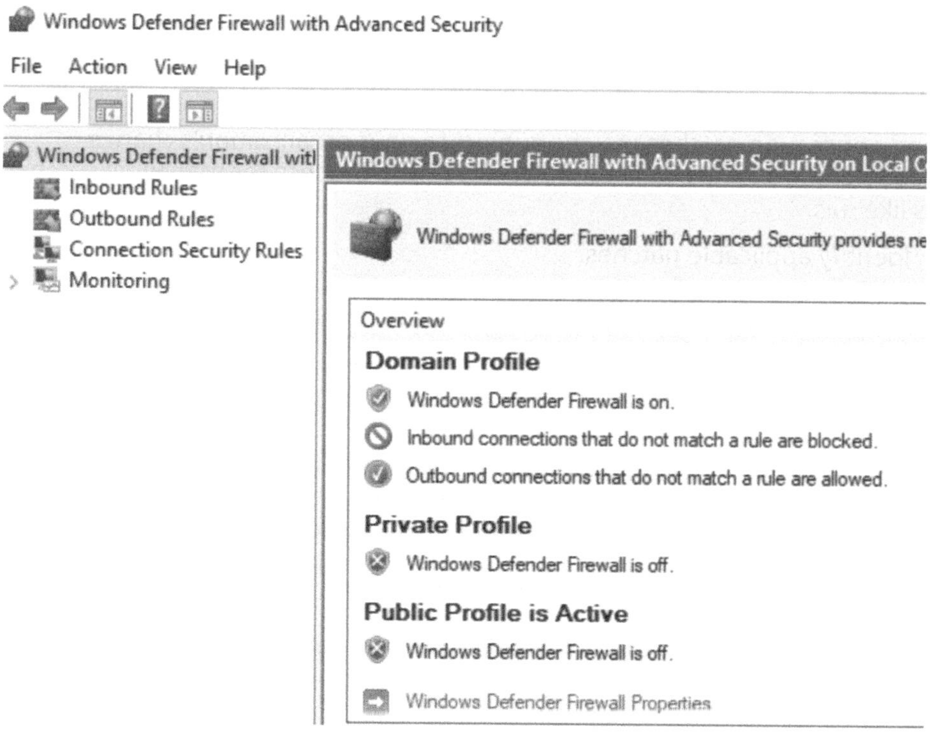

The Windows Firewall console. (Screenshot courtesy of Microsoft.)

The Linux firewall may also be manually configured to permit or deny specific traffic. You can identify that traffic by name or by port number, as well.

```
[root@localhost ~]# firewall-cmd --zone=public --add-service=http
success
[root@localhost ~]# firewall-cmd --list-all --zone=public
public
  target: default
  icmp-block-inversion: no
  interfaces:
  sources:
  services: dhcpv6-client ftp http mdns ssh
  ports:
  protocols:
  masquerade: no
  forward-ports:
  source-ports:
  icmp-blocks:
  rich rules:
[root@localhost ~]#
```

Add the http service to the Linux firewall.

Manage Patches

Patching

OS and application patches may be subject to your organization's change management processes. In general, however, the process for managing patches looks like this:

1. Identify applicable patches.
2. Download and deploy patches to test systems.
3. Verify functionality of test systems.
4. Deploy patches to destination systems.

Patch management may be automated. For example, Microsoft provides a free online service for updating the OS and many Microsoft applications. In most business settings, administrators configure a Windows Server Update Service (WSUS) server to manage the patching process, including approval, staged deployments, and reporting.

In some cases, it is possible to uninstall or remove the patch. If that's not possible, it may be necessary to roll the system back to a restore point before the patch was applied.

Starting in 2003, Microsoft established the second Tuesday of the month as the predictable release date for patches. Zero-day fixes and other services, such as anti-malware updates, are more frequent.

Scheduled Reboots

You may wish to schedule server reboots regularly. Doing so may free up memory from poorly written applications or kill processes that did not shut down correctly.

Consider adding scheduled reboots to your patch management process. Most patches require that the system be rebooted to complete anyway.

Manage Software Packages

Software applications may be delivered as executable installers or as packages. Packages contain everything needed to deploy the application: metadata, executables, scripts, application descriptors, etc. Package managers install, update, uninstall, and inventory software on the system.

The Microsoft Installer Service manages .msi packages. Linux distributions derived from Red Hat Linux use the Red Hat Package Manager (RPM) or the Yellowdog Updater Modified (YUM) package managers. Debian Linux-derived distributions use dpkg or Advanced Package Tool (APT) to manage software.

The use of different package managers is one of the main differentiators between two of the splits in the Linux family of distributions. Those distributions derived from Red Hat use RPM-based management, while those derived from Debian use dpkg-based package management.

The following commands can be used on a Red Hat-derived Linux server to manage software:

To install software:

```
rpm -ivh software.rpm
```

To remove software:

```
rpm -evh software.rpm
```

To redirect a list all installed packages to a file named sw-inventory.txt:

```
rpm -qa > sw-inventory.txt
```

To display information on installed Apache web server software:

```
rpm -qi apache
```

```
[root@localhost ~]# rpm -ivh nmap-7.91-1.x86_64.rpm
Verifying...                          ################################# [100%]
Preparing...                          ################################# [100%]
Updating / installing...
   1:nmap-2:7.91-1                    ################################# [100%]
[root@localhost ~]#
```

Use the rpm command to install a software package on Linux.

Red Hat-derived distributions use software packages with a .rpm file extension.

The YUM package manager can also be used on Red Hat–derived distributions.

To redirect a list of all installed packages to a file named software.txt:

```
yum list installed > software.txt
```

The following commands can be used on a Debian-derived Linux server to manage software:

To install software:

```
apt install software-package
```

To uninstall software:

```
apt remove software-package
```

To display all installed packages:

```
apt list --installed
```

Debian-derived distributions use software packages with a .deb file extension.

Check the Windows Applications and Features console for installed software. Software, roles, and features may be displayed in multiple places.

Manage Time Services

As noted earlier, a small battery on the motherboard powers the clock. It may eventually fail. If that happens, the system time will not be accurate. Servers (and workstations) usually synchronize their time from a central network source, however, to ensure that they all agree on exactly what the current time is.

Time agreement is essential in a network environment. Some services, such as the **Kerberos** authentication service, use timestamps to ensure that authentication attempts are legitimate. Other network tasks, like scheduled backups or reboots, need to be carefully managed to ensure availability.

The **Network Time Protocol (NTP)** manages time synchronization. NTP uses a client/server model that designates a time source for all other systems in the network agree to use. That time source synchronizes its time with external time services.

```
[root@localhost ~]# cat /etc/chrony.conf
# Use public servers from the pool.ntp.org project.
# Please consider joining the pool (https://www.pool.ntp.org/join.html).
pool 2.fedora.pool.ntp.org iburst
```

The Linux NTP /etc/chrony.conf configuration file.

Configure Recovery

OS recovery options are essential if a patch or other configuration change renders the server nonfunctional.

Windows Server includes Safe Mode to boot the server with nothing but the essential OS components. It bypasses device drivers and services to give you access to the bare-bones system.

For example, what if you deployed a new device driver for your server's video card, but you accidentally installed the incorrect driver? Now when the system boots, the GUI interface fails to appear, so you cannot reverse your changes. You would boot into Safe Mode, which does not load the third-party video driver, and configure the system with a different driver.

Safe Mode is also used for performing virus scans.

The Linux single-user mode is similar to Safe Mode. It loads the OS with minimal drivers and services, and it permits only the root user account to authenticate. The root user corrects the misconfigurations that caused startup problems on the server.

Reload the OS

In some cases, you have no option but to reload or reinstall the OS. This task tends to be cumbersome. You may have an automated method for installing OSs, such as imaging. You may also have automated systems for configuring the server, such as Group Policy, Ansible, or Chef. Finally, you might also use automated patch management. Even with all of this automation, the process of rebuilding a server can be very time consuming. You also need to restore any user data that was stored on the server.

While reloading the OS, reconfiguring it, and restoring user data might be necessary and reliable, it should not be your first choice in most instances.

The reload process:

1. Wipe old OS
2. Deploy new OS
3. Install applications
4. Install patches
5. Manage configurations
6. Restore user data
7. Test
8. Return to service

Snapshots

Snapshots are a copy of a system's configuration at a given point in time. The system can later be reverted to that documented configuration, often reversing changes that might have occurred.

Windows snapshots may be scheduled, taken by the OS before significant configuration changes, or manually recorded before an administrator alters settings on the server.

Virtualization software can also take snapshots of VMs, allowing you to roll a VM back to an earlier state.

Review Activity:

OS and Applications

Answer the following questions:

1. **List the six general troubleshooting categories:**

2. **What are some possible reasons a user is not able to access resources or files?**

3. **What are the administrator-level accounts for Linux, local Windows administration, and Microsoft AD administration?**

4. **What tools or commands are used in Linux and Windows to elevate privileges?**

5. **List the common Linux package managers:**

6. **What is the Windows package manager?**

Topic 8B

Troubleshoot Network Configurations

EXAM OBJECTIVES COVERED
4.5 Given a scenario, troubleshoot network connectivity issues

Network troubleshooting varies significantly from troubleshooting server OS and application issues. First, there are far more variables. Second, as a systems administrator, you may not have access to all of the network resources and nodes.

Some IT departments have a very defined split between the role of the systems administrator (server administration) and network administrator (network administration). If that's the case, then you, as a sysadmin, may have to pass off some troubleshooting to members of the network administrator's groups.

Begin troubleshooting by determining whether the issue is internal or external. Internal problems are wholly encompassed inside your network. You have an internal client machine using the internal network to access an internal server. External issues usually involve issues accessing the Internet.

External Issues

You may find that your client computers and servers have trouble accessing Internet resources. Perhaps users cannot browse web pages or send/receive email. Even more troublesome, they cannot access cloud-based resources. With the prevalence of cloud computing, a great many resources that users need must be accessible over the Internet. Many organizations host some or all of their internal services in the cloud. The Internet connection is the pipe used to access those resources.

Recall that the service provider may have issues, including cable failure or other outages.

Common problem	Common causes
No Internet connectivity	Improper IP configuration Component failures Firewall misconfiguration DNS failure Misconfigured edge router Failure of service provider Bad cables

External network problems.

Internal Issues

Troubleshooting internal network issues may be a little easier, since your organization has direct control of the environment. Troubleshooting involves ensuring that physical connectivity is available, client and server configurations are correct, switch and router settings are correct, and IP addressing and name resolution are working.

Common problems	Common causes
Resource unavailable	Improper IPv4 or IPv6 configuration due to a DHCP misconfiguration or failure Improper IPv4 or IPv6 configuration due to a static IP assignment mistake VLAN misconfiguration Network port security misconfigured at the switch Cable failure Firewall misconfiguration NIC misconfiguration DNS failure DNS/hosts file misconfiguration
Receiving incorrect or no DHCP information	DHCP service failure or disabled DHCP service misconfiguration DHCP server out of IP addresses DHCP server not authorized in Active Directory DHCP server on the other side of router from clients
Ping failures	"Destination host unreachable" is usually a misconfiguration of the ping sender. "Unknown host" may be a name resolution issue "Timeout" is usually a misconfiguration of the ping destination.
Unable to reach remote subnets	Router misconfigured OS route tables misconfigured Router failure
Failed name resolution	Improper IPv4 or IPv6 configuration Misconfigured or failed DNS Misconfigured hosts file DNS server failure Unknown host

Internal network problems.

Network Troubleshooting Tools

There are many useful tools for troubleshooting network connectivity. Most of these tools are command-line commands that display configurations or send test messages.

It is usually best to verify physical connectivity before using software tools.

Common steps	Common indicators or tools
Verify physical connectivity	Check link lights on NICs and switches Confirm power supply Verify cable integrity Check appropriate cable selection
Confirm basic IP configurations	ipconfig ifconfig or ip addr route
Test connectivity	ping the destination first ping the router second ping on the same subnet nc (netcat) telnet
Verify network path	traceroute (Linux) or tracert (Windows) nc (netcat)
Update IP configurations	ipconfig /release, ipconfig /renew
Display current connections to the server	netstat nbtstat
Verify name resolution	nslookup dig host ping by hostname

Troubleshooting.

Review Activity:

Network Configurations

Answer the following questions:

1. **List common causes of failed Internet connectivity:**

2. **List common causes of failed name resolution:**

3. **List the Windows and Linux command-line tools to display and configure basic IP settings:**

4. **List the Windows and Linux command-line tools to display and troubleshoot name resolution settings:**

Lesson 8

Summary

It is useful to categorize troubleshooting by layer. For example, there are OS issues, application issues, and network issues. Your troubleshooting approach changes depending on which of those three layers is involved. One of the earliest steps is identifying the layer. From there, log files, user information, and diagnostic utilities can all help to determine the cause and ultimate resolution of the problem.

1. **List three or more network diagnostic utilities.**
2. **How can log files be used as part of the troubleshooting process?**

Lesson 9

Managing Post-Installation Administrative Tasks

LESSON INTRODUCTION

Post-installation administrative tasks are essential to the performance, utility, and security of servers. These tasks are governed by good administrative practices, proper service configuration, and server hardening.

Lesson Objectives

In this lesson, you will:

- Understand secure administration practices.
- Configure services.
- Configure server hardening.

Topic 9A

Understand Secure Administration Practices

EXAM OBJECTIVES COVERED

3.3 Explain important concepts pertaining to identity and access management for server administration

Secure administration begins with managing user identities, which are represented by user accounts and typically proven via passwords. The passwords are governed by password policies. Groups represent collections of users that have similar security requirements, such as access to particular files, folders, printers, and other resources. Permissions are used to control access to these resources. Windows and Linux users, groups, and permissions are managed differently from each other. You will examine both in this Topic.

Managing Users and Groups

One of the most fundamental concepts of system administration is user accounts. Users must identify themselves to the system so that it can configure security settings and user preferences. This concept is straightforward but very important. Once the system knows who you are, it knows what you should and should not be allowed to do.

The management of user accounts is directly related to **access control** through permissions. You will see more about permissions later in this Lesson.

Local User Accounts in Windows

Most sysadmins who work with Windows Server use the GUI. To create a local user account, open the Local Users and Groups console. One way to access this console is from the Computer Management console. You can configure a user name, first name, last name, description, and other settings in the user account. This console is also where you set the local user account password.

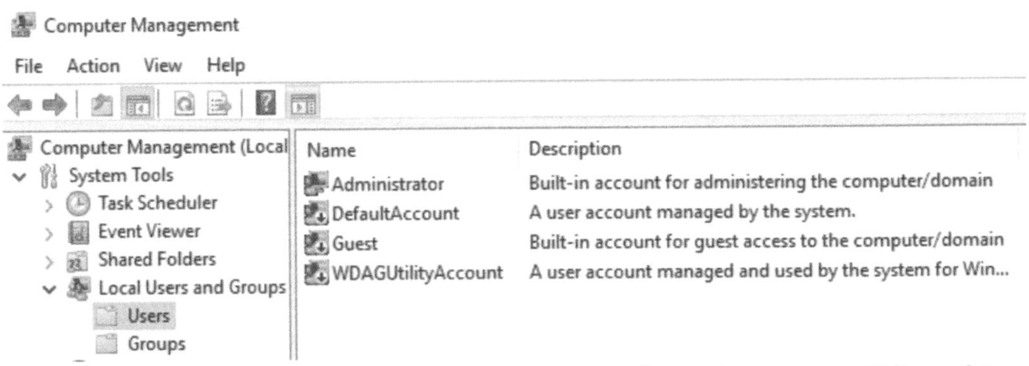

The Local Users and Groups console on Windows Server. (Screenshot courtesy of Microsoft.)

For networks larger than ten users, Microsoft recommends a centralized approach to managing users. This AD approach centralizes the user accounts to a database so that any modifications to them occurs in one place. Local user accounts, such as those discussed above, are stored only on the individual server where they are created, and they only have access to that server's resources.

Configuring passwords in Windows is covered later in this section.

Local User Accounts in Linux

Linux servers are usually managed from the command line. There are three Linux commands to keep in mind for managing user accounts.

Command	Description
useradd	Create a new local user
usermod	Modify an existing local user
userdel	Delete an existing local user

Three common commands to manage local Linux users.

```
[root@localhost ~]# useradd user01
[root@localhost ~]#
```

Creating a new local user by using the useradd command in Linux.

Some Linux distributions rely on the adduser command to create local user accounts. You may need to use one command or the other, depending on your distribution.

Configuring passwords in Linux is covered later in this section.

Local Groups

Managing user accounts and their access to resources, such as files and folders, is cumbersome in large networks. By using **group accounts**, administrators can associate many users with similar security or organizational requirements into a single unit and then just manage that unit.

Imagine if your company purchased a print device for all 100 members of the Sales department to use. Without groups, you would have to grant each of the 100 user accounts access to the printer individually.

Local Windows Groups

You use the same console to create groups in Windows Server that you used to create users. You can configure settings, such as group name, description, and members.

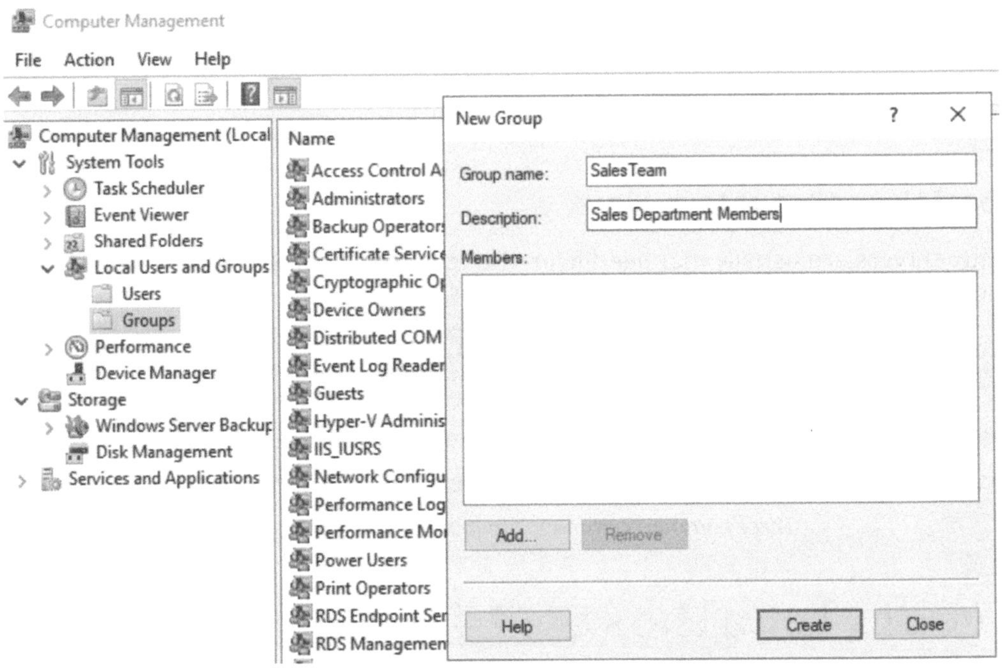

Creating a new local group account in the Local Users and Groups console on Windows Server. (Screenshot courtesy of Microsoft.)

Local Linux Groups

You use three commands to manage groups that are similar to user management commands.

Command	Description
groupadd	Create a new local group
groupmod	Modify an existing local group
groupdel	Delete an existing local group

Three common commands to manage local Linux groups.

Adding a user to a group in Linux is considered to be a modification of the user. The command to add the user01 user account to the Sales group is

```
usermod -aG Sales user01
```

Recall that you can use man usermod to display an explanation of the available command options. In this case, the options are -aG (remember that these are case sensitive).

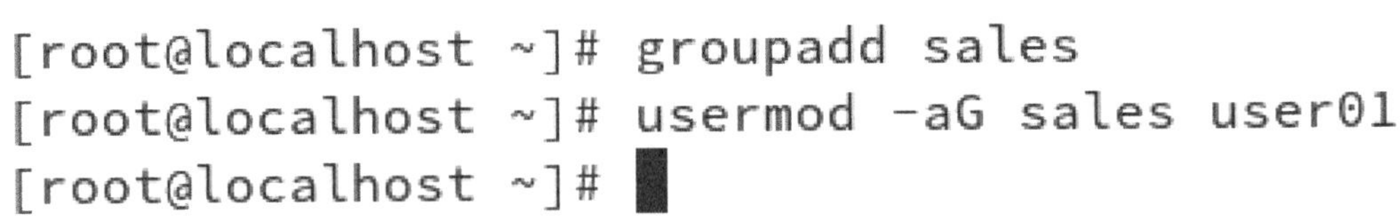

Using the usermod command to add a user to a group.

Users can be members of multiple groups in both Windows and Linux. This feature is useful, but it can make troubleshooting permissions issues more challenging.

Delegation

The management of user accounts and groups is a great example of administrative delegation. In many cases, junior IT staff members are given a specific area of responsibility, such as account management. Rather than grant them full privileges, such as with the Linux root user account or the Windows Domain Administrator account, it is better to delegate the specific level of access required—no more and no less. If the administrator should only be able to manage accounts, then there is no reason to grant them privileges to manage DNS configurations.

Password Policies

It seems as though passwords have always been a challenge for sysadmins to manage. Users do not understand that they really are the targets of a great many attacks and that they are responsible for business security. Users often seem to spend a lot of time thinking about how to circumvent password polices.

Standard Password Guidelines

Complexity—Use combinations of words, letters (uppercase and lowercase), numbers, and special characters.

Passphrases—Use passphrases rather than passwords.

Acronyms—Use the first letters of a common phrase. "To be or not to be" becomes "2B0n2b."

Password length—Use 8–14 characters for standard user passwords.

Do not use personally recognizable values, such as birth dates or names.

Do not use common words found in the dictionary.

Do not use combinations of adjacent keyboard keys, such as 1234 or qwerty.

Do not use the same password on multiple sites or for work and home accounts.

Some administrators advise changing passwords regularly, but that practice is falling out of favor.

Account lockouts—Set lockouts for failed login attempts.

Use MFA.

Audit passwords—Test passwords with password auditing tools.

Privileged accounts—Change the passwords of privileged accounts when an IT employee leaves the company.

If your password policy is too long or too strict, users will write down their passwords.

NIST has released modified guidelines for password management (nvlpubs.nist.gov/nistpubs/SpecialPublications/NIST.SP.800-63b.pdf). These guidelines deprecate many of the standard password management practices, including the following:
Do not enforce complexity.
Do not age passwords.
Do not permit password hints to be used.

Password Auditing

There are many threats to user passwords. Again, this is a fact that users often don't accept. They simply don't believe that their passwords or identities are essential enough to be of interest to hackers.

Hackers will not always use technology to defeat passwords. They will also use **social engineering**. Social engineering manipulates people into giving up confidential information that they would not normally expose.

For example, have you ever seen the quizzes on social media that say something like "Let's compare notes! List your answers to the following questions:

- What's your birth date?
- What are the names of your children? Grandchildren?
- What's your mother's maiden name?"

The answers to these questions make great starting points for hackers.

Of course, hackers also have many technologies available to circumvent passwords.

Common Password Attacks

Dictionary attacks—software that encrypts and attempts to use simple or common dictionary words or words that are easily associated with you personally (such as birth dates).

Brute force attacks—attempts to use random strings of characters.

Password stuffing—the use of authentication credentials from one site against other sites. This vulnerability works because users often use the same name/password combinations with multiple sites.

Password attacks start with word lists, common words or strings of text that contain potential passwords. However, these word lists can be edited to add information the attacker has explicitly learned about the target (their birth date, family birth dates, family names, and more). Such edits significantly increase the efficiency of the attack.

You can download password lists from the Web. Be aware that many of these lists contain vulgarity. It can be interesting, however, to see what passwords are common.

You can manage password auditing by using the available password cracking utilities, such as Cain and Abel, John the Ripper, Rainbow Crack, and others. Some of these tools are specific to Windows or Linux. You can place password hashes into the tools and let them attempt to crack the passwords.

The best place to begin might be to download the Kali Linux distribution, which comes with a great many security tools preinstalled. You can run Kali in a VM, and there are many tutorials online for it.

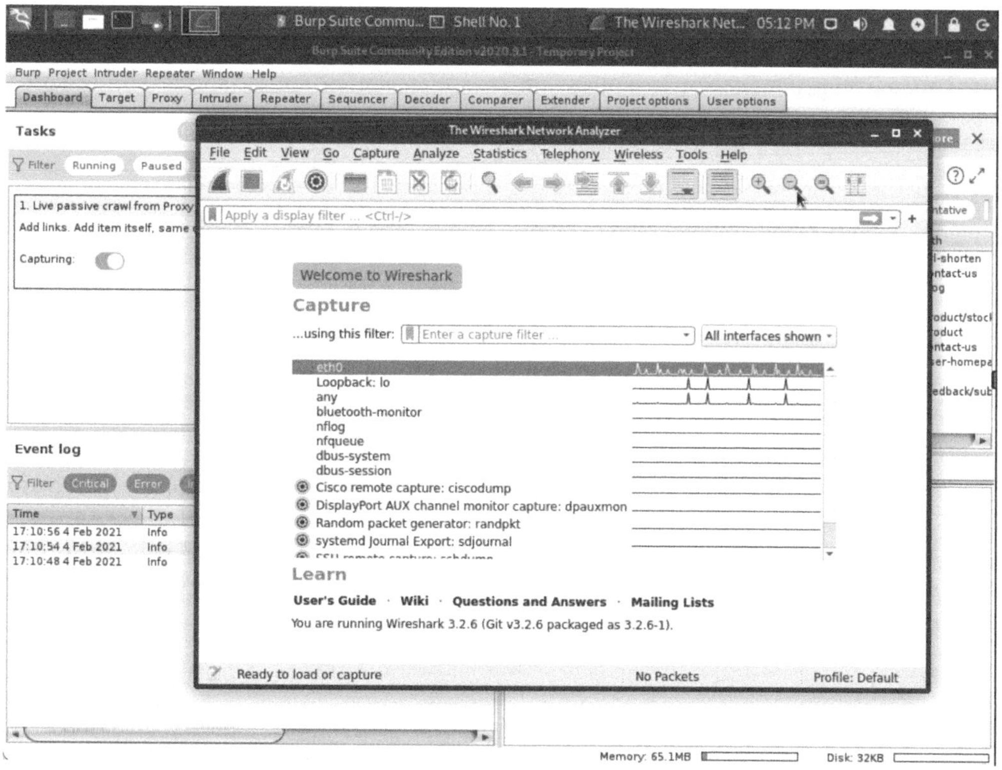

The Kali Linux penetration testing distribution. (Screenshot courtesy of Wireshark.)

Enforcing Password Policies

Both Windows and Linux provide ways to enforce your organization's password policies. Windows relies on local security policies, while Linux uses Pluggable Authentication Modules (PAM).

Enforce Password Policies in Windows

Microsoft Windows Server has multiple methods for managing passwords. First, you can configure password policies for local user accounts. Second, you can set password policies that apply to all user accounts in the AD domain. Finally, you can use Fine-Grained Password Policies to manage passwords on a per-group basis in an AD environment.

Local security policies, including password settings, apply only to the individual machine where they are configured. Locally managed settings are a challenge in business environments because they are set on each workstation or server manually. If you have 100 servers, you would have to configure the policies on each of them . This isn't time efficient or consistent.

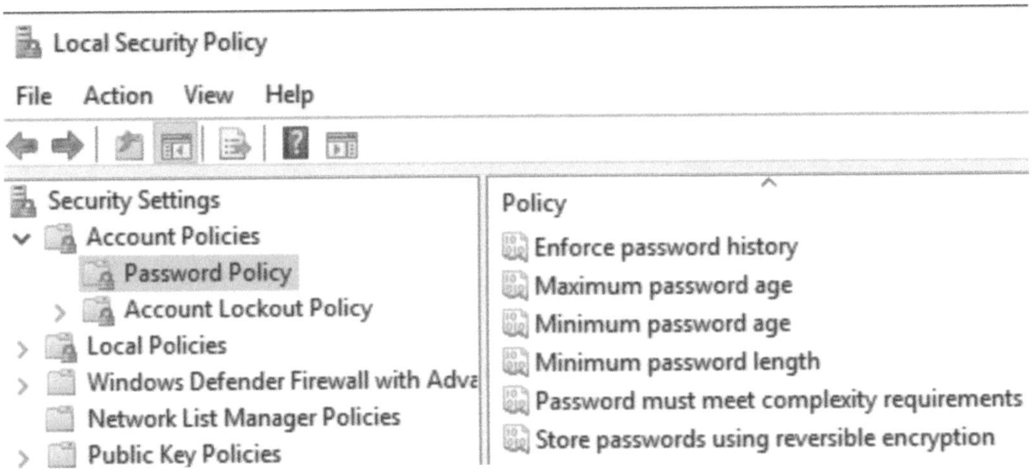

The path in Local Security Policies to configure password settings. (Screenshot courtesy of Microsoft.)

AD uses Group Policy to configure thousands of different settings on the computers in the AD domain. Domain admins can use the Default Domain Policy to define a single password policy for all user accounts in the domain.

The interface in AD Group Policy for managing passwords is similar to that of the Local Security Policies. The primary difference is that the AD Group Policy settings apply to all users in the domain, and the Local Security Policy settings apply only to the users on that specific computer.

Windows uses Fine-Grained Password policies to permit domain admins to configure different password policies for various AD users or global groups. For example, the Finance department may have a more stringent password policy than the Sales department. Fine-Grained Password policies are not enforced through Group Policy.

Enforce Password Policies in Linux

In the past, Linux systems used the /etc/login.defs file to define password settings. While this file usually still exists on modern Linux distributions, it is ignored in favor of the settings found in PAM. The PAM configuration file is edited to enforce password requirements.

Distribution	PAM configuration file
Red Hat distributions	/etc/pam.d/system-auth
Debian distributions	/etc/pam.d/common-password

The location of the PAM configuration file varies depending on whether the Linux distribution is derived from Red Hat or Debian.

For example, the PAM configuration file in Red Hat can be editing with the following information to define an eight-character password:

```
authconfig --passminlen=8 --update
```

Depending on your Linux distribution, you may be able to test the quality of your password by using the pwscore command.

Password Best Practices Review

- Consider complex passwords.
- Do not use easily guessed or personally related password strings.
- Do not use dictionary words.
- Do not use the same password for different accounts, especially between personal and work accounts.
- Change privileged account passwords when administrators leave the organization.
- Implement MFA.

Multifactor Authentication

One of the strongest ways to supplement authentication security is MFA.

Initially, **authentication** consisted of three factors:

- What you know (password)
- What you have (token or smart card)
- Who you are (biometrics such as a fingerprint)

MFA consists of at least two of these authentication factors.

Modern MFA implementations offer a great many additional options, including the following:

- Codes generated by apps
- USB or other storage devices
- Certificates
- GPS location
- Codes sent to an email address or a text number
- Facial recognition, retinal scans, fingerprints
- Personal security questions
- Time limitations for authentication codes

Single Sign-On

Single sign-on permits authentication against a single authentication source, such as Microsoft AD, which is then accepted by other sources.

For example, an employee authenticates at 8 am to AD. The employee then connects to a file server (which accepts the AD authentication) and prints a document (the print server accepts the AD authentication). The user also connects to a Microsoft Exchange email server (which accepts the AD authentication). Finally, the user queries a Microsoft SQL Server database (which accepts the AD authentication). The user only had to enter their name and password once, and they were authorized to access a wide variety of resources. Without SSO, they would have had to enter a name and password to use each service.

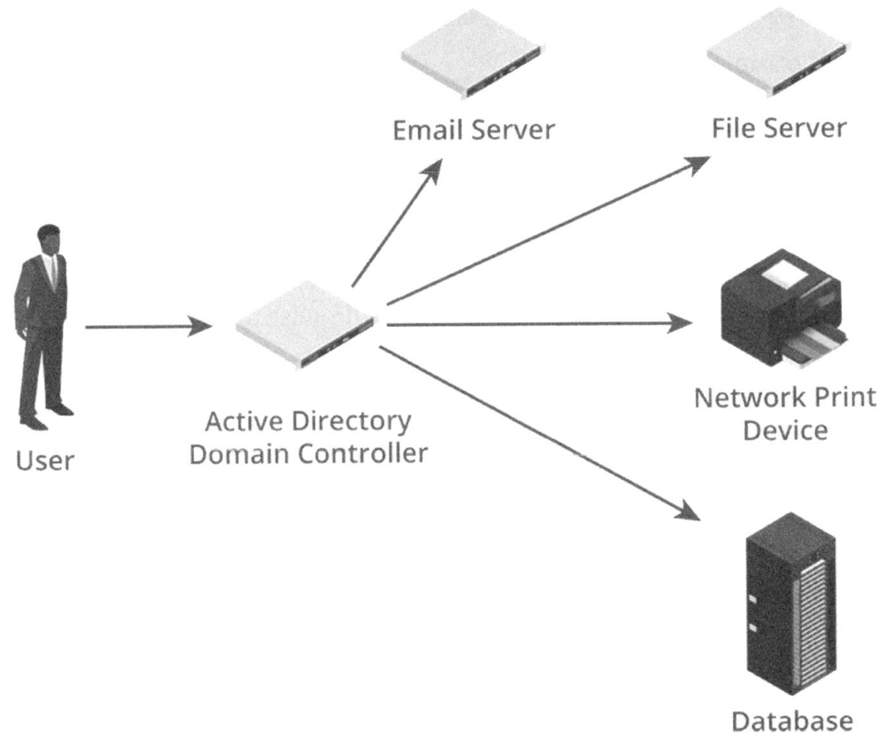

After authenticating to AD, the user has access to file, print, email, and database resources. (Images © 123RF.com)

Access Controls

One of the ways to manage security is to use segregation or **separation of duties**. For example, you could grant one administrator the ability to back up system data (including user account information), and a different administrator the ability to restore system data. Such a separation helps with accountability.

With **role-based access controls**, the administrator defines specific roles and assigns these roles to users. When a user attempts to access a resource, their role determines their level of access.

For example, a user account assigned to the Finance department will be configured with a finance label. The label is checked when the user attempts to access a resource. If the user's label reads something other than finance, access is denied.

Rule-based access controls permit the administrator to define a list of rules (for files and folders, these rules are permissions). When a user attempts to access a resource, rules determine their level of access.

For example, to access a finance resource, such as a payroll application, the user may be required to be logged on to a workstation assigned to the Finance department. A connection from a Sales workstation would be refused.

Scope-based access controls are commonly used with external applications to control their level of access to resources. Applications may be permitted to manage files, including backup, deduplication, and archiving functions. Users may be given a scope of access to permit the ability to view or modify content depending on the application scope.

For example, applications that routinely scan directories may be limited to certain files. One such application is Microsoft's Data Deduplication feature.

Permissions

Permissions utilize the user's authenticated credentials. The user's credentials are then compared to ACLs or file properties that define a level of access for that identity. Access is controlled at the file level with local or standard permissions and at the network level with shared or NFS permissions.

Windows local file and folder permissions are called NTFS permissions. Linux permissions are referred to as standard permissions.

Windows NTFS Permissions

Windows NTFS permissions are an attribute of the files and folders. These permissions control access to the resource whether the user is logged in to the system locally or accessing it from across the network. NTFS permissions for a file or a folder can be assigned to as many users and groups as you wish.

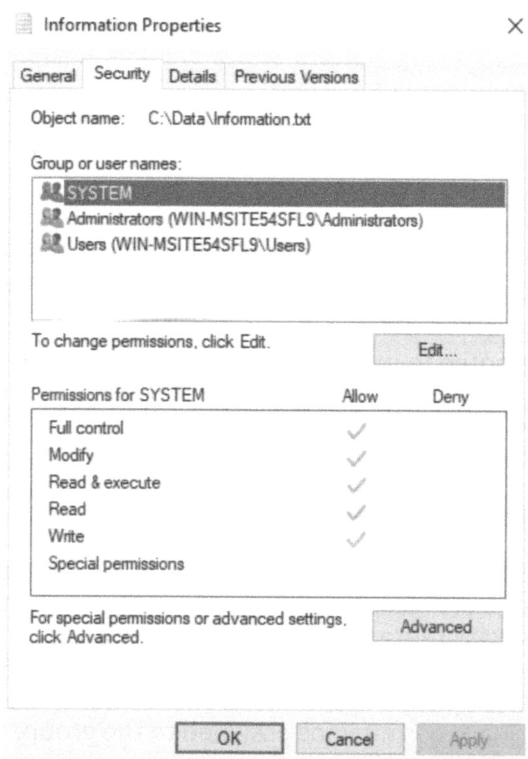

The Security tab in the Properties of a file. (Screenshot courtesy of Microsoft.)

The Security tab in the Properties of a folder. (Screenshot courtesy of Microsoft.)

Permissions can be granted to individual users, but it is usually more efficient to assign access to groups of users. Doing so is a Microsoft best practice. If a user is a member of multiple groups, the user's level of access to a file or folder will the cumulative or most permissive of all the NTFS permissions assigned to the group.

Windows Share Permissions

Windows uses **Share permissions** to control user access to network resources. These permissions control access to folders shared from network servers. Assuming that the user is granted access to the folder from across the network by the Share permissions, their access is controlled by the NTFS permissions. If a user is a member of multiple groups, their level of access is the cumulative or most permissive of all the Share permissions assigned to the group.

If there is a conflict between the NTFS and Share permissions as to the user's level of access, Windows grants the least permissive of the two as the effective permissions.

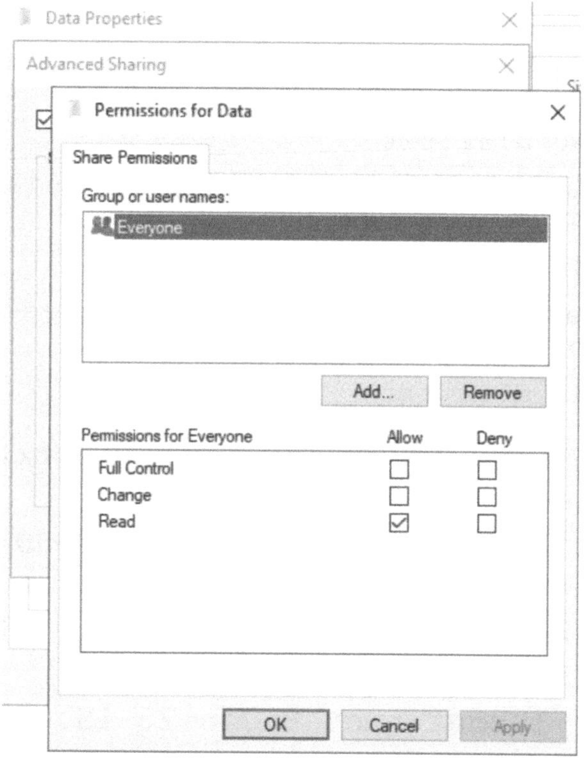

The Sharing tab in the Properties of a folder. (Screenshot courtesy of Microsoft.)

Standard Linux Permissions

Linux permissions are applied to files and directories. You can assign permissions to three identities: one user (owner), one group, and everyone else (others).

Identity	Description
u	User (sometimes referred to as "owner")
g	Group
o	Others—any ID that is not the user or the group

Linux identities.

There are three levels of access for Linux permissions: read, write, and execute.

Depending on the GUI your chosen Linux distribution uses (if there is a GUI), you can set permissions in the files or folder's properties. At the command line, you will use the chmod (change mode) command to configure permissions.

There are two methods for using chmod—absolute mode and symbolic mode. Absolute mode uses octal values, and symbolic mode uses abbreviations.

Permission	Abbreviation	Octal value
Read	r	4
Write	w	2
Execute	x	1

Linux permissions, abbreviations, and octal values.

Linux Standard Permissions Examples

Absolute mode example 1: To grant the user rwx, the group rw, and others no access to file1.txt, issue the following command:

```
chmod 760 file1.txt
```

Absolute mode example 2: To grant the user r, the group r, and all others no access to file1.txt, issue the following command:

```
chmod 440 file1.txt
```

Absolute mode example 3: To grant the user rw, the group read-only, and others read-only to file1.txt, issue the following command:

```
chmod 644 file1.txt
```

```
[root@localhost ~]# chmod 760 file1.txt
[root@localhost ~]# ls -l file1.txt
-rwxrw----. 1 root root 0 Jan 26 15:00 file1.txt
[root@localhost ~]#
[root@localhost ~]# chmod 440 file1.txt
[root@localhost ~]# ls -l file1.txt
-r--r-----. 1 root root 0 Jan 26 15:00 file1.txt
[root@localhost ~]#
[root@localhost ~]# chmod 644 file1.txt
[root@localhost ~]# ls -l file1.txt
-rw-r--r--. 1 root root 0 Jan 26 15:00 file1.txt
[root@localhost ~]#
```

Examples of using absolute mode to configure permissions.

Symbolic mode example 1: To grant the user rwx, the group rw, and others no access to file1.txt, issue the following command:

```
chmod u=rwx,g=rw,o= file1.txt
```

Symbolic mode example 2: To grant the user r, the group r, and all others no access to file1.txt, issue the following command:

```
chmod ug=r,o= file1.txt
```

Symbolic mode example 3: To grant the user rw, the group read-only, and others read-only to file1.txt, issue the following command:

```
chmod u=rw,go=r file1.txt
```

```
[root@localhost ~]# chmod u=rwx,g=rw,o= file1.txt
[root@localhost ~]# ls -l file1.txt
-rwxrw----. 1 root root 0 Jan 26 15:00 file1.txt
[root@localhost ~]#
[root@localhost ~]# chmod ug=r,o= file1.txt
[root@localhost ~]# ls -l file1.txt
-r--r-----. 1 root root 0 Jan 26 15:00 file1.txt
[root@localhost ~]#
[root@localhost ~]# chmod u=rw,go=r file1.txt
[root@localhost ~]# ls -l file1.txt
-rw-r--r--. 1 root root 0 Jan 26 15:00 file1.txt
[root@localhost ~]#
```

Examples of using symbolic mode to configure permissions.

Linux also uses Access Control Lists (ACLs) to manage permissions for multiple users and groups to access files and directories.

Linux NFS

Linux directories are exported, or made available on the network, by using NFS. You can configure network access by using the /etc/exports file. Users who are allowed to connect to the directory via NFS must still satisfy the standard Linux permissions, too.

Account Auditing

You can also view system log files to discover user activity and login attempts (successful and failed). Log files will also display information about deleted user accounts.

Windows Server can be configured for file **auditing**. This auditing logs attempted access to specified folders and files and whether the access was successful or not. A folder containing confidential Human Resources files can be audited. Successful access by HR department members is logged, but so are failed access attempts by non-HR department members.

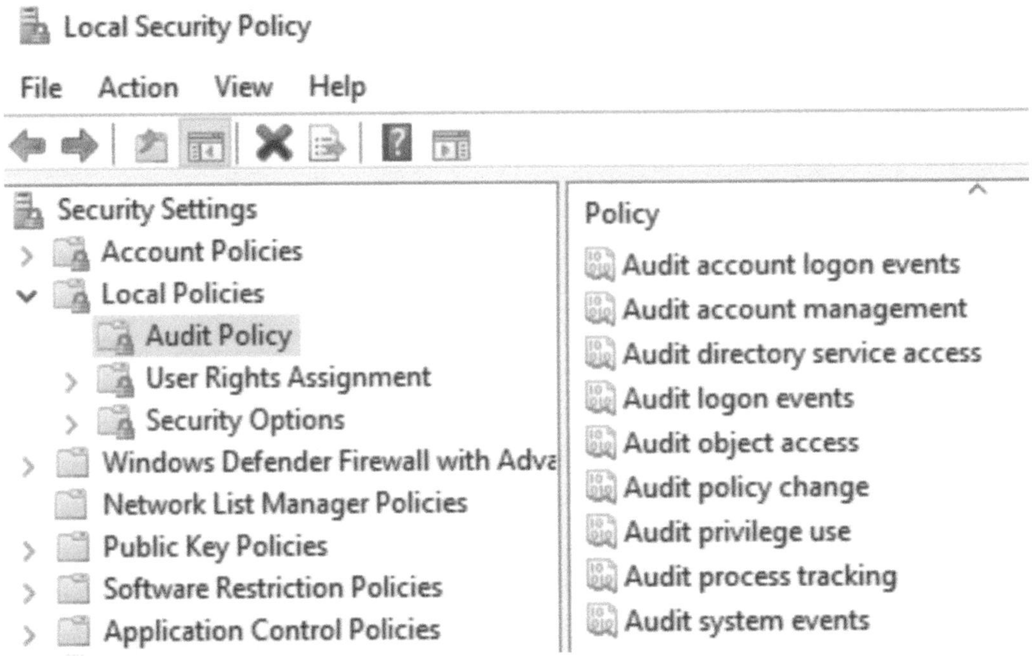

Audit policy options in Windows Server. (Screenshot courtesy of Microsoft.)

One challenging aspect of user management is group membership. As discussed earlier, you can grant access to files and folders based on group membership. It is essential to carefully control group membership and periodically verify that the appropriate users are in the correct groups.

Basic User Auditing Commands

It is easy to list the local users on both Windows and Linux servers. This list is useful to ensure that all accounts are legitimate and current.

Use the following PowerShell cmdlet to audit the local users on a Windows server:

```
get-localuser
```

Use the following command to audit the local users on Linux server:

```
cat /etc/passwd
```

Basic Group Auditing Commands

Use the following PowerShell cmdlet to audit the Administrators group membership in Windows:

```
Get-ADGroupMember -Identity Administrators
```

Use the following commands to audit the wheel group membership in Linux:

```
cat /etc/group | grep -i wheel
getent group wheel
```

Third-Party Auditing

You can outsource your password auditing to organizations that specialize in testing the quality of passwords. Outsourcing is much more cost effective if you attempt to audit AD user account passwords or review more than a few passwords.

Guidelines for Secure Administration Practices

- Do not share user accounts between employees.
- Use groups to organize users with similar security requirements.
- Review password policies with users.
- Audit passwords.
- Use MFA.
- Enforce password requirements in Windows with Group Policy.
- Enforce password requirements in Linux with PAM.
- Windows uses NTFS permissions for local files and folders.
- Windows uses Share permissions to access resources across the network.
- Linux uses standard permissions for local files and folders.
- Linux uses NFS permissions to access resources across the network.
- Sysadmins manage user accounts to provide authentication and access control.
    - Use groups to associate users with similar security requirements, and grant privileges to groups rather than individual users whenever possible.
    - User accounts are managed by password policies to ensure security.
- Windows uses NTFS and Share permissions to control access to files and folders.
- Linux uses standard permissions, ACLs, and NFS permissions to control access to files and directories.

Review Activity:

Secure Administration Practices

Answer the following questions:

1. **What three Linux commands are used to manage local user accounts?**

2. **What are the three primary forms of MFA?**

3. **Explain the single sign-on concept.**

4. **What are the two types of Windows permissions?**

5. **What are the three identities used with Linux permissions?**

6. **What are the three access levels used with Linux permissions?**

Topic 9B

Manage Server Functions

EXAM OBJECTIVES COVERED

2.3 Given a scenario, configure and maintain server functions and features

Servers need different specifications and configurations depending on the role they play in the organization. Some roles emphasize various hardware subsystems more than others. It is essential to take this into account when specifying the server's hardware requirements.

Server Roles Requirements

When it is time to stand up a new server, one of the earliest steps is to define the device's primary role. Depending on your company's service management or change management process, this has probably already been done for you.

Recall that computers consist of four major subsystems: CPU, memory, storage, and networking. Evaluate performance with at least these four subsystems in mind.

It is possible that the server will play multiple roles. For example, services such as DNS and DHCP may be co-located on the same box.

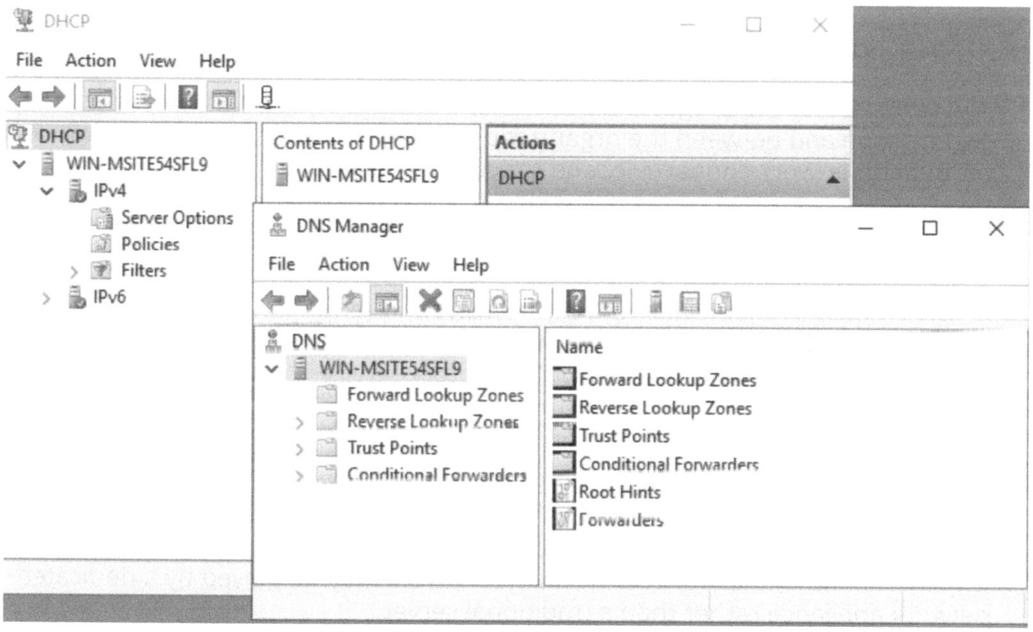

The DNS service and the DHCP service co-located on a single server. (Screenshot courtesy of Microsoft.)

Server Roles

The following points describe typical server roles and which of the four major subsystems they utilize the most heavily.

General Servers

The most fundamental servers on the network are file and print servers. File servers provide a centralized storage location for business data, making it easier to secure and back up. Print servers allow for shared print devices, which is far more cost effective than managing the devices per user. Web servers are also common. Basic websites consist of relatively small files and are straightforward to host.

- File—storage for user and business data files, requires a large amount of storage capacity, redundant storage, and fast storage IO. It also requires fast network connectivity.
- Print—storage and management of print jobs during the printing process, requires adequate storage capacity, speed, and fast network connectivity.
- Web—hosts one or more web sites, requires redundant and efficient network connectivity.

Application Servers

Application servers host major network multiuser applications. For example, an organization might have a very large customer database or a company-wide collaboration solution.

- Database—stores database files and processes queries, requires a large amount of fast storage capacity, redundancy, and high availability. It also requires sufficient processor power to handle queries. It is not usually a good idea to co-locate any other services on a database server.
- Application/Middleware—hosts middleware applications that may connect databases with web or client front-end applications. Requirements vary depending on use.
- Messaging/email—manages the transfer and storage of email within the organization and between the organization and the Internet. It also requires redundant network connectivity and storage capacity.
- Network infrastructure—supports network functionality, including name resolution (DNS) and IP address management (DHCP).
    - DNS requires reliable network connectivity and redundancy—it is one of the most critical services on your network. DNS is often co-located with Microsoft AD Domain Controllers (Microsoft's directory services role).
    - DHCP is a very lightweight service, requiring little in the way of hardware resources.
- VPN—provides remote access to client computers that are physically outside of the business network but need secured access to internal data. VPN servers require redundant network connectivity. This role may be played by a dedicated network appliance rather than a traditional server.
- Collaboration—hosts sites where business units can collaborate on projects and initiatives, including document management, communications, versioning, etc. It requires sufficient storage for user data.

- VM hosts—servers whose sole purpose is to host VMs. These servers must have sufficient resources among all four of the major subsystems to support the role of the VMs deployed on them. VM hosts have a great deal of processing power, memory, redundant and fast storage, and redundant networking. Any of the other servers listed may be hosted as VMs on a VM host.

Directory Services Servers

Directory services manage the authentication and storage of user and computer accounts. Directory services provide a centralized location for administrators to create, modify, or delete the accounts. Microsoft AD is an example of a directory service.

- Directory services—hosts an authentication database to verify the identity of client computers and end users on the network. When users log in, their name and password are checked, and any limitations or configurations are applied. Directory services require redundancy and efficient network connectivity.
    - User account storage—stores and organizes user accounts, making account management easier for administrators, help desk technicians, etc. Authenticates the identity of users attempting to log on to the network. For example, user passwords are verified.
    - Computer account storage—stores and organizes computer accounts. Proves the identity of client, mobile, and server devices attempting to log on to the network. For example, Microsoft AD checks computer account passwords (in much the same way that it checks user account passwords).

Directory Services Configuration Controls

Directory services may also provide configuration settings for client computers, depending on the identity of the authenticated user and the specific workstation. Microsoft AD uses Group Policy to provide configuration management based on the user and the workstation identity. A computer in the Sales department, with a Sales user logged on, may be configured differently than a Marketing user's workstation. Configurations might include deployed applications, security settings, network configurations, or mapped network printers.

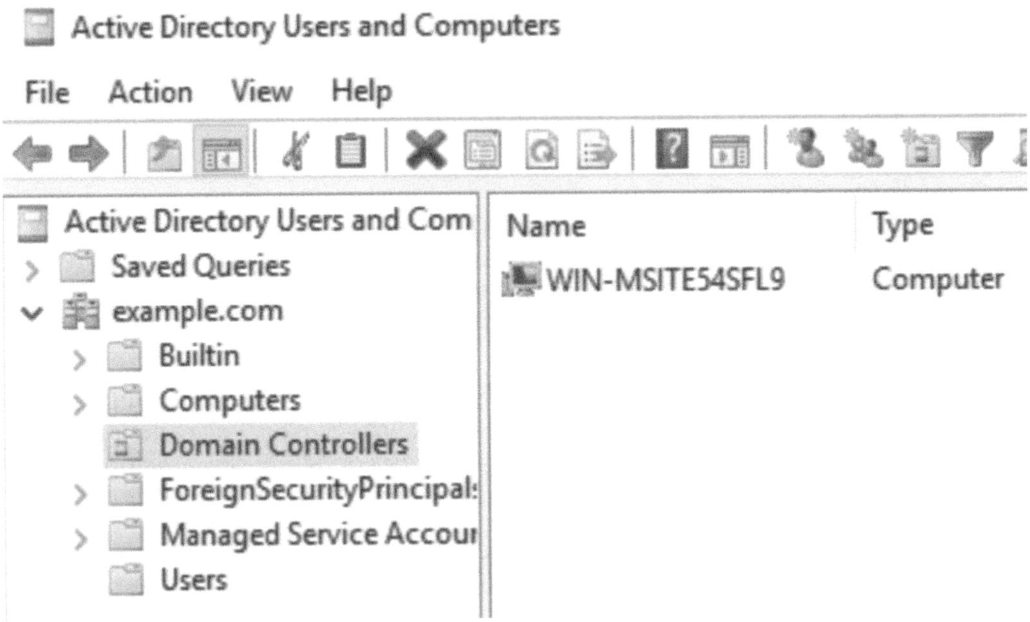

The AD Users and Computers console is used to organize accounts, partly for the purpose of configuration management via Group Policy. (Screenshot courtesy of Microsoft.)

Storage Management

Hardware performance has the most impact on your users' experience with the file server. Effective storage utilization requires fast HDDs, dedicated hardware controllers, and efficient network connectivity.

Directory connectivity relies on the network infrastructure. Efficient network connectivity is critical for access to data. Most file servers make stored data available by sharing out folders/directories. Workstations use the network to connect to these directories. Even though server storage configuration is emphasized, it is dependent on network performance.

There are many tools to help manage storage effectively on servers. File servers, in particular, often need your attention. End users may not follow policies for data storage in home folders or department directories. Some services, such as databases, also perform more efficiently with specific configurations set.

Basic file servers, such as those hosting user data, can be configured with quotas to control the storage capacity that individual users consume. Also, data can be compressed, ensuring that there is sufficient storage space on the server. Finally, data deduplication can be enabled to help reduce the amount of storage capacity consumed by redundant data.

Depending on the needs of your users, you will also consider the appropriate file system. With Windows, this choice is limited to NTFS, or perhaps ReFS. On Linux systems, you will likely choose either the ext4 file system or XFS. The XFS file system is the default for RHEL, for example, and may provide significant performance and reliability improvements.

Storage Management Example 1

One typical configuration is the separation of the OS and data storage to different physical drives (not different logical partitions that share the same physical drive). The idea is to separate IO competition between the OS and applications to different drives and busses. This is a common configuration on Windows systems.

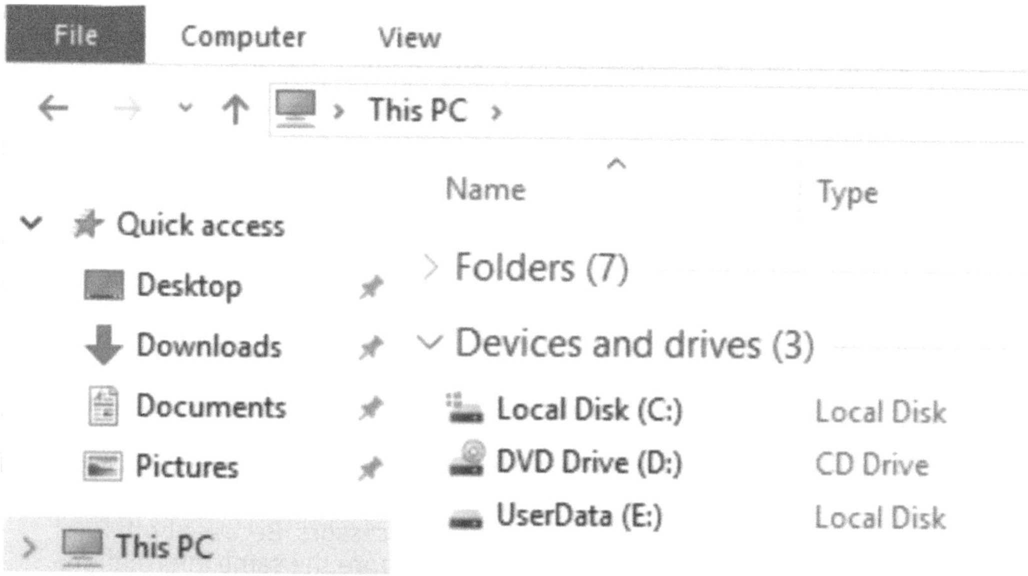

A Windows server with the OS on C: and user data on E: (Screenshot courtesy of Microsoft.)

Storage Example 2

A slightly more complex setup than the first example is to place the operating system on a RAID 1 disk mirror. If one drive fails, the other still has the ability to run the OS. Data is placed on a RAID 5 disk striping with parity array, which makes more efficient use of storage space and provides fault tolerance.

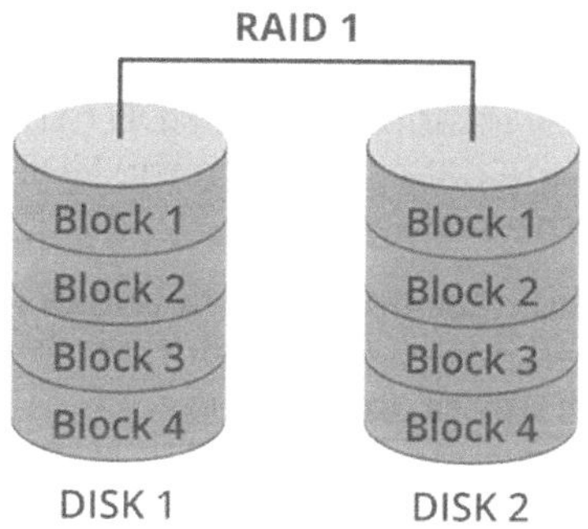

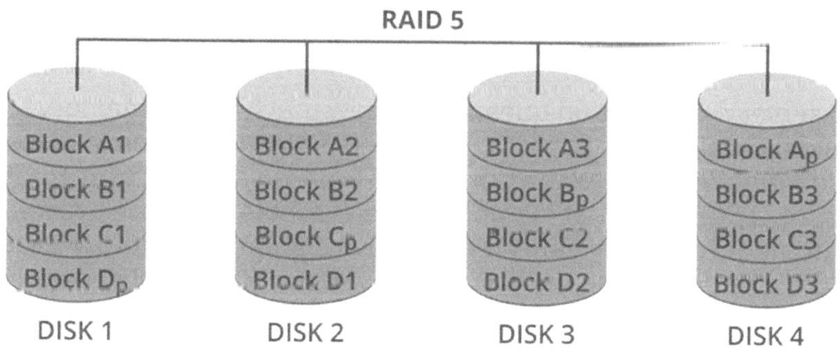

RAID 1 holds the operating system while RAID 5 holds the user data. (Images © 123RF.com)

Storage Example 3

Linux servers may use a more complex storage scheme than Windows servers. Several partitions may be used to store specific parts of the OS.

Here are some of the Linux directories that may be stored on dedicated partitions:

- / - root of the file system
- `/home` - end-user home directories
- `/var` - log files, web sites, print **spool** files
- `swap` - storage space for virtual memory

Virtual Memory

RAM and HDDs are both storage locations. Servers typically have less RAM installed than HDD. RAM is a relatively limited storage area compared to HDDs. However, RAM is also very fast and easily accessible to the processors. Because both RAM and HDDs are storage, it is possible to use them to store the same information. Specifically, HDD storage space can be used as if it were RAM. This borrowed space is called **virtual memory**.

If a server (or workstation) consumes all of its physical RAM, it borrows storage capacity from one or more HDDs. The upside to this feature is that the system has far more potential storage capacity for data it wants to store in RAM. The downside is that the HDD subsystem is substantially slower than RAM.

Windows virtual memory is usually a dedicated file on the C: drive that is written to as if it were RAM. Linux can use a dedicated file, but it is more common to use a dedicated partition on the hard drive.

If all the RAM's storage capacity is consumed, the system can move some data to the designated virtual memory location on the HDD (which frees up some space in RAM). If the system needs the data stored on the HDD, it can move it back and transfer some other data to the storage drive.

The above process swaps data back and forth between RAM and the HDD. The data is moved in chunks called pages. Linux refers to the use of virtual memory as swapping, and Windows calls this process paging.

As a general rule, relying on virtual memory is bad. It indicates that the system does not have enough available RAM to manage its services. The real solution is to either increase the amount of RAM or decrease the server's workload. Virtual memory is a short-term measure that keeps the server functioning until the underlying memory issue is resolved.

A standard server configuration question is "How much virtual memory space should be available on the HDD?" In the past, virtual memory space recommendations were 1.5-2x the quantity of RAM (so a server with 16 GB of RAM would have 24–32 GB of virtual memory space available). However, this guideline is pretty outdated. Today's systems tend to have a great deal more available memory. Furthermore, virtual memory space varies a great deal depending on the anticipated need. Remember, you do not want virtual memory used at all—it is an indicator that your server doesn't have enough RAM for its workload, and it slows the system.

Recommended Virtual Memory Settings

Ubuntu Linux—consider setting the swap partition at the quantity of RAM + .5 GB. A system with 8 GB of RAM would have a swap partition of 8.5 GB.

System Memory (physical)	Recommended swap space (virtual memory)
2 GB or less	2 x RAM
2-8 GB	Equal to RAM
8-64 GB	4 GB or more

Recommendations for virtual memory for RHEL.

Windows Server uses the pagefile to store system crash dump information, so it should be at least as large as RAM's quantity. You will need to use the Committed Bytes Performance Monitor counter when your system is in production to see how large the dump file might be and ensure that there is sufficient space for the dump file on the partition where the pagefile.sys file exists.

Windows dynamically manages the pagefile.sys file for you and grows the file as needed to a predefined maximum size. It is usually best to let Windows manage the pagefile for you.

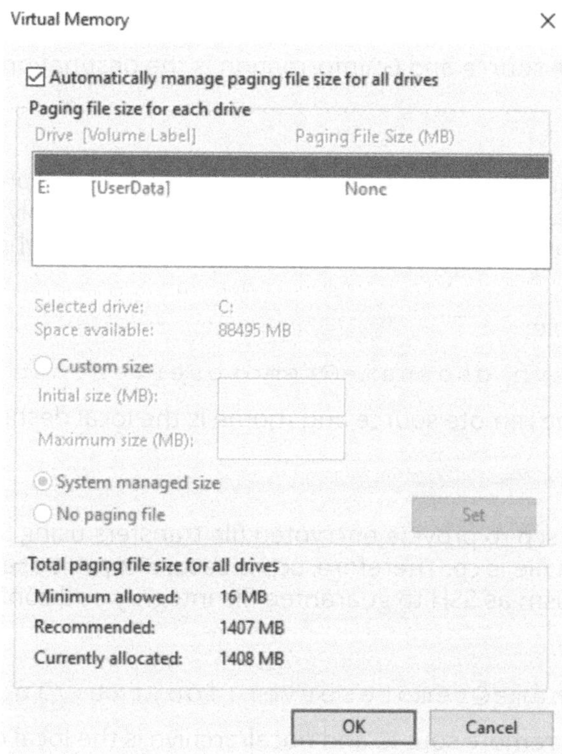

Windows Virtual Memory pagefile configuration. (Screenshot courtesy of Microsoft.)

Some sysadmins will configure the initial size of the Windows pagefile.sys file to be the maximum allowed size of the file. The advantage of this trick is to keep Windows from having to dynamically grow the file. Instead, the file is already at its maximum size and ready for utilization.

Data Transfers

Data may be transferred on or off of your servers legitimately or illegitimately. In this section, you will see some Windows and Linux administrative tools used to transfer data.

Data Transfers Using Administrative Tools

Legitimate transfers occur in many ways. File sharing, such as SMB or NFS, is probably the most common way . The FTP and **HTTP** are also ways of moving data on and off servers.

Many of these methods permit data transfers between disparate OSs. For example, HTTP transfers usually occur between Linux webservers and Windows or macOS clients.

Robocopy

At the command prompt, one of the most powerful Windows file transfer tools is **Robocopy**. It transfers entire directory trees, including permissions, attributes, and ownership. It is worth noting that Robocopy itself does not encrypt the contents of the file transfer.

Robocopy syntax example:

```
robocopy D:\data G:\information
```

Where D:\data is the source and G:\information is the destination.

Rsync

Linux uses a tool named rsync to provide a similar file transfer process. One of the interesting attributes of rsync is that it may be configured to only transfer changed files within a directory tree, rather than all data, regardless of whether that data has changed.

Rsync syntax example:

```
rsync -azvh username@remoteserver:/archive /home
```

Where /archive is the remote source and /home is the local destination.

Scp

Linux also relies on scp to provide encrypted file transfers using SSH. The Linux command to copy a file is cp. Therefore, scp is secure copy. It uses the same encryption mechanism as SSH to guarantee file integrity and confidentiality.

Scp syntax example:

```
scp username@remoteserver:foo.txt /local/archive
```

where foo.txt is the remote source and /local/archive is the local destination.

The WinSCP tool is commonly used to transfer files between Linux and Windows systems. WinSCP has an easy GUI and encrypts the contents of the file transfer.

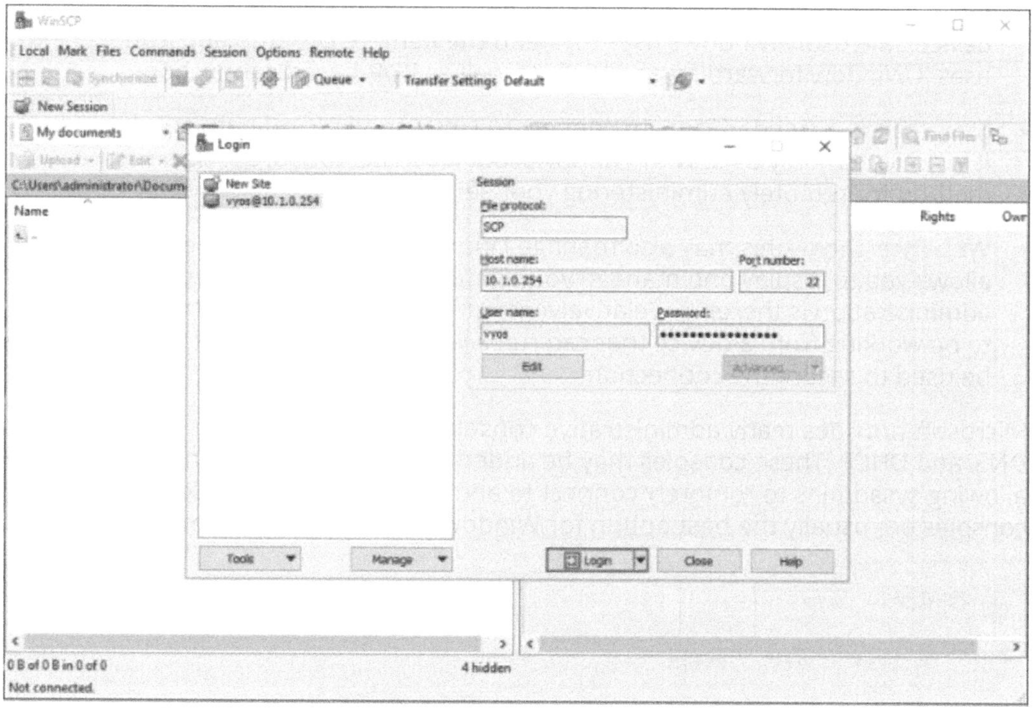

WinSCP. (Screenshot courtesy of Microsoft.)

Security Breaches/Data Exfiltration

File transfers may also be illegitimate. For example, **data exfiltration** describes the content copied from a server in a security breach. The corresponding term, **data infiltration**, describes data transferred to a server.

Data exfiltration examples:

- Confidential HR files copied from the server to an attacker's laptop.
- Ransomware delivered to a file server via file transfer.

Data infiltration examples:

- Data uploaded from a remote workstation, such as images uploaded by a photographer to an FTP server.
- Data replicated from a database. Such replication may be part of a data redundancy configuration.
- Files uploaded from a user's workstation. The files were created while the laptop was disconnected from the network and need to be stored on file server.

Administrative Interfaces

Maintaining server functionality requires the ability to connect to the server and gather information. As you learned earlier, there are many ways of connecting to the server to issue commands or display information.

- Console—this is a direct connection, where the sysadmin stands at the server using a keyboard and mouse directly connected to the device. Console connections include KVM connectivity.

- **Remote desktop**—there are many ways of accessing the GUI on a remote device. Microsoft Windows uses RDP and the Remote Desktop application. Linux uses X Window forwarding and VNC, as well as RDP-based connections.
- **SSH**—this is a standard tool to connect to Linux servers and network devices. It is not commonly used with Windows, but it can be added. SSH is a secure method for remotely administering your servers.
- **Web interface**—this may also manage Linux servers. For example, Linux Cockpit allows you to display and manage your Linux servers via a web browser. Such administration is therefore relatively universal, since the administrator only has to be working from a device that can run a web browser. SSL VPN protocols may be used to secure the connection.

Microsoft provides many administrative consoles to manage services such as AD, DNS, and DHCP. These consoles may be added to Windows 10 admin workstations, allowing sysadmins to remotely connect to and configure Windows servers. These consoles are usually the best option for Windows server configuration.

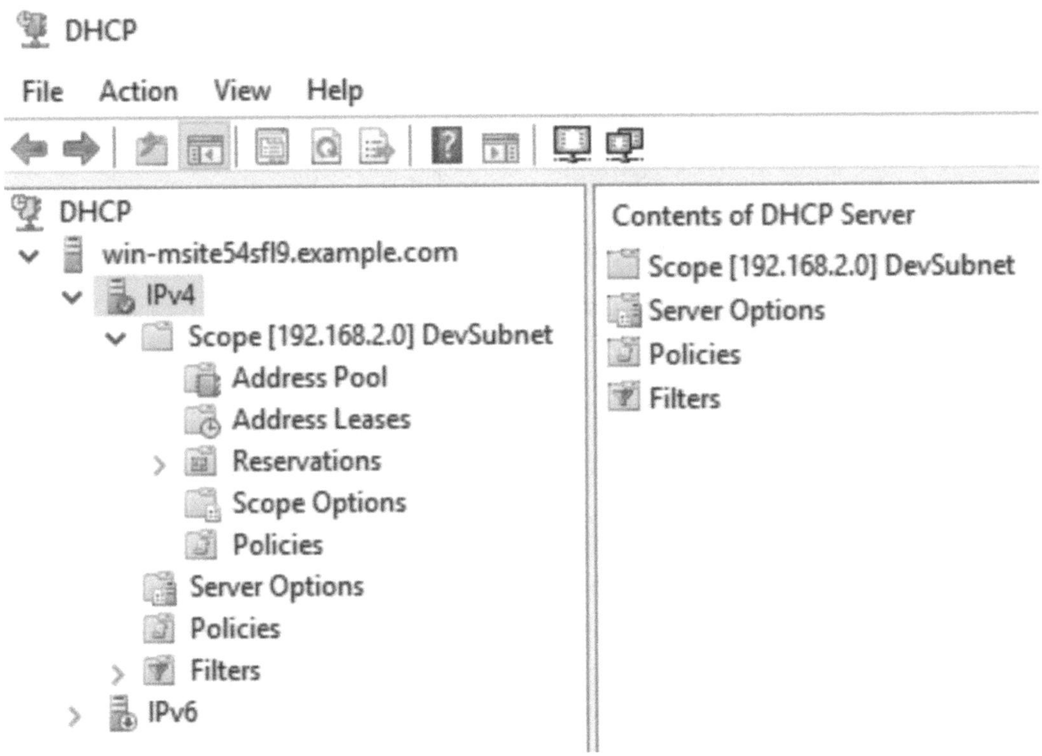

DHCP console in Windows Server. (Screenshot courtesy of Microsoft.)

Windows administrators may connect to remote servers by using the Remote Desktop service. This solution is easy in an entirely Windows network. The administrator uses a Windows client computer to remotely connect to Windows servers to make configuration changes. While SSH can be added to Windows computers, it is not native and therefore not usually the best choice.

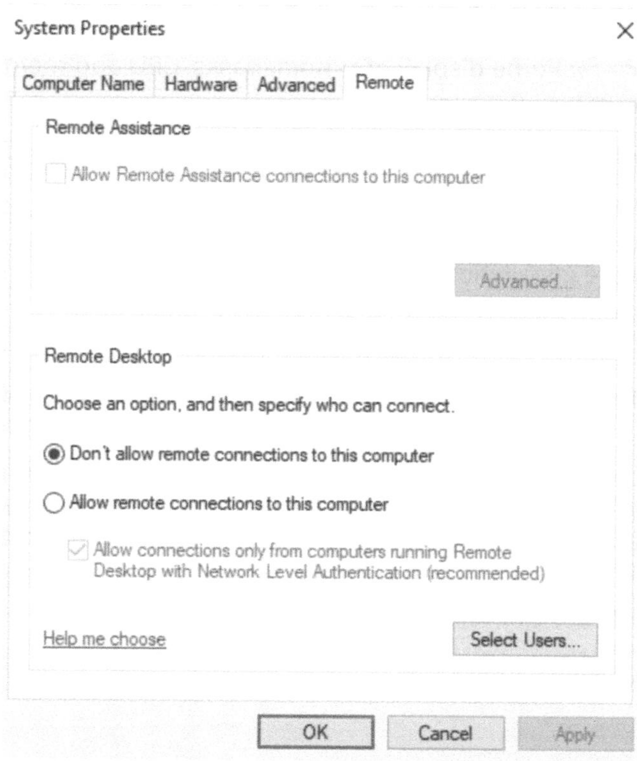

Remote Desktop configuration. (Screenshot courtesy of Microsoft.)

Linux servers rely on the SSH for remote connectivity. SSH services are almost always running on Linux services, and the SSH client is installed by default. SSH is secure and convenient, especially for Linux servers without a GUI. Remote desktop clients can be added to Linux workstations for connectivity to Windows servers.

```
[user01@CentOS7-A ~]$ ssh root@192.168.1.100
root@192.168.1.100's password:
Last login: Mon Aug  3 15:15:09 2020 from 172.20.0.2
[root@CentOS7-A ~]# 
```

SSH connection to 192.168.1.100.

Monitoring

Recall that in Lesson 4, you examined server baselining and monitoring. The purpose of baselining is to document a system's performance when it is first brought online. Continuous monitoring after that allows sysadmins to understand how a server's performance changes as the demands on it change over time. Because of this, you will usually use the same performance monitoring criteria.

Windows Monitoring

Microsoft Windows Server includes many performance monitoring utilities that give you real-time or historical data. Sysadmins use these tools regularly to maintain the server and troubleshoot specific issues.

Windows Monitoring Tools

- Task Manager—real-time display of running tasks, CPU and memory load, network performance data
- Resource Monitor—real-time display broken down into the four major subsystems
- Reliability Monitor—historical data documenting system crashes, application crashes, software installations, and updates, and system changes

Windows Performance Monitor

The primary monitoring tools in Windows Server are Performance Monitor and Event Viewer.

Performance Monitor tracks real-time data, but it also records historical information for later analysis. Many categories can be tracked with Performance Monitor, and each category has many counters. It is easy to track too much information and become overwhelmed. Begin monitoring with the following counters:

- Processor—% Processor time
- Processor—% User time
- Memory—Pages/sec
- Network Interface—Transfers/sec
- Physical Disk—Transfers/sec
- Physical Disk—Average disk queue length

Alerts and Thresholds

Performance monitor can also be configured to alert administrators when specific thresholds are met. For example, a file server administrator might configure a server to send an alert when the data stored on the server's HDD exceeds 80% of the drive's capacity.

CPU Monitoring

Microsoft recommends that the Processor % Processor Time threshold should not exceed 80%. In other words, the processor should use less than 80% of its capacity.

Input Output Operations per Second (IOPS)

Disk drive performance is usually measured as IOPS. Four common Windows Performance Monitor counters for IOPS are the following:

- Current disk queue length
- Disk reads/sec
- Disk transfers/sec
- Disk writes/sec

If IOPS requirements are not met, services such as Microsoft SQL Server can report errors. Depending on the service, users might also notice performance problems.

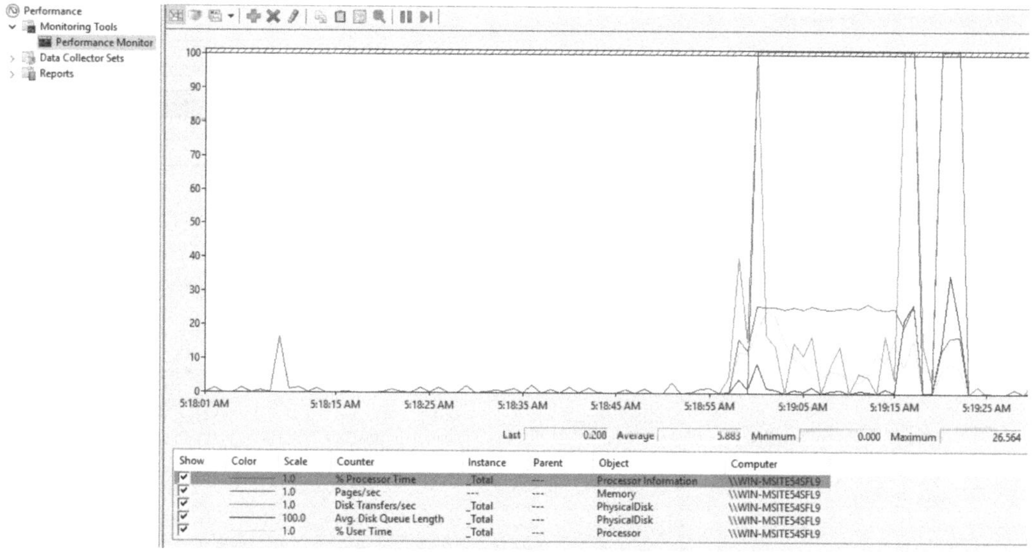

Windows Performance Monitor. (Screenshot courtesy of Microsoft.)

System Uptime

The Performance tab in Task Manager displays the system uptime.

Windows Event Viewer

Windows Event Viewer logs system and application information, including security events, the status of services, and application events. Event Viewer has a practical filtering utility to help you gather exactly the information you need. Reviewing Event Viewer logs is a common task for both day-to-day system management and troubleshooting.

Logs	Description
Application	Logs for applications on the system
Security	Logs for security and auditing information
System	Logs for Windows-related events

Event Viewer logs.

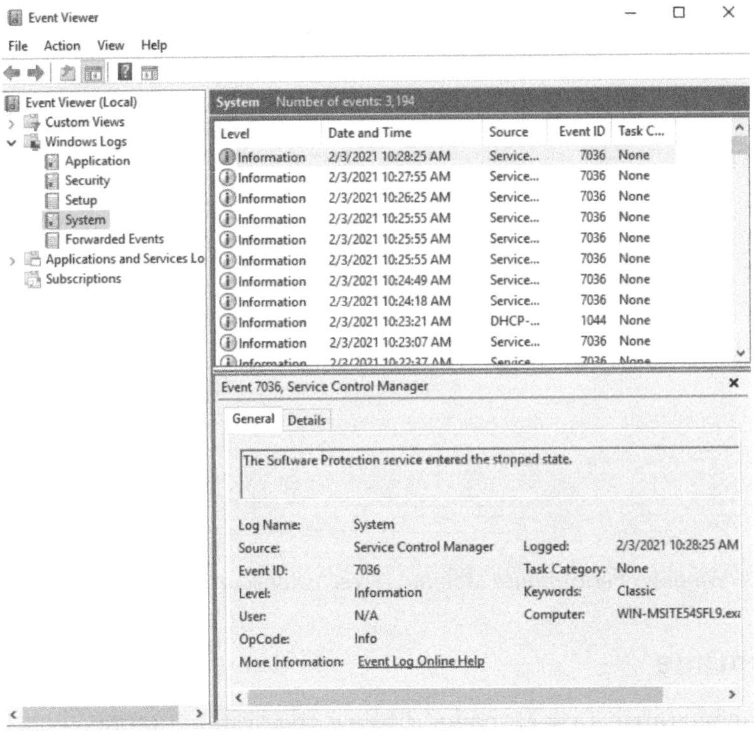

Windows Event Viewer. (Screenshot courtesy of Microsoft.)

Linux Monitoring

Assuming that you are working in the bash shell in Linux, you can use several tools to display and monitor the system's performance.

Monitoring Linux with Top

One of the most useful tools to monitor your Linux server is top. Top displays the processes on the system that are consuming the most CPU time and the most RAM. Top is dynamic and recalculates its information every few seconds.

- To organize the data by the processes consuming the most processor time, select P (note that this display is the default).
- To organize the data by the processes consuming the most memory, select M.

Both the P and M options in top are upper case.

```
top - 15:11:45 up 22 min,  1 user,  load average: 0.00, 0.02, 0.07
Tasks: 216 total,   1 running, 215 sleeping,   0 stopped,   0 zombie
%Cpu(s):  0.7 us,  0.0 sy,  0.0 ni, 98.3 id,  0.3 wa,  0.7 hi,  0.0 si,  0.0 st
MiB Mem :   3927.9 total,   1917.2 free,    776.6 used,   1234.1 buff/cache
MiB Swap:   1963.0 total,   1963.0 free,      0.0 used.   2906.3 avail Mem

    PID USER      PR  NI    VIRT    RES    SHR S  %CPU  %MEM     TIME+ COMMAND
   1691 damon     20   0 3835420 255780 122460 S   0.7   6.4   0:05.34 gnome-shell
   2977 root      20   0  234964   4604   3960 R   0.3   0.1   0:00.02 top
      1 root      20   0  174992  17428  11556 S   0.0   0.4   0:01.27 systemd
      2 root      20   0       0      0      0 S   0.0   0.0   0:00.00 kthreadd
      3 root       0 -20       0      0      0 I   0.0   0.0   0:00.00 rcu_gp
```

Output from the top command.

Monitoring Linux with Sar

The sar utility displays system performance information. It can be configured to update regularly and to repeat itself a specific number of times.

The syntax of the sar command is

```
sar (intervals) (repeats)
```

where intervals is the refresh rate and repeats is the number of times the tool refreshes.

Example:

```
sar - u 2 5
```

Displays CPU utilization information, updating every two seconds, and repeating for a total of five times.

Option	Description
-S	Swap information
-u	CPU information
-r	Memory/RAM information
-b	I/O disk information
-n	Network information

Common options for the sar command.

Linux Uptime

The uptime command displays how long the system has been up, the current number of users, and the CPU load for the last one, five, and fifteen minutes.

```
[root@localhost ~]# uptime
 15:13:06 up 24 min,  1 user,  load average: 0.00, 0.01, 0.06
[root@localhost ~]#
```

Output of the uptime command.

Displaying Linux Storage Information

You have already seen information on monitoring storage in other lessons. You should recall that the df and du commands can display useful information about available and consumed storage capacity.

- df—displays information about used and free space. Use the -h option to display the information in a more useable, human-readable format.
- du—displays information about the quantity of storage space consumed by specific files and folders. Like df, you should add the -h option.

```
[root@localhost ~]# du -h /var/log/audit
2.2M    /var/log/audit
[root@localhost ~]#
```

The output of the du command.

```
[root@localhost ~]# df -h
Filesystem      Size  Used Avail Use% Mounted on
devtmpfs        1.9G     0  1.9G   0% /dev
tmpfs           2.0G     0  2.0G   0% /dev/shm
tmpfs           786M  1.4M  785M   1% /run
/dev/sda2        13G  6.8G  5.7G  55% /
tmpfs           2.0G  392K  2.0G   1% /tmp
/dev/sda2        13G  6.8G  5.7G  55% /home
/dev/sda1       976M  229M  681M  26% /boot
tmpfs           393M  156K  393M   1% /run/user/1000
```

The output of the df command.

Linux Log Files

Log files are a great way to discover information about your server. Linux uses rsyslog to track system and application events. By default, Linux stores log files in the /var/log directory. Linux itself, services, and applications such as Apache all use in this location.

```
[root@localhost log]# head boot.log
         Starting Authorization Manager...
[  OK  ] Finished Rotate log files.
[  OK  ] Started ABRT Automated Bug Reporting Tool.
[  OK  ] Started Creates ABRT problems from coredumpctl messages.
[  OK  ] Started ABRT kernel log watcher.
[  OK  ] Started ABRT Xorg log watcher.
[  OK  ] Started Authorization Manager.
[  OK  ] Finished Builds and install new kernel modules through DKMS.
[  OK  ] Started Disk Manager.
[  OK  ] Started System Security Services Daemon.
[root@localhost log]#
```

Linux boot log file located in the /var/log directory.

Log File Reporting and Retention

Because log files record detailed server events, industry or governmental regulations may define how the logs are made available to systems administrators as well as auditors.

Many log file management tools, such as rsyslog and Event Viewer, are capable of centralizing logs. Such centralization makes reporting much easier.

Windows Server log files can be configured for a maximum size and further configured to overwrite the oldest events once that maximum size is reached. Many Windows administrators will manually rotate or backup log files before then.

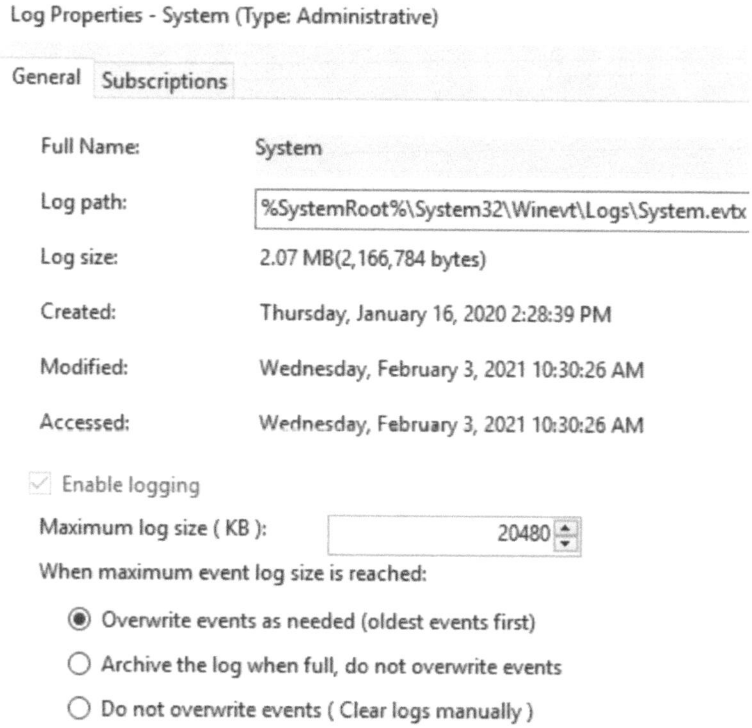

Windows log overwrite screen. (Screenshot courtesy of Microsoft.)

Linux sysadmins will use tools such as logrotate to automatically archived older log files, preventing them from being overwritten or deleted and also from ballooning to immense sizes if the server begins to experience issues.

Log files may also be governed by retention rules that state how long the logs must be available. Depending on the business type, legal requirements may define your retention policies. Luckily, since older log files are probably not accessed frequently, they can be compressed, archived, and placed in offline storage.

Log Shipping

Log shipping refers to a process that is different from log forwarding or centralization. Log shipping is used with database servers such as MYSQL or Microsoft SQL Server. The goal is to provide increased database availability by ensuring a secondary database server has the same changes as a primary.

With log shipping, changes to the primary database server that are recorded in the logs are mimicked on the secondary database server. If the primary server fails, the secondary is configured to take over with little to no downtime.

Review Activity:

Server Functions

Answer the following questions:

1. **Which type of server hosts an authentication database to verify the identity of users and computers?**

2. **Which type of server leases IP address configurations to client computers?**

3. **Which type of server provides name resolution to client computers?**

4. **What is virtual memory?**

5. **What term describes Windows virtual memory? Linux virtual memory?**

6. **List at least two examples of administrative interfaces:**

7. **List at least two Windows monitoring utilities:**

8. **List two Linux monitoring utilities:**

9. **What Windows PowerShell cmdlet displays the system's current uptime? What command displays a Linux system's current uptime?**

10. **List two Linux commands used to monitor storage space:**

Topic 9C

Configure Server Hardening

EXAM OBJECTIVES COVERED

3.5 Given a scenario, apply server hardening methods

Server administration best practices include the proper configuration of the server from a security perspective. This concept is known as hardening, and it applies to hardware, the server OS, and applications.

Hardware Hardening

Hardening means to remove services and applications from the server that aren't needed and update the necessary software. You can break the hardening process down into components.

Hardening begins with the physical server itself. First, disable any hardware components not needed by the system. Often, these settings are configured in the BIOS. These might include USB ports, devices, such as local DVD drives, or functionality, such as multiple NICs. These examples would help to prevent intruders from accessing the server locally or installing unauthorized software.

The next step is to configure the server's boot order to bypass USB devices and DVDs, ensuring the server will only boot from its own internal HDDs or via a network service, such as PXE.

Finally, configure a BIOS password. The BIOS configuration manages the ports and boot order, and so protecting those configurations with a password helps to maintain the server's security profile.

Device drivers allow the OS to understand how to work with a specific hardware device's features.

OS Hardening

Recall that the concept behind hardening is to remove what isn't needed, keep the OS up to date, and change default settings. Server hardening is one of several layers of security to better protect your data and services.

Remove Unneeded Services

Server OSs may include certain services as part of the installation process by default. The role of that particular server, however, may not require those services. For example, an OS installation may include a web server service, which immediately makes the server available to host web sites. This is convenient if the server you're standing up is supposed to be a web server. However, if the device is supposed to be a file server instead, with no web services required, then the additional service leaves open a potential vulnerability. Hardening the server's OS means removing these types of services.

Change Default Settings

A critical part of hardening OSs is to change default settings, which varyby OS (Windows Server, Red Hat Enterprise Linux, Ubuntu Server, etc) and by version (Windows Server 2012 vs Windows Server 2019). Here are some general categories of defaults to consider:

Configure the Firewall

Hardening includes controlling network access to the server. The firewall filters inbound and outbound traffic. By default, most firewalls deny all traffic, and then the administrator explicitly configures certain services or ports to be permitted through the firewall.

Firewall configurations vary depending on the role of the server. Webservers, for instance, will typically permit inbound port 80 and port 443 connections, while DNS servers will permit port 53.

- Default accounts should be managed. This may encompass disabling guest and administrative accounts.
- Password requirements should be configured (complexity, etc), and single sign-on or MFA should be considered.
- Servers are typically configured with a static IP address, and this IP address should be part of an isolated subnet. Most server OSs install with a dynamic IP address setting.
- Automated updates need to point to your preferred update suite and not necessarily to the default update site.
- Remote access settings for PowerShell, SSH, RDP, and other tools should be enabled or disabled according to your company's policies.
- Configure logging to manage log file sizes and rotation schedules. These settings may be subject to industry or legal requirements.
- Remove Windows permissions for the Everyone group and use the Authenticated Users group instead.
- Enable data encryption such as **Encrypting File System (EFS)**, BitLocker, and LUKS.

OS patching is covered later in this section. It was also covered in Lesson 8.

Application Hardening

As noted before, the server should only have the required applications installed on it. However, many applications are modular, and you may only be using a subset of the application's functionality. Either remove or disable its unused roles or features.

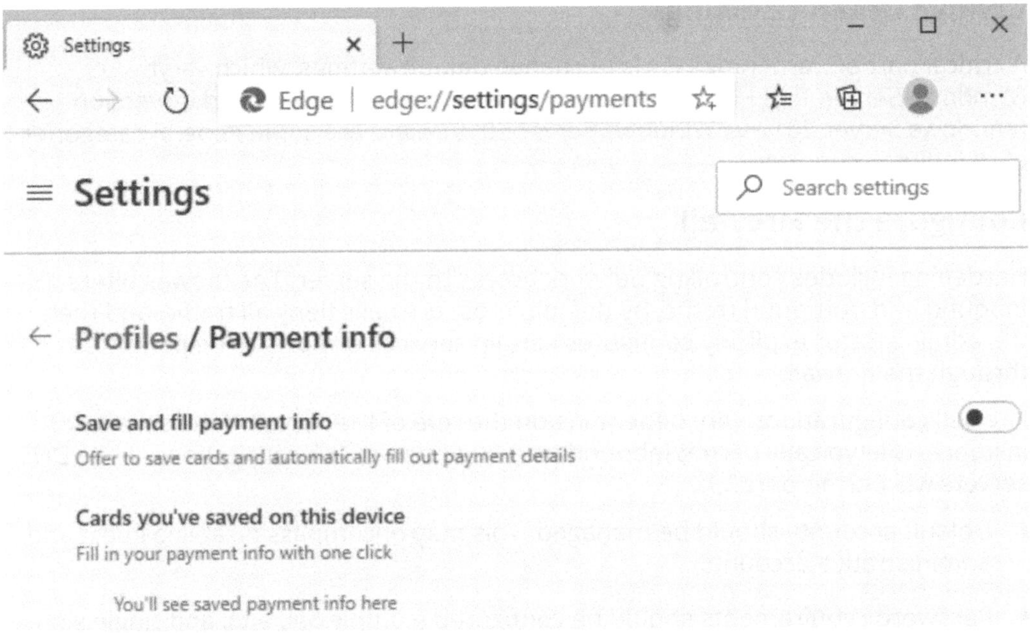

Disable Payment info in Microsoft Edge. (Screenshot courtesy of Microsoft.)

For example, a database server running Microsoft SQL Server should only have the components of SQL Server required for its functionality, and the others should be removed or disabled. However, the SQL Server installation should be the latest supported version, and application patching must be managed.

Following the practice of application hardening can be difficult. It requires that the sysadmin carefully examine the server's role and understands which components of the application are required for the environment. Application hardening checklists for web servers, database servers, file servers, and so forth will vary.

Host Security

Many organizations also rely on **host-based intrusion detection systems (HIDS)** or **host-based intrusion prevention systems (HIPS)** to identify or prevent unauthorized data access or system configuration changes.

There are plenty of additional actions you can take as the sysadmin to secure your servers better. Antivirus and antimalware software should be installed. In many cases, these applications are already installed. For example, Windows Server includes antimalware software by default.

Windows Security console. (Screenshot courtesy of Microsoft.)

Patching

Hardening relies heavily on patching at the firmware, OS, application, and device driver layers. Your organization needs a patch management process that includes identifying the necessary patches, downloading them, testing their functionality, approving their distribution, and finally deploying them to the impacted servers.

Approach patching by considering the systems layers. Begin with firmware, or patching the hardware layer. Device drivers are also managed at this layer. Next, manage OS patching. Application patching comes after the OS.

Firmware and Drivers

Firmware and device driver updates will typically describe any security or stability issues that they address. Vendors publish descriptions of the problems the update is designed to fix.

Firmware and driver updates were covered in more detail in Lesson 5.

OS Updates

OS vendors, such as Microsoft and Linux, release system updates regularly. These updates address security, performance, and stability issues that have been discovered and corrected.

OS updates were covered in more detail in Lesson 8.

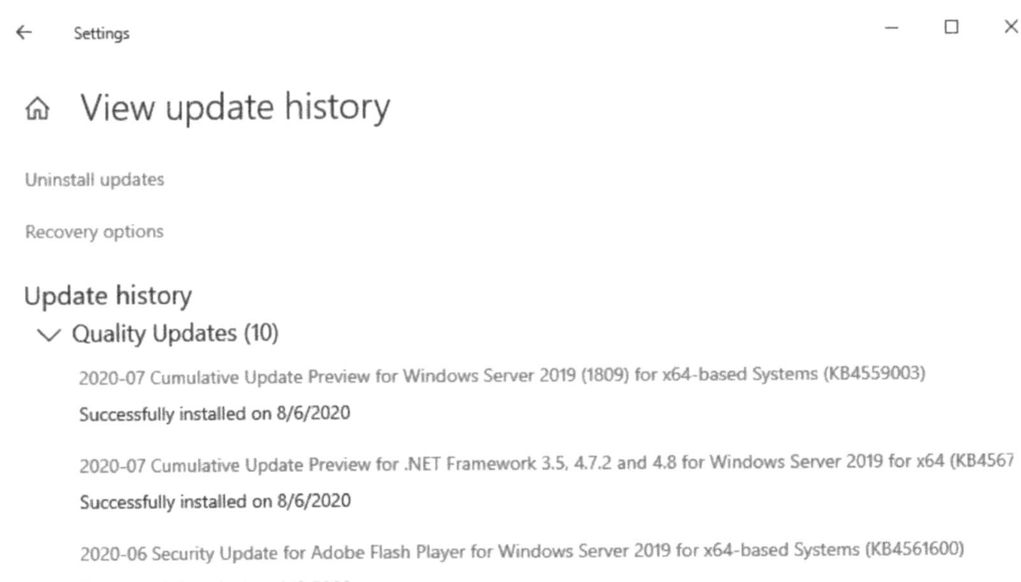

Windows Updates history. (Screenshot courtesy of Microsoft.)

Recall that one of the primary goals of security is availability. Ensure that patches don't have unintended consequences or downtime that might impact availability.

Application Updates

Like firmware, device drivers, and OSs, applications also need to be kept current. Microsoft provides patches for both end-user applications, such as Microsoft Office, and larger applications, such as Microsoft SQL Server. These patches also need to be tested to ensure there are no unexpected functionality or feature changes.

The 2020 SolarWinds Orion attack is an example of an exploitation of vulnerable enterprise-class software.

Guidelines for Server Hardening

- Hardening servers includes removing unneeded software, features, and services. It also includes using current and patched OSs and applications.
- Carefully test device driver updates.
- Patches should be tested and applied regularly.
- Automate the patch management process.
- Security includes availability, so make sure that patches do not interrupt services.

Review Activity:

Server Hardening

Answer the following questions:

1. **List at least two examples of physical hardening for servers:**

2. **List three types of host security software that may be installed on servers:**

Lesson 9

Summary

Once the OS is installed, it needs to be configured to securely provide services. Sysadmins usually access servers remotely by using tools such as SSH and Remote Desktop. Administrator tasks may include user and group management and auditing. The installed and running services should be limited to only the primary function of the server, and hardware, such as storage and virtual memory, must be configured. Finally, security hardening is configured. Hardening may be summed up as removing what is not needed and then using the most current version of whatever applications and services remain. Server hardware should match the specific resource requirements of the services.

1. **What process does your organization use to test OS, application, and device driver update?**

2. **Why would you not want to rely on virtual memory on a busy server?**

Lesson 10

Managing Data Security

LESSON INTRODUCTION

Data security is one of the most important jobs of the sysadmin. In the first portion of the lesson, you will view data security concepts. Next, you'll manage data security configurations. Finally, security troubleshooting will be covered.

Lesson Objectives

In this lesson, you will:

- Understand data security concepts.
- Manage data security.
- Troubleshoot data security.

Topic 10A

Understand Data Security Concepts

EXAM OBJECTIVES COVERED
3.1 Summarize data security concepts

Data security has a tangible impact on business practices and results. It is essential to understand the value of data, data security priorities, and the data lifecycle. Finally, you must determine the cost of security versus the risk of loss or replacement.

The Business Impact of Data Security

Data security begins with understanding the value of your organization's data, the data lifecycle, and the cost of security mitigation versus the loss of the data. It is difficult to protect organizational resources if you do not know their value or priority.

Data Value Prioritization

One key aspect of security is that the organization must recognize and prioritize the value of its data. An organization that does not consciously value its data will have no reason to dedicate resources to that data. Once the organization deliberately decides that the information has value and perhaps even goes so far as to assign a monetary value, there is an incentive to manage that data from a security perspective.

Lifecycle Management

Data, from **PII** to research and development projects, is an essential part of businesses. Data goes through a lifecycle that is addressed by a data management policy.

Data Management Policy

An organization uses a data management policy to govern data throughout its lifecycle. Aspects of this management include data creation (applications), internal data storage (file servers or databases), external data storage (on-premises vs. off-site), data backup, data security (permissions, encryption), data policies (acceptable use), and data transmission (network encryption).

Some aspects of the data management lifecycle may be dictated to your organization by government or industry regulations and standards. For example, the PCI DSS governs information security related to credit cards. If your company takes credit card payments, then it likely falls under these standards.

Recall that security goals follow the CIA triad—confidentiality, integrity, and availability. When an organization values its data, it manages that data with those goals in mind.

The Cost of Security Versus Risk and/or Replacement

There may be pushback in some organizations against the value of data security. This cost may be measured in actual expenditures, on applications or redundant hardware, or in terms of resources and staff time. Most likely, it is measured in both. Regardless, it is a useful practice to compare the relative cost of proposed security measures against the cost of loss of access to the data or the exposure of data to unauthorized viewers.

The first step is to identify the level of risk or likelihood that a threat will be executed against the organization. Next, estimate the cost of mitigating that risk. You might break the information down into the categories displayed in the table.

Risk/cost	Description
High likelihood/high cost	May be worth the expense to address
Low likelihood/low cost	May be worth the expense to address
High likelihood/low cost	Is worth the expense to address
Low likelihood/high cost	May not be worth the expense to address

Risks and associated costs.

Exactly what the threats, risks, vulnerabilities, and associated costs are varies depending on the industry and the organization itself.

Data Encryption

There are various ways in which data is vulnerable to abuse, including unauthorized access or distribution. One aspect of data security is **encryption**. Data may be encrypted for several reasons, including confidentiality, integrity, and non-repudiation. Data encryption is used when data is at rest (stored on a drive) or in transit on the network, or both. Finally, data is governed by retention policies that define how long data must be kept and at what point the data must be deleted.

Encryption is the process of encoding data so that only those with the proper decryption key can access it. Those without the key cannot decrypt the data and access its contents. There are many different encryption algorithms available. Applications such as email clients and web browsers often integrate encryption solutions.

Goals of Encryption

It is important to note that there are three goals of encryption. When the word encryption is used, most people immediately equate it with confidentiality, or keeping something secret. While confidentiality is one goal of encryption, it is not the only possible goal.

Goal	Description
Confidentiality	Making data available only to authorized users
Integrity	Ensuring that data has not changed unexpectedly
Non-repudiation	Ensuring that a particular transaction cannot be denied or renounced

The three goals of encryption.

Confidentiality

Encrypting data for confidentiality is pretty self-evident. Data is encrypted such that only authorized users with the decryption key can view the data. Confidentiality provides privacy and is a common use of encryption.

Integrity

Encrypting data for integrity provides a simple way of checking whether data has changed. For example, on a Linux server, you can run the command `md5 file1.txt` to generate a hash result. If you run that same command on that same file in the future, you can compare the two hash results to determine whether the file has changed.

```
[root@localhost ~]# md5sum file1.txt
d41d8cd98f00b204e9800998ecf8427e  file1.txt
[root@localhost ~]#
[root@localhost ~]#
```

Generate a checksum by using the md5sum command.

In Linux, the command to generate a hash is md5sum. Windows does not have a built-in tool for generating hashes.

Non-Repudiation

Encrypting data may also result in non-repudiation, or making it impossible for someone to deny that an action occurred. For example, if your organization routinely uses encrypted email, all email messages are encrypted using the sender's private key. That key, by definition, is private and related only to that specific sender. Only that sender has access to that key. If you receive an encrypted email from that sender, you know that they are the only person who could have sent it. That sender cannot deny, or repudiate, the message.

Try to break yourself of the habit of assuming that encrypted data is private. Encrypted data may be private, but there are other possible purposes behind data encryption.

Administrators and applications use different encryption techniques depending on the required result and how the data is accessed.

Data in Transit Versus Data at Rest

There are two different times when data encryption protects information: when the **data is in transit** across the network or at rest on the drive.

Data in Transit

It is essential to understand that a great deal of network traffic on most internal networks and the Internet is not encrypted for data confidentiality. Network traffic is relatively easy to intercept using **packet sniffers** (also known as **packet analyzers** or **protocol analyzers**). If the data payload is unencrypted, its contents can be read.

Network communications can be encrypted for confidentiality. Here are some tools that provide encryption for network communications:

- SSH—used primarily for remote administration
- HTTPS—secure, mainly used for encrypted web browsing
- RDP—encrypts the remote desktop connection when used for remote administration with Windows Servers

Data at Rest

Data stored on a drive is not usually encrypted for confidentiality. Permissions protect the data in Linux and Windows. However, there are various methods for circumventing permissions. Data encryption adds another layer of security to **data at rest** by ensuring that only the authorized users possessing the decryption key can access the data.

There are two approaches to protecting data at rest: drive/partition encryption and file encryption.

Drive encryption encrypts the entire drive (or designated partitions on it) during the shutdown process and decrypts the driveduring the startup process. Such encryption protects the contents while the server is powered off. For example, if someone steals the drive, the data is encrypted. Individual files are encrypted when they are closed and decrypted when opened. Drive encryption, therefore, protects data from unauthorized access when the system is powered on.

Examples of drive encryption:

- Microsoft **BitLocker**
- Linux LUKS (Linux Unified Key Setup)

Examples of file encryption:

- Microsoft BitLocker
- TrueCrypt (Linux, Windows, macOS)
- 7Zip (Linux, Windows)
- GnuPG (Linux)

By default, neither Linux nor Windows servers encrypt at the drive or file levels, so encrypting data at rest is something you, as the sysadmin, have to enable if you wish to use it.

Retention Policies

Most organizations have a data management policy that governs the company's ability to secure, track, update, and store data. The data retention policy is a subset of that data management policy.

Data Retention

Data retention policies are the company's standardized approach to keeping data for a specific period and disposing of that data once it expires. Data must be accessible to the appropriate users, which requires planning. This planning may be relatively simple, like a particular folder hierarchy, or much more complex, like a full-fledged document management system.

Companies should retain data as long as required and no longer. Retaining data for longer than necessary incurs storage and management costs that do not contribute to the organization's business objectives. Document management systems label data with expiration dates and enforce those dates by archiving or deleting data that is no longer current. In some cases, legal or regulatory requirements govern data retention policies.

Businesses must be aware of electronically stored information (ESI). It has become increasingly difficult to keep track of where data might be stored: personal devices belonging to users, company-issued laptops, USB flash drives, servers, cloud-based storage, email (personal and professional), and text messages. In the context of **subpoenas**, knowledge of and ability to track such data is critical.

Physical Storage

Another aspect of data security is the physical storage location. Data stored on-site can be carefully managed by systems administrators. The organization retains complete control over the data. This type of control requires that the on-site staff be fully knowledgeable in security best practices. In some cases, regulatory requirements might force organizations to retain data on-site.

Backup media may be stored off-site to protect the backups from incidents that occur on-site, such as a building fire or flood. Relying on a separate physical location means that the organization gives up some control of its data and must rely on the storage location's expertise.

The cloud is one interesting example of off-site storage. Storing data in the cloud, whether it be a relatively simple solution, such as Dropbox, or a more robust solution, such as Microsoft Azure or Amazon AWS, introduces other security concerns. Not only is your data stored off-site, but it is probably put in a shared storage implementation alongside other organizations' data. Data management policies and regulatory requirements may govern cloud-based storage differently than on-site storage.

Location	Description
On-site storage	Business retains control, and sysadmins must be security experts
Off-site storage	Business gives up some control and relies on the security expertise of the remote storage staff

Comparing storage location options.

Additional Data Security Measures

You may also protect data from unauthorized access by restricting access to the servers where data is stored. UEFI/BIOS passwords add an additional layer of authentication to servers. Boot loader password help to protect the server against unauthorized changes that might make data vulnerable.

UEFI/BIOS Passwords

One fundamental way of managing data security is to ensure that system access is locked down. As you've seen elsewhere in the course, the system's BIOS or UEFI settings are protected by a password.

Example: Your organization is concerned about data leaving the premises on USB flash drives. To mitigate this concern, USB ports on the servers are disabled in the BIOS settings. You configure a BIOS password to stop potential data thieves from re-enabling the USB ports in the BIOS and then copying data to USB flash drives.

Boot Loader Passwords

During the boot process, the BIOS configurations are enabled. The next phase in the start process is launching a boot loader to manage the actual startup of the installed OS. The boot loader contains many settings that impact security and data access. Sysadmins configure passwords to prevent unauthorized users from making changes to OS startup settings that might expose data to access.

Guidelines for Understanding Data Security

- Encryption has three goals: confidentiality, integrity, and non-repudiation.
- Balance the cost of data security against the likelihood of a risk.
- Retention policies govern the minimum and maximum amount of time data is kept.
- Data in transit is vulnerable on the network.
- Data in transit may be protected by SSH, HTTPS, RDP, and other protocols.
- Data at rest is vulnerable on the drive.
- Data at rest may be protected by drive encryption (BitLocker, LUKS) or file encryption (BitLocker, TrueCrypt, 7Zip, GnuPG).
- Tools such a md5sum in Linux can determine whether data has changed unexpectedly.
- On-site storage allows a business to retain complete control of its data, but the full responsibility for security rests on the sysadmins.
- Off-site or cloud storage causes a business to lose some control over data, but the responsibility for security is shared.
- UEFI/BIOS and boot loader passwords provide an additional authentication layer.

Review Activity:

Data Security Concepts

Answer the following questions:

1. **What is the purpose of a data management policy?**
2. **What are the three goals of encryption?**
3. **What does it mean to ensure data integrity?**
4. **What does it mean to ensure non-repudiation?**
5. **List at least one tool used for secure network communications:**
6. **List two examples of disk encryption technologies:**
7. **List at least two examples of file encryption technologies:**

Topic 10B

Manage Data Security

EXAM OBJECTIVES COVERED
3.4 Explain data security risks and mitigation strategies

There are many risks to your server and its content. It is useful to categorize those risks and then to list possible mitigation strategies. In the following section, you see several examples of risks and a brief list of possible mitigation techniques.

Risks and Mitigation

Sometimes it is thought that risks to data can be eliminated. That's not really true. Rather, risks are mitigated. Mitigation is an effort to reduce the severity of a data loss event.

The table below displays several kinds of risks along with possible mitigation techniques.

Risk	Mitigation techniques
Hardware failure	Log analysis (SIEM), redundancy
Malware	Data monitoring, log analysis (SIEM)
Data corruption	Data monitoring, backups
Insider threats	Log analysis (SIEM), two-person integrity, separation of roles, role rotation, regulatory constraints
Data Loss Prevention (DLP)	Data monitoring, two-person integrity, regulatory constraints, data retention
Unwanted duplication (theft)	Log analysis (SIEM), data monitoring, two-person integrity, regulatory constraints, data retention
Unwanted publication (theft)	Log analysis (SIEM), data monitoring, two-person integrity, regulatory constraints, data retention
Unwanted access (backdoor, social engineering)	Log analysis (SIEM), two-person integrity
Breach	Log analysis (SIEM), data monitoring, regulatory constraints, data retention

Risks and mitigation techniques.

Notice that several mitigation strategies cover multiple types of risks. That indicates that these strategies are particularly useful to you. For example, log file analysis with a robust SIEM solution is a critical security strategy. It is also common for compliance with industry regulations and legal constraints to be listed.

Two-person integrity methods help to mitigate various threats to data. The method relies on at least two entities to agree to decrypt data (or conduct other activities). This form of mitigation supports role separation. Adding role rotation further strengthens security. By separating roles, perpetrators must work together to have access to vulnerable data. Such collusion is far less likely to be successful.

In some data integrity and confidentiality scenarios, encrypted data can be decrypted by a golden key with the ability to decrypt all data within the environment. Think of this like a master key that can open all physical locks in a building. For additional security, split encryption keys can be put in place that require two encryption key holders to combine keys to decrypt data.

Industry and Government Regulations

Industry regulations, including the management of PII and the PCI DSS requirements, may involve some additional research on the part of the security team and the legal department. Government regulations may also impact your mitigation strategies. The United States federal government may have additional regulations and constraints that govern your particular industry.

CSPs often certify their services as PCI compliant. This certification is a useful fact when choosing a cloud solution. It makes management easier because the CSP handles this compliance for you.

Breaches

One of the biggest concerns for security incidents is the exposure of PII. Identity theft is a common cybercrime and when a company's systems are exploited, PII is one of the primary targets. The information could be that of employees or customers (or both).

The NIST includes the following data as part of or associated with PII:

- National identification number (Social Security number in the United States, for example)
- Bank account numbers
- Passport number
- Driver's license number
- Bank card/credit card numbers
- Name
- Address (including street address, city, state, country, postal code)
- Telephone number
- Birth date
- Gender

Accidental disclosure of this information may constitute a crime or breach of contract.

Guidelines for Managing Data Security

- Implement a strong SIEM system.
- Consider separation of roles and role rotations in your organization.
- Log file management and analysis are an essential aspect of your security posture.
- Be aware of industry requirements, such as PCI DSS.
- Be mindful of best practices for managing PII.
- Be aware of any legal considerations surrounding data retention.

Review Activity:

Data Security

Answer the following questions:

1. **What mitigation technique is recommended for the risk of data corruption?**

2. **What mitigation technique is recommended for the risk of unwanted duplication?**

3. **What mitigation technique is recommended for the risk of unwanted access?**

4. **What mitigation technique is recommended for the risk of malware?**

Topic 10C

Troubleshoot Data Security

EXAM OBJECTIVES COVERED
4.6 Given a scenario, troubleshoot security problems

There are some standard techniques and practices for common troubleshooting situations. Sysadmins often see problems in the following areas:

- Network connectivity
- Connectivity to online resources, such as shared folders
- Misconfigured services, permissions, ports, and applications
- Data loss and data integrity
- Firewall misconfiguration, including open ports
- Antivirus and antimalware application misconfiguration

This section displays some common problems and their related causes.

General Troubleshooting

Consider resource access, server configurations, and services when troubleshooting common issues.

Resource Access

Many help desk tickets and user complaints center around access to resources. Frequently, these issues are tied to permissions. In Windows, file access is managed by NTFS permissions and by Share permissions when accessing the file from across the network. In Linux, file access is controlled by standard permissions and by NFS permissions when accessing the data from across the network. Ensuring these permissions are set correctly eases many user frustrations and provides users access to the files that they need. **Viruses** and other malware also impact the ability of users to access resources.

When configuring permissions, remember the principle of Least Privilege, which states that users should be granted as little access as possible while still being able to do their jobs.

Group Policy Configurations

Recall that Windows uses Group Policy at the local and domain levels to manage workstation and server configurations centrally. Misconfigured Group Policy settings impact firewalls, services, applications, anti-malware, and other **data loss prevention** configurations.

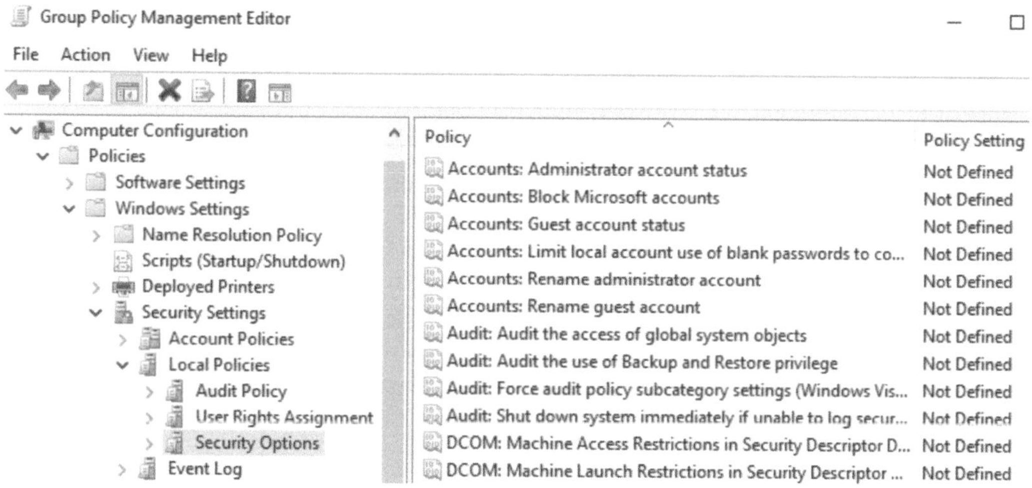

AD Group Policy Security Options. (Screenshot courtesy of Microsoft.)

Firewall Configurations

Misconfigured firewall settings may cause users to be unable to access network resources. For example, an internal web site might be made available to users to manage time off requests, but if the local host-based firewall on the web server does not permit port 80/443 connections, then users will not be able to access the resource.

Firewalls may also be configured to be too open—ports that are unused and should be closed expose servers to unauthorized access. Most firewalls default to closing all or most ports and requiring administrators to specifically open desired ports.

Service Configurations

Services enable or disable additional functionality on the server. Security hardening includes disabling all services not required on the server. A service misconfiguration that disables an essential service limits the server's functionality.

The Services console manages Windows services. Linux services are usually managed from the command-line, often by using the systemctl command. For example, to start the SSH **daemon (service)**, the command syntax is

```
systemctl start sshd
```

Orphan (zombie) and rogue processes may interfere with the proper execution of new processes and consume system resources that otherwise would be dedicated to current processes. These processes can be detected in Linux by tools such as sar and top.

```
top - 15:11:45 up 22 min,  1 user,  load average: 0.00, 0.02, 0.07
Tasks: 216 total,   1 running, 215 sleeping,   0 stopped,   0 zombie
%Cpu(s):  0.7 us,  0.0 sy,  0.0 ni, 98.3 id,  0.3 wa,  0.7 hi,  0.0 si,  0.0 st
MiB Mem :   3927.9 total,   1917.2 free,    776.6 used,   1234.1 buff/cache
MiB Swap:   1963.0 total,   1963.0 free,      0.0 used.   2906.3 avail Mem

    PID USER      PR  NI    VIRT    RES    SHR S  %CPU  %MEM     TIME+ COMMAND
   1691 damon     20   0 3835420 255780 122460 S   0.7   6.4   0:05.34 gnome-shell
   2977 root      20   0  234964   4604   3960 R   0.3   0.1   0:00.02 top
      1 root      20   0  174992  17428  11556 S   0.0   0.4   0:01.27 systemd
      2 root      20   0       0      0      0 S   0.0   0.0   0:00.00 kthreadd
      3 root       0 -20       0      0      0 I   0.0   0.0   0:00.00 rcu_gp
```

Managing processes by using top.

Common concerns	Possible causes
File integrity	Misconfigured permissions, viruses, malware
Improper privilege escalation (excessive access)	Misconfigured Local/Group Policy settings, misconfigured permissions
Applications won't load	Misconfigured services, misconfigured anti-malware, misconfigured Local/Group Policy settings, misconfigured permissions, zombie/orphan processes
Cannot access network shares	Misconfigured services, misconfigured anti-malware, misconfigured Local/Group Policy settings, misconfigured permissions, misconfigured data loss prevention tools, misconfigured intrusion detection systems
Unable to open files	Misconfigured services, misconfigured anti-malware, misconfigured Local/Group Policy settings, misconfigured permissions, misconfigured data loss prevention tools, misconfigured intrusion detection systems

Troubleshooting Tools and Their Uses

Knowing when to use the tools at your disposal is one of the most useful skills you can develop. There are so many tools, built in and third party, that it can be challenging to know when to use what. Of course, the available tools vary depending on whether you're using Linux or Windows servers (or both).

Using Troubleshooting Tools

Tools	Use
Port scanners	Ensure firewalls and services are configured correctly
Packet sniffers	Ensure firewalls are configured correctly
Telnet clients	Ensure firewalls and services are configured correctly
Anti-malware	Ensure servers are free of malware
Antivirus	Ensure servers are free of viruses
File integrity (checksums, monitoring, detection, enforcement)	Ensure files have not changed unexpectedly
User access controls (SELinux, User Account Control (UAC))	Ensure proper privilege escalation, ensure file access
Service management tools (systemctl, Services console)	Ensure service configuration, manage rogue processes and services
Group Policy console, gpresult	Ensure Local/Group Policies are configured correctly

Review Activity:

Data Security Troubleshooting

Answer the following questions:

1. **Explain the concept of the Principle of Least Privilege.**

2. **List two common causes for issues of improper privilege escalation:**

3. **List at least three common causes for issues where users cannot properly access network shares:**

4. **What is the purpose of port scanning tools?**

5. **What is the purpose of packet sniffing tools?**

6. **What is the purpose of user access control services, such as SELinux and User Account Control?**

Lesson 10

Summary

Use the data lifecycle to manage data security. Understand the value of your data, balance risk and cost, and manage data retention policies. Use encryption to provide information confidentiality, integrity, and non-repudiation.

1. **Does your organization maintain PII? What steps are taken to protect that information?**

2. **Does your organization use an SIEM system to help manage incidents?**

Lesson 11

Managing Service and Data Availability

LESSON INTRODUCTION

Frequently, service and data availability are functions of redundancy. That redundancy may entail duplication of data, such as with backups, or duplication of servers, such as with clustering, or even duplication of locations, such as with disaster recovery sites. Each of these strategies also has a corresponding recovery method that must be properly planned and tested.

Lesson Objectives

In this lesson, you will:

- Manage data backup and restore.
- Manage high availability.
- Manage disaster recovery.

Topic 11A

Manage Data Backup and Restore

EXAM OBJECTIVES COVERED
3.7 Explain the importance of backups and restores

There are many reasons to regularly back up data on computers. Users may inadvertently delete or alter data, or storage devices could fail. Incidents on a larger scale, such as a fire or a flood, might cause damage to the physical building. Additionally, industry regulations may require that you retain data for a specific length of time. This section will discuss backup frequency, media types, and validation as well as data restoration.

Managing Backups and Restores

Managing **backups** is a balance between the time the backup job takes and the time the restoral process takes. There are several backup types and backup strategies that are used to properly manage data backup and recovery. Backup strategies also vary depending on whether a physical server or a VM is used.

Full Backups

Full Backups are a complete backup of the system. They often take a relatively long time, especially when there is a lot of data on the server. The restoral process is relatively quick because only one backup job needs to be used.

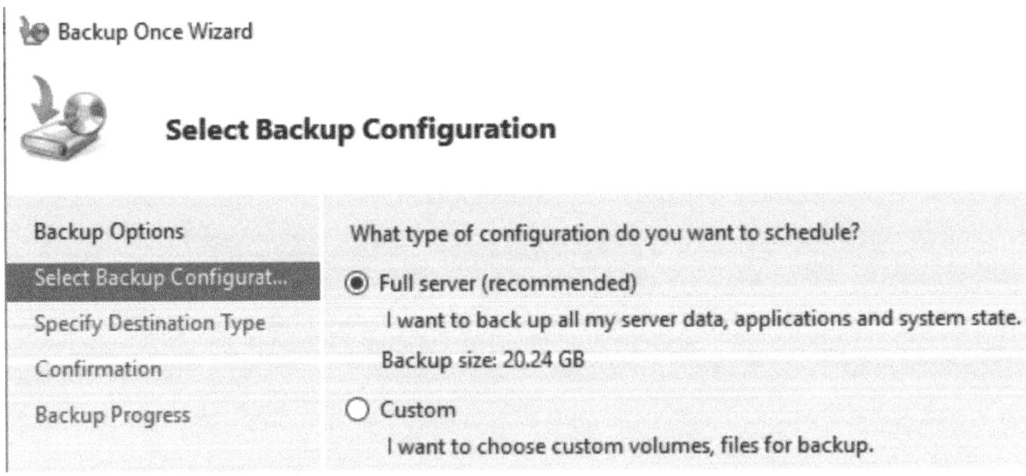

Full server backup on Windows Server. (Screenshot courtesy of Microsoft.)

Synthetic Full Backups

Synthetic full backups are backup jobs created by combining the most recent full backup and the subsequent incremental backups. The result in a single aggregated backup job. Synthetic full backups are not generated directly from the original data but instead assembled from other backup jobs.

Incremental Backups

An **incremental backup** is a backup of changes since a specified marker (usually a full backup) and resets the archive bit. Backups are quicker than differentials, but the restoral process is slower (must use each backup job after the full).

Differential Backups

Backup of changes since a specified marker (usually a full backup), without resetting the archive bit. **Differential backups** are slower as the week progresses, but restorals are faster (must only use two backup jobs to accomplish the restoral).

Continuous Data Protection (CDP)

Immediate backup of all changes to the data.

Near CDP

Incremental backups at a specified frequent interval, such as every 15 minutes.

Snapshot

A **snapshot** is a read-only copy of data at a specific point in time. Snapshots are often used with VMs and some services, such as AD and Microsoft Exchange. Snapshots are usually most useful for retaining system settings. Snapshots may also be referred to as images (and images are often used for system deployments, rather than data protection).

Archive

Archives are not precisely the same thing as backups. The archives retain data for long periods and are optimized for storage space efficiency. While backups are used for data protection, archives are used for long-term data retention for legal or regulatory purposes. Archives often contain data the company must keep but is not likely to actually reference.

Open File

Typical backup programs require files to be closed and static to capture their state. In some cases, closing all files may not be possible. Some organizations are 24 x 7, meaning there is always some data being accessed. Other services, such as databases, contain critical information that needs to be backed up without closing the files that make up the database (which would render it inaccessible during the backup process). Special backup programs exist for resources such as email and database services.

System-State Backups Versus File-Level Backups

System state backups duplicate the essential OS configurations. These configurations can then be quickly restored to the same machine in the event of corrupted system files or misconfigurations. System state backups are small and fast because they do not include the entire drive or user data.

File-level backups protect user data, application configuration files, etc. They are often scheduled much more frequently than system-state backups, because regular data changes often and system configurations change less often.

Backup Frequency

The frequency of backup jobs, and the type of jobs run during a given backup event, varies based on several criteria. The first question is, "How much data is your organization willing to lose?" The initial response, of course, is "none!" That's not very realistic, however, as CDP backups are costly. A balance is found between cost, the time needed for a backup, and the time required for a restoral.

Backup type	Result
Full	Slow backup, fast restore
Full+Incremental	Fast backup, slow restore (compared to Full+Differential)
Full+Differential	Slow backup, fast restore (compared to Full+Incremental)

Comparing backup scenarios.

The terms fast and slow in this discussion are relative. The actual speeds vary by the amount of data, the backup media type and related hardware, and the server storage hardware's performance.

Example Backup Schemes

- Option 1—Saturday night—Full, Sunday–Friday—Incrementals
- Option 2—Saturday night—Full, Sunday–Friday—Differentials

An organization chooses Option 1 for its file servers if it does not anticipate the need to do many restorals, because of reliable hardware, and access to the data stored on the file servers is not mission critical. The organization values fast backups.

An organization chooses Option 2 for its file servers if it values fast restorals over fast backup jobs because the data on the file servers is mission critical.

Common incremental example:

- Full backup is done at the first of the month.
- Incremental to the previous Friday done each weekday—catches all files changed since that Friday. Wednesday's tape has changed files since the previous Friday.
- Incremental to the first of the month is done on each Friday. Catches changes since the first of the month—all changes made during the month to that Friday.

	Floating	Mon	Tue	Weds	Thurs	Fri
Week 1	Full					
Week 2		Incr	Incr	Incr	Incr	Incr*
Week 3		Incr	Incr	Incr	Incr	Incr*
Week 4		Incr	Incr	Incr	Incr	Incr*
Week 5		Incr	Incr	Incr	Incr	Incr*

Weekly incremental backup since the last full. The Week 4 Friday incremental has all changes since the first of the month.

Backup Media Types

Backup jobs can be written to tape cartridges. Tapes often have a good cost-to-capacity ratio, have excellent long-term archive ability, and are easy to move and store. Many backup providers also suggest writing backup jobs to disk. Disks also have very beneficial attributes. For example, they are quite fast (for both backup and restore), are often easy to move and store, and are efficient for general backup use (as recovery points, rather than long-term archive media).

In addition to tape and disk backup media, there are also many cloud-based backup solutions. Cloud backups have many advantages, as well. For example, the initial investment in media and tape or disk drive devices is small. Cloud-based storage is easy to expand and easy to maintain.

A different way to consider the cloud versus tape/disk discussion is this: Does your organization want to maintain the backup infrastructure (manage your own tapes/disks), or does it want someone else to do it (CSP)? That's the whole premise of cloud services. In this case, you're looking at Backup-and-Restore as a Service (which is really SaaS).

Backup Media Types Considerations

- Disk and tape solutions are likely to have a higher initial cost in media and tape drives than cloud solutions are.
- Cloud solutions introduce your Internet connection as a variable when determining speed.
- Cloud solutions are likely to be much more future proof than tape solutions.
- Cloud backups are globally accessible, and you won't have to manage off-site storage.
- Your organization physically secures disk and tape solutions.
- Disk and tape solutions allow your organization to retain full control of all data.

Print Backups

Some backup products write to paper. These products translate data to codes, similar to QR codes, and then print them to paper. The code is reread by the application to convert the information back to your data. Typically, acid-free paper and high-quality ink are used to ensure longevity. Paper-based backups are an interesting option. Paper is durable for long periods of time and may be more future proof than disk drives or tapes. Think of it this way—will your organization be able to recover data from SATA HDDs 20 years from now?

Media Rotation

Backup media may need to be rotated to make more efficient use of storage capacity when preserving data for long-term access. There are many methods of rotating media.

First-In, First-Out (FIFO)

This is the most straightforward backup scheme. The organization decides how many days of backups are required, and that is the number of tapes (or drives) used. When the next tape is put into the **tape drive** for a backup job, the oldest tape is used.

For example, you are constructing a backup media rotation. The company has determined that backups are available for 14 days, so 14 tapes are used. Tonight's backup job will use the tape with the oldest backup file on it. The same criteria are selected for tomorrow night's backup job.

Grandfather-Father-Son

This scheme labels the backup tapes in generations. Sons are the most recent backups, and grandfathers are the oldest. As time passes, a backup job gets older and older relative to the date when the job occurred.

Full backups are done weekly, and incremental backups occur daily. Full backups are also done monthly (let's say on the last day of the month). The weekly fulls are fathers, the daily incrementals are sons, and the monthly fulls are grandfathers. There is a dedicated set of tapes for each role. In other words, there are 12 tapes labeled by month and dedicated to the grandfather role. There are four (or five, for long months) tapes labeled and dedicated to the father role.

Tower of Hanoi

This backup method is based on the Tower of Hanoi puzzle. It is designed to optimize backup media rotations. It uses three backup sets that are rotated regularly. It allows for the recovery of older information but is not as efficient for the restoral of recent information. It is an effective archiving scheme.

Backup Validation

Backup validation ensures that you're actually backing up what you think you're backing up and that the backed up data can be restored as expected. One way of testing this to actual perform restorals. VMs are handy for this. Spin up a virtual server, restore the data, and delete the VM after the data is validated. Testing restoral procedures is also a good exercise to prove that you are comfortable with the restore process.

Backup validation equipment, therefore, can be very simple. VMs, whether hosted on-premises or in the cloud, are quick and cheap. Log files can help pinpoint failed or partial backup attempts. Testing backups regularly will verify that they are complete, recoverable, and reliable. By confirming the integrity of the data on the backup media, your organization is more confident in its ability to recover from a storage failure. Few organizations tend to test their backups regularly, but conventional wisdom indicates that they should.

Restoring Data

Backing up data is useless without the ability to restore it. There are many ways of restoring data. Restore processes might occur due to data loss or corruption or to test the efficiency and effectiveness of backup jobs. Restore processes also validate the storage media.

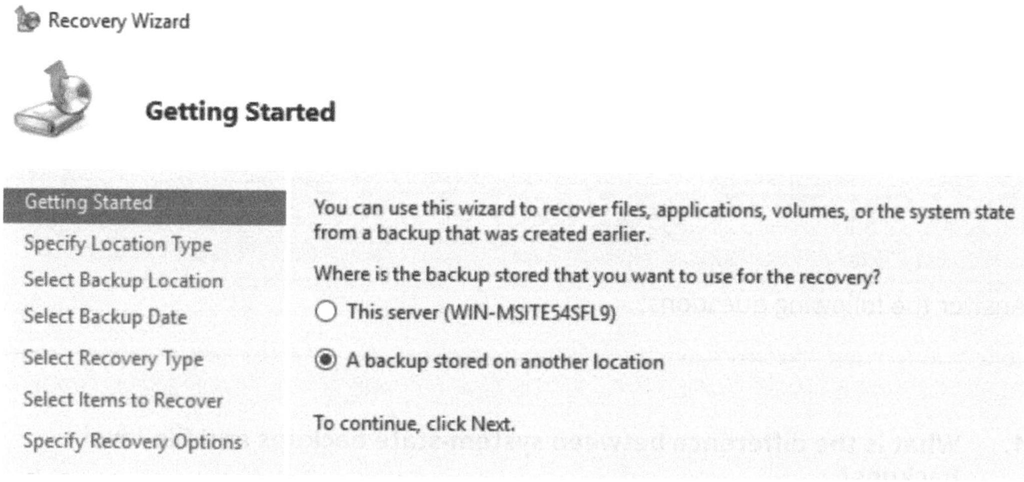

Restoring data from remote storage. (Screenshot courtesy of Microsoft.)

Media Inventory Before Restoration

Many enterprise-class backup utilities index backup jobs, allowing you to recover your data more accurately. Backup schemes such as grandfather-father-son or Tower of Hanoi are complex, and you need to be able to restore the correct version of the data as efficiently as possible.

Many backup solutions implement an entire workflow for managing your backup processes. This workflow helps with media rotation, backup frequency, backup validation and testing, and indexing. The backup infrastructure is a critical system in your environment.

Restore Methods

When restoring data, whether in a recovery process from an incident or during testing, carefully consider where you'll restore the data to. One consideration is security—the restoral destination must be secure, since it will have a full copy of the backed up data.

You may specify different restore locations, depending on your needs.

Overwrite

In the case of an actual incident, you may recover data back to its original location, overwriting whatever data currently resides there. For example, you may be rolling data back to a known point in time or setting a server back to an original configuration.

Side-by-Side

You may wish to restore data to the original production server without overwriting the existing data on that server. One of the reasons for this type of restoral is that you need to compare the backed-up versions of the files against those currently residing on the production server.

Alternate Location

In the restore program, specify an alternate location path to define where to restore the data. This is a great option when testing to ensure that the backup jobs are working as intended and that you know the recovery procedure. In a test scenario, the production server is still up and in use, so you need to restore data to another location. VMs are often great targets for alternate location restorals for testing.

Review Activity:

Data Backup and Restoration

Answer the following questions:

1. **What is the difference between system-state backups and file-level backups?**

2. **Which backup method tends to provide quicker backups but slower restores?**

3. **List the traits associated with cloud backups:**

4. **Which backup method is described by the following: A set number of backup tapes is used, and the tape containing the oldest backup job is the next tape to be overwritten with the next scheduled backup job.**

5. **What makes a virtual machine a good candidate for testing restores?**

Topic 11B

Manage High Availability

EXAM OBJECTIVES COVERED
2.4 Explain the key concepts of high availability for servers

Availability is a critical aspect of the sysadmin's job. Many systems rely on various high availability practices to ensure their services are accessible. Server clusters and NIC teaming are two examples of such practices. Both approaches provide redundancy as a way of guaranteeing availability. Server clusters consist of at least two servers, allowing services to continue even if one device fails. NIC teaming associates network adapters together, providing redundancy and aggregated bandwidth.

High Availability

High availability keeps services accessible to users in the event of hardware failures, OS or application issues, network outages, etc. Availability is measured by a common system. This section covers server clusters and NIC teaming.

System of Nines

Availability is often measured uses a system displayed as the percentage of uptime expected per year. Almost always, this measurement begins at two nines, or 99% uptime. An estimation of four nines would be 99.99% uptime.

Percentage of System Uptime per Year	Downtime per Year	Term
99.999%	5.26 minutes	Five nines
99.99%	52.6 minutes	Four nines
99.9%	8.77 hours	Three nines
99%	87 hours, 40 minutes	Two nines

System of nines measuring availability.

Server Clusters

Server **clusters** are a group of two or more integrated servers and often use the same data storage source. Each cluster member is referred to as a "node," and all of the nodes are all configured the same way. Each node does the same tasks as the other nodes. Each server is an independent device within the cluster. A cluster of servers is treated as a single entity by clients, and their network identity is a single IP address.

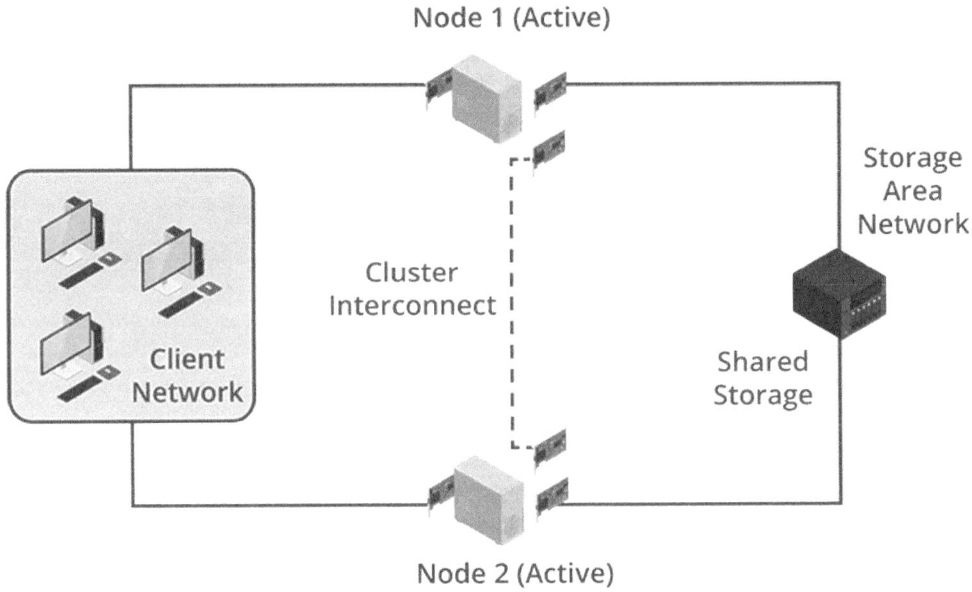

A server cluster. (Images © 123RF.com)

The purpose behind server clusters is to provide high availability of services and data, scalability, and load balancing.

Consider the following example: You have a web site hosting critical customer data. A BIA determined that if the website becomes unavailable, there will be severe consequences for the organization. As the sysadmin, you decide to create a two-node cluster of web servers. The two servers each host duplicate copies of the files that make up the web site. If one server fails, the other server is configured to automatically and immediately take over. Since both nodes share the same IP address, there is no interruption or reconfiguration necessary. Also, if you need to take the servers down for maintenance, you can do so one at a time, allowing the site to remain available during patching or upgrade procedures.

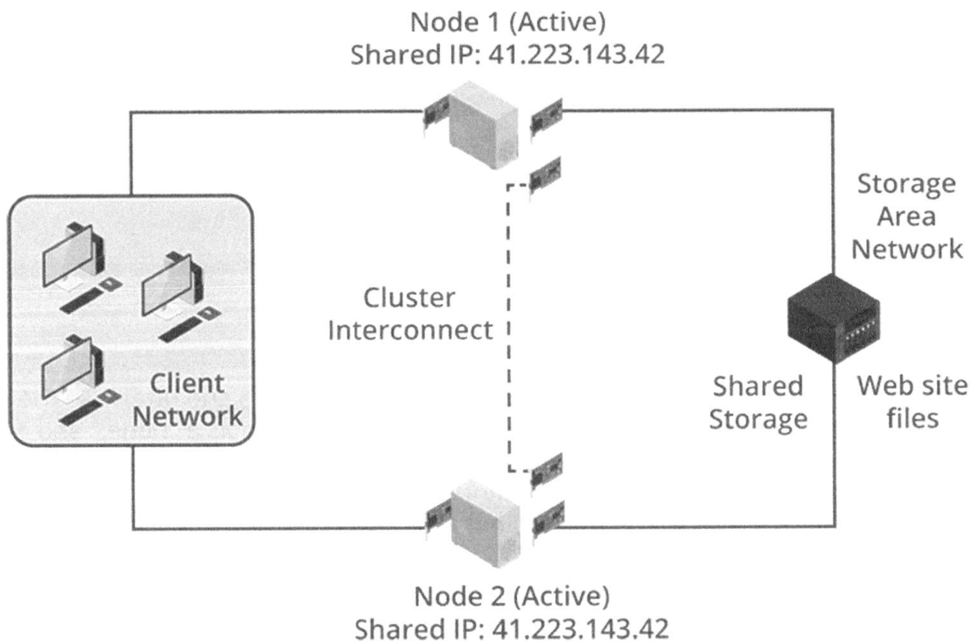

Standard functionality with two web servers sharing the same IP address and web site files. (Images © 123RF.com)

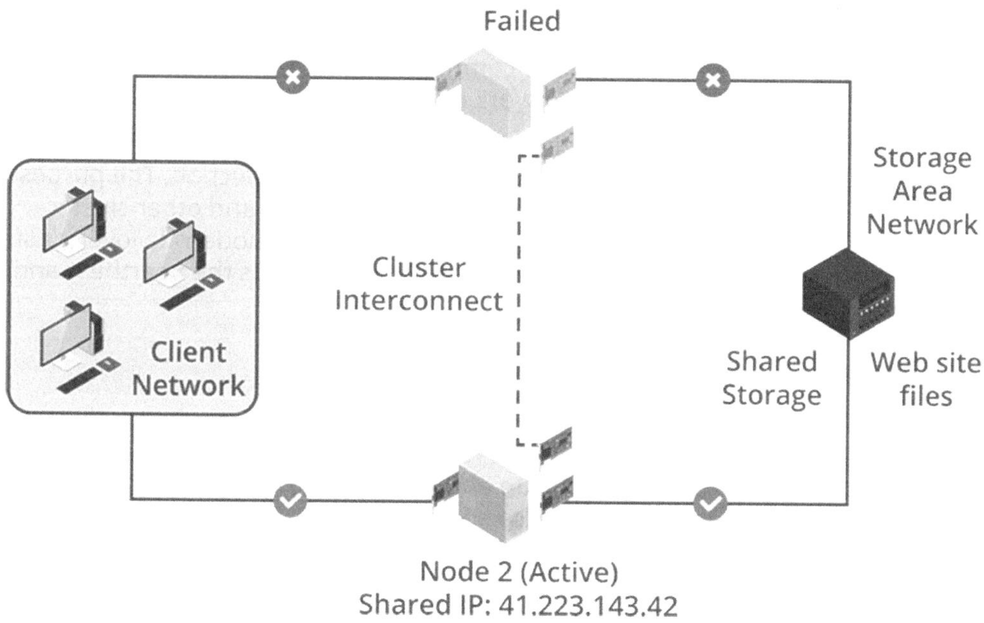

One server has failed, but the site remains accessible. (Images © 123RF.com)

Failover clusters are different from load balancing clusters. Load balancing distributes the workload across functioning servers. Failover clusters provide fault tolerance. The two cluster mechanisms are not necessarily mixed.

Avoiding Single Points of Failure

The goal of server clusters is high availability. The cluster nodes are redundant servers, ensuring the server services are always available. But what about the connection between the cluster and the client computers? You must also consider the connection between the cluster servers and their data source. The cluster implementation must include redundancy in these areas.

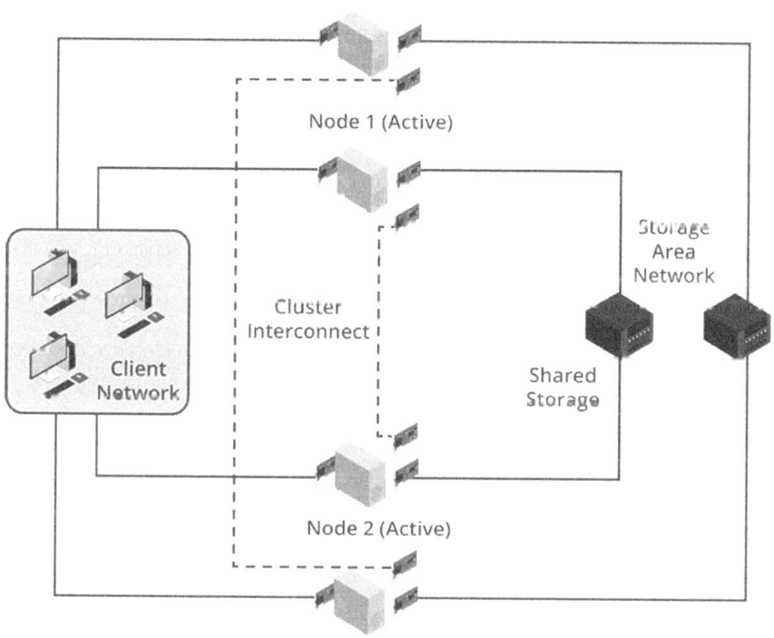

Server cluster with several redundancies. (Images © 123RF.com)

Network Redundancy

The two cluster nodes must be able to communicate with each other. This communication occurs over an IP network connection.

In older clustering schemes, multiple network connections were configured directly between the nodes as a dedicated **heartbeat network** connection. The purpose of these two connections was to carry the cluster heartbeat and other cluster-specific traffic while avoiding a single point of failure. With modern failover clusters, Microsoft now recommends using the production network as the heartbeat and cluster communication path.

Cluster Heartbeat

The heartbeat's primary purpose is to confirm the status of the other node(s) in the cluster. It is a signal passed back and forth between the nodes that confirms to each node that the other node is still up and running. If one node does not receive a heartbeat signal from the other within a specified period, it assumes the other node has failed and acts accordingly.

While the heartbeat does not actually use IP ping packets, it may be useful to think of the heartbeat signal like a continuous ping that ensures network communications.

Types of Server Clusters

There are many server cluster variations. Common differences include the number of participating nodes, whether or not a node is active during normal operations, and how a cluster determines normal activities.

Active-Active Versus Active-Passive

There are two configuration types for clusters: active-active and active-passive.

Active-active clusters use a load balancer device to distribute server requests between the nodes. This design provides high availability and also increases performance. The load balancer distributes the workload among the cluster nodes.

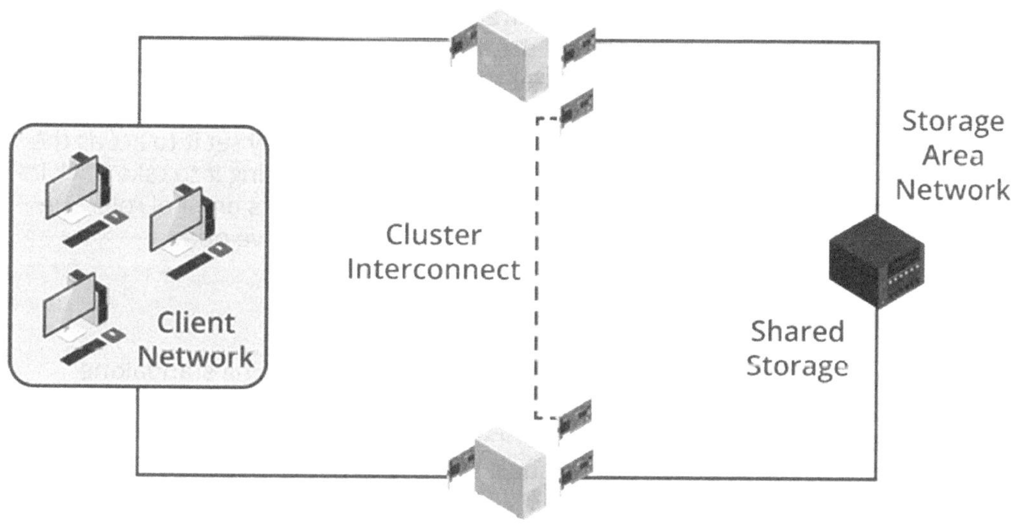

An active-active cluster and load balancer distribute the workload. (Images © 123RF.com)

Active-passive clusters provide only high availability and not load balancing. All requests go to the active server. If that node fails, however, the requests go to the second server.

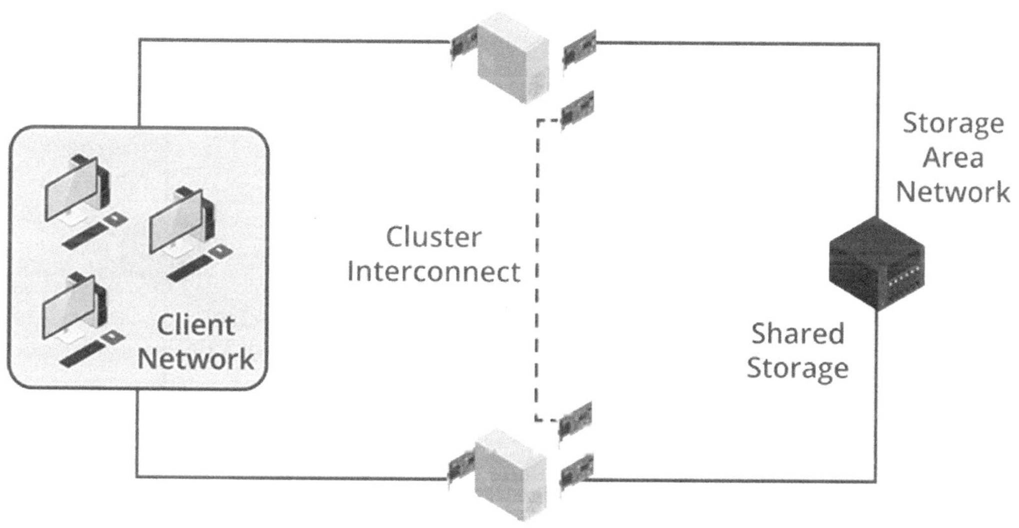

An active-passive cluster. (Images © 123RF.com)

As an administrator, you configure the cluster as active-active or active-passive depending on the design and requirements.

Failover and Failback

When you research server clustering, you frequently hear the terms failover and failback. **Failover** refers to the failure of the active service provider node and passive node's taking over of its responsibilities. At that point, the server that was the passive node becomes the active node. It services clients and handles the cluster's duties. Once the original active node returns to service, you may set it to act as the new passive node, or you may shift the services back to it, causing it to take back its active node role and relegating the formerly passive server to its original role. The term **failback** refers to the service returning to the original active node.

Patching Failover Clusters

Patching clusters is a far more complicated process than patching standalone servers. Because the cluster exists to provide continuous service (high availability), administrators must be cautious not to bring down the entire cluster during the patching process. Consider resource issues.

Cluster Patching Process

The process to patch cluster nodes is to bring down one node at a time for patching (and the subsequent reboot) and then return it to service. This process is accomplished for each cluster member, never bringing down all of the nodes simultaneously. It is not usually realistic to manage this process manually. Services such as Microsoft SCCM and Microsoft Cluster Aware Updating can automate the process.

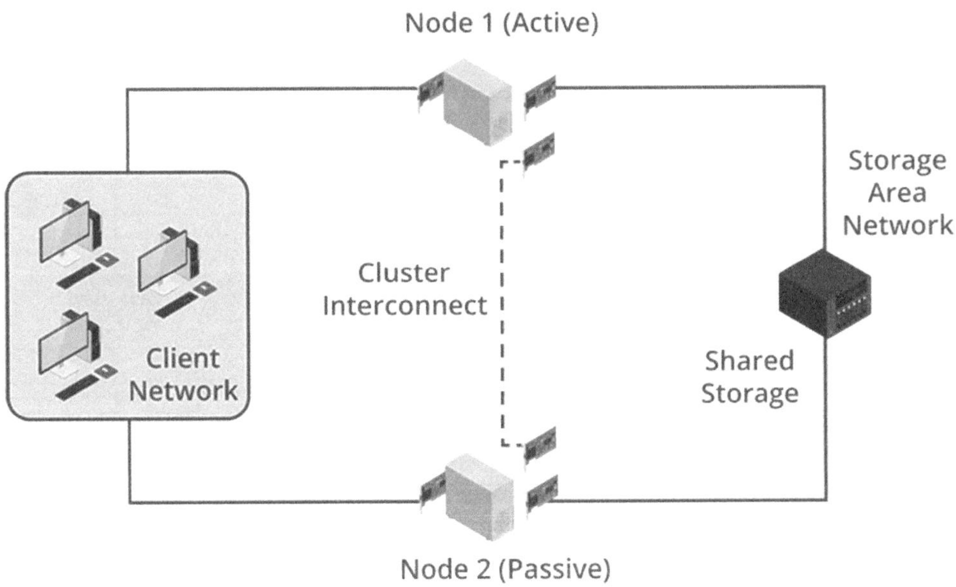

Node 2 (Passive) is patched and then made active; Node 1 is made passive and then patched. (Images © 123RF.com)

To add to the complexity of cluster management in general, and patching specifically, consider the following scenario: you have a failover cluster consisting of two physical servers configured as active-passive. Each server hosts a failover cluster consisting of two VMs. In other words, the two physical host servers are configured in a cluster to ensure high availability for the VMs that they are hosting. In turn, those VMs are configured in a cluster to ensure high availability for the services hosted on the VMs. Managing this structure gets complex in a hurry!

Fault Tolerance

Redundancy may occur in many areas. With failover clustering, the entire server and its services are redundant. Component redundancy is within the server or network. For example, a single server may have multiple NICs or multiple power supplies.

Redundancy

Server redundancy may be automated, as in failover clusters, or manual. Manual redundancy means that your organization maintains a separate server, configured identically to an essential server, that remains offline. It is brought online immediately should the primary fail. In this case, it is very similar to an active-passive failover cluster, but without the actual failover management software.

Server-level redundancy is a much more cost-effective proposition with VMs. Because the VM does not contain dedicated hardware, it is really just consuming HDD space, and nothing else, until it is needed.

Component redundancy refers to server hardware. As noted earlier in the book, many servers ship with redundant components, including power supplies and NICs. It is also important to have replacement components available on hand for server components.

Load Balancing

In many cases, servers hosting popular services would be overwhelmed by demand. Web servers, for example, might have hundreds or thousands of connections at any given time. A single server would not be able to handle that many connections. **Load balancers** do precisely what their name suggests: they balance inbound client connections across two or more servers.

Load balancers may be hardware or software-driven.

- Hardware load balancer—network appliance that distributes a workload across servers. It resides between the client computers and the servers.
- Software load balancer—installed directly on the servers.

Load Balancing Schedules

There are many scheduling types for load balancers. Three of them are **round robin**, most recently used, and weighted scheduling.

Type	How load is distributed
Round robin	Assigns connections in order
Most recently used (MRU)	Attempts to use existing machines for the workload but can spin up new VMs if needed
Weighted scheduling	Used when the server's hardware capabilities vary, allocating more connections to the more powerful servers

Load balancing schedules.

NIC Teaming

One of the common single points of failure in a server is the NIC. Also, the NIC may be overwhelmed by the amount of traffic flowing in and out of the server. NIC teaming combines two or more NICs into a single virtual NIC with a single IP address configuration. The virtual NIC aggregates the bandwidth of the physical NICs, allowing a lot more traffic through the connection. When one NIC in the team fails, however, the remaining NICs continue functioning, eliminating the NIC as a single point of failure. NIC teaming provides both failover capabilities and link aggregation.

Red Hat Linux Enterprise 6, 7, and 8 and Windows Server 2016 have NIC teaming capabilities built in. Before these OSs provided the functionality, proprietary software from the NIC vendors provided teaming.

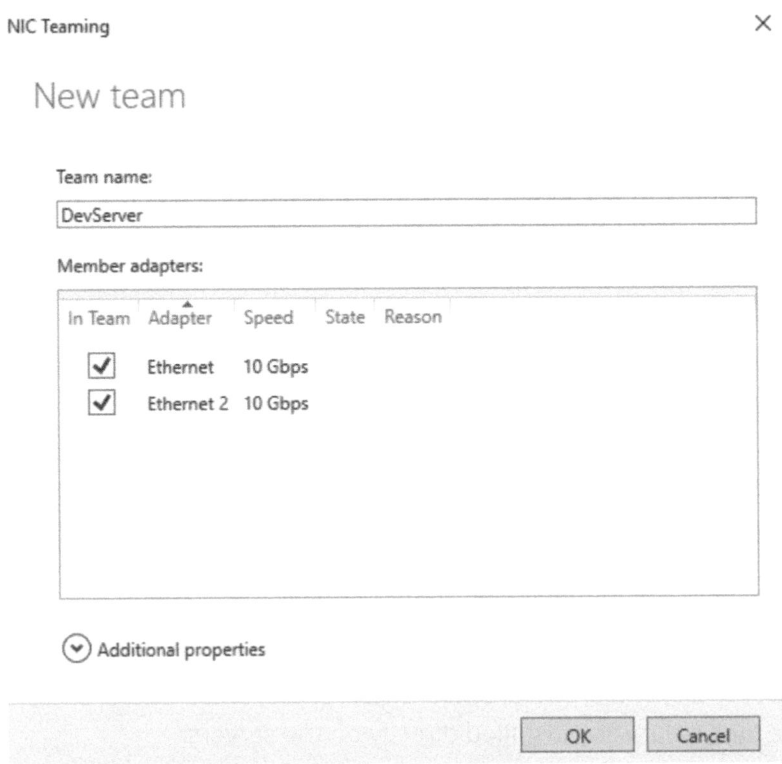

Configuring NIC Teaming in Windows Server. (Screenshot courtesy of Microsoft.)

The switch the NICs are connected to must also be configured for NIC teaming. Not all switches support NIC teaming.

Microsoft Windows Server 2016 supports up to 32 NICs in a single team.

Review Activity:

High Availability

Answer the following questions:

1. **Explain the difference between failover and failback.**

2. **What is the function of the cluster heartbeat?**

3. **What is the difference between server redundancy and component redundancy?**

4. **Which load balancing mechanism allocates connections in a specified order, regardless of workload or capability?**

5. **List the two features of NIC Teaming:**

Topic 11C

Manage Disaster Recovery

EXAM OBJECTIVES COVERED

3.8 Explain the importance of disaster recovery

Most organizations have DRPs in place. The plans address the balance between mitigation cost and the cost of lost assets/time/resources. Disaster recovery planning includes alternate sites where business functions can be transferred. DRPs must be tested regularly.

Sites

One aspect of disaster recovery is the management of the physical business site. If there is a major catastrophe that damages the organization's primary business, a second location may be designated to take over operations. The key to defining this secondary site is based on how quickly the site can return the business to normal operations.

Hot Sites

Hot sites are designed for an immediate takeover of operations in the event of a disaster. They have all the equipment necessary for the business—servers, workstations, network devices, office furniture, power, Internet connectivity, etc. A hot site is a fully capable location ready at a moment's notice. Because of this, hot sites are costly—they are essentially a mirror of the primary site, with all associated costs. Data is replicated to the hot site regularly to ensure that it has up-to-date content.

Warm Sites

Warm sites contain the necessary space for your data center and business offices and some of the required computer and network hardware. For the site to take over from the primary, some equipment needs to be brought in, and some configuration needs to occur. Data has to be migrated to the warm site. This makes the warm site less expensive up front than a hot site, but it also requires more time to get the business up and running again if there's a disaster.

Cold Sites

Cold sites contain the necessary office space, without the essential equipment (workstations, servers, network devices, office furniture, etc.). Data has to be migrated to the cold site. A cold site is basically just the building, and the rest of the equipment must be brought in before the site can take over operations. Power, HVAC, and physical space are all that are provided.

Separate Geographic Locations

Whether your DR site is hot, warm, or cold, it is important to consider the importance of geographically dispersed locations. If the DR site is far enough from the primary site, then large-scale natural disasters or regional conflicts should not affect it. Unfortunately, using separate geographic locations brings its own challenges, including legal requirements for different countries, data replication time, and onsite staff.

Cloud Sites

Many organizations now look to the cloud as a replacement for traditional hot, warm, or cold sites. CSPs offer DRaaS options. It's relatively easy to replicate a VM configuration from your onsite data center to the cloud. CSPs have their own geographically dispersed locations, redundancy, and disaster recovery capabilities. A cloud-based DR solution may meet the needs of many smaller organizations that couldn't normally consider a traditional multi-site solution.

Type	Cost	Data	On-site equipment
Hot	High	Immediate replication	All
Warm	Medium	Data migrated	Some
Cold	Low	Data migrated	None
Cloud	Varies	Varies	None

Disaster recovery site types.

Data Replication

Replication is copying data to another server or another site to retain business continuity, maintain scalability, or keep data near to users.

Replication may occur on several scales, from server-to-server to site-to-site.

Replication Example 1

A virtualization server replicates its VMs to a second virtualization server. If the primary virtualization server fails, the second takes over with fully up-to-date VMs. In this case, both virtualization servers exist at the same site, and the goal is high availability for the VMs.

Replication Example 2

A virtualization server replicates its VMs to a second virtualization server. If the primary virtualization server fails, the second takes over with fully up-to-date VMs. In this case, both virtualization servers exist at different sites, and the goal is high availability for the VMs.

Replication Example 3

Servers replicate their stored data to other servers, in either the same site or a remote site. This structure ensures current copies of the data and keeps a copy of the data "near" the users. AD Domain Controllers, for example, replicate user and computer account data among each other.

The following replication types may be used in the scenarios displayed above.

Constant Replication

The primary system replicates data changed data blocks continually. Constant replication is also referred to as "continuous replication." The replication process occurs in the background, permitting users to access the data without interruption. Constant replication is different than regular backups, where files must be closed to be duplicated.

Periodic Replication

Replication of changed data between the primary and the destination device occurs based on a preconfigured schedule, such as every 30 minutes.

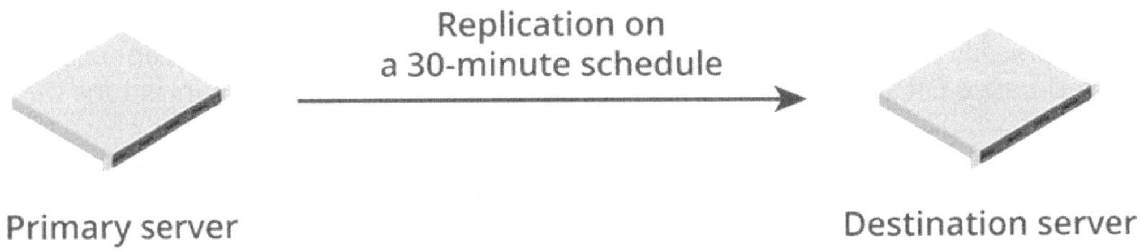

Data replication on a regular timetable. (Images © 123RF.com)

Asynchronous Versus Synchronous Replication

These two replication types vary by how they confirm to the client machine, or replication control, that the replication process was successful.

With asynchronous replication, data is sent to the primary storage (a database, for example). Confirmation that the data was written is sent to the client machine. The data is then replicated to the second database server, and it responds to the first database server with a confirmation. The problem arises if the primary server fails. The secondary may not actually have the replicated data, but the client computer believes that it does. The data is then lost.

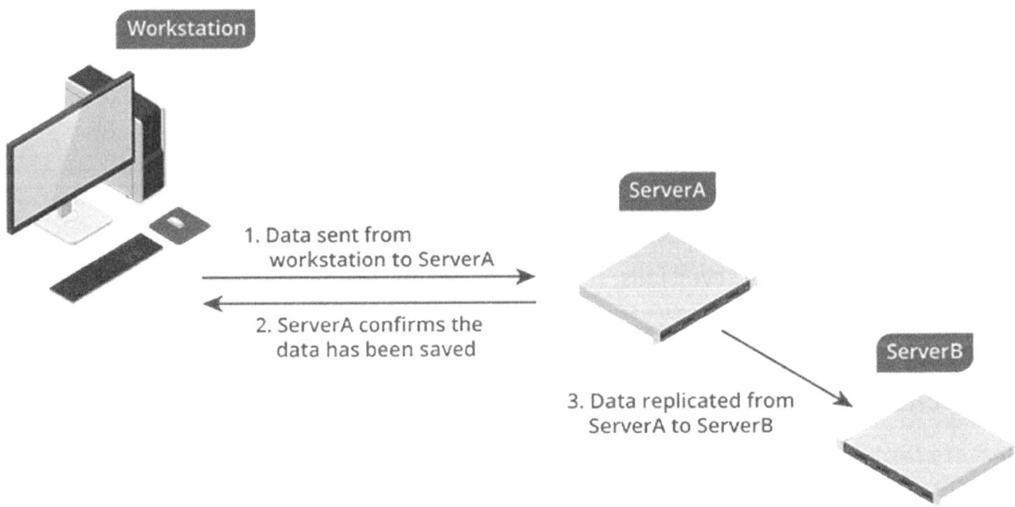

The workstation is updated that the data was saved, even though the data has not yet been replicated to ServerB. (Images © 123RF.com)

With synchronous replication, the client machine is not informed that the transaction was successful until both servers have a copy of the data.

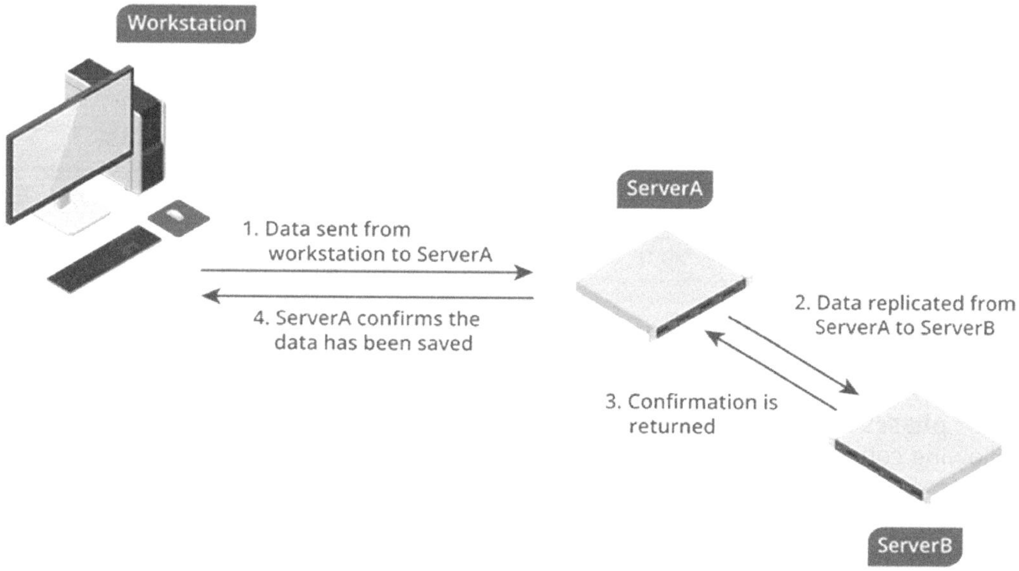

The workstation is not updated that the data was saved until the data has been replicated to ServerB. (Images © 123RF.com)

Application Consistent Replication

Application consistent replication (or backup) can see data on the HDD, like other replication methods. However, it can also see application data stored in RAM and pending I/O operations. This backup process is more comprehensive, resulting in a quicker restore process.

File Locking Replication

File locking occurs when multiple copies of a file exist, and one of those copies is opened for editing. When that happens, the other copies are locked and unchangeable. The goal is to avoid a situation where a user in one location modifies a file at the same time that a user in another location modifies a copy of that file. In that situation, there will be three copies of the file: the original, unmodified copy, the copy edited by the first user, and the copy modified by the second user. This situation is untenable. File locking mitigates this by denying the second user the ability to modify the file until the first user has committed the changes.

Mirroring Versus Replication

When working with databases, you must recognize the difference between mirroring and replication. Mirroring is a complete duplicate of the database on a different server (probably at a different site). The mirrored copy acts as an immediate failover data source. The main focus of mirroring is database availability.

Replication is concerned with data availability. Data and database objects replicate to different databases to ensure the data is near the users who will consume it. This replication provides greater efficiency.

BiDi Replication

Some replication services use a multi-master structure, where two or more servers replicate data between them. Bidirectional replication updates information in either direction.

Because changes are made at multiple servers, client computers do not have to maintain expensive WAN connections to update or access information.

In other replication infrastructures, a single master server maintains the definitive copy of the data, and it replicates that data to secondary servers.

Replication takes many forms. It is frequently configured in conjunction with backups to ensure service and data availability. There are many replication technologies, and they vary by application and by application requirements.

Replication should be a part of your organization's overall DRP.

Data Recovery

Disaster Recovery Planning

There are distinct phases of disaster recovery planning. Organizations can adjust these phases as needed, but in general, all companies will need to address the following concerns:

1. Audit all IT resources—on-premises, cloud, public, private
2. Identify mission-critical services, data, and vendors
3. Define responsibilities and assign them to specific roles
4. Define achievable recovery goals
5. Manage remote data storage and remote sites
6. Test the components of the DRP

The DRP should include realistic RTO and RPO targets, as well as backup and restore goals.

A DRP is just that: a plan. It needs to be reviewed and tested periodically to ensure that it works as expected. Testing is the only way to be sure that the plan covers all aspects of the business.

Disaster Recovery Testing

One key consideration is how often the DRP should be tested (at least annually). Testing needs to have clear and measurable goals. Next, roles and responsibilities are carefully defined. Finally, a debriefing process is used to apply what was learned from the test. All of these test components should be standardized and documented for clarity and consistency.

Testing Types

- Paper test—critical stakeholders examine the disaster recovery procedures in the organization, and suggestions are considered.
- Walk-through—the disaster recovery procedures are stepped through to confirm their viability. No changes are made, and no data is restored.
- **Tabletop**/Simulated failover—the disaster recovery procedures are implemented on a limited scale. Participants engage in role-playing to ensure comprehension and realism.
- Parallel recovery using a non-production test environment—the disaster recovery procedures are implemented in a non-production environment. VMs work especially well for this kind of test. The production environment remains unaffected.

- Live failover (cutover)—the disaster recovery procedure is tested on the production environment where customers and employees reside. The goal is to prove zero interruption of service.
- Sandbox—there are a great many different types of cloud services, including environments for disaster recovery testing. These services may also be the designated recovery environment in an actual disaster. The service goes beyond backups by providing the ability to stand up virtual servers, web applications, and databases on-demand as part of a recovery process. This cloud service is Recovery as a Service (RaaS) or DRaaS.

Guidelines for Managing Disaster Recovery

- Hot sites are the most expensive alternate sites but the quickest to take over business operations.
- Warm sites are less expensive than hot sites but do not take over business operations as quickly.
- Cold sites are the least expensive alternate sites but take the most time to bring online.
- Use replication to duplicate data and store data nearer to the consumers.
- Test DRPs regularly.
  - Paper tests allow for discussion and review.
  - Walkthrough tests allow resource confirmation.
  - Tabletop/simulation tests permit administrators to practice procedures.
  - Live failover tests are the best way to guarantee uninterrupted services.

Review Activity:

Disaster Recovery

Answer the following questions:

1. **Which type of disaster recovery site has the following attributes: relatively high cost, immediate failover, all equipment is on-site?**

2. **What is the relative cost difference between hot, warm, and cold disaster recovery sites?**

3. **Which type of disaster recovery testing has the following attributes: critical stakeholders examine the disaster recovery procedures in the organization, and suggestions are considered.**

4. **Which type of disaster recovery testing has the following attributes: the disaster recovery procedures are implemented in a non-production environment. VMs work especially well for this kind of test. The production environment remains unaffected.**

5. **Which type of disaster recovery testing has the following attributes: the disaster recovery procedure is tested on the production environment where customers and employees reside. The goal is to prove zero interruption of service.**

Lesson 11

Summary

Backup and restore procedures are critical elements of data availability. Recovery processes should be tested regularly to guarantee backed-up data can be recovered and that IT staff is comfortable with the process. Server clusters help to ensure service availability, even in the event of server failure or downtime due to updates and patches.

Traditionally, businesses have relied on alternate sites—whether hot, warm, or cold—as disaster recovery locations. Many current DRPs now use cloud-based services to accomplish the same goal.

1. **How frequently does your organization test data restore processes?**
2. **What alternate disaster recovery site(s) does your organization use?**

Lesson 12

Decommissioning Servers

LESSON INTRODUCTION

Removing servers from the network must be accomplished in a deliberate way. Sysadmins must ensure the server is no longer supporting services in use, whether those services have been migrated to another physical server, a virtual server, the cloud, or retirement. This lesson covers the decommissioning process.

Lesson Objectives

In this lesson, you will decommission servers by addressing:

- Removal procedures, including documentation.
- Media destruction.
- Recycling.

Topic A

Decommission Servers

EXAM OBJECTIVES COVERED
3.6 Summarize proper server decommissioning concepts

Decommissioning processes are more involved than one might anticipate. The processes are not complex, but they play an important role in making sure that the business's inventory is properly accounted for.

Removal plans are often governed by change management and integrated into the standard policies and procedures for the organization. While servers are the focus of this decommissioning lesson, cable remediation and component recycling are also covered.

Decommissioning Policies

Most organizations have server decommissioning policies. The decommissioning project is likely to be categorized under change management. These policies cover service management, non-utilization, documentation updates, media retention and destruction, and recycling.

Plan for Server Decommissioning

There are several steps for decommissioning a server. These steps vary by organization and the regulations that govern the organization. However, there are some general tasks to be aware of.

The owners of the services hosted on the server must be notified. The services themselves may be retired, moved to a different server, or migrated to the cloud. The allocation of the services must be verified before the original server can be removed from the network.

Once the services are removed or migrated, place the server in an offline state. The change management program typically defines a time during which the server and its data are preserved but inaccessible to clients. This trial period ensures that there were no unexpected clients or services that still rely on the retiring server.

It is possible to migrate the physical server you are decommissioning to a VM. The VM files (including data) can be easily archived and brought back online if necessary.

Don't forget the importance of notifying users regarding the status of the service.

Finally, a designated end-of-service date is defined. At this point, the server is removed entirely and assumed to no longer be necessary. Resources are removed from it (such as technical support personnel).

Document the Decommissioning Process

Document the decommissioning process itself. Again, it's likely that your change management process accounts for and provides the decommissioning documentation. The organization's overall documentation must also be updated. For example, amend the IT service catalog to acknowledge that the server is no longer available. Management software, such as AD, SCCM, and centralized log file services, also needs to be updated.

For example, your organization uses centralized Windows Server log files through Event Viewer. Over a year, you decommission five servers. It would be disruptive to have continual alert messages logged for the apparently missing servers.

The documentation process includes inventory management procedures. Most IT resources have an asset management tag that is used to track the server throughout its lifecycle. The asset is marked as decommissioned at the end of the process.

On many servers, you can place asset tag numbers in the system BIOS.

Company Policies

A decommissioning process should be integrated into company policies and procedures. Milestones such as service migration, end-user notification, documentation updates, and support procedure updates are clearly outlined in such a document.

Verify Server Status

There are many methods to ensure that a service is no longer accessed on a server scheduled for decommissioning. One of the easiest approaches is to examine the log files for connections created to the server and what resources are consumed. Packet sniffing utilities, such as Nmap or tcpdump, also help identify network connection attempts addressed to the server. You can query service owners and service consumers to discover whether they connect to the server.

Media Destruction

Data stored on HDDs (and other forms of permanent storage media) represents a major security risk during the decommissioning process. If the data is not effectively removed and the drive ends up in the hands of unauthorized persons, confidential company information may be exposed. This is a common and a very serious concern.

Dumpster diving is an example of this sort of security risk. It refers to acquiring computer hardware that a company has disposed of and looking for stored data.

HDD Disposal

The process of properly disposing of HDDs and the data stored on them is sanitization.

HDDs may be logically wiped by using software processes, such as reformatting or zeroing. These processes are not particularly effective. Those with the knowledge and computer forensics tools at their disposal can recover a lot of data from a drive that's been overwritten.

Recall that deleting a file does not remove it from the drive; it merely marks the file's location as available for future writes if needed.

The physical destruction of drives is a more reliable approach to protecting your organization's stored data.

Process	Explanation	Reliability
Degaussing	Magnetically destroys stored data	Highly reliable
Shredding	Physically destroys the drive	Reliable
Crushing/drilling	Physically damages the drive	Somewhat reliable
Incineration	Physically destroys the drive	Highly reliable

Techniques for physical sanitization.

It is worth noting that for the risk of data exposure to adequately mitigated, the drives must be secured during transport to any destruction or disposal facilities.

Media Retention Requirements

As you observed during the backup/restore portion of the course, backup media must be carefully managed, rotated, and secured. The backup media is governed by a retention policy that defines how long backup jobs must be maintained and how that content is secured. Industry regulation and legal requirements inform this retention policy.

Cable Remediation

Another aspect of decommissioning is removing necessary network and power cable. These resources can be recycled. In addition, removing them helps to ensure that proper cabling is in use and physical security is maintained.

Network Cable Remediation

Cable management was discussed earlier in the course. During the decommissioning process, however, there are additional network media considerations. One concern is abandoned network cable that was not removed by previous tenants of the space that your organization is leasing. This cable leads to confusion about what media is yours and what was left behind by another organization. Using abandoned media leads to issues with reliability, security, and network performance.

Cable remediation does not just cover the removal of existing media. It also ensures that cabling is properly routed near electronics, HVAC, and sprinkler systems that also exist in the ceiling. These requirements may be defined in building codes that your organization is required to satisfy. In addition, many fire codes require **plenum cable** to protect people from toxic gasses during a fire.

Power Cable Remediation

Server rooms have unique power requirements compared to most other parts of the facility. Data centers have even more concerns. Power must be clean (a very steady current). Often, for reliability, your organization will have two electrical circuits for the server room. A certified professional electrician should perform all electrical installations and upgrades.

Device	Connected power
UPS	Connected to the electrical circuit
PDU	Connected to the UPS
Servers, routers, switches, KVM	Connected to the PDU
Crash cart	Connected to the electrical circuit or PDU
Repair bench	Connected to the electrical circuit or PDU
Air conditioning unit	Connected to the electrical circuit or UPS
Backup AC unit	Connected to the electrical circuit or UPS

Devices connected by power cables.

Electronics Recycling and Repurposing

So once your server is out of completely out of your network, what do you physically do with it?

Repurpose Within the Organization

One way to dispose of older hardware resources is by repurposing them elsewhere in your organization.

Device	Alternate use
Server	Location for testing disaster restoral procedures
	Training center devices
	Updates-testing box
	Print server for a small branch office location
Laptop	Crash cart computer
Network devices	Training center devices

Alternate uses for decommissioned devices.

Older system repurposed as a crash cart. (Image by Aleksei Gorodenkov © 123RF.com)

Donations

You may be able to donate older hardware to charities, schools, or other social programs. Keep in mind that these donations may provide a tax deduction for your organization.

Recycling

Electronics hardware contains many valuable metals and plastics. These components can be recycled. There are authorized recycling centers that will take your devices. It is typically illegal to simply place your electronics in garbage dumpsters or generic recycling bins. Electronics often contain toxic substances that must be managed appropriately. Network cables contain a lot of copper and should also be recycled.

Guidelines for Decommissioning Servers

- Ensure services hosted on the server are no longer necessary or have been migrated to another server.
- Data sanitization refers to the proper removal of data stored on HDDs.
- It is not difficult to recover deleted data from storage media, so magnetic or physical destruction of the drive is required.
- Remove and recycle unused network cable media.
- Consider repurposing older hardware with the organization.
- Consider donating older hardware.
- Recycle computer components properly, because many contain toxic or harmful substances.

Review Activity:

Server Decommissioning

Answer the following questions:

1. **What are the steps in the decommissioning process?**

2. **Why is it necessary to update management software after decommissioning a server?**

3. **What is sanitization?**

4. **What HDD disposal technique is described by the phrase "magnetically destroys stored data"?**

5. **List three ways of physically destroying HDDs:**

6. **What risks exist for using network media left behind by former tenants?**

7. **Where in the organization might you repurpose a laptop?**

Lesson 12

Summary

Decommissioning a server usually falls under the auspices of the change management process. The services hosted on the server must be transferred or removed, documentation and inventory information updated, and proper disposal managed.

In particular, it is critical to dispose of storage devices properly, because data can be recovered from these devices fairly easily. In many cases, storage devices will be destroyed to prevent data recovery.

1. **How does your organization currently dispose of server hardware that is no longer needed?**

2. **What method does your organization use to destroy physical HDDs? Do you use a similar method for personal HDDs?**

Appendix A

Mapping Course Content to CompTIA Certification

Achieving CompTIA Server+ certification requires candidates to pass Exam SK0-005. This table describes where the exam objectives for Exam SK0-005 are covered in this course.

Domain and Objective	Covered in
1.0 Server Hardware Installation and Management	Lesson 5, Topic A Lesson 5, Topic B Lesson 6, Topic A
1.1 Given a scenario, install physical hardware	Lesson 5, Topic A Lesson 5, Topic B
Racking	Lesson 5, Topic A
Enclosure sizes	Lesson 5, Topic A
Unit sizes	Lesson 5, Topic A
1U, 2U, 3U, etc.	Lesson 5, Topic A
Rack layout	Lesson 5, Topic A
Cooling management	Lesson 5, Topic A
Safety	Lesson 5, Topic A
Proper lifting techniques	Lesson 5, Topic A
Rack balancing	Lesson 5, Topic A
Floor load limitations	Lesson 5, Topic A
Power distribution unit (PDU)	Lesson 5, Topic A
Keyboard-video-mouse (KVM) placement	Lesson 5, Topic A
Rail kits	Lesson 5, Topic A
Power cabling	Lesson 5, Topic A
Redundant power	Lesson 5, Topic A
Uninterruptible power supply (UPS)	Lesson 5, Topic A
Separate circuits	Lesson 5, Topic A
Separate providers	Lesson 5, Topic A
Power connector types	Lesson 5, Topic A
Cable management	Lesson 5, Topic A
Network cabling	Lesson 5, Topic A
Redundant networking	Lesson 5, Topic A
Twisted pair	Lesson 5, Topic A
Fiber	Lesson 5, Topic A
SC	Lesson 5, Topic A
LC	Lesson 5, Topic A

Domain and Objective	Covered in
Single mode	Lesson 5, Topic A
Multimode	Lesson 5, Topic A
Gigabit	Lesson 5, Topic A
10 GigE	Lesson 5, Topic A
Small form factor pluggable (SFP)	Lesson 5, Topic A
SFP+	Lesson 5, Topic A
Quad small form factor pluggable (QSFP)	Lesson 5, Topic A
Cable management	Lesson 5, Topic A
Server chassis types	Lesson 5, Topic A
Tower	Lesson 5, Topic A
Rack mount	Lesson 5, Topic A
Blade enclosure	Lesson 5, Topic A
Server components	Lesson 5, Topic B
Hardware compatibility list (HCL)	Lesson 5, Topic B
Central processing unit (CPU)	Lesson 5, Topic B
Graphics processing unit (GPU)	Lesson 5, Topic B
Memory	Lesson 5, Topic B
Bus types	Lesson 5, Topic B
Interface types	Lesson 5, Topic B
Expansion cards	Lesson 5, Topic B
1.2 Given a scenario, deploy and manage storage	Lesson 6, Topic A
RAID levels and types	Lesson 6, Topic A
0	Lesson 6, Topic A
1	Lesson 6, Topic A
5	Lesson 6, Topic A
6	Lesson 6, Topic A
10	Lesson 6, Topic A
Just a bunch of disks (JBOD)	Lesson 6, Topic A
Hardware vs. software	Lesson 6, Topic A
Capacity planning	Lesson 6, Topic A
Hard drive media types	Lesson 6, Topic A
Solid state drive (SSD)	Lesson 6, Topic A
Wear factors	Lesson 6, Topic A
Read intensive	Lesson 6, Topic A
Write intensive	Lesson 6, Topic A
Hard disk drive (HDD)	Lesson 6, Topic A
Rotations per minute (RPM)	Lesson 6, Topic A
15,000	Lesson 6, Topic A
10,000	Lesson 6, Topic A
7,200	Lesson 6, Topic A
Hybrid	Lesson 6, Topic A

Domain and Objective	Covered in
Interface types	Lesson 6, Topic A
Serial attached SCSI (SAS)	Lesson 6, Topic A
Serial ATA (SATA)	Lesson 6, Topic A
Peripheral component interconnect (PCI)	Lesson 6, Topic A
External serial advanced technology attachment (eSATA)	Lesson 6, Topic A
Universal serial bus (USB)	Lesson 6, Topic A
Secure digital (SD)	Lesson 6, Topic A
Shared storage	Lesson 6, Topic A
Network attached storage (NAS)	Lesson 6, Topic A
Network file system (NFS)	Lesson 6, Topic A
Common Internet file system (CIFS)	Lesson 6, Topic A
Storage area network (SAN)	Lesson 6, Topic A
Internet small computer systems interface (iSCSI)	Lesson 6, Topic A
Fibre Channel	Lesson 6, Topic A
Fibre Channel over Ethernet (FCoE)	Lesson 6, Topic A
1.3 Given a scenario, perform server hardware maintenance	Lesson 5, Topic B
Out-of-band management	Lesson 5, Topic B
Remote drive access	Lesson 5, Topic B
Remote console access	Lesson 5, Topic B
Remote power on/off	Lesson 5, Topic B
Internet protocol keyboard-video-mouse (IP KVM)	Lesson 5, Topic B
Local hardware administration	Lesson 5, Topic B
Keyboard-video-mouse (KVM)	Lesson 5, Topic B
Crash cart	Lesson 5, Topic B
Virtual administration console	Lesson 5, Topic B
Serial connectivity	Lesson 5, Topic B
Console connections	Lesson 5, Topic B
Components	Lesson 5, Topic B
Firmware upgrades	Lesson 5, Topic B
Drives	Lesson 5, Topic B
Hot-swappable hardware	Lesson 5, Topic B
Drives	Lesson 5, Topic B
Cages	Lesson 5, Topic B
Cards	Lesson 5, Topic B
Power supplies	Lesson 5, Topic B
Fans	Lesson 5, Topic B
Basic input/output system (BIOS)/Unified Extensible Firmware Interface (UEFI)	Lesson 5, Topic B

Domain and Objective	Covered in
2.0 Server Administration	Lesson 1, Topic C Lesson 2, Topic A Lesson 2, Topic B Lesson 4, Topic A Lesson 4, Topic B Lesson 5, Topic B Lesson 6, Topic A Lesson 6, Topic B Lesson 7, Topic A Lesson 7, Topic B Lesson 7, Topic C Lesson 7, Topic D Lesson 9, Topic B Lesson 11, Topic B
2.1 Given a scenario, install server operating systems	Lesson 7, Topic A Lesson 7, Topic B Lesson 7, Topic C Lesson 7, Topic D
Minimum operating system (OS) requirements	Lesson 7, Topic A
Hardware compatibility list (HCL)	Lesson 7, Topic A
Installations	Lesson 7, Topic A
Graphical user interface (GUI)	Lesson 7, Topic A
Core	Lesson 7, Topic A
Bare metal	Lesson 7, Topic A
Virtualized	Lesson 7, Topic A
Remote	Lesson 7, Topic A
Slipstreamed/unattended	Lesson 7, Topic A
Scripted installations	Lesson 7, Topic D
Additional drivers	Lesson 7, Topic A
Additional applications and utilities	Lesson 7, Topic A
Patches	Lesson 7, Topic A
Media installation type	Lesson 7, Topic A
Network	Lesson 7, Topic A
Optical	Lesson 7, Topic A
Universal serial bus (USB)	Lesson 7, Topic A
Embedded	Lesson 7, Topic A
Imaging	Lesson 7, Topic A
Cloning	Lesson 7, Topic A
Virtual machine (VM) cloning	Lesson 7, Topic A
Physical clones	Lesson 7, Topic A
Template deployment	Lesson 7, Topic A
Physical to virtual (P2V)	Lesson 7, Topic A
Partition and volume types	Lesson 7, Topic B
Global partition table (GPT) vs. master boot record (MBR)	Lesson 7, Topic B

Domain and Objective	Covered in
Dynamic disk	Lesson 7, Topic B
Logical volume management (LVM)	Lesson 7, Topic B
File system types	Lesson 7, Topic B
ext4	Lesson 7, Topic B
New technology file system (NTFS)	Lesson 7, Topic B
VMware file system (VMFS)	Lesson 7, Topic B
Resilient file system (ReFS)	Lesson 7, Topic B
Z file system (ZFS)	Lesson 7, Topic B
2.2 Given a scenario, configure servers to use network infrastructure services	Lesson 7, Topic C
IP configuration	Lesson 7, Topic C
Virtual local area network (VLAN)	Lesson 7, Topic C
Default gateways	Lesson 7, Topic C
Name resolution	Lesson 7, Topic C
Domain name service (DNS)	Lesson 7, Topic C
Fully qualified domain name (FQDN)	Lesson 7, Topic C
Hosts file	Lesson 7, Topic C
Addressing protocols	Lesson 7, Topic C
IPv4	Lesson 7, Topic C
Request for comments (RFC) 1918 address spaces	Lesson 7, Topic C
IPv6	Lesson 7, Topic C
Firewall	Lesson 7, Topic C
Ports	Lesson 7, Topic C
Static vs. dynamic	Lesson 7, Topic C
Dynamic host configuration protocol (DHCP)	Lesson 7, Topic C
Automatic private IP address (APIPA)	Lesson 7, Topic C
MAC addresses	Lesson 7, Topic C
2.3 Given a scenario, configure and maintain server functions and features	Lesson 4, Topic B Lesson 5, Topic B Lesson 6, Topic A Lesson 6, Topic B
Server role requirements	Lesson 9, Topic B
Print	Lesson 9, Topic B
Database	Lesson 9, Topic B
File	Lesson 9, Topic B
Web	Lesson 9, Topic B
Application	Lesson 9, Topic B
Messaging	Lesson 9, Topic B
Baselining	Lesson 9, Topic B
Documentation	Lesson 9, Topic B
Performance metrics	Lesson 9, Topic B
Directory connectivity	Lesson 9, Topic B

Domain and Objective	Covered in
Storage management	Lesson 5, Topic B Lesson 6, Topic A Lesson 6, Topic B Lesson 9, Topic B
Formatting	Lesson 6, Topic A
Connectivity	Lesson 9, Topic B
Provisioning	Lesson 9, Topic B
Partitioning	Lesson 6, Topic B
Page/swap/scratch location and size	Lesson 9, Topic B
Disk quotas	Lesson 6, Topic A
Compression	Lesson 6, Topic A
Deduplication	Lesson 6, Topic A Lesson 9, Topic B
Monitoring	Lesson 4, Topic B Lesson 9, Topic B
Uptime	Lesson 4, Topic B Lesson 9, Topic B
Thresholds	Lesson 9, Topic B
Performance	Lesson 6, Topic A Lesson 9, Topic B
Memory	Lesson 5, Topic B Lesson 9, Topic B
Disk	Lesson 6, Topic A Lesson 9, Topic B
Input output operations per second (IOPS)	Lesson 9, Topic B
Capacity vs. utilization	Lesson 6, Topic A
Network	Lesson 9, Topic B
Central processing unit (CPU)	Lesson 5, Topic B
Event logs	Lesson 9, Topic B
Configuration	Lesson 9, Topic B
Shipping	Lesson 9, Topic B
Alerting	Lesson 9, Topic B
Reporting	Lesson 9, Topic B
Retention	Lesson 9, Topic B
Rotation	Lesson 9, Topic B
Data migration and transfer	Lesson 9, Topic B
Infiltration	Lesson 9, Topic B
Exfiltration	Lesson 9, Topic B
Disparate OS data transfer	Lesson 9, Topic B
Robocopy	Lesson 9, Topic B
File transfer	Lesson 9, Topic B
Fast copy	Lesson 9, Topic B
Secure copy protocol (SCP)	Lesson 9, Topic B

Domain and Objective	Covered in
Administrative interfaces	Lesson 9, Topic B
Console	Lesson 9, Topic B
Remote desktop	Lesson 9, Topic B
Secure shell (SSH)	Lesson 9, Topic B
Web interface	Lesson 9, Topic B
2.4 Explain the key concepts of high availability for servers	Lesson 11, Topic B
Clustering	Lesson 11, Topic B
Active-active	Lesson 11, Topic B
Active-passive	Lesson 11, Topic B
Failover	Lesson 11, Topic B
Failback	Lesson 11, Topic B
Proper patching procedures	Lesson 11, Topic B
Heartbeat	Lesson 11, Topic B
Fault tolerance	Lesson 11, Topic B
Server-level redundancy vs. component redundancy	Lesson 11, Topic B
Redundant server network infrastructure	Lesson 11, Topic B
Load balancing	Lesson 11, Topic B
Software vs. hardware	Lesson 11, Topic B
Round robin	Lesson 11, Topic B
Most recently used (MRU)	Lesson 11, Topic B
Network interface card (NIC) teaming and redundancy	Lesson 11, Topic B
Failover	Lesson 11, Topic B
Link aggregation	Lesson 11, Topic B
2.5 Summarize the purpose and operation of virtualization	Lesson 2, Topic A Lesson 2, Topic B
Host vs. guest	Lesson 2, Topic A
Virtual networking	Lesson 2, Topic A
Direct access (bridged)	Lesson 2, Topic A
Network address translation (NAT)	Lesson 2, Topic A
vNICs	Lesson 2, Topic A
Virtual switches	Lesson 2, Topic A
Resource allocation and provisioning	Lesson 2, Topic A
CPU	Lesson 2, Topic A
Memory	Lesson 2, Topic A
Disk	Lesson 2, Topic A
NIC	Lesson 2, Topic A
Overprovisioning	Lesson 2, Topic A
Scalability	Lesson 2, Topic A
Management interfaces for virtual machines	Lesson 2, Topic A

Domain and Objective	Covered in
Cloud models	Lesson 2, Topic B
Public	Lesson 2, Topic B
Private	Lesson 2, Topic B
Hybrid	Lesson 2, Topic B
2.6 Summarize scripting basics for server administration	Lesson 7, Topic D
Script types	Lesson 7, Topic D
Bash	Lesson 7, Topic D
Batch	Lesson 7, Topic D
PowerShell	Lesson 7, Topic D
Virtual basic script (VBS)	Lesson 7, Topic D
Environment variables	Lesson 7, Topic D
Comment syntax	Lesson 7, Topic D
Basic script constructs	Lesson 7, Topic D
Loops	Lesson 7, Topic D
Variables	Lesson 7, Topic D
Conditionals	Lesson 7, Topic D
Comparators	Lesson 7, Topic D
Basic data types	Lesson 7, Topic D
Integers	Lesson 7, Topic D
Strings	Lesson 7, Topic D
Arrays	Lesson 7, Topic D
Common server administration scripting tasks	Lesson 7, Topic D
Startup	Lesson 7, Topic D
Shut down	Lesson 7, Topic D
Service	Lesson 7, Topic D
Login	Lesson 7, Topic D
Account creation	Lesson 7, Topic D
Bootstrap	Lesson 7, Topic D
2.7 Explain the importance of asset management and documentation	Lesson 4, Topic A Lesson 4, Topic B
Asset management	Lesson 4, Topic A
Labeling	Lesson 4, Topic A
Warranty	Lesson 4, Topic A
Leased vs. owned devices	Lesson 4, Topic A
Lifecycle management	Lesson 4, Topic A
Procurement	Lesson 4, Topic A
Usage	Lesson 4, Topic A
End of life	Lesson 4, Topic A
Disposal/recycling	Lesson 4, Topic A
Inventory	Lesson 4, Topic A
Make	Lesson 4, Topic A

Domain and Objective	Covered in
Model	Lesson 4, Topic A
Serial number	Lesson 4, Topic A
Asset tag	Lesson 4, Topic A
Documentation management	Lesson 4, Topic B
Updates	Lesson 4, Topic B
Service manuals	Lesson 4, Topic B
Architecture diagrams	Lesson 4, Topic B
Infrastructure diagrams	Lesson 4, Topic B
Workflow diagrams	Lesson 4, Topic B
Recovery processes	Lesson 4, Topic B
Baselines	Lesson 4, Topic B
Change management	Lesson 4, Topic B
Server configurations	Lesson 4, Topic B
Company policies and procedures	Lesson 4, Topic B
Business impact analysis (BIA)	Lesson 4, Topic B
Mean time between failure (MTBF)	Lesson 4, Topic B
Mean time to recover (MTTR)	Lesson 4, Topic B
Recovery point objective (RPO)	Lesson 4, Topic B
Recovery time objective (RTO)	Lesson 4, Topic B
Service level agreement (SLA)	Lesson 4, Topic B
Uptime requirements	Lesson 4, Topic B
Document availability	Lesson 4, Topic B
Secure storage of sensitive documentation	Lesson 4, Topic B
2.8 Explain licensing concepts	Lesson 1, Topic C
Models	Lesson 1, Topic C
Per-instance	Lesson 1, Topic C
Per-concurrent-user	Lesson 1, Topic C
Per-server	Lesson 1, Topic C
Per-socket	Lesson 1, Topic C
Per-core	Lesson 1, Topic C
Site-based	Lesson 1, Topic C
Physical vs. virtual	Lesson 1, Topic C
Node-locked	Lesson 1, Topic C
Signatures	Lesson 1, Topic C
Open source	Lesson 1, Topic C
Subscription	Lesson 1, Topic C
License vs. maintenance and support	Lesson 1, Topic C
Volume licensing	Lesson 1, Topic C
License count validation	Lesson 1, Topic C
True up	Lesson 1, Topic C

Domain and Objective	Covered in
Version compatibility	Lesson 1, Topic C
Backward compatible	Lesson 1, Topic C
Forward compatible	Lesson 1, Topic C
3.0 Security and Disaster Recovery	Lesson 3, Topic A Lesson 9, Topic A Lesson 9, Topic C Lesson 10, Topic A Lesson 10, Topic B Lesson 11, Topic A Lesson 11, Topic C Lesson 12, Topic A
3.1 Summarize data security concepts	Lesson 10, Topic A
Encryption paradigms	Lesson 10, Topic A
Data at rest	Lesson 10, Topic A
Data in transit	Lesson 10, Topic A
Retention policies	Lesson 10, Topic A
Data storage	Lesson 10, Topic A
Physical location storage	Lesson 10, Topic A
Off-site vs. on-site	Lesson 10, Topic A
UEFI/BIOS passwords	Lesson 10, Topic A
Bootloader passwords	Lesson 10, Topic A
Business impact	Lesson 10, Topic A
Data value prioritization	Lesson 10, Topic A
Lifecycle management	Lesson 10, Topic A
Cost of security vs. risk and/or replacement	Lesson 10, Topic A
3.2 Summarize physical security concepts	Lesson 3, Topic A
Physical access controls	Lesson 3, Topic A
Bollards	Lesson 3, Topic A
Architectural reinforcements	Lesson 3, Topic A
Signal blocking	Lesson 3, Topic A
Reflective glass	Lesson 3, Topic A
Datacenter camouflage	Lesson 3, Topic A
Fencing	Lesson 3, Topic A
Security guards	Lesson 3, Topic A
Security cameras	Lesson 3, Topic A
Locks	Lesson 3, Topic A
Biometric	Lesson 3, Topic A
Radio frequency identification (RFID)	Lesson 3, Topic A
Card readers	Lesson 3, Topic A
Mantraps	Lesson 3, Topic A
Safes	Lesson 3, Topic A
Environmental controls	Lesson 3, Topic A
Fire suppression	Lesson 3, Topic A

Domain and Objective	Covered in
Heating, ventilation, and cooling (HVAC)	Lesson 3, Topic A
Sensors	Lesson 3, Topic A
3.3 Explain important concepts pertaining to identity and access management for server administration	Lesson 9, Topic A
User accounts	Lesson 9, Topic A
User groups	Lesson 9, Topic A
Password policies	Lesson 9, Topic A
Length	Lesson 9, Topic A
Lockout	Lesson 9, Topic A
Enforcement	Lesson 9, Topic A
Permissions and access controls	Lesson 9, Topic A
Role-based	Lesson 9, Topic A
Rule-based	Lesson 9, Topic A
Scope-based	Lesson 9, Topic A
Segregation of duties	Lesson 9, Topic A
Delegation	Lesson 9, Topic A
Auditing	Lesson 9, Topic A
User activity	Lesson 9, Topic A
Logins	Lesson 9, Topic A
Group memberships	Lesson 9, Topic A
Deletions	Lesson 9, Topic A
Multifactor authentication (MFA)	Lesson 9, Topic A
Something you know	Lesson 9, Topic A
Something you have	Lesson 9, Topic A
Something you are	Lesson 9, Topic A
Single sign-on (SSO)	Lesson 9, Topic A
3.4 Explain data security risks and mitigation strategies	Lesson 10, Topic B
Security risks	Lesson 10, Topic B
Hardware failure	Lesson 10, Topic B
Malware	Lesson 10, Topic B
Data corruption	Lesson 10, Topic B
Insider threats	Lesson 10, Topic B
Theft	Lesson 10, Topic B
Data loss prevention (DLP)	Lesson 10, Topic B
Unwanted duplication	Lesson 10, Topic B
Unwanted publication	Lesson 10, Topic B
Unwanted access methods	Lesson 10, Topic B
Backdoor	Lesson 10, Topic B
Social engineering	Lesson 10, Topic B

Domain and Objective	Covered in
Breaches	Lesson 10, Topic B
Identification	Lesson 10, Topic B
Disclosure	Lesson 10, Topic B
Mitigation strategies	Lesson 10, Topic B
Data monitoring	Lesson 10, Topic B
Log analysis	Lesson 10, Topic B
Security information and event management (SIEM)	Lesson 10, Topic B
Two-person integrity	Lesson 10, Topic B
Split encryption key tokens	Lesson 10, Topic B
Separation of roles	Lesson 10, Topic B
Regulatory constraints	Lesson 10, Topic B
Governmental	Lesson 10, Topic B
Individually privileged information	Lesson 10, Topic B
Personally identifiable information (PII)	Lesson 10, Topic B
Payment Card Industry Data Security Standard (PCI DSS)	Lesson 10, Topic B
Legal considerations	Lesson 10, Topic B
Data retention	Lesson 10, Topic B
Subpoenas	Lesson 10, Topic B
3.5 Given a scenario, apply server hardening methods	Lesson 9, Topic C
OS hardening	Lesson 9, Topic C
Disable unused services	Lesson 9, Topic C
Close unneeded ports	Lesson 9, Topic C
Install only required software	Lesson 9, Topic C
Apply driver updates	Lesson 9, Topic C
Apply OS updates	Lesson 9, Topic C
Firewall configuration	Lesson 9, Topic C
Application hardening	Lesson 9, Topic C
Install latest patches	Lesson 9, Topic C
Disable unneeded services, roles, or features	Lesson 9, Topic C
Host security	Lesson 9, Topic C
Antivirus	Lesson 9, Topic C
Anti-malware	Lesson 9, Topic C
Host intrusion detection system (HIDS)/Host intrusion prevention system (HIPS)	Lesson 9, Topic C
Hardware hardening	Lesson 9, Topic C
Disable unneeded hardware	Lesson 9, Topic C
Disable unneeded physical ports, devices, or functions	Lesson 9, Topic C
Set BIOS password	Lesson 9, Topic C
Set boot order	Lesson 9, Topic C
Patching	Lesson 9, Topic C
Testing	Lesson 9, Topic C

Domain and Objective	Covered in
Deployment	Lesson 9, Topic C
Change management	Lesson 9, Topic C
3.6 Summarize proper server decommissioning concepts	Lesson 12, Topic A
Proper removal procedures	Lesson 12, Topic A
Company policies	Lesson 12, Topic A
Verify non-utilization	Lesson 12, Topic A
Documentation	Lesson 12, Topic A
Asset management	Lesson 12, Topic A
Change management	Lesson 12, Topic A
Media destruction	Lesson 12, Topic A
Disk wiping	Lesson 12, Topic A
Physical	Lesson 12, Topic A
Degaussing	Lesson 12, Topic A
Shredding	Lesson 12, Topic A
Crushing	Lesson 12, Topic A
Incineration	Lesson 12, Topic A
Purposes for media destruction	Lesson 12, Topic A
Media retention requirements	Lesson 12, Topic A
Cable remediation	Lesson 12, Topic A
Power	Lesson 12, Topic A
Networking	Lesson 12, Topic A
Electronics recycling	Lesson 12, Topic A
Internal vs. external	Lesson 12, Topic A
Repurposing	Lesson 12, Topic A
3.7 Explain the importance of backups and restores	Lesson 11, Topic A
Backup methods	Lesson 11, Topic A
Full	Lesson 11, Topic A
Synthetic full	Lesson 11, Topic A
Incremental	Lesson 11, Topic A
Differential	Lesson 11, Topic A
Archive	Lesson 11, Topic A
Open file	Lesson 11, Topic A
Snapshot	Lesson 11, Topic A
Backup frequency	Lesson 11, Topic A
Media rotation	Lesson 11, Topic A
Backup media types	Lesson 11, Topic A
Tape	Lesson 11, Topic A
Cloud	Lesson 11, Topic A
Disk	Lesson 11, Topic A
Print	Lesson 11, Topic A
File-level vs. system-state backup	Lesson 11, Topic A

Domain and Objective	Covered in
Restore methods	Lesson 11, Topic A
Overwrite	Lesson 11, Topic A
Side by side	Lesson 11, Topic A
Alternate location path	Lesson 11, Topic A
Backup validation	Lesson 11, Topic A
Media integrity	Lesson 11, Topic A
Equipment	Lesson 11, Topic A
Regular testing intervals	Lesson 11, Topic A
Media inventory before restoration	Lesson 11, Topic A
3.8 Explain the importance of disaster recovery	Lesson 11, Topic C
Site types	Lesson 11, Topic C
Hot site	Lesson 11, Topic C
Cold site	Lesson 11, Topic C
Warm site	Lesson 11, Topic C
Cloud	Lesson 11, Topic C
Separate geographic locations	Lesson 11, Topic C
Replication	Lesson 11, Topic C
Constant	Lesson 11, Topic C
Background	Lesson 11, Topic C
Synchronous vs. asynchronous	Lesson 11, Topic C
Application consistent	Lesson 11, Topic C
File locking	Lesson 11, Topic C
Mirroring	Lesson 11, Topic C
Bidirectional	Lesson 11, Topic C
Testing	Lesson 11, Topic C
Tabletops	Lesson 11, Topic C
Live failover	Lesson 11, Topic C
Simulated failover	Lesson 11, Topic C
Production vs. non-production	Lesson 11, Topic C
4.0 Troubleshooting	Lesson 1, Topic B Lesson 5, Topic C Lesson 6, Topic B Lesson 8, Topic A Lesson 8, Topic B Lesson 10, Topic C
4.1 Explain the troubleshooting theory and methodology	Lesson 1, Topic B
Identify the problem and determine the scope.	Lesson 1, Topic B
Question users/stakeholders and identify changes to the server/environment.	Lesson 1, Topic B
Collect additional documentation/logs.	Lesson 1, Topic B
If possible, replicate the problem as appropriate.	Lesson 1, Topic B
If possible, perform backups before making changes.	Lesson 1, Topic B
Escalate, if necessary.	Lesson 1, Topic B

Domain and Objective	Covered in
Establish a theory of probable cause (question the obvious).	Lesson 1, Topic B
Determine whether there is a common element or symptom causing multiple problems.	Lesson 1, Topic B
Test the theory to determine the cause.	Lesson 1, Topic B
Once the theory is confirmed, determine the next steps to resolve the problem.	Lesson 1, Topic B
If the theory is not confirmed, establish a new theory.	Lesson 1, Topic B
Establish a plan of action to resolve the problem.	Lesson 1, Topic B
Notify impacted users.	Lesson 1, Topic B
Implement the solution or escalate.	Lesson 1, Topic B
Make one change at a time and test/confirm the change has resolved the problem.	Lesson 1, Topic B
If the problem is not resolved, reverse the change, if appropriate, and implement a new change.	Lesson 1, Topic B
Verify full system functionality and, if applicable, implement preventive measures.	Lesson 1, Topic B
Perform a root cause analysis.	Lesson 1, Topic B
Document findings, actions, and outcomes throughout the process.	Lesson 1, Topic B
4.2 Given a scenario, troubleshoot common hardware failures	Lesson 5, Topic C
Common problems	Lesson 5, Topic C
Predictive failures	Lesson 5, Topic C
Memory errors and failures	Lesson 5, Topic C
System crash	Lesson 5, Topic C
Blue screen	Lesson 5, Topic C
Purple screen	Lesson 5, Topic C
Memory dump	Lesson 5, Topic C
Utilization	Lesson 5, Topic C
Power-on self-test (POST) errors	Lesson 5, Topic C
Random lockups	Lesson 5, Topic C
Kernel panic	Lesson 5, Topic C
Complementary metal-oxide-semiconductor (CMOS) battery failure	Lesson 5, Topic C
System lockups	Lesson 5, Topic C
Random crashes	Lesson 5, Topic C
Fault and device indication	Lesson 5, Topic C
Visual indicators	Lesson 5, Topic C
Light-emitting diode (LED)	Lesson 5, Topic C
Liquid crystal display (LCD) panel readouts	Lesson 5, Topic C
Auditory or olfactory cues	Lesson 5, Topic C
POST codes	Lesson 5, Topic C
Misallocated virtual resources	Lesson 5, Topic C

Domain and Objective	Covered in
Causes of common problems	Lesson 5, Topic C
Technical	Lesson 5, Topic C
Power supply fault	Lesson 5, Topic C
Malfunctioning fans	Lesson 5, Topic C
Improperly seated heat sink	Lesson 5, Topic C
Improperly seated cards	Lesson 5, Topic C
Incompatibility of components	Lesson 5, Topic C
Cooling failures	Lesson 5, Topic C
Backplane failure	Lesson 5, Topic C
Firmware incompatibility	Lesson 5, Topic C
CPU or GPU overheating	Lesson 5, Topic C
Environmental	Lesson 5, Topic C
Dust	Lesson 5, Topic C
Humidity	Lesson 5, Topic C
Temperature	Lesson 5, Topic C
Tools and techniques	Lesson 5, Topic C
Event logs	Lesson 5, Topic C
Firmware upgrades or downgrades	Lesson 5, Topic C
Hardware diagnostics	Lesson 5, Topic C
Compressed air	Lesson 5, Topic C
Electrostatic discharge (ESD) equipment	Lesson 5, Topic C
Reseating or replacing components and/or cables	Lesson 5, Topic C
4.3 Given a scenario, troubleshoot storage problems	Lesson 6, Topic B
Common problems	Lesson 6, Topic B
Boot errors	Lesson 6, Topic B
Sector block errors	Lesson 6, Topic B
Cache battery failure	Lesson 6, Topic B
Read/write errors	Lesson 6, Topic B
Failed drives	Lesson 6, Topic B
Page/swap/scratch file or partition	Lesson 6, Topic B
Partition errors	Lesson 6, Topic B
Slow file access	Lesson 6, Topic B
OS not found	Lesson 6, Topic B
Unsuccessful backup	Lesson 6, Topic B
Unable to mount the device	Lesson 6, Topic B
Drive not available	Lesson 6, Topic B
Cannot access logical drive	Lesson 6, Topic B
Data corruption	Lesson 6, Topic B
Slow I/O performance	Lesson 6, Topic B
Restore failure	Lesson 6, Topic B

Domain and Objective	Covered in
Cache failure	Lesson 6, Topic B
Multiple drive failure	Lesson 6, Topic B
Causes of common problems	Lesson 6, Topic B
Disk space utilization	Lesson 6, Topic B
Insufficient disk space	Lesson 6, Topic B
Misconfigured RAID	Lesson 6, Topic B
Media failure	Lesson 6, Topic B
Drive failure	Lesson 6, Topic B
Controller failure	Lesson 6, Topic B
Host bus adapter (HBA) failure	Lesson 6, Topic B
Loose connectors	Lesson 6, Topic B
Cable problems	Lesson 6, Topic B
Misconfiguration	Lesson 6, Topic B
Corrupt boot sector	Lesson 6, Topic B
Corrupt filesystem table	Lesson 6, Topic B
Array rebuild	Lesson 6, Topic B
Improper disk partition	Lesson 6, Topic B
Bad sectors	Lesson 6, Topic B
Cache battery failure	Lesson 6, Topic B
Cache turned off	Lesson 6, Topic B
Insufficient space	Lesson 6, Topic B
Improper RAID configuration	Lesson 6, Topic B
Mismatched drives	Lesson 6, Topic B
Backplane failure	Lesson 6, Topic B
Tools and techniques	Lesson 6, Topic B
Partitioning tools	Lesson 6, Topic B
Disk management	Lesson 6, Topic B
RAID and array management	Lesson 6, Topic B
System logs	Lesson 6, Topic B
Disk mounting commands	Lesson 6, Topic B
net use	Lesson 6, Topic B
mount	Lesson 6, Topic B
Monitoring tools	Lesson 6, Topic B
Visual inspections	Lesson 6, Topic B
Auditory inspections	Lesson 6, Topic B
4.4 Given a scenario, troubleshoot common OS and software problems	Lesson 8, Topic A
Common problems	Lesson 8, Topic A
Unable to log on	Lesson 8, Topic A
Unable to access resources	Lesson 8, Topic A
Unable to access files	Lesson 8, Topic A
System file corruption	Lesson 8, Topic A

Domain and Objective	Covered in
End of life/end of support	Lesson 8, Topic A
Slow performance	Lesson 8, Topic A
Cannot write to system logs	Lesson 8, Topic A
Service failures	Lesson 8, Topic A
System or application hanging	Lesson 8, Topic A
Freezing	Lesson 8, Topic A
Patch update failure	Lesson 8, Topic A
Causes of common problems	Lesson 8, Topic A
Incompatible drivers/modules	Lesson 8, Topic A
Improperly applied patches	Lesson 8, Topic A
Unstable drivers or software	Lesson 8, Topic A
Server not joined to domain	Lesson 8, Topic A
Clock skew	Lesson 8, Topic A
Memory leaks	Lesson 8, Topic A
Buffer overrun	Lesson 8, Topic A
Incompatibility	Lesson 8, Topic A
Insecure dependencies	Lesson 8, Topic A
Version management	Lesson 8, Topic A
Architecture	Lesson 8, Topic A
Update failures	Lesson 8, Topic A
Missing updates	Lesson 8, Topic A
Missing dependencies	Lesson 8, Topic A
Downstream failures due to updates	Lesson 8, Topic A
Inappropriate application-level permissions	Lesson 8, Topic A
Improper CPU affinity and priority	Lesson 8, Topic A
OS and software tools and techniques	Lesson 8, Topic A
Patching	Lesson 8, Topic A
Upgrades	Lesson 8, Topic A
Downgrades	Lesson 8, Topic A
Package management	Lesson 8, Topic A
Recovery	Lesson 8, Topic A
Boot options	Lesson 8, Topic A
Safe mode	Lesson 8, Topic A
Reload OS	Lesson 8, Topic A
Snapshots	Lesson 8, Topic A
Proper privilege escalations	Lesson 8, Topic A
runas/Run As	Lesson 8, Topic A
sudo	Lesson 8, Topic A
su	Lesson 8, Topic A
Scheduled reboots	Lesson 8, Topic A

Domain and Objective	Covered in
Software firewalls	Lesson 8, Topic A
Adding or removing ports	Lesson 8, Topic A
Zones	Lesson 8, Topic A
Clocks	Lesson 8, Topic A
Network time protocol (NTP)	Lesson 8, Topic A
System time	Lesson 8, Topic A
Services and processes	Lesson 8, Topic A
Starting	Lesson 8, Topic A
Stopping	Lesson 8, Topic A
Status identification	Lesson 8, Topic A
Dependencies	Lesson 8, Topic A
Configuration management	Lesson 8, Topic A
System center configuration manager (SCCM)	Lesson 8, Topic A
Puppet/Chef/Ansible	Lesson 8, Topic A
Group Policy Object (GPO)	Lesson 8, Topic A
Hardware compatibility list (HCL)	Lesson 8, Topic A
4.5 Given a scenario, troubleshoot network connectivity issues	Lesson 8, Topic B
Common problems	Lesson 8, Topic B
Lack of Internet connectivity	Lesson 8, Topic B
Resource unavailable	Lesson 8, Topic B
Receiving incorrect DHCP information	Lesson 8, Topic B
Non-functional or unreachable	Lesson 8, Topic B
Destination host unreachable	Lesson 8, Topic B
Unknown host	Lesson 8, Topic B
Unable to reach remote subnets	Lesson 8, Topic B
Failure of service provider	Lesson 8, Topic B
Cannot reach server by hostname / fully qualified domain name (FQDN)	Lesson 8, Topic B
Causes of common problems	Lesson 8, Topic B
Improper IP configuration	Lesson 8, Topic B
IPv4 vs. IPv6 misconfigurations	Lesson 8, Topic B
Improper VLAN configuration	Lesson 8, Topic B
Network port security	Lesson 8, Topic B
Component failure	Lesson 8, Topic B
Incorrect OS route tables	Lesson 8, Topic B
Bad cables	Lesson 8, Topic B
Firewall (misconfiguration, hardware failure, software failure)	Lesson 8, Topic B
Misconfigured NIC	Lesson 8, Topic B
DNS and/or DHCP failure	Lesson 8, Topic B
DHCP server misconfigured	Lesson 8, Topic B
Misconfigured hosts file	Lesson 8, Topic B

Domain and Objective	Covered in
Tools and techniques	Lesson 8, Topic B
Check link lights	Lesson 8, Topic B
Confirm power supply	Lesson 8, Topic B
Verify cable integrity	Lesson 8, Topic B
Check appropriate cable selection	Lesson 8, Topic B
Commands	Lesson 8, Topic B
ipconfig	Lesson 8, Topic B
ip addr	Lesson 8, Topic B
ping	Lesson 8, Topic B
tracert	Lesson 8, Topic B
traceroute	Lesson 8, Topic B
nslookup	Lesson 8, Topic B
netstat	Lesson 8, Topic B
dig	Lesson 8, Topic B
telnet	Lesson 8, Topic B
nc	Lesson 8, Topic B
nbtstat	Lesson 8, Topic B
route	Lesson 8, Topic B
4.6 Given a scenario, troubleshoot security problems	Lesson 10, Topic C
Common concerns	Lesson 10, Topic C
File integrity	Lesson 10, Topic C
Improper privilege escalation	Lesson 10, Topic C
Excessive access	Lesson 10, Topic C
Applications will not load	Lesson 10, Topic C
Cannot access network fileshares	Lesson 10, Topic C
Unable to open files	Lesson 10, Topic C
Causes of common problems	Lesson 10, Topic C
Open ports	Lesson 10, Topic C
Services	Lesson 10, Topic C
Active	Lesson 10, Topic C
Inactive	Lesson 10, Topic C
Orphan/zombie	Lesson 10, Topic C
Intrusion detection configurations	Lesson 10, Topic C
Anti-malware configurations	Lesson 10, Topic C
Improperly configured local/group policies	Lesson 10, Topic C
Improperly configured firewall rules	Lesson 10, Topic C
Misconfigured permissions	Lesson 10, Topic C
Virus infection	Lesson 10, Topic C
Malware	Lesson 10, Topic C
Rogue processes/services	Lesson 10, Topic C
Data loss prevention (DLP)	Lesson 10, Topic C

Domain and Objective	Covered in
Security tools	Lesson 10, Topic C
Port scanners	Lesson 10, Topic C
Sniffers	Lesson 10, Topic C
Telnet clients	Lesson 10, Topic C
Anti-malware	Lesson 10, Topic C
Antivirus	Lesson 10, Topic C
File integrity	Lesson 10, Topic C
Checksums	Lesson 10, Topic C
Monitoring	Lesson 10, Topic C
Detection	Lesson 10, Topic C
Enforcement	Lesson 10, Topic C
User access controls	Lesson 10, Topic C
SELinux	Lesson 10, Topic C
User account control (UAC)	Lesson 10, Topic C

Solutions

Review Activity: Server Administration Concepts

1. **List several examples of systems administrator job roles.**

- Manage hardware, applications, networking
- Manage the server's lifecycle
- Monitor server performance, capacity planning, growth
- Manage user and group accounts
- Accept and troubleshoot escalated service desk tickets
- Work with other IT teams
- Manage disparate technologies
- Advise the organization on new technologies
- Manage network services
- Advise the organization on cybersecurity topics
- Create documentation
- Sharpen communications and presentation skills

2. **List at least three differences between workstations and servers.**

Servers contain redundant hardware, servers may be more powerful, servers are secured differently than workstations, there are specific OSs for servers and for workstations, workstations are assigned to individual users, servers have a rack form factor and workstations have a desktop or laptop form factor

3. **What are the four phases of the server lifecycle?**

Purchase, install/deploy, maintain/update, decommission

4. **What are the four main subsystems of a computer?**

Processor, memory, storage, network

5. **What is a Linux distribution?**

As a general rule, Linux distributions are purpose-specific variations of the Linux OS

6. **What are the two main branches of the Linux family of distributions?**

Debian and Red Hat

7. **How do these two branches differ?**

Mainly by software management

Review Activity: Discuss a Troubleshooting Methodology

1. **While troubleshooting a printing problem with a network print device, you check to see that the print device is powered, is turned on, has paper, and does not have an alarm indicating that the paper path is jammed. Which step of the troubleshooting methodology are you applying?**

Theory of Probable Cause/Question the Obvious

2. **While troubleshooting a permissions issue on a file server, you check to verify that a user that should be able to access a particular folder can access that folder. You also check that a user that should not be able to access the folder cannot access it. It appears that you have successfully solved the permissions issue. Which step of the troubleshooting methodology are you applying?**

Verify Full System Functionality

3. **The service desk escalates a ticket to you that indicates a user cannot access any network servers or any websites. While troubleshooting, you ask several employees near the user whether they can access the network servers and websites. Those users all indicate that they can access the requested resources. You have now determined that only one user is experiencing issues. Which step of the troubleshooting methodology are you applying?**

Determine the Scope of the Problem

Review Activity: Licenses

1. **List at least three attributes of FOSS licensing and at least three attributes of proprietary licensing.**

FOSS:

- No cost
- Free to modify and redistribute
- Not necessarily reliable vendor support
- Not necessarily reliable documentation

Proprietary:

- Not free to use
- Not free to modify
- More likely reliable vendor support
- More likely reliable documentation

2. **Anne, a developer, creates a piece of software named "SuperSolver" and licenses the software as open source. She places the source code and the compiled software executable on her website. John, another developer, downloads the source code for SuperSolver and modifies the code to add several new features. He places the modified source code on his website. This is an example of what kind of licensing?**

FOSS

3. You are a systems administrator, and you are responsible for managing the licenses for a piece of cloud-based software. Currently, you have 100 users that access the software. Your organization is billed monthly for these users. Your organization hires an additional 50 users who also need access. You increase your licenses by using a web-based management tool. You also notice that the vendor has automatically given your users access to the newly released 2.0 version of the software. This is an example of what kind of licensing?

Subscription

4. You are systems administrator, and you are responsible for managing the license for a piece of server-based software. The software license requires you to pay based on the number of physical CPUs enabled on the server's motherboard. This is an example of what kind of license?

Per-socket

Review Activity: Virtualization Concepts

1. How does virtualization improve scalability as compared to physical server deployments?

It is much easier to add resources, such as compute or memory, to virtualized servers than to physical servers.

2. What is the difference between Type 1 and Type 2 hypervisors?

Type 1 hypervisors are installed directly on the server, without an underlying OS. Type 2 hypervisors rely on a host OS that is installed directly on the server.

3. What is the role of virtual networking in virtualization?

Virtual networking provides VMs with access to the physical network.

Review Activity: Cloud Computing

1. What are the five characteristics of cloud computing, according to NIST?

- On-demand self-service
- Broad network access
- Resource pooling
- Rapid elasticity
- Measured services

2. What are the four cloud deployment models?

- Private cloud
- Public cloud
- Community cloud
- Hybrid cloud

3. **What are the three cloud service models?**

- SaaS
- PaaS
- IaaS

4. **What is the cloud shared security model?**

The CSP is responsible for the security of the cloud, and the consumer is responsible for security in the cloud. The CSP must secure its datacenter and the cloud platform. The consumer must securely configure and manage cloud-based resources.

Review Activity: Deployment Models

1. **List at least two advantages of on-premises deployments over cloud deployments.**

Better security, control of administration, data, deployment environment

2. **List at least two disadvantages of on-premises deployments over cloud deployments.**

Organization bears the cost of hardware, installation, maintenance, expert staff, security, and a higher initial CapEx.

Review Activity: Physical Security Concepts

1. **Explain the outside-in approach to physical security.**

Start managing physical security by securing the property, followed by the building perimeter, the building interior, the datacenter, the NOC, and the physical server racks.

2. **List at least three examples of building or property security measures:**

- Gates
- Fences
- Landscaping
- Lighting
- Cameras/surveillance
- Bollards

3. **List at least three examples of perimeter security measures:**

- Door buzzers
- Turnstiles
- Mantraps
- Guest badges
- Cameras/surveillance
- One-way doors

Review Activity: Network Security Concepts

1. **Why might it be useful to intercept network traffic as a server administrator, and what are two tools you could use to accomplish this task?**

Intercepting network traffic to the server is useful for identifying what traffic is sent to and from the server for troubleshooting and security audits.

Wireshark and tcpdump are both packet sniffers that can intercept network traffic.

2. **List two reasons an administrator might segment a network.**

Networks might be segmented to isolate traffic for security and performance reasons.

3. **What types of services might reside on servers located in a DMZ?**

DMZ-based servers usually contain services that need direct Internet connections, such as VPN, DNS, web, email, and FTP.

4. **What is the purpose of the IP address subnet mask?**

The subnet mask is used to calculate which part of the IP address is the Network ID and which part is the Host ID.

5. **What are the Class A, B, and C reserved IP address ranges, and what is their purpose?**

- Class A = 10.0.0.0/8
- Class B = 172.16.0.0/12
- Class C = 192.168.0.0/16

The purpose of the reserved IP address ranges is to provide IP addresses for internal use.

6. **What is the difference between a host-based firewall and a network-based firewall?**

Host-based firewalls control the flow of network traffic into and out of a single server. Network-based firewalls control the flow of traffic into and out of a network segment.

7. **What is the default port for the SSH protocol, and when might you need to use that port number?**

The default port is 22/tcp, and you may need to use that information to configure a firewall, configure a service, or review a log file.

Review Activity: Asset Management Concepts

1. **What are the four phases of the server lifecycle?**

- Procurement
- Usage
- End of life
- Disposal/recycling

2. **What are some risks of not tracking inventory?**

- License violations
- Misinformed purchasing decisions
- Inadequate security (you can't secure what you don't know about)

3. **What inventory information might you track for servers?**

- Make and model
- Serial number
- Asset tag
- Basic input/output system (BIOS) asset tag
- OS

Review Activity: Documentation

1. **List server components (hardware and software) that are commonly standardized.**

OS, antivirus/anti-malware software, local account information, storage and RAID configurations, BIOS passwords

2. **What is the purpose of an architectural diagram?**

Architectural diagrams display the service components and the flow of data through a service.

3. **Explain the difference between MTBF and MTTR.**

- MTBF—estimates mean time between service or system failure for the purpose of mitigation.
- MTTR—estimates recovery time for failed services for the purpose of developing SLAs.

4. **Explain the difference between RPOs and RTOs.**

RPO—Time from the most recent backup or recovery point to a disaster. This value estimates how much data an organization can acceptably lose in the event of a disaster.

RTO—Time needed to recover from a disaster for business continuity purposes. This allows prioritization of services to recover.

5. **What information is contained on an infrastructure diagram?**

Network segments, network devices, IP address ranges, servers, clients

6. **What are the goals of a document management system?**

- Capture
- Store
- Locate
- Update
- Securely share

Review Activity: Physical Server Management

1. **What are the standard width and height measurements for rack-mounted devices?**

The standard width is 19 inch, and height is 1.75 inch increments (also known as "units").

2. **List at least two benefits of using rack-mounted devices:**

Cooling, space management, security, standardized form factors, cable organization within racks.

3. **What are hot and cold aisles in a server room?**

Servers are mounted into racks so that they all pull cool air from one aisle (the cold aisle) and blow hot air into one aisle (the hot aisle). This maximizes the efficiency of air circulation in the server room.

4. **How is a KVM switch useful in a server room?**

The KVM switch saves space and money by providing administrative connectivity to multiple servers through only one keyboard, video, and mouse interface. An administrator can therefore connect to multiple servers without having to provide keyboard, video, and mouse devices for each individual server.

5. **List at least three ways of providing redundant power to servers:**

- Provide power from at least two utility companies.
- Provide generators in addition to the utility company.
- Provide multiple circuits in the server room.
- Use multiple UPSs.
- Use multiple PDUs.
- Install multiple power supplies in the server.

Review Activity: Administration and Storage

1. **List at least one situation where out of band management of a server may be necessary:**

The server has no OS installed or is down.

2. **List one Linux and one Windows tool that may be used to verify storage disk file systems for errors:**

chkdsk (Windows) and fsck (Linux)

3. **What is the advantage of using an HCL when considering a server purchase?**

Servers listed on the HCL of a given OS, such as Windows Server or RHEL, have been verified to work with the OS.

Review Activity: Server Hardware

1. **List at least two common sources of information for predictive failure analysis:**

- Hardware vendors
- System log files
- Service desk tickets
- Personal experience

2. **List at least two environmental factors that might contribute to server failures:**

- Heat
- Humidity/static electricity
- Dust

3. What is the recommended level of humidity for a server room?

40–60% (rH)

4. What is the recommended temperature range for a server room?

68–71 degrees F (20–21.6 degrees C)

Review Activity: Storage Management

1. List at least two ways to mitigate storage capacity issues:

- Enforced user quotas
- Data deduplication
- Data compression

2. What is the balance of cost versus performance between SATA, SAS, and NVMe drives?

- SATA— used when cost savings is more important than performance
- SAS—used when cost savings and performance are balanced
- NVMe—used when performance is more important than cost savings

3. Which RAID solution writes data to two drives simultaneously, so that if one drive fails, the other contains all of the data?

RAID 1 mirroring

4. List at least four differences between software RAID and hardware RAID:

- Hardware RAID is more flexible than software RAID.
- Hardware RAID is faster than software RAID.
- Hardware RAID is independent of the OS, and software RAID is managed by the OS.
- OSs typically cannot boot from software RAID implementations.
- Software RAID is less expensive than hardware RAID.
- Software RAID contains fewer components to manage.
- Software RAID is less complex than hardware RAID.

5. What is the common file sharing protocol for Linux? For Windows?

- Linux—NFS
- Windows—SMBs or CIFS

6. List at least one advantage and one disadvantage of using NAS:

Advantages: easy to implement, relatively inexpensive, flexible

Disadvantages: performance is impacted by network traffic

Review Activity: Common Storage Problems

1. **What storage failure causes are often associated with the OS not being found?**

- Drive failure
- Controller or HBA failure
- Corrupt boot sector
- Boot loader misconfiguration
- Corrupt file system table

2. **What storage failure causes are often associated with failed backups or restores?**

- Media failure
- Drive failure
- Misconfiguration of backup software

3. **List at least two partitioning tools:**

fdisk, parted, Windows Disk Management Console

4. **What Linux command is used to attach a partition to a directory so that users can access the partition?**

The mount command attaches a partition to a directory.

Review Activity: OS Installation

1. **List common attributes of manual installations:**

- Slow
- Inconsistent
- Simple

2. **List common attributes of automated installations:**

- Fast
- Consistent
- More complex to set up initially

3. **Why might an administrator conduct at V2V conversion?**

If moving from one virtualization platform to another

4. **List at least three advantages of command-line administration:**

- Consumes fewer resources
- May be faster
- Can be scripted or automated
- May be more secure

5. What is an advantage of GUI administration?

Easier

6. List at least three remote administration methods:

- SSH
- RDP
- VNC

Review Activity: Storage Configuration

1. List two advantages that the GPT format has over MBR:

- Supports more partitions
- Supports drives and partitions greater than 2 TB

2. What are the three components of a Linux LVM deployment?

PVs, VGs, LVs

3. What content is typically stored on the C: drive on a Windows Server? On the D: drive?

- C: drive contains the OS and applications.
- D: drive contains user data.

4. List three common Linux file systems. List two common Windows file systems.

- Linux—ext4, XFS, ZFS
- Windows—ReFS, NTFS

Review Activity: Network Settings

1. What are the seven layers of the OSI model?

- Application
- Presentation
- Session
- Transport
- Network
- Data Link
- Physical

2. **What are the four layers of the TCP/IP stack?**

- Application
- Transport
- Internet
- Network Access

3. **List the Class A, B, and C reserved IP address ranges:**

- A - 10.0.0.0—10.255.255.255
- B - 172.16.0.0—172.31.255.255
- C - 192.168.0.0—192.168.255.255

4. **List the loopback address and the Automatic Private IP Address range:**

- Loopback—127.0.0.1
- APIPA—169.254.0.0

5. **What are the three identities a network node has?**

Hostname, IP address, and MAC address

6. **What are two reasons a network administrator segments a network?**

Security and performance

7. **What is the purpose of name resolution?**

Name resolution relates an easy-to-remember name with a difficult-to-remember IP address.

Review Activity: Configure Servers with Scripts

1. **What is the difference between a for loop and a while loop?**

For loops repeat a specific number of times, such as eight, before ending. While loops repeat as long as a particular test is true, such as the existence of a file.

2. **Why are comments important in scripts?**

Comments are used to provide information to script users. Scripts may be downloaded from the Internet or used by someone other than the original author, so comments provide a way for the author to communicate what a section of the script does, examples, what the options are for the script, or other notes.

3. **You are configuring a server in a lab environment and need a script that clears user-specific information, such as temp files and downloaded files, after students ends their session. What kind of script would you write?**

You would write a logout script.

Review Activity: OS and Applications

1. **List the six general troubleshooting categories:**

- Hardware
- OS
- Applications
- Misconfigurations
- Patching
- User error

2. **What are some possible reasons a user is not able to access resources or files?**

- Incompatible drivers/modules
- Unstable drivers or software
- Server not joined to the domain
- Inappropriate application-level permissions

3. **What are the administrator-level accounts for Linux, local Windows administration, and Microsoft AD administration?**

Linux administrator account is named "root," the local Windows administration account is named "administrator," and the Microsoft Active Directory administration account is named "Domain Administrator."

4. **What tools or commands are used in Linux and Windows to elevate privileges?**

- In the Windows GUI, use Run As, and at the Windows command line, use runas.
- In the Linux command line, use su or sudo.

5. **List the common Linux package managers:**

RPM, YUM, dpkg, APT

6. **What is the Windows package manager?**

MSI

Review Activity: Network Configurations

1. **List common causes of failed Internet connectivity:**

- Improper IP configuration
- Component failure
- Firewall misconfiguration
- DNS failure
- Edge router misconfiguration

2. **List common causes of failed name resolution:**

- Improper IP configuration
- Misconfigured or failed DNS
- Misconfigured hosts file
- DNS server failure

3. **List the Windows and Linux command-line tools to display and configure basic IP settings:**

- Linux—ip addr or ifconfig or route
- Windows—ipconfig or route

4. **List the Windows and Linux command-line tools to display and troubleshoot name resolution settings:**

- nslookup
- dig
- host
- ping by hostname

Review Activity: Secure Administration Practices

1. **What three Linux commands are used to manage local user accounts?**

useradd, usermod, userdel

2. **What are the three primary forms of MFA?**

- What you know
- What you have
- Who you are

3. **Explain the single sign-on concept.**

Single sign-on refers to a single authentication process that provides access to multiple resources, such as email, databases, and files.

4. **What are the two types of Windows permissions?**

NTFS permissions and Share permissions.

5. **What are the three identities used with Linux permissions?**

User (owner), group, others

6. **What are the three access levels used with Linux permissions?**

Read (r), write (w), execute (x)

Review Activity: Server Functions

1. **Which type of server hosts an authentication database to verify the identity of users and computers?**

Directory Services server

2. **Which type of server leases IP address configurations to client computers?**

DHCP server

3. **Which type of server provides name resolution to client computers?**

DNS server

4. **What is virtual memory?**

When a system consumes its available physical memory (RAM), it may be configured to borrow HDD storage space. That borrowed space is virtual memory.

5. **What term describes Windows virtual memory? Linux virtual memory?**

The use of Windows virtual memory is referred to as paging, and the use of Linux virtual memory is referred to as swapping.

6. **List at least two examples of administrative interfaces:**

- Console
- Remote desktop
- SSH
- Web interface

7. **List at least two Windows monitoring utilities:**

- Task Manager
- Resource Monitor
- Reliability Monitor
- Performance Monitor

8. **List two Linux monitoring utilities:**

sar and top

9. **What Windows PowerShell cmdlet displays the system's current uptime? What command displays a Linux system's current uptime?**

- Windows PowerShell cmdlet: Get-Uptime
- Linux command: uptime

10. **List two Linux commands used to monitor storage space:**

du and df

Review Activity: Server Hardening

1. **List at least two examples of physical hardening for servers:**

- Disable unused ports, such as USB in the system BIOS
- Disable DVD drives in the system BIOS
- Change the boot order to bypass USB and DVD drives
- Configure a BIOS password

2. **List three types of host security software that may be installed on servers:**

- Anti-virus
- Anti-malware
- HIDS

Review Activity: Data Security Concepts

1. **What is the purpose of a data management policy?**

The data management policy governs business data throughout its lifecycle.

2. **What are the three goals of encryption?**

Confidentiality, integrity, non-repudiation

3. **What does it mean to ensure data integrity?**

To prove that data has not changed unexpectedly (such as from corruption or changes made by unauthorized users or software).

4. **What does it mean to ensure non-repudiation?**

To prove the source of a file, network transfer, or other data by showing that the data could only have originated from that source.

5. **List at least one tool used for secure network communications:**

- SSH
- HTTPS
- RDP

6. **List two examples of disk encryption technologies:**

- BitLocker (Windows)
- LUKS (Linux)

7. List at least two examples of file encryption technologies:

- BitLocker
- TrueCrypt
- 7Zip
- Gnu-PG

Review Activity: Data Security

1. What mitigation technique is recommended for the risk of data corruption?

Data monitoring, Backups

2. What mitigation technique is recommended for the risk of unwanted duplication?

Log analysis, Data monitoring, Two-person integrity, Regulatory constraints, Data retention

3. What mitigation technique is recommended for the risk of unwanted access?

Log analysis, Two-person integrity

4. What mitigation technique is recommended for the risk of malware?

Data monitoring, Log analysis

Review Activity: Data Security Troubleshooting

1. Explain the concept of the Principle of Least Privilege.

The Principle of Least Privilege means to grant the least amount of access to resources possible.

2. List two common causes for issues of improper privilege escalation:

Misconfigured Local/Group Policy settings, misconfigured permissions.

3. List at least three common causes for issues where users cannot properly access network shares:

Misconfigured services, misconfigured anti-malware, misconfigured Local/Group Policy settings, misconfigured permissions, misconfigured data loss prevention tools, misconfigured intrusion detection systems.

4. What is the purpose of port scanning tools?

To confirm that firewalls and services are configured correctly.

5. What is the purpose of packet sniffing tools?

To confirm that firewalls are configured correctly.

6. What is the purpose of user access control services, such as SELinux and User Account Control?

To ensure proper privilege escalation and file access.

Review Activity: Data Backup and Restoration

1. **What is the difference between system-state backups and file-level backups?**

System-state backups copy information about the OS and application configurations and tend to be scheduled less frequently than file-level backups. File-level backups capture user data and tend to be scheduled more frequently than system-state backups.

2. **Which backup method tends to provide quicker backups but slower restores?**

Incremental backups

3. **List the traits associated with cloud backups:**

Relatively future proof, introduces Internet connectivity as a variable with backup jobs, backup jobs are globally available.

4. **Which backup method is described by the following: A set number of backup tapes is used, and the tape containing the oldest backup job is the next tape to be overwritten with the next scheduled backup job.**

FIFO

5. **What makes a virtual machine a good candidate for testing restores?**

VMs can easily be reverted or destroyed after the test. Restoring sensitive data to a physical server makes it much more difficult to securely dispose of the data after the test.

Review Activity: High Availability

1. **Explain the difference between failover and failback.**

Failover occurs when a cluster node fails and the service is moved over to another node. Failback occurs when the original node is restored and the service is returned to that node.

2. **What is the function of the cluster heartbeat?**

The heartbeat is a signal transmitted between cluster nodes that proves a node is online.

3. **What is the difference between server redundancy and component redundancy?**

Server redundancy refers to multiple complete servers that can manage a service, such as the server nodes in a cluster. Component redundancy refers to components inside the server or on the network that are duplicated, such as NICs, HDDs, or power supplies.

4. **Which load balancing mechanism allocates connections in a specified order, regardless of workload or capability?**

Round robin

5. **List the two features of NIC Teaming:**

- Redundancy for fault tolerance
- Link aggregation for better performance

Review Activity: Disaster Recovery

1. **Which type of disaster recovery site has the following attributes: relatively high cost, immediate failover, all equipment is on-site?**

Hot site

2. **What is the relative cost difference between hot, warm, and cold disaster recovery sites?**

Hot sites are the most expensive, warm sites are the next most expensive, and cold sites are the least expensive.

3. **Which type of disaster recovery testing has the following attributes: critical stakeholders examine the disaster recovery procedures in the organization, and suggestions are considered.**

Paper test

4. **Which type of disaster recovery testing has the following attributes: the disaster recovery procedures are implemented in a non-production environment. VMs work especially well for this kind of test. The production environment remains unaffected.**

Parallel test

5. **Which type of disaster recovery testing has the following attributes: the disaster recovery procedure is tested on the production environment where customers and employees reside. The goal is to prove zero interruption of service.**

Live failover (cutover)

Review Activity: Server Decommissioning

1. **What are the steps in the decommissioning process?**

Notify the service owner, migrate or retire the application, take the server offline, remove the server

2. **Why is it necessary to update management software after decommissioning a server?**

Management software may generate errors if expected servers are not found.

3. **What is sanitization?**

Sanitization is the proper disposal of HDDs and data.

4. **What HDD disposal technique is described by the phrase "magnetically destroys stored data"?**

Degaussing

5. **List three ways of physically destroying HDDs:**

Shredding, crushing/drilling, incinerating

6. **What risks exist for using network media left behind by former tenants?**

Performance issues, reliability issues, security issues.

7. **Where in the organization might you repurpose a laptop?**

Training center, crash cart, update testing station

Glossary

access control The process of determining and assigning privileges to resources, objects, and data. Each resource has an access control list (ACL) specifying what subjects (users and hosts) can do.

Active Directory The standards-based directory service from Microsoft that runs on Microsoft Windows servers. Also known as AD.

Automatic Private IP Addressing Developed as a means for Windows clients configured to obtain an address automatically that could not contact a DHCP server to communicate on the local subnet. The host randomly selects an address from the range 169.254.x.y. Also called APIPA and a link-local address.

application server Any server making a software application available to clients. Applications are developed on different models (dedicated, distributed, and peer-to-peer).

array Identifier for a group of variables of the same type. The number of possible elements in an array is fixed when the array is declared.

auditing A detailed and specific evaluation of a process, procedure, organization, job function, or system in which results are gathered and reported to ensure that the target of the audit is in compliance with the organization's policies, regulations, and legal responsibilities.

authentication A method of validating a particular entity's or individual's unique credentials.

Backplane A high-speed bus that can be used to interconnect multiple devices (such as switches, servers, or drive arrays).

backup Recovery of data can be provided via a backup system. Most backup systems offer support for tape devices. This provides a reasonably reliable and quick mechanism for copying critical data. Different backup types (full, incremental, or differential) balance media capacity, time required to backup, and time required to restore.

bandwidth Generally used to refer to the amount of data that can be transferred through a connection over a given period. Bandwidth more properly means the range of frequencies supported by transmission media, measured in hertz.

baseline The point from which something varies. A configuration baseline is the original or recommended settings for a device, while a performance baseline is the originally measured throughput.

bash A command shell and scripting language for Unix-like systems. Bash is short for Bourne again shell.

beep codes During Power-On Self-Test (POST), errors in hardware or the system firmware data can be brought to the attention of the user by beep noises. Each beep code is able to draw attention to a particular fault with the hardware. It was once customary for a computer to beep once to indicate that POST was successful, though most modern computers boot silently.

biometric authentication Physical characteristics stored as a digital data template can be used to authenticate a user. Typical features used include facial pattern, signature recognition, and iris, retina, or fingerprint pattern.

Basic Input/Output System A firmware interface that initializes hardware for an operating system boot. Also known as BIOS.

BitLocker Feature of Windows allowing for encryption of NTFS-formatted drives. The encryption key can be stored in a TPM chip on the computer or on a USB drive.

blade server A thin server form factor designed to optimize density, or the amount of space taken up in a rack. Blades are connected in an enclosure that provides a common power, cooling, and interconnect solution.

bollards A sturdy, short, vertical post. The term originally referred to a post on a ship or quay used principally for mooring boats, but it is now also used to refer to posts installed to control road traffic and posts designed to prevent ram-raiding and vehicle-ramming attacks.

Bootstrap Protocol TCP/IP protocol enabling a host to acquire IP configuration information from a server or download a configuration program using TFTP. BOOTP is an earlier, simpler form of DHCP and also works over UDP port 67. Unlike DHCP, the configuration settings for each host must be manually configured on the server.

bridge Used to divide an overloaded network into separate segments. Intrasegment traffic (traffic between devices on the same segment) remains within this segment and cannot affect the other segments. A bridge works most efficiently if the amount of intersegment traffic (traffic between devices on different segments) is kept low. Segments on either side of a bridge are in separate collision domains but the same broadcast domain. The function of bridges is now typically performed by switches.

British Thermal Unit A measure of heat energy generated by equipment. One watt is 3.41 British Thermal Units. Also known as BTU.

Blue Screen Indicates an error from which the system cannot recover (also called a stop error). Blue screens are usually caused by bad driver software or hardware faults (memory or disk). Also known as Blue Screen of Death or BSOD.

bus Buses are the connections between components on the motherboard and peripheral devices attached to the computer. Buses are available in industry standard formats, each with its own advantages and disadvantages. The standard functions of a bus are to provide data sharing, memory addressing, power supply, and timing. Common bus types include PCI, PCI Express, and USB.

business impact analysis A systematic activity that identifies organizational risks and determines their effect on ongoing, mission-critical operations. Also known as BIA.

cache Caching is a technique used for maintaining consistent performance during file access and data processing. It generally is required when components are mismatched in terms of the speed at which they can operate. Caching allows a slow component to store data it cannot process at that moment (a disk drive storing up write instructions, for instance) or a fast component to pre-fetch data that it might need soon (a CPU storing instructions from system memory for reuse, for example).

capacity planning A practice that involves estimating the storage, computer hardware, software and connection infrastructure resources required over some future period of time.

Cat Cable Standards Twisted pair cabling is rated by the ANSI/TIA/EIA cat standards for different Ethernet applications. Cat3 is rated for 10 Mbps applications at up to 100m, Cat5 for 100 Mbps, and Cat5e and Cat6 for 1 Gbps. Cat6 and Cat6a are also rated for 10 Gbps at 55m and 100m, respectively.

change management The process through which changes to the configuration of information systems are implemented, as part of the organization's overall configuration management efforts.

chkdsk A program that verifies the integrity of a disk's file system.

cloud deployment model Classifying the ownership and management of a cloud as public, private, community, or hybrid.

cloud service model Classifying the provision of cloud services and the limit of the cloud service provider's responsibility as software, platform, infrastructure, and so on.

cluster Disk sectors are grouped in clusters of 2, 4, 6, 8, or more. The smaller the cluster size, the lower the data overhead in terms of wasted space, but larger clusters can improve performance. Clusters are also known as allocation units.

cold site A predetermined alternate location where a network can be rebuilt after a disaster.

community cloud A cloud that is deployed for shared use by cooperating tenants.

compression Reducing the amount of space that a file takes up on disk using various algorithms to describe it more efficiently. File storage compression uses lossless techniques. NTFS-formatted drives can compress files automatically, while ZIP compression adds files to a compressed archive. Lossy compression, such as that used by JPEG and MPEG image and video formats, discards some information in the file more or less aggressively, allowing for a trade-off between picture quality and file size.

cooling device A central processing unit (CPU) generates a large amount of heat that must be dissipated via a cooling system to prevent damage to the chip. Generally, a CPU will be fitted with a heatsink (a metal block with fins) and fan. Thermal compound is used at the contact point between the chip and the heatsink to ensure good heat transfer. The power supply unit also incorporates a fan to expel warm air from the system. Modern motherboards have temperature sensors that provide warning of overheating before damage can occur. Very high performance or overclocked systems or systems designed for quiet operation may require more sophisticated cooling systems, such as liquid cooling. Cooling systems that work without electricity are described as passive; those requiring a power source are classed as active.

CPU (Central Processing Unit) The principal microprocessor in a computer or smartphone responsible for running operating system and applications software.

crash cart A wheeled cart, containing a secured laptop or a keyboard, monitor, and mouse, that can be directly connected to the server for local out-of-band management. The cart is typically designed to be used while standing and carries all necessary cables to connect to any device in the server room.

cloud service provider A vendor offering public cloud service models, such as PaaS, IaaS, or SaaS. Also known as a CSP.

data at rest Information that is primarily stored on specific media, rather than moving from one medium to another.

data exfiltration The process by which an attacker takes data that is stored inside of a private network and moves it to an external network.

data in transit Information that is being transmitted between two hosts, such as over a private network or the Internet. Also referred to as data in motion.

data infiltration The process by which an attacker takes data that is stored inside of an external network and moves it to an internal network.

data loss (leak) prevention A software solution that detects and prevents sensitive information from being stored on unauthorized systems or transmitted over unauthorized networks. Also known as DLP.

data retention The process an organization uses to maintain the existence of and control over certain data in order to comply with business policies and/or applicable laws and regulations.

Double Data Rate SDRAM Standard for SDRAM where data is transferred twice per clock cycle (making the maximum data rate 64x the bus speed in bps). DDR2/DDR3/DDR4 SDRAM uses lower voltage chips and higher bus speeds. Also known as DDR SDRAM.

default gateway The default gateway is an IP configuration parameter that identifies the location of a router on the local subnet that the host can use to contact other networks.

device driver A small piece of code that is loaded during the boot sequence of an operating system. This code, usually provided by the hardware vendor, offers access to a device, or hardware, from the OS kernel. Under Windows, a signing system is in place for drivers to ensure that they do not make the OS unstable.

Dynamic Host Configuration Protocol A protocol used to automatically assign IP addressing information to hosts that have not been configured manually. Also known as DHCP.

differential backup A backup type in which all selected files that have changed since the last full backup are backed up.

directory A file system object used to organize files. Directories can be created on any drive (the directory for the drive itself is called the root) and within other directories (subdirectory). Different file systems put limits on the number of files or directories that can be created on the root or the number of subdirectory levels. In Windows, directories are referred to as folders.

diskpart Command-line utility used to configure disk partitions.

demilitarized zone A segment isolated from the rest of a private network by one or more firewalls that accepts connections from the Internet over designated ports. Also known as a DMZ.

Domain Name System The service that maps names to IP addresses on most TCP/IP networks, including the Internet. Also known as DNS.

domain controller Windows-based server that provides domain authentication services (logon services). Domain controllers maintain a master copy of the database of network resources. Also known as DC.

disaster recovery plan A documented and resourced plan showing actions and responsibilities to be used in response to critical incidents. Also known as a DRP.

Encrypting File System Microsoft's file-level encryption feature available for use on NTFS. Also called EFS.

encryption Scrambling the characters used in a message so that the message can be seen but not understood or modified unless it can be deciphered. Encryption provides for a secure means of transmitting data and authenticating users. It is also used to store data securely. Encryption uses different types of cipher and one or more keys. The size of the key is one factor in determining the strength of the encryption product.

electrostatic discharge Metal and plastic surfaces can allow a charge to build up. This can discharge if a potential difference is formed between the charged object and an oppositely charged conductive object. This electrical discharge can damage silicon chips and computer components if they are exposed to it. Also known as ESD.

Ethernet (802.3) Popular Local Area Networking technology defining media access and signaling methods. Ethernet has been developed for use with coax (thicknet [10BASE-5] and thinnet [10BASE-T]), UTP cable (10BASE-TX, 100BASE-TX, 1000BASE-T, and 1000BASE-TX), and fiber optic (10BASE-F, 100BASE-FX, 1000BASE-X, and 10G standards). Wireless devices can also connect to Ethernet networks via a Wireless Access Point.

external serial advanced technology attachment A variant of SATA meant for external connectivity. It uses a more robust connector, longer shielded cables, and stricter (but backward-compatible) electrical standards. Also called eSATA.

failback The return of service to a previously failed asset, making it an active node once more.

failover A technique that ensures a redundant component, device, or application can quickly and efficiently take over the functionality of an asset that has failed.

File Allocation Table File Allocation Table is a basic disk format allowing the OS to write data as files on a disk. The original 16-bit version (FAT16, but often simply called "FAT") was replaced by a 32-bit version that is almost universaly supported by different operating systems and devices. A 64-bit version (exFAT) was introduced with Windows 7 and is also supported by XP SP3 and Vista SP1 and some versions of Linux and MacOS. There is also a 12-bit version used to format floppy disks. Also known as FAT.

fault tolerance Protection against system failure by providing extra (redundant) capacity. Generally, fault-tolerant systems identify and eliminate single points of failure. Fault tolerance is also known as redundancy.

Fibre Channel High-speed network communications protocol used to implement SANs. Also called FC.

Fibre Channel over Ethernet Standard allowing for a mixed use Ethernet network with both ordinary data and storage network traffic. Also called FCoE.

fiber optic cable Fiber optic cable employs light signals as the basis for data transmission, as opposed to the electrical signals that are used by the other main cable types. The light pulses travel down the glass core of the fiber (known as the waveguide). The cladding that surrounds this core reflects light back to ensure transmission efficiency. Two main categories of fiber are available: multi-mode, which uses cheaper, shorter-wavelength LEDs or VCSEL diodes, or single-mode, which uses more expensive longer wavelength laser diodes. At the receiving end of the cable, light-sensitive diodes reconvert the light pulse into an electrical signal. Fiber optic cable is immune to eavesdropping and EMI, has low attenuation, supports rates of 10 Gbps+, and is light and compact.

file server In file-server-based networks, a central machine provides dedicated file and print services to workstations. Benefits of server-based networks include ease of administration through centralization.

fire suppression Fire detection and suppression systems are mandatory in most public and private commercial premises. Water-based fire suppression is a risk to computer systems, both in the event of fire and through the risk of flood. Alternatives include dry pipe and gas systems.

firewall A software or hardware device that protects a system or network by blocking unwanted network traffic.

firmware Software instructions stored semipermanently (embedded) on a hardware device. Modern types of firmware are stored in flash memory and can be updated more easily than legacy programmable Read Only Memory (ROM) types.

form factor The size and shape of a component, determining its compatibility. Form factor is most closely associated with PC motherboard, case, and power supply designs.

Fully Qualified Domain Name A name in DNS specifying a particular host within a subdomain within a top-level domain. Also called FQDN.

File Transfer Protocol A protocol used to transfer files between network hosts. Variants include S(ecure)FTP, FTP with SSL (FTPS and FTPES) and T(rivial)FTP. FTP utilizes ports 20 and 21.

full backup A backup type in which all selected files, regardless of prior state, are backed up.

gateway A computer or other device that acts as a translator between two completely dissimilar computer systems. For example, a connection from a PC LAN to an IBM mainframe would require a gateway. Gateways tend to be slower than bridges or routers. The term default gateway is also used to denote a router on a TCP/IP network, though this is not a gateway in the sense described above.

gigabit ethernet Gigabit Ethernet operates at 1000 Mbps (1 Gbps) and is now the standard for networking. It can be used with devices designated as 10/100/1000 Mbps (devices will adjust to the highest common speed between sender and receiver).

GUID Partition Table Modern disk partitioning system allowing large numbers of partitions and very large partition sizes. Also known as GPT.

graphics processing unit Type of microprocessor used on dedicated video adapter cards or within a CPU with integrated graphics capability. GPUs can also perform cryptographic operations efficiently and are often used for password cracking.

group account A group account is a collection of user accounts that are useful when establishing file permissions and user rights because when many individuals need the same level of access, a group could be established containing all the relevant users.

Graphical User Interface A GUI provides an easy-to-use, intuitive interface for a computer operating system. Most GUIs require a pointing device, such as a mouse, to operate efficiently. One of the world's first GUI-based operating systems was the Apple Mac OS, released in 1984. Thereafter, Microsoft produced its Windows family of products based around its GUI. In fact, recognizing that GUI covers a whole range of designs, the Windows interface is better described as a WIMP (Windows, Icons, Menus, Pointing [device]) interface.

high availability The property that defines how closely systems approach the goal of providing data availability 100 percent of the time while maintaining a high level of system performance. Also called HA.

half-duplex Network link where simultaneously sending and receiving is not possible.

hazard Any source of potential damage, harm or adverse health effects on something or someone. As part of health and safety, employers must identify and mitigate workplace hazards. Employees must not cause hazards and must report any hazards they detect. PC maintenance can expose a technician to a number of hazards, notably electric shock, laser light, and thermal (burns). Hazards such as heat, dust, EMI, or ESD can also affect PC operation.

hardware compatibility list A database of hardware models and their compatibility with a given operating system. Before installing an OS, it is vital to check that all the PC components have been tested for compatibility with the OS (that they are on the Hardware Compatibility List [HCL] or Windows Logo'd Product List). Incompatible hardware may not work or may even prevent the installation from completing successfully.

hard disk drive Device providing persistent mass storage. Data is stored using platters with a magnetic coating that are spun under disk heads that can read and write to locations on each platter (sectors). Also called an HDD.

heartbeat network A private network that is shared only by the nodes in the cluster and is not accessible from outside the cluster. It is used by cluster nodes in order to monitor each node's status and communicate with each other messages necessary for maintaining operation of the cluster.

host-based intrusion detection system A type of intrusion detection system that monitors a computer system for unexpected behavior or drastic changes to the system's state. Also called HIDS.

host-based intrusion prevention system Endpoint protection that can detect and prevent malicious activity via signature and heuristic pattern matching. Also known as HIPS.

host bus adapter A component allowing storage devices to exchange data with a computer system using a particular interface (PATA, SATA, SCSI, and so on). Motherboards will come with built-in host adapters, and more can be added as expansion cards if necessary. Also referred to as HBA.

hot site A fully configured alternate network that can be online quickly after a disaster.

hot-swappable Denoting a device that can be added or removed without having to restart the operating system.

HTTP/HTTPS The protocol used to provide web content to browsers. HTTP uses port 80. HTTPS(ecure) provides for encrypted transfers, using SSL/TLS and port 443. Also known as HyperText Transfer Protocol/HTTP Secure.

heating, ventilation, air conditioning Building control systems maintain an optimum heating, cooling, and humidity level working environment for different parts of the building. Also known as HVAC.

hybrid cloud A cloud deployment that uses both private and public elements.

Infrastructure as a Service A computing method that uses the cloud to provide any or all infrastructure needs. Also known as IaaS.

image A duplicate of an operating system installation (including installed software, settings, and user data) stored on removable media. Windows makes use of image-based backups, and they are also used for deploying Windows to multiple PCs rapidly.

imaging Copying the structure and contents of a physical disk device or logical volume to a single file, using a tool such as dd.

incremental backup A backup type in which all selected files that have changed since the last full or incremental backup (whichever was most recent) are backed up.

Integer Data type supporting storage of whole numbers.

internet protocol keyboard-video-mouse KVM over IP (KVMoIP) access technology extends keyboard, video, and mouse (KVM) signals from any computer or server over TCP/IP via a LAN, WAN, or Internet connection. Through this KVMoIP connection, remote users can access and control a number of servers simultaneously from wherever they are, inside or outside the organization, and anywhere in the world. This technology works in diverse hardware environments and is ideal for managing multilocation data centers and branch offices.

IP Address Each IP host must have a unique IP address. This can be manually assigned or dynamically allocated (using a DHCP server). In IPv4, the 32-bit binary address is expressed in the standard four byte, dotted decimal notation: 10.0.5.1. In IPv6, addresses are 128-bit expressed as hexadecimal (for example, 2001:db8::0bcd:abcd:ef12:1234).

ipconfig command A Windows-based utility used to gather information about the IP configuration of a workstation.

Internet Protocol security A set of open, nonproprietary standards that are used to secure data through authentication and encryption as the data travels across the network or the Internet. Also called IPSec.

iSCSI IP tunneling protocol that enables the transfer of SCSI data over an IP-based network to create a SAN.

Just a Bunch Of Disks Configuring a spanned volume across a number of disks without any sort of RAID striping functionality. Also called JBOD.

Kerberos A single sign-on authentication and authorization service that is based on a time-sensitive ticket-granting system.

kernel A low-level piece of code in all operating systems responsible for controlling the rest of the operating system.

Keyboard Video Mouse A switch supporting a single set of input and output devices controlling a number of PCs. KVM are more typically used with servers, but two-port versions allow a single keyboard, mouse, and display to be used with two PCs.

Lucent Connector Small Form Factor version of the SC push-pull fiber optic connector; available in simplex and duplex versions. Also called LC.

Linux An open-source operating system supported by a wide range of hardware and software vendors.

load balancer A type of switch or router that distributes client requests between different resources, such as communications links or similarly configured servers. This provides fault tolerance and improves throughput.

logical partition A partition created within an extended partition to divide the disk space between logical drives, each of which can be allocated a drive letter.

logs OS and applications software can be configured to log events automatically. This provides valuable troubleshooting information. Security logs provide an audit trail of actions performed on the system and warning of suspicious activity. It is important that log configuration and files be made tamperproof.

Media Access Control address A unique hardware address hard-coded into a network adapter. This provides local addressing on Ethernet and Wi-Fi networks. A MAC address is 48 bits long, with the first half representing the manufacturer's Organizationally Unique Identifier (OUI).

master boot record Sector on a mass storage device that holds information about partitions and the OS boot loader. Also referred to as MBR.

mirroring A type of RAID that using two hard disks, providing the simplest way of protecting a single disk against failure. Data is written to both disks and can be read from either disk.

Multimode Fiber Category of fiber optic cable. Compared to SMF, MMF is cheaper (using LED optics rather than lasers) but supports shorter distances (up to about 500m).

mean time between failures The rating on a device or component that predicts the expected time between failures. Also known as MTBF.

mean time to repair/replace/recover The average time taken for a device or component to be repaired, be replaced, or otherwise recover from a failure. Also known as MTTR.

network attached storage A storage device with an embedded OS that supports typical network file access protocols (TCP/IP and SMB, for instance). Also referred to as NAS.

network address translation A routing mechanism that conceals internal addressing schemes from the public Internet by translating between a single public address on the external side of a router and private, non-routable addresses internally. Also called NAT.

Network File System Remote file access protocol used principally on UNIX and Linux networks. Also known as NFS.

network interface card Implements the physical and data link connection between a host and transmission media. Also known as NIC and network adapter.

nmap Versatile port scanner used for topology, host, service, and OS discovery and enumeration.

New Technology Filing System The 64-bit default file system for Windows, with file-by-file compression and RAID support as well as advanced file attribute management tools, encryption, and disk quotas. Also known as NTFS.

Network Time Protocol TCP/IP application protocol allowing machines to synchronize to the same time clock that runs over UDP port 123. Also known as NTP.

out-of-band management Accessing the administrative interface of a network appliance using a separate network from the usual data network. This could use a separate VLAN or a different kind of link, such as a dial-up modem. Also known as OOB.

open-source The programming code used to design the software is freely available.

operating system Software that facilitates the control and configuration of the computer device via device drivers, services, and one or more user interfaces. Commonly abbreviated as OS.

Open Systems Interconnection reference model Assigns network and hardware components and functions at seven discrete layers: Physical, Data Link, Network, Transport, Session, Presentation, and Application. Also called the OSI model.

platform as a service A computing method that uses the cloud to provide any platform-type services. Also known as PaaS.

packet analyzer Software that decodes a network traffic capture (obtained via a packet sniffer) and displays the captured packets for analysis, allowing inspection of the packet headers and payload (unless the communications are encrypted).

packet sniffing Recording data from frames as they pass over network media, using methods such as a mirror port or tap device.

parity Data parity is an integral feature of network transmission. When a data packet is sent, it contains a specific number of bits—either an odd or an even number of bits. If parity is set to odd, the computer that is sending the data adds the required number of bits so that the number becomes odd. This is the same principle if parity is set to even. Parity provides a simple error-checking system through which transmission faults can be overcome. If two computers have been set up to transmit using the same parity, any fault that causes the data to be disrupted may lead to an altering of parity, which is used to signify data error.

partition A discrete area of storage defined on a hard disk using either the Master Boot Record (MBR) or GUID Partition Table (GPT) scheme. Each partition can be formatted with a different file system, and a partition can be marked as active (made bootable).

patch panel A type of wiring cross-connect with IDCs to terminate fixed cabling on one side and modular jacks to make cross-connections to other equipment on the other. Patch panels simplify moves, adds, and changes (MACs) in network administration.

Payment Card Industry Data Security Standard Information security standard for organizations that process credit or bank card payments. Also called PCI DSS.

PCI express Expansion bus standard using serial communications. Each device on the bus can create a point-to-point link with the I/O controller or another device. The link comprises one or more lanes (x1, x2, x4, x8, x12, x16, or x32). Each lane supports a full-duplex transfer rate of 250 MBps (v1.0), 500 MBps (v2.0), or 1 GBps (v3.0). The standard is software compatible with PCI, allowing for motherboards with both types of connector. Also called PCIe.

power distribution unit Advanced strip socket that provides filtered output voltage. A managed unit supports remote administration. Also called PDU.

Performance Monitor Tool in Windows for viewing CPU, memory, and pagefile utilization, accessible through the Performance and Reliability Monitor. You can also view statistics on the Performance tab in Task Manager. Actual performance needs to be measured against a baseline, usually taken when the system is first installed. Most software can also generate alerts if performance breaches defined thresholds.

permissions Security settings that control access to objects, including file system items and network resources.

personally identifiable information Data that can be used to identify or contact an individual (or, in the case of identity theft, to impersonate them). Also known as PII.

plenum cable Local fire and safety regulations may require the use of special types of cable for specific situations, such as plenum cable in plenum spaces (the space above false ceilings in an office that contains the HVAC system). Plenum cable is designed to be fire resistant and has Teflon coatings for the jacket material so it produces a minimal amount of smoke.

port In TCP and UDP applications, a port is a unique number assigned to a particular application protocol (such as HTTP or SMTP). The port number (with the IP address) forms a socket between client and server. A socket is a bidirectional pipe for the exchange of data. For security, it is important to allow only the ports required to be open (ports can be blocked using a firewall).

Power-On Self-Test The POST procedure is a hardware checking routine built into the PC firmware. This test sequentially monitors the state of the memory chips, the processor, system clock, display, and firmware itself. Errors that occur within vital components such as these are signified by beep codes emitted by the internal speaker of the computer. Further tests are then performed and any errors displayed as on-screen error codes and messages.

PowerShell A command shell and scripting language built on the .NET Framework.

primary partition A partition that is primary can be marked as active and hence made bootable.

print server Windows-based machine sharing its printer with other computers. Standalone print servers are also available.

private cloud A cloud that is deployed for use by a single entity.

protocol Rules and formats enabling systems to exchange data. A single network will involve many different protocols. In general terms, a protocol defines header fields to describe each packet, a maximum length for the payload, and methods of processing information from the headers.

protocol analysis Analysis of per-protocol utilization statistics in a packet capture or network traffic sampling.

public cloud A cloud that is deployed for shared use by multiple independent tenants.

quad small form factor pluggable A compact, hot-pluggable transceiver used for data communications applications. The form factor and electrical interface are specified by a multi-source agreement (MSA) under the auspices of the Small Form Factor Committee. It interfaces networking hardware (such as servers and switches) to a fiber optic cable or active or passive electrical copper connection. Also known as QSFP.

rack A storage solution for server and network equipment. Racks are designed to a standard width and height (measured in multiples of 1U or 1.75 inches). Racks offer better density, cooling, and security than ordinary office furniture.

redundant array of independent/ inexpensive disks Specifications that support redundancy and fault tolerance for different configurations of multiple-device storage systems. Commonly known as RAID.

random access memory Volatile storage space for computer data and program instructions while the computer is turned on. Also known as RAM and system memory.

redundancy Overprovisioning resources at the component, host, and/or site level so that there is failover to a working instance in the event of a problem.

remote desktop A Windows remote control feature allowing specified users to log onto the Windows computer over the network and work remotely. Remote Desktop uses the RDP protocol over TCP port 3389.

replication Automatically copying data between two processing systems, either simultaneously on both systems (synchronous) or from a primary to a secondary location (asynchronous).

resilient file system A Microsoft file system designed to maximize data availability, scale efficiently to large data sets across diverse workloads, and provide data integrity by means of resiliency to corruption. Also known as ReFS.

request for comments A collection of documents that detail standards and protocols for Internet-related technologies. Also called RFC.

Radio Frequency ID A means of encoding information into passive tags, which can be easily attached to devices, structures, clothing, or almost anything else. Also called RFID.

robocopy Command-line file copy utility recommended for use over the older xcopy.

role-based access control An access control model where resources are protected by ACLs that are managed by administrators and that provide user permissions based on job functions. Also called RBAC.

router A network device that links dissimilar networks and can support multiple alternate paths between location-based parameters, such as speed, traffic loads, and price.

recovery point objective The longest period of time that an organization can tolerate lost data being unrecoverable. Also known as RPO.

round robin DNS A load balancing technique where multiple DNS A records are created with the same name. Also known as RRDNS.

recovery time objective The length of time it takes after an event to resume normal business operations and activities. Also known as RTO.

rule-based access control A non-discretionary access control technique that is based on a set of operational rules or restrictions to enforce a least privileges permissions policy.

software as a service A computing method that uses the cloud to provide application services to users. Also known as SaaS.

storage area network A network dedicated to data storage, typically consisting of storage devices and servers connected to switches via host bus adapters. Also known as SAN.

Serial Attached Small Computer Systems Interface Developed from parallel SCSI, SAS represents the highest-performing hard disk interface available. Also known as SAS.

Serial ATA Serial ATA is the most widely used interface for hard disks on desktop and laptop computers. It uses a seven-pin data connector with one device per port. There are three SATA standards specifying bandwidths of 1.5 Gbps, 3 Gbps, and 6 Gbps, respectively. SATA drives also use a new 15-pin power connector, though adapters for the old style 4-pin Molex connectors are available. External drives are also supported via the eSATA interface.

scalability The property by which a computing environment is able to gracefully fulfill its ever-increasing resource needs.

Secure Digital Card The most popular type of flash memory card. There are also mini and micro form factors and SDHC, SDXC, and SDUC capacity variants plus UHS-I, UHS-II, UHS-III, and NVMe bus speeds. Also known as SD card.

separation of duties A concept that states that duties and responsibilities should be divided among individuals to prevent ethical conflicts or abuse of powers.

service A service, or daemon, is typically a non-interactive process that runs in the background to support an OS or application function, such as Plug-and-Play, the print spooler, and DHCP. In Windows, services can be viewed, configured, and started/stopped via the Services console, msconfig, and the Processes tab in Task Manager.

service level agreement Operating procedures and standards for a service contract. Also called an SLA.

Share Permissions When a resource is shared over a network, it can be assigned Read, Change, Full Control, or Deny permissions on the share. Windows supports user-level security; users have permissions depending upon who they are. Share permissions only protect the resource from access over the network. Local access can only be secured by NTFS permissions.

Server Message Block Used for requesting files from Windows servers and delivering them to clients. SMB allows machines to share files and printers, thus making them available for other machines to use. SMB client software is available for UNIX-based systems. Samba software allows UNIX and Linux servers or NAS appliances to run SMB services for Windows clients.

Single Mode Fiber Category of fiber optic cable. SMF is more expensive than MMF (using high-quality cable and optics) and supports much longer distances (up to about 70 km).

snapshot backup A type of backup copy used to create the entire architectural instance/copy of an application, disk, or system. It is used in backup processes to restore the system or disk of a particular device at a specific time. Also referred to as image backup.

social engineering An activity where the goal is to use deception and trickery to convince unsuspecting users to provide sensitive data or violate security guidelines.

spool A generic term describing how a print output stream is passed from a client application and stored temporarily at a print server until the print monitor can route the job to the print device.

solid state drive Persistent mass storage device implemented using flash memory.

Secure Shell A remote administration and file-copy program that supports VPNs by using port forwarding and that runs on TCP port 22. Also known as SSH.

Straight Tip Connector Bayonet-style twist-and-lock connector for fiber optic cabling. Also known as ST connector.

shielded twisted pair Copper network cabling with screening or shielding to reduce risks from interference and eavesdropping. Also known as STP.

string Data type supporting storage of a variable length series of characters.

subnet mask An IP address consists of a Network ID and a Host ID. The subnet mask is used in IPv4 to distinguish these two components within a single IP address. The typical format for a mask is 255.255.0.0. Classless network addresses can also be expressed in the format 169.254.0.0/16, where /16 is the number of bits in the mask. IPv6 uses the same / nn notation to indicate the length of the network prefix. Also known as CIDR and network prefix.

subpoena A writ issued by a government agency, most often a court, to compel testimony by a witness or production of evidence under a penalty for failure.

switch In Ethernet, a networking device that receives incoming data, reviews the destination MAC address against an internal address table, and sends the data out through the port that contains the destination MAC address.

synthetic full backup A synthetic backup takes a full backup and combines subsequent incremental backups with it to provide a full backup that is always up to date. Synthetic full backups have the advantage of being easy to restore from while also being easy on bandwidth across the network, as only changes are transmitted.

tabletop exercise A discussion of simulated emergency situations and security incidents.

tape Tape media provide robust, high-speed, high-capacity backup storage. Tape drives and autoloader libraries can be connected to the SATA and SAS buses or accessed via a SAN.

Transmission Control Protocol Protocol in the TCP/IP suite operating at the transport layer to provide connection-oriented, guaranteed delivery of packets. Hosts establish a session to exchange data and confirm delivery of packets using acknowledgements. This overhead means the system is relatively slow. Also known as TCP.

tower server A server mounted in standard PC-like tower case. Server cases are normally larger than ordinary PCs, with better cooling designs.

transceiver Converts the signal from the computer to a signal that can be sent over the network medium (and vice versa—that is, it transmits and receives). Transceivers are usually incorporated onto the network adapter and specific to a particular media type. There are also modular transceivers, such as Small Form Factor Pluggable (SFP/SFP+/QSFP/QSFP+) and Gigabit Interface Converter (GBIC), designed to plug into switches and other network equipment.

troubleshooting Troubleshooting requires a methodical approach. Having ensured that any data has been backed up, the first step is to gather information (from the user, error messages, diagnostic tools, or inspection). The next is to analyze the problem, again consulting documentation, web resources, or manufacturer's help resources if necessary. When analyzing a problem, it helps to categorize it (for example, between hardware and software). The next step is to choose and apply the most suitable solution. Next, test the system and related systems to verify functionality. The last step is to document the problem, steps taken, and the outcome. If the problem cannot be solved, it may be necessary to escalate it to another technician or manager.

twisted pair cable Twisted pair is two insulated copper wires twisted about each other; a cable is made up of a number of pairs (usually four in data networking). The twisting of the wires acts to reduce interference and crosstalk. Each pair of wires is twisted at a different rate to ensure that the pairs do not interfere with each other. The drawbacks of twisted pair cabling are sensitivity to EMI and eavesdropping and attenuation (it cannot be used for long-distance transmission). Cabling is categorized according to EIA/TIA standards; Cat3 cable was specified for 10 Mbps Ethernet and Cat5 for 100 Mbps (Fast Ethernet). Cabling is now either Cat5e or Cat6, both of which support Gigabit Ethernet. Most cabling is unshielded (UTP), although in continental Europe, foil screened cabling is commonly used (Foil Twisted Pair [FTP] or Screened Twisted Pair [ScTP]). Screened cable is less susceptible to EMI and eavesdropping but is more complex to install and consequently more expensive.

Unified Extensible Firmware Interface A type of system firmware providing support for 64-bit CPU operation at boot, full GUI and mouse operation at boot, and better boot security. Also known as UEFI.

Universal Naming Convention Standard naming convention for local network resources, in the format \\server\share\file, where server is the name of a remote machine, share is the name of a folder on that machine, and "file" is the file you wish to access. Also known as UNC.

UNIX Systems UNIX is a family of more than 20 related operating systems that are produced by various companies. UNIX can run on a wide variety of platforms. UNIX offers a multitude of file systems in addition to its native system. UNIX remains widely deployed in enterprise data centers to run mission-critical applications and infrastructure.

uninterruptible power supply A battery-powered device that supplies AC power that an electronic device can use during a power failure.

uptime Uptime is the amount of time that the server is powered on and running. This is not to be confused with availability.

Universal Serial Bus The main type of connection interface used on PCs. A larger Type A connector attaches to a port on the host; Type B and Mini- or Micro-Type B connectors are used for devices. USB 1.1 supports 12 Mbps, while USB 2.0 supports 480 Mbps and is backward compatible with 1.1 devices (which run at the slower speed). USB devices are hot swappable. A device can draw up to 2.5W power. USB 3.0 and 3.1 define 5 Gbps (SuperSpeed) and 10 Gbps (SuperSpeed+) rates and can deliver 4.5W power.

unshielded twisted pair Copper cabling that supports Ethernet, as rated to EIA/TIA Cat standards. Also referred to as UTP.

vbs Extension for the Visual Basic Script file format.

virtual memory An area on the hard disk allocated to contain pages of memory. When the operating system doesn't have sufficient physical memory (RAM) to perform a task, pages of memory are swapped to the paging file. This frees physical RAM to enable the task to be completed. When the paged RAM is needed again, it is reread into memory. Also known as pagefile and swapfile.

virus Code designed to infect computer files (or disks) when it is activated.

virtual local area network A logically separate network, created by using switching technology. Even though hosts on two VLANs may be physically connected to the same cabling, local traffic is isolated to each VLAN, so they must use a router to communicate.

virtual machine A guest operating system installed on a host computer using virtualization software (a hypervisor), such as Microsoft Hyper-V or VMware. Also known as a VM.

VMware file system A virtual machine file system used in VMware ESX Server software to store files in a virtualized environment. VMware VMFS was designed to store files, images, and screenshots within a virtual machine. Multiple virtual machines can share a single virtual machine file system. Its storage capacity can be increased by spanning multiple VMFSs.

voltage The potential difference between two points (often likened to pressure in a water pipe) measured in volts (V). In the UK, mains power is supplied at 220–240V. In the US, mains power is 110–120V.

volume A storage area formatted with the same file system. A volume might be mapped to a single hard disk partition or span multiple disks or represent a storage media that cannot be partitioned (such as an optical disc).

virtual private network A secure tunnel created between two endpoints connected via an insecure network (typically the Internet). Also called a VPN.

virtualization technology CPU extensions to allow better performance when a host runs multiple guest operating systems or VMs. Also called VT.

warm site A location that is dormant or performs noncritical functions under normal conditions but can be rapidly converted to a key operations site if needed.

web interface A programming interface that applications use to access services in a Web server.

workstation Client devices connecting to the network. These represent one of the most vulnerable points, as they are usually harder to monitor than centrally located equipment, such as servers and switches. As well as secure configuration of the OS and applications, workstations should be protected with anti-malware software. Users should be trained in security best practices and educated about common threats.

XaaS Expressing the concept that most types of IT requirements can be deployed as a cloud service model. Also called anything as a service.

Z file system ZFS (previously: Zettabyte file system) combines a file system with a volume manager.

Index

Note: Page numbers in *italics* represent pages with charts, graphs, and diagrams.

C

N

O

P